# GOVERNMENT
## IN THE
# CLOUDS

How to Restore
Our Democracy and Empower Voters

PATRICK E. PETERSON

*For Mollie and Lucy*

# TABLE OF CONTENTS

Introduction                                                                    vii

Chapter 1  |  1776                                                                1

Chapter 2  |  The Federal Behemoth                                               37

Chapter 3  |  Government Subsidies                                               63

Chapter 4  |  Our Litigious Society                                              89

Chapter 5  |  Healthcare                                                        129

Chapter 6  |  The Natives are Restless…                                         163

Chapter 7  |  Voting                                                            203

Chapter 8  |  The Romans and the U.S.                                           217

Chapter 9  |  Thomas Jefferson, George Washington, and Abraham Lincoln          239

Chapter 10  |  Imagine….                                                        255

References                                                                      279

Acknowledgments                                                                 285

# INTRODUCTION

Our country is in a real mess and the people aren't happy about it. Democrats are angry at the Republicans, Republicans are angry at the Democrats. Each blames the other for our many problems. The people are blaming the government, yet waiting and expecting them to fix our problems. All the people have is the right to vote. Accordingly, we have to wait for elections to change our politicians, but really, isn't it like changing rooms on the Titanic? We know what politicians are going to do before they do it. One party has their agenda and dependants — the people whose entitlements are based on their party being in power, and the other party, with their agenda and dependants and entitlements. Each party is fighting for an ever increasing slice of the federal pie, the greatest money machine ever created. Yet, the government doesn't generate any income, doesn't produce anything, and doesn't sell anything (except influence). The government simply redistributes money that it takes in, or borrows money it doesn't have. Our forefathers wrote *The Declaration of Independence* and independence used to be our defining characteristic. Nowadays, more people are dependent on the government for their livelihood than ever before.

Politicians have created an entitlement nation, where people, special interests and companies belly up to the trough and gorge on government money. Subsidies for businesses, farmers, oil companies, foreign nations we support, and ordinary people who just don't want to work drain hundreds of billions of dollars from our country. The people—the taxpayers and voters—seem powerless. People are powerless in the face of big government, big business, and big money. The people are told their vote matters. Are they going to vote for the right or left? If people don't want what they have, they vote politicians out of office, and others take their place. Yet, the spending, subsidizing, entitlements, waste and fraud continue. Politicians got us into this mess, yet we hope they are going to get us out of the mess *they created*. We can't vote the lobbyists and special interests in or out of office, because they aren't in office. Yet, they exert more influence over our government than anybody else.

Spending and deficits have grown to unimaginable levels. Under President Bush, spending continued to climb as we dealt with our terrorist threat and bailed out banks and Wall Street. President Obama was able to ram through a healthcare bill and stimulus spending. The healthcare bill (which will forthwith be referred to as "ObamaCare" in the book) weighed in at over 2000 pages. Many senators and congressmen didn't even read this massive bill, but should have since it solves none of the problems with our healthcare system. Stimulus spending failed to stimulate anything, except more wasteful government spending.

When times were good, it was easy to be apathetic about what the government was doing. Yet, the government stood by and watched as our economy collapsed, fraudsters like Bernie Madoff and many others bilked tens of billions of dollars from investors, big banks that perpetuated lending fraud were bailed out while millions of people lost their homes and millions more lost their jobs. Well, the government didn't exactly sit by while all this was happening; they ramped up deficit spending, so that now it runs to more than $100 billion per month. The government is currently spending $100 billion more *per month* than it is taking in. Seen another way, the total combined wealth of two of America's wealthiest individuals, Bill Gates, founder of Microsoft, and Warren Buffett, who runs Berkshire Hathaway is around $100 billion. *The government is spending their combined wealth every month!* And it's deficit spending, borrowed money that is being added to our already mind-boggling federal debt of $13.8 trillion (as of 12/10). At the current rate of deficit-spending brinkmanship, politicians will reach their own self-imposed federal debt ceiling of $14.2 trillion sometime in early 2011. It imposed this limit on itself in Feb. 2010, and then exceeded it in a little more than a year. In spring of 2011, politicians will have to decide whether to raise the debt ceiling again or let the government shut down—because the U.S. government will be broke, out of money. While it's hard for the average American to even imagine a trillion dollars, the government and politicians spend more than $1 trillion per year that they don't have. This over-spending is financed via treasury bills, many of which are bought by foreigners like Middle Easterners and China. Politicians are mortgaging our country and future courtesy of wealthy and not-always friendly nations.

As a result, there is an undercurrent of anger and hostility in the U.S., especially at political types, bureaucracy, and the size of our government. Spending by politicians and our national debt is even threatening our national security. The people are fed up and they should be. They are watching our national debt and spending spiral out of control, knowing the whole time who is going to have to pay—the people. They are facing increased taxes – they are going to have to pay more and more just to service the national debt, much of which is going to foreign investors. Yet, the politicians keep spending money like it's going out of style—and it is. Our public discourse has become us versus them, right vs. left. It's interesting that you hear about a class-war coming in the U.S. from *economists* instead of social scientists. The "class war" is between those expecting entitlements like government employee pensions, Social Security, Disability, Welfare, and all the rest and the people that are going to have to pay for them.

It's interesting that politics is considered a science. It lacks all the logic and reasoning of science, but it takes someone with a scientific mind to figure it out. Who in their right mind wants to be involved in politics? Does anyone believe our best and brightest minds are politicians? Of course not. Most politicians are lawyers, everyone knows that. To get into law school, you usually get a degree in political science. Getting into law school is not very difficult. There are more law schools opening all the time and they keep turning out lawyers onto our society like the plague even though we already have more lawyers than any other country. Some go to work representing "the people," meaning they are district attorneys, judges or prosecutors, and some are state or federal employees. Many are busy suing whoever they can for lottery-like fortunes and many more are cleaning up the wreckage of a disappearing middle class—in the form of bankruptcies (1.4 million in 2009) and divorce. From whatever job they may have had, as lawyers, a small percentage decides to run for office. They become involved in the election process, and have to raise huge amounts of money so they can run T.V. ads, print ads, radio ads, and any other publicity they can manage. If they can get elected and go to Washington, they are welcomed with open arms by a shadow government of lobbyists, special interests, and political action committees.

We saw the Democrats lose a recent election (2010), and Republicans win. This has quieted the voters for awhile. Elections in the last twenty years have differed little. Some politicians will offer a ray of hope to the people they represent, and will attack their counterpart in the election with such ferocity that they win the election. Then they get sent off to Washington to perform their duty. They use their "political capital" to raise more money. They need to raise money for the next election cycle, and they only think in terms of the next election. Depending on the party they are affiliated with, they have a ready group of supporters. Their supporters will fund their campaign, as long as their interests are looked after. All you have to do is look at who gives the most money to each political party to see the way they are going to vote, and where their allegiance lies. Once politicians get elected, they are suddenly placed on a different shelf. They can now spend federal or state tax dollars. They can now spend *our* money, and its more money than they could ever spend if they were CEOs or bank presidents. Their political capital in now translated into real capital – real money that they can spend. They are told what to spend it on, once again, by special interests, lobbyists, political action committees and the like. And their spending is jeopardizing our national security.

Politicians are elected by the people they represent, but represent the people that give them money. It's become a horrible mess, and it's the same "usual suspects" that are to blame in every case. I hope to take an outsider's view of politics, to research and look at how things got this bad. I also have a solution to the whole problem. As a physician, my mind works to diagnose and treat problems, why should politics be any different? We will either get this problem solved, or it will consume us, as a nation, just like cancer. It already is. Our politicians have driven us much closer to financial collapse than most people realize; and people feel like they are drowning, politically, and they are. But like those who are drowning, they will do just about anything to keep their head above water. From the Tea Party movement to the local barber shop, people are getting more and more desperate. They have a feeling that another election, another change in politicians, isn't going to change anything. It hasn't solved anything yet.

When the system is broken, but you keep trying and trying to get it to work, it gets frustrating. It's plain to see that people are frustrated, some would say desperate. People do funny things when they are angry, and the more desperate they become, the angrier they get. Anger boils over at "town hall meetings," when politicians poke their heads out in public. Politicians are the target of voter anger at every turn, and it's only going to get worse. This book takes a look back to see what happened. How things went so wrong, when things went wrong. How much we are spending, on who, and what the results are. You might be surprised at how factually bad things really are, and what others are saying about our situation.

There is still hope, however. This book will constantly look and listen to what the patriots who started this country were trying to do and say over 224 years ago. Their ideas will be superimposed in chapters that deal with how things are now. This book will also look even further back into history to see if *we are different*, which is what we all want to think, or if we are simply following the same path to collapse that all other nations have followed. This book brings up some tough issues that must be examined and confronted if we are ever going to get ourselves out of the mess we currently find ourselves in. This book *is not* intended to be political in terms of conservative or liberal. It *is* political in that it examines our current political system and outside influences that are promoting our ruin. Most importantly, this book proposes a solution to some of our problems. Things didn't get this bad over night, but if we don't do something about it now, we are headed off a cliff. It seems everyone is wrestling for the steering wheel, but maybe we need to switch to an airplane instead, and airplane that flies in the clouds. Maybe the solution to the whole mess of politics, the power and corruption, is in the clouds...

# CHAPTER 1

# *1776*

*"We the People of the United States, in Order to form a more perfect Union, establish Justice, insure domestic Tranquility, provide for the common defense, promote the general Welfare, and secure the Blessings of Liberty to ourselves and our Posterity, do ordain and establish this Constitution for the United States of America."* Right after some of the most famous words in our history, we give everything away *"All legislative Powers herein granted shall be vested in a Congress of the United States, which shall consist of a Senate and House of Representatives."* And the President and Vice President. The key phrase, however, is "We the People of the United States." Our great forefathers set up this form of government, this form of representation, more than 224 years ago. It promises to *establish justice, insure domestic tranquility, provide for the common defense, promote the general Welfare*, and *secure the blessings of liberty to ourselves* (224 years ago) *and to our posterity* (us, today). We'll call the part in italics "the promises" or "guarantees" set up by those who started our country. Let's take a look at these individually, and see if we are getting what our forefathers promised, and how well it's working today.

## *"Establish Justice"*

### Fear is the foundation of most governments.
### *John Adams*

Nobody will argue that we have established justice. In fact, as a result of our justice system, we have more people in prison, per capita, than any other country in the world. Like many businesses, our justice system runs on results—the bottom line. If our justice system didn't put more and more people in jail, its budgets would be cut and people would lose their jobs. If our justice system can put more people in jail, it can increase its budgets and hire more people. So, as we will see, our justice system has been very productive.

In 2008, over 7.3 million people were under some form of correctional supervision including:

> **Probation** - court-ordered period of correctional supervision in the community generally as an alternative to incarceration. In some cases probation can be a combined sentence of incarceration followed by a period of community supervision. These data include adults under the jurisdiction of probation agency, regardless of supervision status (i.e., active supervision, inactive supervision, financial conditions only, warrant status, absconder status, in a residential/other treatment program, or supervised out of jurisdiction).

**Prison** - confinement in a state or federal correctional facility to serve a sentence of more than 1 year, although in some jurisdictions the length of sentence which results in prison confinement is longer.

**Jail** - confinement in a local jail while pending trial, awaiting sentencing, serving a sentence that is usually less than 1 year, or awaiting transfer to other facilities after conviction.

**Parole** - period of conditional supervised release in the community following a prison term, including prisoners released to parole either by a parole board decision (discretionary parole) or according to provisions of a statute (mandatory parole). These data include adults under the jurisdiction of a parole agency, regardless of supervision status (i.e., active supervision, inactive supervision, financial conditions only, absconder status, or supervised out of state).

---

*The number of adults in the correctional population has been increasing:*

---

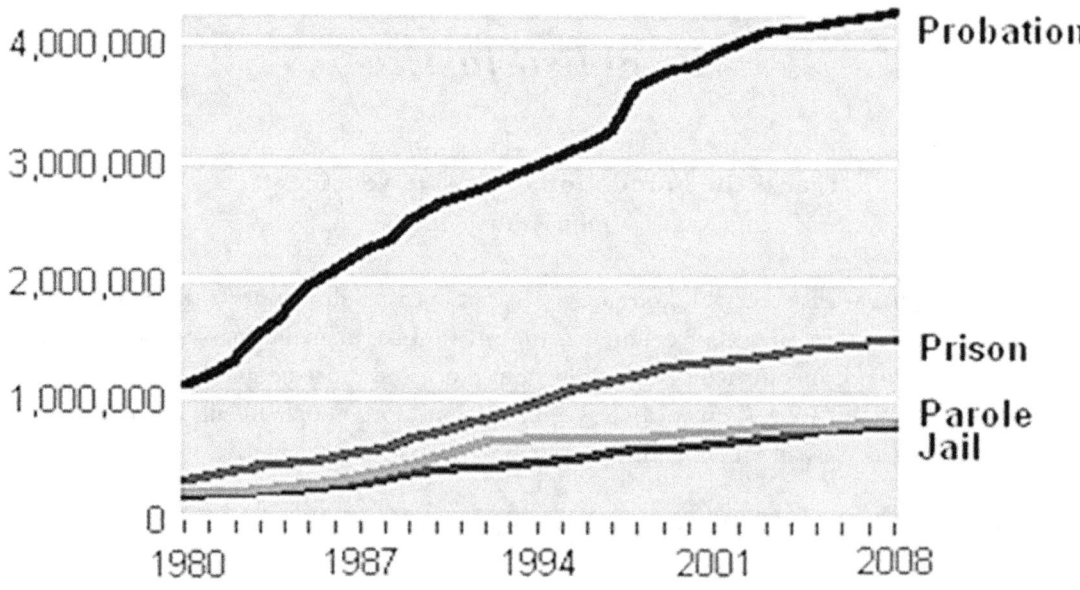

## Adult correctional populations, 1980-2008

Source: Bureau of Justice Statistics Correctional Surveys (The Annual Probation Survey, National Prisoner Statistics Program, Annual Survey of Jails, and Annual Parole Survey, as presented in Correctional Populations in the United States, annual, Prisoners in 2008, and Probation and Parole in the United States, 2008, http://bjs.ojp.usdoj.gov/content/glance/corr2.cfm)

From this graph presented by the Justice Department, the number of people in prison has at least tripled in thirty years. The number of people on probation has quadrupled, and the number of people on parole or in jail has at least doubled. It would appear that there has been a crime wave in the U.S. over this time, but no such crime wave shows up in the data (excluding drug arrests). Many more people are getting justice now than thirty years ago, however, and the penal population has increased dramatically.

*Direct expenditures for each of the major criminal justice functions (police, corrections, judicial) have also been increasing:*

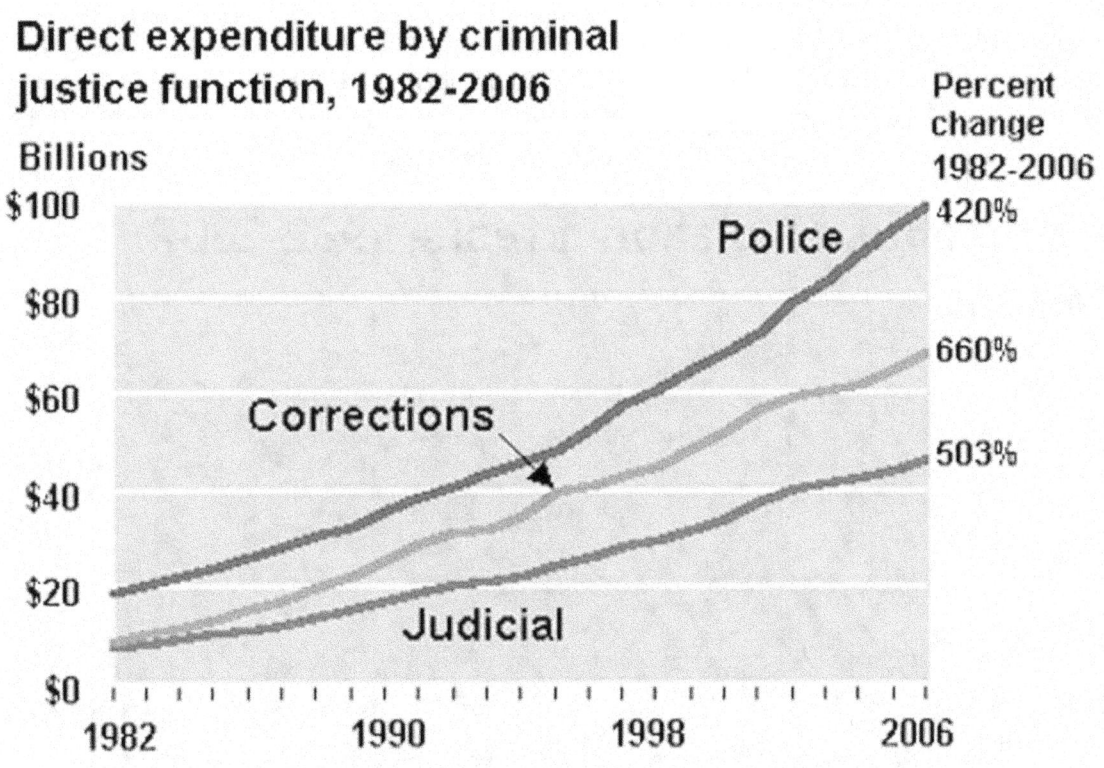

(Source: Justice Expenditure and Employment Extracts, Bureau of Justice Statistics Correctional Surveys, http:// bjs.ojp.usdoj.gov/content/glance/corr2.cfm )

In twenty five years, spending for police has grown from $20 billion to $100 billion, an increase of 420%. Corrections increased 660%, to more than $60 billion, and the judicial system grew by more than 500% to over $40 billion, and this was just up until 2006. The U.S. now spends at least $200 billion a year on our justice system (up from about $40 billion in 1982). The money we spend on our justice system ($200 billion per year) is *more than the entire* GDP of the following nations: Czech Republic $194B, Israel $195B, Malaysia $191B, Egypt $188B, Singapore $177B, Nigeria $169B, Pakistan $166B, Chile $162B, Romania $161B, Philippines $161B, Algeria $141B, Hungary $129B, Peru $127B, New Zealand $118B, and many others. One has to ask, did crime increase at the same rate during this period—more than at least 400%? Were more cops, lawyers and judges, and more corrections officers needed to lower crime? Let's take a look at who has received all this justice.

(Source: List of countries by GDP {nominal}, From Wikipedia, the free encyclopedia. en.wikipedia.org)

---

### *Arrests*

---

Federal, state, and local agencies share responsibility for enforcing the Nation's drug laws, although most arrests are made by state and local authorities. In 2007 the Federal Bureau of Investigation's Uniform Crime Reports (UCR) estimated that there were about 1,841,200 state and local arrests for drug abuse violations in the United States.

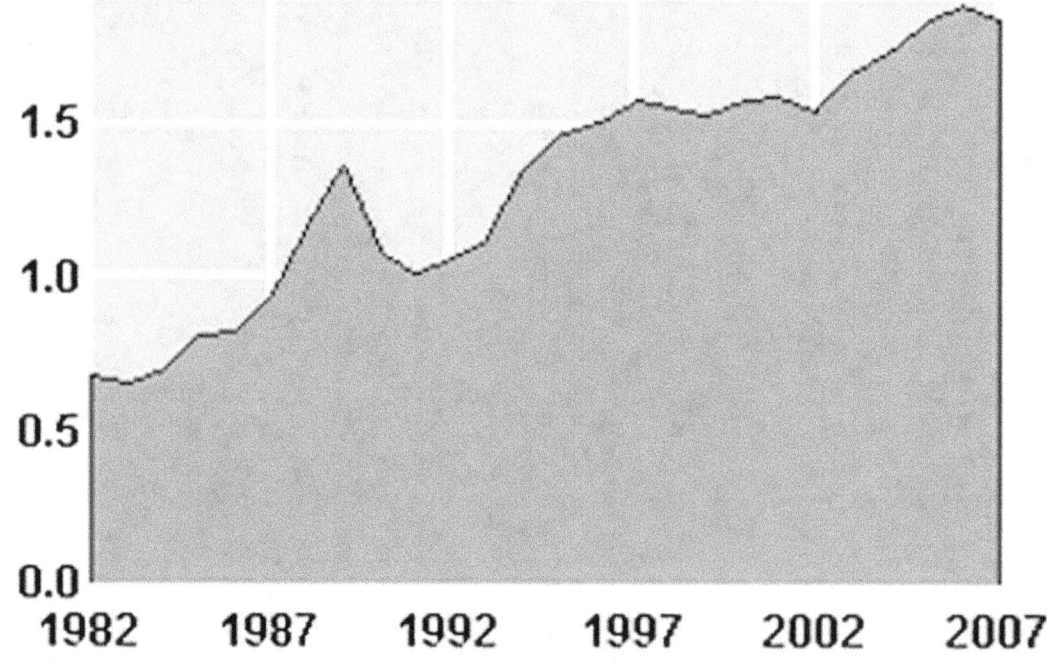

(Source: FBI, Uniform Crime Reports, *Crime in the United States,* annually, FBI.gov)

According to the Uniform Crime Reports (UCR), drug abuse violations are defined as state and/or local offenses relating to the unlawful possession, sale, use, growing, manufacturing, and making of narcotic drugs including opium or cocaine and their derivatives, marijuana, synthetic narcotics, and dangerous non-narcotic drugs such as barbiturates.

---

*More than four-fifths of drug law violation arrests are for possession:*

---

## Number of arrests, by type of drug law violations, 1982-2007

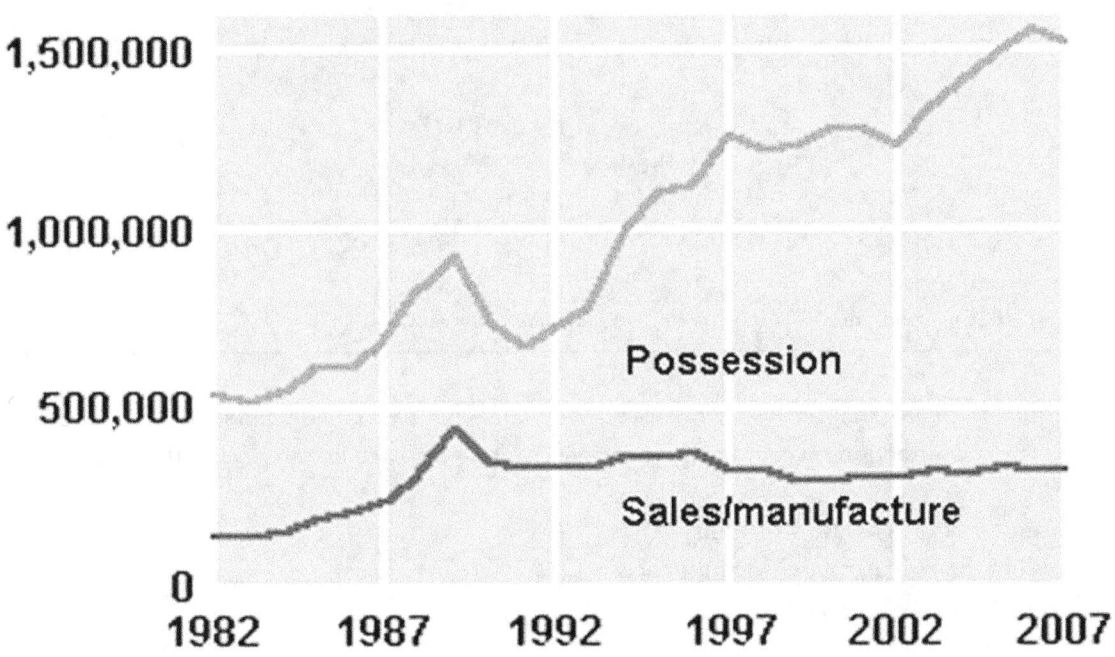

(Source: FBI, Uniform Crime Reports, *Crime in the United States,* annually, FBI.gov)

---

The increase in police, justice, and corrections looks surprising similar to the increases in the amount of arrests for drug possession, which almost tripled during the same period. The estimated number of arrests for drug abuse violations continues to increase. Arrests of adults increased in recent years, while arrests of juveniles decreased slightly. Juveniles are defined as persons under age 18. Adults are defined as persons age 18 or older.

In 1987 drug arrests were 7.4% of the total of all arrests reported to the FBI; by 2007, drug arrests had risen to 13.0% of all arrests, although the actual number had almost tripled since 1982.

## Drug arrests by age, 1970-2007

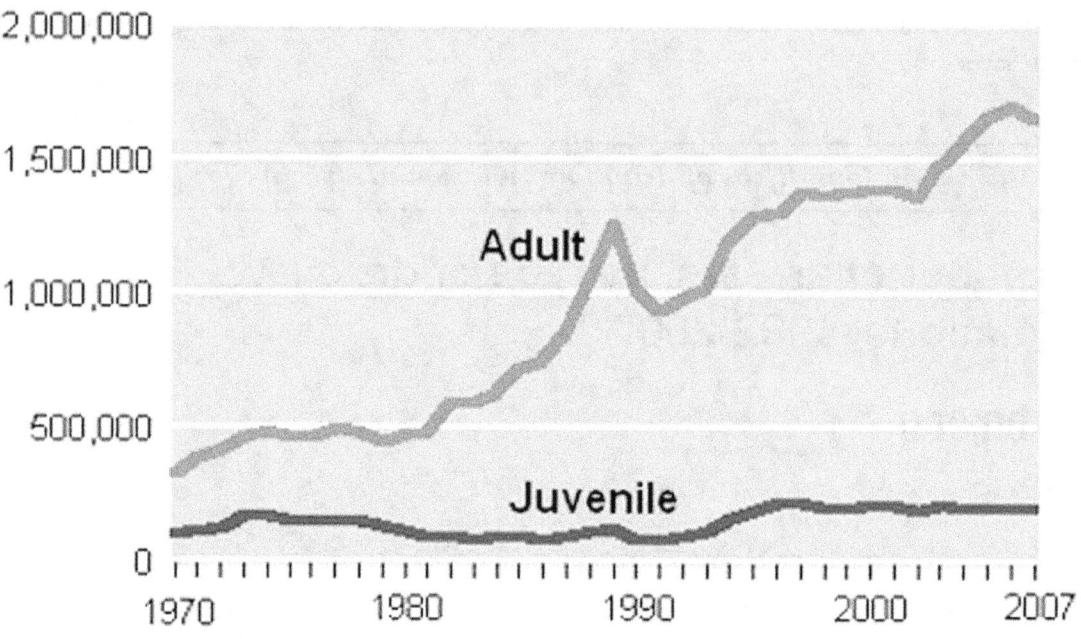

(Source: FBI, Uniform Crime Reports, *Crime in the United States,* annually, FBI.gov)

In 2007, according to the UCR, law enforcement agencies nationwide made an estimated 14 million arrests for all criminal infractions except traffic violations. Among the specific categories, the highest arrest counts were —

- 1.8 million for drug abuse violations;
- 1.4 million for driving under the influence;
- 1.3 million for simple assaults; and
- 1.2 million for larceny-thefts.

Look at the top figure, 1.8 million people arrested for drug abuse violations. If you compare the charts for the rises in prison population with the chart for drug abuse violations, you will see that they almost perfectly overlap.

There is no mention in the Constitution of locking away people for drug possession (the highest increase in number of arrests from 1982-2007). Sales and manufacture numbers peaked in the late 1980's, then dropped, and then started to plateau. It's clear from the data provided here by the FBI that it is possession of drug violations that has ballooned the prison population to what it is today. Again, the cost of this justice has been high, police, corrections, and judicial budgets have increased 420%, 660%, and 503% respectively from 1982-2006. The resulting cost: $200 billion dollars.

As everyone is aware, this is due to the "War on Drugs." Failing to stem the tide of sales and manufacture of drugs, despite spending tens of billions on programs within the U.S. and billions more in countries like Colombia, data show arrests for sales and manufacture haven't increased. So, with ever increasing budgets available, enforcement turned to users and possession, whose arrest totals went up three fold since 1982. As a result, we have by far the most people, per capita, in prison of any country in the world.

| # 1 | United States | 715 per 100,000 people |
| # 2 | Russia | 584 per 100,000 people |
| # 3 | Belarus | 554 per 100,000 people |
| # 4 | Palau | 523 per 100,000 people |
| # 5 | Belize | 459 per 100,000 people |
| # 6 | Suriname | 437 per 100,000 people |
| # 7 | Dominica | 420 per 100,000 people |
| # 8 | Ukraine | 416 per 100,000 people |
| # 9 | Bahamas, The | 410 per 100,000 people |
| # 10 | South Africa | 402 per 100,000 people |
| # 11 | Kyrgyzstan | 390 per 100,000 people |
| # 12 | Singapore | 388 per 100,000 people |
| # 13 | Kazakhstan | 386 per 100,000 people |
| # 14 | Barbados | 367 per 100,000 people |
| # 15 | Panama | 354 per 100,000 people |
| # 16 | Trinidad and Tobago | 351 per 100,000 people |
| # 17 | Thailand | 340 per 100,000 people |
| # 18 | Estonia | 339 per 100,000 people |
| # 19 | Latvia | 339 per 100,000 people |
| # 20 | Saint Kitts and Nevis | 338 per 100,000 people |
| # 21 | Grenada | 333 per 100,000 people |
| # 22 | Botswana | 327 per 100,000 people |
| # 23 | Swaziland | 324 per 100,000 people |
| # 24 | Mongolia | 303 per 100,000 people |
| # 25 | Antigua and Barbuda | 278 per 100,000 people |

(Data source: Crime Statistics > Prisoners > Per capita (most recent) by country. nationmaster.com)

According to our founding fathers, we have attained justice, but at what price? According to the U.S. Bureau of Justice Statistics (BJS): "In 2008, over 7.3 million people were on probation, in jail or prison, or on parole at year-end — 3.2% of all U.S. adult residents or 1 in every 31 adults." An American has a 1 in 10 chance of catching the flu, and a 1 in 31 chance of ending up in prison, jail, or otherwise in trouble with the legal system.

2,304,115 were incarcerated in U.S. prisons and jails in 2008. In addition, according to a December 2009 BJS report, there were 92,854 held in juvenile facilities as of the 2006 Census of Juveniles in Residential Placement

(CJRP), conducted by the *Office of Juvenile Justice and Delinquency Prevention*. The "War on Drugs" now looks more like a civil war, with the losers – those using and possessing drugs – ending up in jail. Our war on drugs is, if nothing else, very expensive. $200 billion dollars is quite a lot of money, all courtesy of American taxpayers.

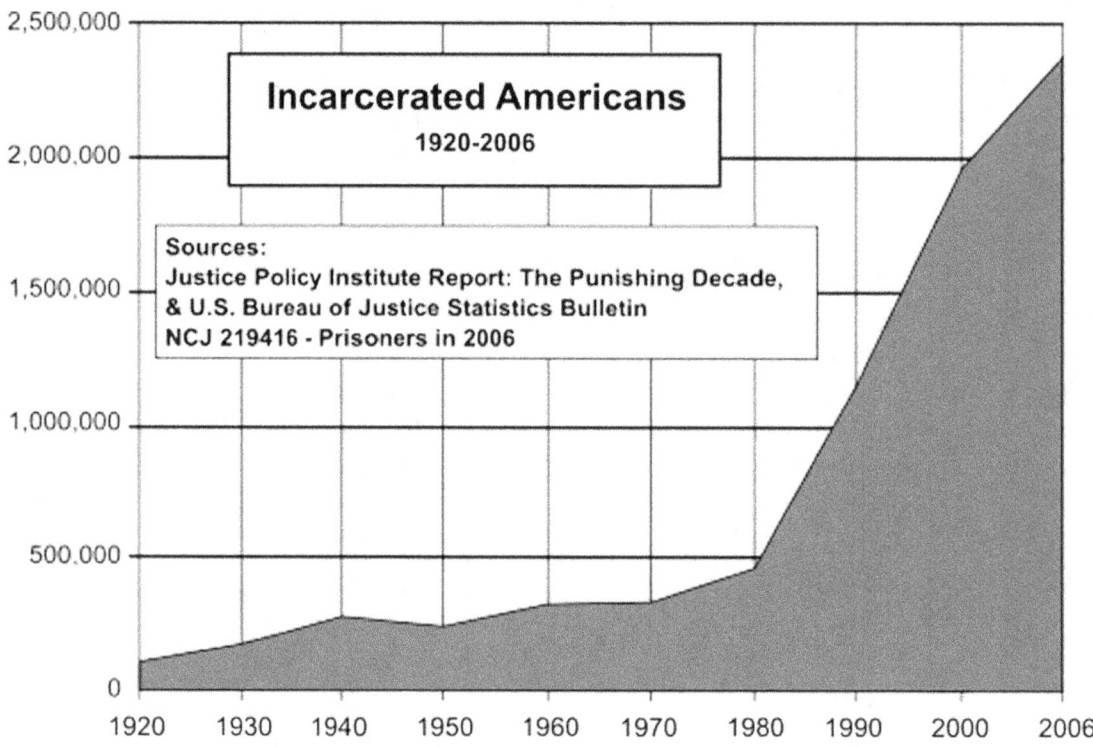

**Incarcerated Americans**
**1920-2006**

Sources:
Justice Policy Institute Report: The Punishing Decade,
& U.S. Bureau of Justice Statistics Bulletin
NCJ 219416 - Prisoners in 2006

We have more people in jail than the *entire populations* of some countries: Latvia: 2,234,800, Qatar: 1,696,563, Estonia: 1,340,127, Trinidad and Tobago: 1,317,714, Fiji: 854,000, Solomon Islands: 530,669, Western Sahara: 530,000, Suriname: 524,000, Luxembourg: 502,100, Bahamas: 353,658, Belize: 333,200, Iceland: 318,200. *We have almost eight times the entire population of Iceland in prison.*

Here's another sobering fact: It is estimated by the U.S. Bureau of the Census that in 1776 there were a total of 2.5 million people living in the U.S. So, in 2010, we now have almost as many people incarcerated as *the entire population of our country when it was founded*. Putting people in jail is obviously very lucrative for federal, state, and local law enforcement, judges and lawyers, and prison workers and builders of prisons. But paying the bill for almost 2.3 million prisoners is staggering, and the untold effects on the people and families. The budget for law enforcement, judicial, and prisons was more than $200 billion dollars per year, and probably higher now. Is this justice, as the founding fathers wanted, or is it something else?

*Lawmakers, lawyers and bureaucrats are making more and more things "illegal"*

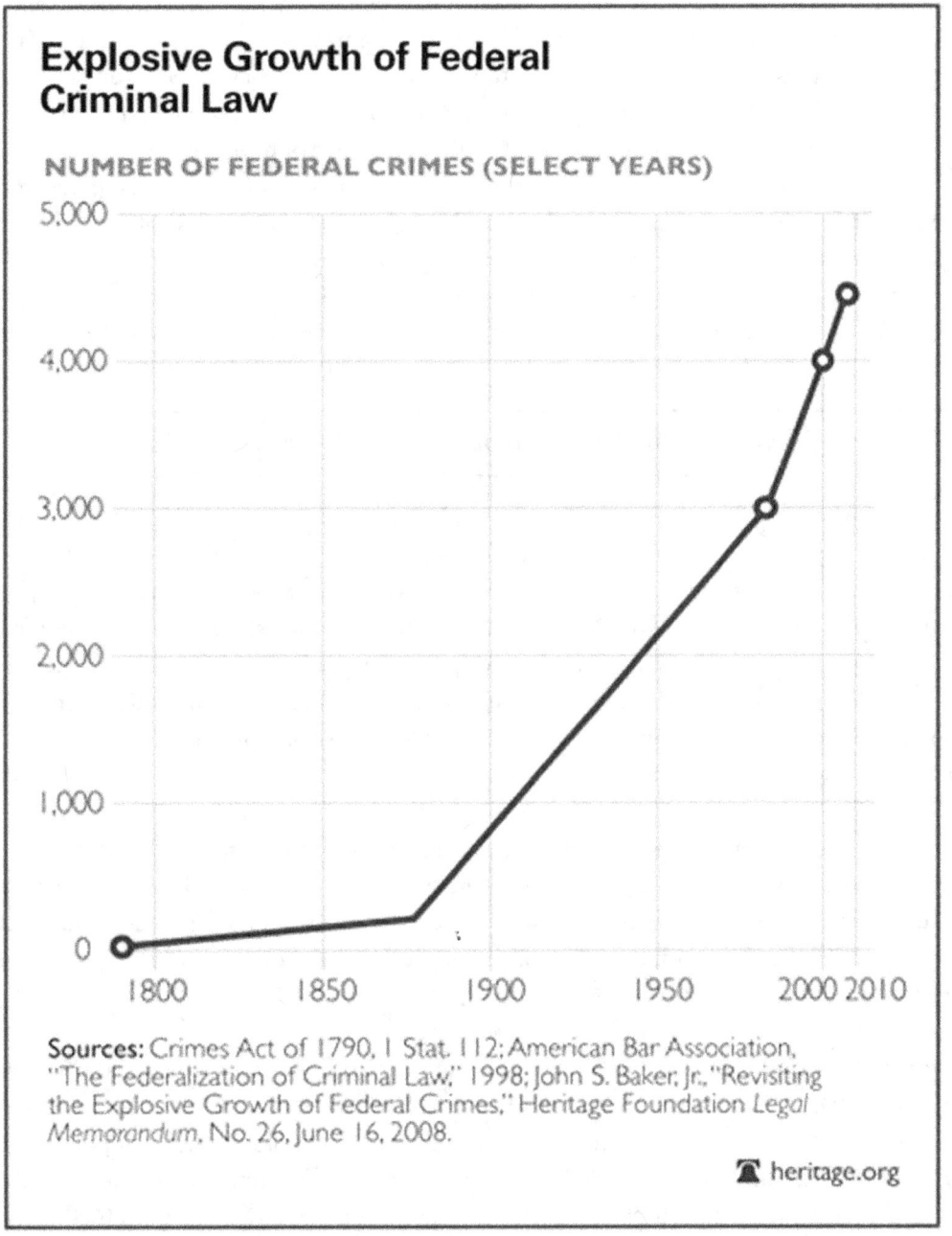

**Explosive Growth of Federal Criminal Law**

NUMBER OF FEDERAL CRIMES (SELECT YEARS)

**Sources:** Crimes Act of 1790, 1 Stat. 112; American Bar Association, "The Federalization of Criminal Law," 1998; John S. Baker, Jr. "Revisiting the Explosive Growth of Federal Crimes," Heritage Foundation *Legal Memorandum*, No. 26, June 16, 2008.

heritage.org

(Source: The Heritage Foundation, Hertitage.org, copyright The Heritage Foundation, used with permission)

How do so many people end up in jail? By making more laws, of course. There has been an explosion of federal criminal laws. The number of criminal offenses in the U.S. Code increased from 3,000 in the early 1980s to 4,000 by 2000 to over 4,450 by 2008. Moreover, there is no letup in sight; rather, the pace appears to be constant or even accelerating. Many federal departments and agencies have created so many criminal offenses that the *Congressional Research Service* itself admitted that it was unable even to count all of the offenses. The Service's best estimate? "Tens of thousands." In short, not even Congress's own experts have a clear understanding of the size or scope of federal criminalization. *The Heritage Foundation and the National Association of Criminal Defense Lawyers* reported in May 2010 the results of a joint study finding that three out of every five new nonviolent offenses lack a "criminal-intent" requirement that is adequate to protect citizens from unjust criminal punishment—A person who lacked criminal intent engaged in conduct that they did not know was illegal or otherwise wrongful. Despite this rampant over-criminalization, Congress continues to add offenses at an average rate of one new crime for every week of every year (including when its members are not in session). All inherently wrongful conduct has been criminalized several times over, yet from 2000 through 2007, Congress enacted 452 new criminal offenses

## High Cost of Prisons Not Paying Off, Report Finds

Let's look at how much it costs to keep people in prison. According to a report filed in 2006 (the last time this study was done) by the Commission on Safety and Abuse in America's Prisons *Confronting Confinement*, the U.S. spends more than any other nation – $60 billion a year – to house inmates, but sees little benefit as a result. The Commission was a bipartisan panel looking at the cost of prison on taxpayers. Americans spend $60 billion a year to imprison 2.2 million people — exceeding any other nation — but receive a dismal return on the investment (the prison population was up to 2.3 million by 2008). The commission concluded there needed to be greater public scrutiny of what goes on behind bars.

The report goes on to say legislators have passed get-tough laws that have packed the nation's jails and prisons to overflowing with convicts, most of them poor and uneducated. However, politicians have done little to help inmates emerge as better citizens upon release. The consequences of that failure include financial strain on states, public health threats from parolees with communicable diseases, and a cycle of crime and victimization driven by a recidivism rate of more than 60%, the report says.

"If these were public schools or publicly traded corporations, we'd shut them down," said Alexander Busansky, executive director of the Commission. Rather, the commission said, Americans view prisons with detachment or futility, growing interested when a riot makes the news and then looking away, "hoping the troubles inside the walls will not affect us." In 2006, $68,747,203,000 was spent on corrections. "The average annual operating cost per state inmate in 2001 was $22,650, or $62.05 per day; among facilities operated by the Federal Bureau of Prisons, it was $22,632 per inmate, or $62.01 per day."

Housing the approximately 500,000 people in jail awaiting trial who cannot afford bail costs $9 billion a year. Most jail inmates are petty, nonviolent offenders. Twenty years ago most nonviolent defendants were released on their own recognizance (trusted to show up at trial). Now most are given bail, and most pay a bail bondsman to afford it. 62% of local jail inmates are awaiting trial.

To ease jail overcrowding, many states consider building new jails every year. As an example Lubbock County, Texas has decided to build a $110 million mega-jail to ease jail overcrowding. Jail costs an average of $60 a day nationally. In Broward County, Florida supervised pretrial release costs about $7 a day per person while jail costs $115 a day. The jail system costs a quarter of every county tax dollar in Broward County, and is the single largest expense to the county taxpayer The report also mentioned that it is estimated that 1 in 9 state government employees works in corrections.

The report stated that almost $70 billion was spent on corrections alone (to house 2.2 million prisoners). Did our founding fathers really want us to be known as the country that puts the most people in jail of any nation in the world? Does anyone think this is what Thomas Jefferson, George Washington, or Abraham Lincoln would have wanted?

# *"Insure domestic tranquility"*

One has to ask, does our form of government today insure *domestic tranquility* (def: quality or state of being tranquil; calmness; peacefulness; quiet; serenity). There is no question that, as a nation, we have high levels of domestic tranquility. We are as safe and protected as any free society can be. We have more than enough police and other forms of protection, and the greatest military in the world. But, let's look at the home front; each person's domestic tranquility, each family's peacefulness, quiet and serenity. The U.S. used to pride itself on its large middle class. After World War Two, the great middle class was born. As far as a bell-curve, most people were in the middle, had good jobs, and had an excellent standard of living. That was 60 years ago. Let's look at what is happening to the middle class today.

The rich are getting richer and the poor are getting poorer at a staggering rate. Once upon a time, the United States had the largest and most prosperous middle class in the history of the world, but now that is changing at a blinding pace.

So why are we witnessing such fundamental changes? Well, the globalism and "free trade" that our politicians and business leaders insisted would be so good for us has had some rather nasty side effects. It turns out that they didn't tell us that the "global economy" would mean that middle class American workers would eventually have to directly compete for jobs with people on the other side of the world where there is no minimum wage, no litigation and very few regulations. The big global corporations have greatly benefited by exploiting third world labor pools over the last several decades, but middle class American workers have increasingly found things to be very tough. And, thanks the behavior of huge banks and Wall Street, our economy was thrown into the worst recession since the Great Depression. How has this affected the middle class? It's been a nightmare.

Here are the statistics to prove it:

83 percent of all U.S. stocks are in the hands of 1 percent of the people.

61 percent of Americans "always or usually" live paycheck to paycheck, which was up from 49 percent in 2008 and 43 percent in 2007.

66 percent of the income growth between 2001 and 2007 went to the top 1% of all Americans.

36 percent of Americans say that they don't contribute anything to retirement savings.

A staggering 43 percent of Americans have less than $10,000 saved up for retirement.

24 percent of American workers say that they have postponed their planned retirement age in the past year.

Over 1.4 million Americans filed for personal bankruptcy in 2009, which represented a 32 percent increase over 2008.

Only the top 5 percent of U.S. households have earned enough additional income to match the rise in housing costs since 1975.

For the first time in U.S. history, banks own a greater share of residential housing net worth in the United States than all individual Americans put together.

In 1950, the ratio of the average executive's paycheck to the average worker's paycheck was about 30 to 1. Since the year 2000, that ratio has exploded to between 300 to 500 to one.

As of 2007, the bottom 80 percent of American households held about 7% of the liquid financial assets.

The bottom 50 percent of income earners in the United States now collectively own less than 1 percent of the nation's wealth.

Average Wall Street bonuses for 2009 were up 17 percent when compared with 2008.

In the United States, the average federal worker now earns 60% MORE than the average worker in the private sector.

The top 1 percent of U.S. households own nearly twice as much of America's corporate wealth as they did just 15 years ago.

In America today, the average time needed to find a job has risen to a record 35.2 weeks. More than 40 percent of Americans who actually are employed are now working in service jobs, which are often very low paying.

for the first time in U.S. history, more than 40 million Americans are on food stamps, and the U.S. Department of Agriculture projects that number will go up to 43 million Americans in 2011.

This is what American workers now must compete against: in China a garment worker makes approximately 86 cents an hour and in Cambodia a garment worker makes approximately 22 cents an hour.

Approximately 21 percent of all children in the United States are living below the poverty line in 2010 - the highest rate in 20 years.

Despite the financial crisis, the number of millionaires in the United States rose a whopping 16 percent to 7.8 million in 2009.

The top 10 percent of Americans now earn around 50 percent of our national income.

(*Source: The Middle Class in America Is Radically Shrinking. Here Are the Stats to Prove it*, by Michael Snyder Yahoo! Business, Jul. 15, 2010, courtesy of Business Insider. businessinsider.com. Used with permission)

Far from domestic tranquility for the average American, these statistics show how the middle class in being wiped out. We don't own our houses, the banks own a greater share of residential houses than all individuals put together. The bottom 80% of Americans only hold 7% of all liquid assets. At least 40 million people are on food stamps, and that number is expected to rise. By any measure, the former level of personal "domestic tranquility" for most Americans is almost gone.

What has developed is a situation where the people at the top are doing quite well, while most Americans are finding it increasingly difficult to make it. There are now about five unemployed Americans for every new job opening in the United States, and the number of "chronically unemployed" is absolutely soaring. The recession wiped out almost 8 million jobs. There simply are not nearly enough jobs for everyone. Many of those who are able to get jobs are finding that they are making less money than they used to. In fact, an increasingly large percentage of Americans are working at low wage retail and service jobs. People have turned to the government for help, and have only gotten more food stamps, more unemployment benefits, and more excuses. The truth is, the government can't provide for the middle class as it does for those on Welfare. The government can't make more jobs (at least not more non-government jobs), and, in essence, can't insure our domestic tranquility, at least not economically.

## End of the American Dream?

Despite the "official" end of the recession in 2009, life remains drab for a large portion of the population: Nearly half of the people in the U.S. aren't living what they would call the "American Dream," according to a new survey. StrategyOne surveyed 1,008 Americans and found 48% of those polled answered "no" when asked: "Are you living the American Dream today?"

In households earning between $40,000 and $50,000 a year, just 41% answered the question affirmatively. However, for higher earning households — those at or above $75,000 annually — 71% of respondents said they were living the American Dream. That supports the notion that money might not be everything, but it helps. The survey also suggests a lack of faith in the possibility of upward mobility: Of the 48% who said they aren't living the American Dream, more than half said they didn't think they ever would.

(Source of data: *StrategyOne Public Opinion Survey: The 'American Dream' in today's economy,* Bradley Honan, http://www.strategyone.net/documents/StrategyOne%20American%20Dream%20powerpoint.pdf, Strategyone.net)

## Safe in the Suburbs?  Not Anymore...

The suburbs—the last great bastion for the middle class, American suburbs are no longer a refuge from poverty in cities. A pair of analyses by the nonprofit *Brookings Institution* paints a bleak economic picture for the 100 largest metropolitan areas over the past decade and in coming years, and finds that suburbs now are home to one-third of the nation's poor, and rising.

The study of census data finds that since 2000, the number of poor people in the suburbs jumped by 37.4 percent to 13.7 million. The growth rate of suburban poverty is more than double that of cities and higher than the national rate of 26.5 percent. At the same time, social service providers are spread thin in many suburban areas, according to a detailed Brookings survey of groups in representative metropolitan areas of Chicago, Los Angeles and the District of Columbia. That has forced providers to turn away many poor people due to scarce aid that typically goes to cities first.

"After the recession began in 2007, the suburbs continued to post larger increases in the number of poor — adding 1.8 million, compared with 1.4 million in the cities." Strategies to address poverty in suburbs, as in cities, include both cash assistance programs and social service programs. Five cash assistance programs are particularly prominent today: Temporary Assistance for Needy Families (TANF) Welfare cash assistance; the Supplemental Nutrition Assistance Program (SNAP, formerly the Food Stamp Program); Unemployment Insurance (UI); the

Earned Income Tax Credit (EITC); and the refundable portion of the Child Tax Credit (CTC). Combined these five core cash assistance programs delivered about $230 billion in aid nationally in 2009, driven in part by significant expansions in SNAP and UI that have helped millions of families cope with income losses during the Great Recession. "Millions of Americans at all income levels moved to the suburbs looking for better schools, better jobs, affordable housing, and a sense of security, but in recent years, as incomes have fallen, people had a harder and harder time making ends meet," said Scott Allard, a University of Chicago professor who co-wrote one of the reports. "As a result, Americans who never imagined becoming poor are now asking for assistance and many are not getting the help they need."

## How did this happen?

As the statistics and data show, there is domestic tranquility and serenity for the 10% of people that own and control everything in this country. People have become aware that the government cannot "insure domestic tranquility," at least not economically speaking. In fact, our government did nothing while predatory lenders; mortgage companies, banks, and investment houses, created and perpetrated the whole sub-prime mortgage debacle. Then, instead of helping people save their homes, the government bailed out the banks and financial institutions that perpetrated the fraud with taxpayer dollars.

The crescendo, the crowning moment, happened in Washington. Our politicians were called on to save the U.S. from a supposed financial meltdown, a return to the Great Depression. The biggest threat from the meltdown was that people were told that they would no longer get paychecks due to a freeze-up in credit markets. The House and Senate debated the bailout, but the people also weighed in. Washington was flooded with more phone calls, emails, faxes, and letters than ever before. The people were emphatic that they did not want the financial bailout of Wall Street and Banks. Senators and Congressmen actually listened to their constituents and voted down the bailout. Then, two days later, President Bush, Treasury Secretary Paulson, and a group of politicians (mainly Democrats leaders Nancy Pelosi and Harry Reid) made a back-room deal to go forward with the bailout, and the taxpayer's money was handed over to banks, Wall Street, AIG, and a host of other firms to cover their loses from gambling on sub-prime mortgages, commercial paper, credit default swaps, and all the other financial instruments that lost trillions of dollars.

The result was the victimization of people by mortgage lending they couldn't afford, variable rate mortgages that went up and up, and millions losing their homes to foreclosure. The people spoke; they didn't want tax dollars spent to bailout anything. The Democratic process actually worked, which was surprising in itself. Well, actually, it only worked for two days. Then big money, banking lobbyists, special interests; the people that actually control our country flexed their political muscle, and the bailout went through anyway. The people were outraged. You can almost hear the birth of the Tea Party, it happened shortly after this outrage. People decided to do whatever they could to save their homes, to save their way of life, to save their country from the politicians.

To look at it another way, imagine a car instead of a house, and imagine taxes as savings. You are still paying on your car, but your payment doubled in a few months. Then someone steals your car, and the government, instead of using your "savings" to get your car back, gives the money to the car thieves, and they keep your car. Predatory lenders gave out millions of mortgages people couldn't afford, then leveraged these mortgages, packaged and sold the mortgages, securitized the mortgages, sold the securities, bought insurance against default of these mortgages, and eventually ripped off millions of people. And instead of helping the taxpayer keep his/her home, using tax dollars they paid the government, they gave a trillion dollars to the people that stole your house through foreclosure. Then came the foreclosure scam, where banks were foreclosing on houses without the proper paperwork, without proof, and without cause. As everyone now knows, the process whereby banks actually take your home away has become fraudulent, also while the government stood by and did nothing.

## Foreclosuregate

As if the mortgage lending fraud and the sub-prime debacle wasn't enough, maybe it's becoming clearer why it was done. Big banks, not happy just owning private property via lending have now taken to foreclosures to actually get the properties themselves. At least one politician is doing something about it. Due to "mounting evidence of a state of rampant lawlessness in Central Florida," Rep. Alan Grayson (D-Fla.) last week sent a letter to FBI director Robert Mueller and U.S. Attorney Robert O'Neill imploring them to investigate possible criminal conduct in what's become known as "foreclosuregate." "There are increasing signs that big banks routinely evade laws meant to protect homeowners, It is not enough for big banks only to apologize for fraud, perjury, and even breaking and entering - when they are caught. It is time for handcuffs. Fraud does not become legal just because a big bank does it" Rep. Grayson was quoted as saying.

Barry Ritholtz, CEO of Fusion IQ and author of *The Big Picture* blog, couldn't agree more. "The whole chain of the foreclosure process is rife with lies, with false affidavits, false testimony — with fraud," Ritholtz says. "This is criminal and these people need to go to jail." Unlike some observers, who believe banks only appear guilty of what some have called "sloppy work," Ritholtz says problems in the foreclosure process go far beyond mere technicalities. "This is a systemic approach to foreclosure where the rule of law completely trampled on and property rights have been totally ignored." While some experts fret the impact a foreclosure moratorium will have on the housing market and/or bank balance sheets, Ritholtz says something far more fundamental is at stake. "This is about property rights," he says. "This is about very sacred rights.....and the respect for the rule of law."

This is round two of the fraud perpetrated on common people, first to give them mortgages they couldn't afford, and now breaking laws to seize their properties. Except for Rep. Grayson, there hasn't been much done by our politicians to protect the people of this country. Every day there is some new type of financial fraud reported, and 2000 pages of new regulations forced into law by President Obama has done nothing to protect the people. Once banks get private property away from the people, what will they have left? Absolutely nothing; well there is always Welfare, food stamps, and public housing, all graciously provided by the government and politicians at the expense of the taxpayers.

# "*Provide for the common defense*"

**It may be laid down as a primary position, and the basis of our system, that every Citizen who enjoys the protection of a Free Government, owes not only a proportion of his property, but even of his personal services to the defense of it.**

*George Washington*

**If there is one principle more deeply rooted in the mind of every American, it is that we should have nothing to do with conquest.**

*Thomas Jefferson*

In the time of the birth of our nation, our politicians made sure that we had local militias. We then had a revolutionary army, and today we have the strongest military in the world. While we are providing for the common defense, the cost is eye-opening. The real question that needs to be asked is why do we have military bases in 40 countries? Are we providing for the common defense of the U.S. or the world as a whole? There is no mandate in our constitution to provide for the defense and protection of the rest of the world, yet we seem to respond militarily to every crisis that happens (except those involving Russia). Thomas Jefferson warned against "conquest," that we should have nothing to do with conquest. Does having military bases in 40 countries protect the people living in the continental United States, or is it conquest? You can decide for yourself.

Military spending has almost doubled since 2001 (see chart below), not all of which was due to the Iraq and Afghanistan wars. It's hard to argue against having a strong military, it's something we need, but the people, once again, are far removed from the decision making process on how much military spending is enough. It's a matter of course, and not something that is even debated much in Washington, Yet, at its current rate of increase, will approach a trillion dollars a year within the next decade.

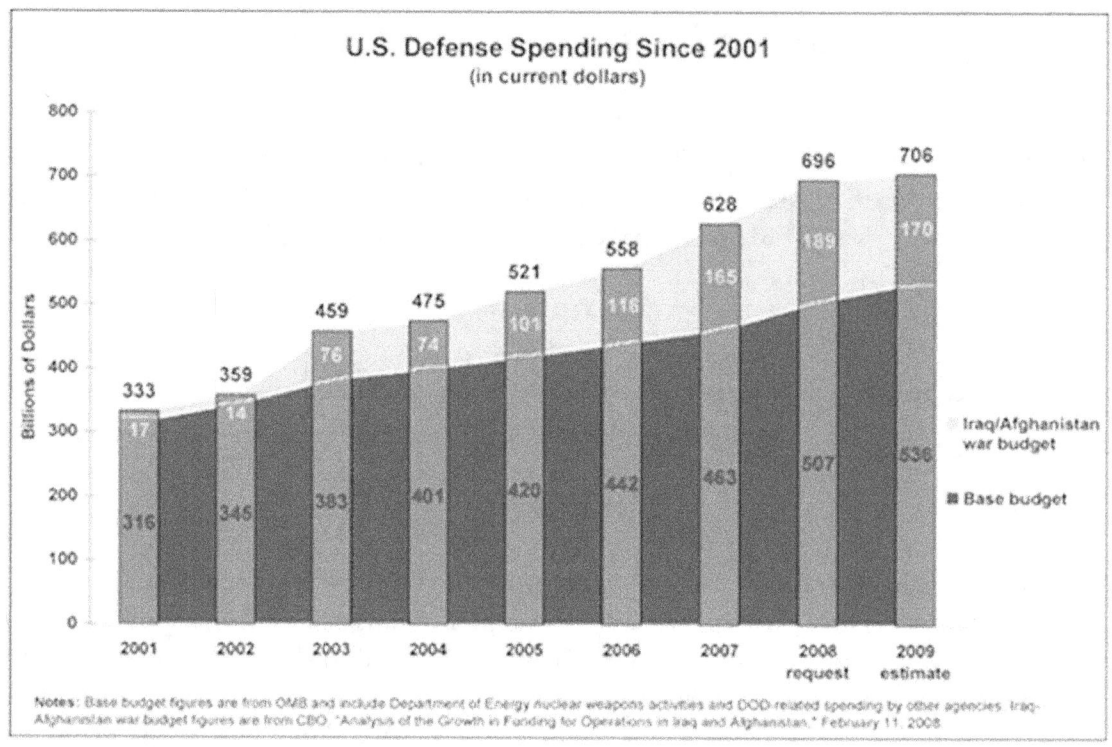

(Graph provided by the U.S. Office of Military Budget, latest available graph of military spending, Defense.gov)

Defense spending will always be a controversial issue, but, defense spending is only the third largest expenditure by the Federal Government. Let's take a look at a much larger expenditure than the military.

# "Promote the General Welfare"

**Government does not solve problems; it subsidizes them.**

*Ronald Reagan*

Our government has indeed promoted the general Welfare, or maybe just Welfare. *The Heritage Foundation* published a report entitled "Obama to spend $10.3 Trillion on Welfare: Uncovering the Full Cost of Means-Tested Welfare or Aid to the Poor." It is very interesting, because although President Obama is not to blame for much of the huge deficit spending accomplished by Speaker of the House Nancy Pelosi and Senate Majority Leader Harry Reid over the years, he is responsible for further inflating Welfare spending in a massive way.

Since the beginning of the "War on Poverty," government has spent vast sums on Welfare or aid to the poor. As this report shows, means-tested Welfare or aid to poor and low-income persons is now the second most expen¬sive government function. Its cost ranks below support for the elderly through Social Security and Medicare, but above spending on national defense. Prior to the current reces¬sion, one dollar in seven in total federal, state, and local government spending went to means-tested Welfare.

Means-tested Welfare spending or aid to the poor consists of government programs that provide assistance delib¬erately and exclusively to poor and lower-income people. By contrast, non-Welfare programs provide benefits and services for the general population. For example, food stamps, public housing, Medicaid, and Temporary Assistance for Needy Families are means-tested aid programs that provide benefits only to poor and lower-income persons. On the other hand, Social Security, Medicare, police protection, and public education are not means-tested; they pro¬vide services and benefits to persons at all income levels.

In fiscal year (FY) 2008, total government spending on means-tested Welfare or aid to the poor amounted to $714 billion. This high level of Welfare spending was the result of steady permanent growth in Welfare spending over several decades rather than a short-term response to temporary economic conditions.

Of the $714 billion in Welfare spending, $522 billion (73 percent) was federal expenditures, and $192 billion (27 percent) was state government funds. Nearly all state government Welfare expenditures are required matching contributions in order to get federal Welfare money. These contributions could be considered a "Welfare tax" that the federal government imposes on the states. Ignoring these matching state payments into the federal Welfare system results in a serious underestimation of spending on behalf of the poor.

Of total means-tested spending in FY 2008, 52 percent was spent on medical care for poor and lower-income persons (Medicaid), and 37 percent was spent on cash, food, and housing aid. The remaining 11 percent was spent on social ser¬vices, training, child development, targeted federal education aid, and community development for lower-income persons and communities (as well as paying the hundreds of thousands of federal and state workers that administer these programs). Roughly half of means-tested spending goes to disabled or elderly persons. The other half goes to lower-income families with children, most of which are headed by single parents.

Means-tested Welfare means that someone is supposed to be checking on income and job status of recipients. In this means-tested system, which has been rubber-stamped over the decades, recipients are *penalized for working*. If you have a job or work, you get less cash, less food stamps, housing, and less healthcare. This system thus adds a huge *disincentive to work* and get off Welfare. It also promotes people to work "off the books," where they are paid cash or in other ways that will not show up as income at the Welfare office, and money that will not be taxed. People that have low paying jobs and medical problems (and aren't offered health insurance at work) find out that they have to quit their jobs to get medical care (Medicaid). So, they quit their job so they can start getting cash, food stamps, housing and healthcare, when all they wanted was healthcare.

Total means-tested Welfare spending in FY 2008 amounted to around $16,800 for each poor person in the U.S.; however, some Welfare spending goes to individuals who have low incomes but are not below the official poverty line (about $22,200 per year for a family of four). Typically, Welfare benefits are received not just by the poor, but also by persons who have incomes below 200 percent of the federal poverty level ($44,400 per year for a family of four). Around one-third of the U.S. population falls within this lower income range. On average, Welfare spending amounts to around $7,000 per year for each individual who is poor or who has an income below 200 percent of the poverty level. This comes to $28,000 per year for each lower-income family of four.

Welfare spending has grown exponentially since President Lyndon B. Johnson launched the "War on Poverty." Welfare spending was *13 times greater* in 2008, after adjusting for inflation, than it was when the War on Poverty started in 1964. Means-tested Welfare spending was 1.2 percent of the gross domestic product (GDP) when President Johnson began the War on Poverty. In 2008, it reached 5 percent of GDP. Like all federal entitlement programs, a good idea and a modest program has mushroomed by 1300% into almost a trillion dollar expense to taxpayers.

Annual means-tested Welfare spending is more than sufficient to <u>eliminate</u> poverty in the United States. The U.S. Census Bureau, which is in charge of measuring poverty and inequality in the nation, defines a family as poor if its annual income falls below official poverty income thresholds. If total means-tested Welfare spending were simply converted into cash benefits, the sum would be nearly *four times the amount* needed to raise the income of all poor families above the official poverty line.

One may reasonably ask how government can spend so much on Welfare and still have great inequality and so many people living in apparent poverty. The answer is that the Census ignores nearly the entire Welfare system in its measurements. In its conventional reports, the Census counts only 4 percent of total Welfare spending as income. Most government discussions of poverty and inequality do not account for the massive transfers to the Welfare state.

Since the beginning of the War on Poverty, government has spent <u>$15.9 trillion</u> (in inflation-adjusted 2008 dol¬lars) on means-tested Welfare. In comparison, the cost of all other wars in U.S. history was $6.4 trillion (in infla-tion-adjusted 2008 dollars). The War on Poverty has cost *twice* as much as all the military wars we have fought in our history. Not to be outdone, President Obama plans to spend *another* $10.3 trillion on Welfare in the years to come.

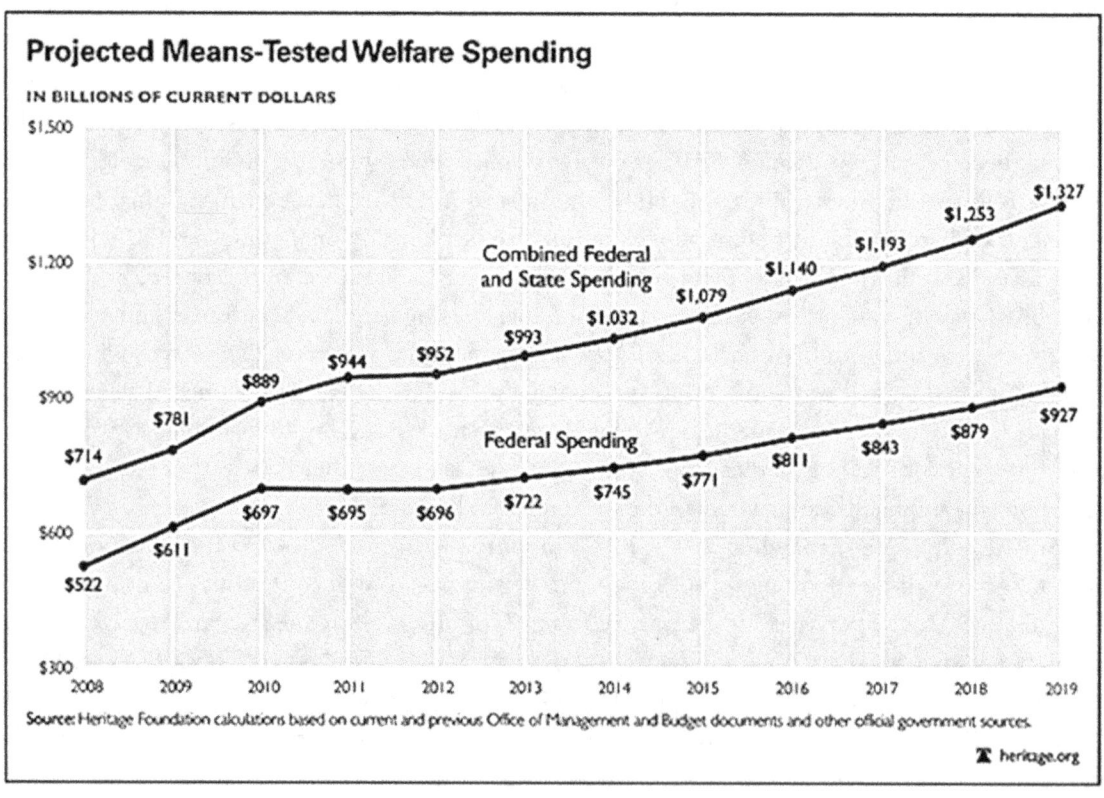

(Source: Originally published by The Heritage Foundation, Hertitage.org. Copyright The Heritage Foundation, used with permission)

### *Spending on Welfare alone is expected to reach $1 trillion by 2014 and $1.3 trillion by 2019.*

In his first two years in office, President Barack Obama increased annual federal Welfare spending by one-third from $522 billion to $697 billion. The combined two-year increase equaled almost $263 billion ($88.2 bil¬lion in 2009 plus $174.6 billion in 2010). After adjusting for inflation, this increase is two and a half times greater than any previous increase in federal Welfare spending in U.S. history. As a share of the economy, annual fed¬eral Welfare spending will rise by roughly 1.2 percent of GDP.

Under President Obama, government will spend more on Welfare in a single year than President George W. Bush spent on the war in Iraq during his entire presidency. According to the *Congressional Research Service*, the cost of the Iraq war through the end of the Bush Administration was around $622 billion. By contrast, annual federal and state means-tested Welfare spending reached $888 billion in 2010.

While campaigning for the presidency, Obama lamented that "the war in Iraq is costing each household about $100 per month." Applying the same standard to means-tested Welfare spending reveals that Welfare costed each household $560 per month in 2009 and $638 per month in 2010.

Most of Obama's increases in Welfare spending are permanent expansions of the Welfare state, not temporary increases in response to the current recession. According to the long-term spending plans set forth in Obama's 2010 budget, combined federal and state spending will not drop significantly after the recession ends. In fact, by 2014, Welfare spending is likely to equal $1 trillion per year. According to President Obama's budget projections, federal and state Welfare spending will total <u>$10.3 trillion</u> over the next 10 years (FY 2009 to FY 2018). This spending will equal $250,000 for each person currently living in poverty in the U.S., or $1 million for a poor family of four. Considering people have a disincentive to get a job, and will actually get less if they do get a job, it is very likely that people that are on Welfare now will also be on Welfare in 2018. To reiterate, a "poor" family of four staying on Welfare benefits the next nine years, will get $1 million dollars transferred to them via Welfare spending.

Over the next decade, federal Welfare spending will equal $7.5 trillion, while state spending will reach $2.8 trillion. These figures do not include any of the increases in healthcare expenditures included in the ObamaCare bill, which is planning to add about 20 million more people to the Medicaid roles (which, you will remember, is 58% of Welfare spending). In the years ahead, average annual Welfare spending will be roughly twice the spending levels under President Bill Clinton after adjusting for inflation. Total means-tested spending is likely to average roughly 6 percent of GDP for the next decade, and these estimates are low, especially considering how many more people are going to be added to the Medicaid and Welfare rolls.

(Source: *Obama to Spend $10.3 Trillion on Welfare: Uncovering the Full Cost of Means-Tested Welfare or Aid to the Poor,* September 16, 2009, by Robert Rector, Kiki Bradley and Rachel Sheffield. Originally published by The Heritage Foundation, Special Report #67. Heritage.org, used with permission)

## The Costly War on Poverty

Incredible as it may seem, Americans transfer close to one trillion dollars each year to low-income families through a bewildering variety of programs, all in the name of fighting poverty and inequality. Its income redistribution on a mammoth scale, and it's equal to the total before-tax cash income of middle-income households. That's right, we transfer to the low-income population an amount equal to the entire income of middle-income households, that is, households in the middle fifth (40th to 60th percentile) of the American income distribution.

What do we get for it? That is the question we should be asking our politicians as they urge us to spend still more on the War on Poverty. When Lyndon Johnson inaugurated the War on Poverty in 1964, he assured the public that ". . .this investment [of tax dollars] will return its cost many fold to our entire economy." Now that this "investment" has cost more than $15.9 trillion, and is costing another trillion dollars per year we should evaluate whether the returns have, in fact, been large.

Some questions to consider: Is the low-income population more independent and self-supporting than before the War on Poverty? Clearly not, the program penalizes those that try to work. Has the $15.9 trillion dollar expenditure eliminated poverty in America? Reduced it dramatically? Nope, more people are in poverty now than in recent years. Has the multi-trillion-dollar expenditure reduced inequality? Are more disadvantaged children being raised in stable two-parent families today than before the War on Poverty? Are the children in low-income families getting good educations that prepare them for productive working lives as adults? The government throws many hundreds of billions of dollars at primary education also, with not much result. Has a trillion dollars in spending a year created more jobs or even people that can or want to work? Welfare spending has resulted in recipients being able to never work. Have the racial gaps in educational achievement been eliminated or greatly narrowed? Has illegitimacy been reduced in the low-income population? Not really, Welfare has resulted in the further collapse of marriage. The collapse of marriage is the predominant cause of child poverty in the U.S. today. When the War on Poverty began, 7% of children were born out of wedlock; today, the figure is over 40%. Most alarmingly, the out-of-wedlock birthrate among minorities is 72%. Is crime lower today than in the 1950s, before the War on Poverty? Well, at least more people are in jail.

The answers to these questions show a dark picture of the accomplishments of the American Welfare state. While some evidence may identify a few positive returns on our "investment," we have a right to expect a lot more for a trillion dollars a year. Perhaps it is time to formulate an exit strategy for the War on Poverty.

(Source: U.S Census Bureau-Poverty, census.gov)

## Spending, Spending, and More Tax-and-Spend Spending...

Another way of looking at what has happened in entitlement spending on Welfare, Medicare, Medicaid, and Social Security is to look at some of the events in government in the last decade:

- 1997: **The State Children's Health Insurance Program (CHIP) is created to subsidize state governments for extending healthcare coverage to families that don't qualify for Medicaid.**
- 2003: **Congress passes the huge Medicare Part D drug benefit in 2003. The new benefit has no funding source, and thus adds enormously to federal debt over the long term. To aid passage of the bill, the Bush administration suppresses internal information from Medicare's chief cost analyst that the new drug benefit will cost more than officially claimed.**
- 2003: **The Bush administration proposes to allow states to receive Medicaid funding in the form of a block grant, which would give the states more flexibility and greater incentive to control costs. Unfortunately, the administration does not push the proposal very hard and it dies.**
- 2009: **The Government Accountability Office estimates that Medicare pays about $17 billion of fraudulent and improper payments each year and Medicaid pays about $33 billion. Those estimates are probably low. Harvard's Malcolm Sparrow, a top specialist in healthcare fraud, estimates that up to 20 percent of healthcare budgets are consumed by fraudulent and improper payments, which would be about $150 billion a year for Medicare and Medicaid combined. As an example of the problem, the *Washington Post* reports that a high-school dropout with a laptop computer single-handedly cheats Medicare out of $105 million by electronically submitting 140,000 fraudulent claims for equipment and services over four years.**
- 2009: **The American Recovery and Reinvestment Act, or "economic stimulus" bill, authorizes about $90 billion of additional spending on healthcare, Welfare, and other HHS activities.**
- 2009: **The Congressional Budget Office projects that Medicaid is expected to double in cost as a share of the nation's economy by 2035 and Medicare is expected to more than double in cost by that date.**
- 2009: **The Department of Treasury reports that the present value of Medicare's unfunded obligations is $36 trillion over the next 75 years. The Treasury's estimate for the funding gap over an "infinite horizon" is a staggering $86 trillion. That means that the government would need to deposit $86 trillion right now in an interest-bearing account to cover all of Medicare's future unfunded liabilities. Thus, unless Medicare spending is cut, young Americans face massive and sustained tax increases that will substantially reduce their standard of living for decades to come.**
- 2010: **An authoritative federal study on Head Start finds that the program provides few if any lasting benefits to participating children. President Barack Obama signs into law the Patient Protection and Affordable Care Act (ObamaCare), which is the largest and most expensive healthcare bill passed since 1965. The legislation expands Medicaid and adds new subsidy programs, and will likely cost more than the advertised $1 trillion over the first decade. Not surprisingly, the health bill expands federal power in many ways, including imposing a**

**mandate on Americans to buy health insurance or pay a fine. The bill also contains large and damaging tax increases, while conferring added power on the Internal Revenue Service.**

While the economy has slowed down due to the recent recession, permanent government spending has only increased in a big way, especially for entitlements. This growth in spending is clearly unsustainable, especially for the next decade. Politicians don't seem to care if entitlement spending is sustainable or affordable, it's popular with voters. There is also typically little action taken against fraudsters of entitlement spending. The reason? If politicians go after fraud in the system, they are often labeled as wanting to cut or decrease entitlements—and entitlement hawks are killed in Washington. Anyone who talks of cutting anything in Medicare, even cutting fraud, are found out and ostracized, especially by organizations like the AARP.

Politicians aren't concerned about the distant future, only the next election cycle. As stated above, the government would have to deposit *$86 trillion* in an interest bearing account just to cover all of Medicare's unfunded liabilities. This is going to be hard considering our nation debt is more than $13.8 trillion dollars. Politicians also like to talk about the Social Security "trust fund." In their book *Seeds of Destruction*, authors Glenn Hubbard and Peter Navarro claim the Social Security / Medicare trust funds are a myth—simple federal accounting hocus-pocus because the money is in treasury bills, which is the same as government debt, there isn't any real trust fund and all future spending will come from either taxation or deficit spending. Chapter nine of their book is entitled "Why ObamaCare Makes Our Economy Sick." ObamaCare expands federal power, includes fines (which may be illegal—several lawsuits are already pending, and will probably have to be resolved in the Supreme Court), increasing taxes, and adds power to the IRS. At a time when our country can least afford it, ObamaCare is a plan that will increase government spending and power. Is anyone surprised?

*Below is a graph of Federal spending, by department or agency, for 2010.*
*Entitlement programs are the top two expenditures by our government:*

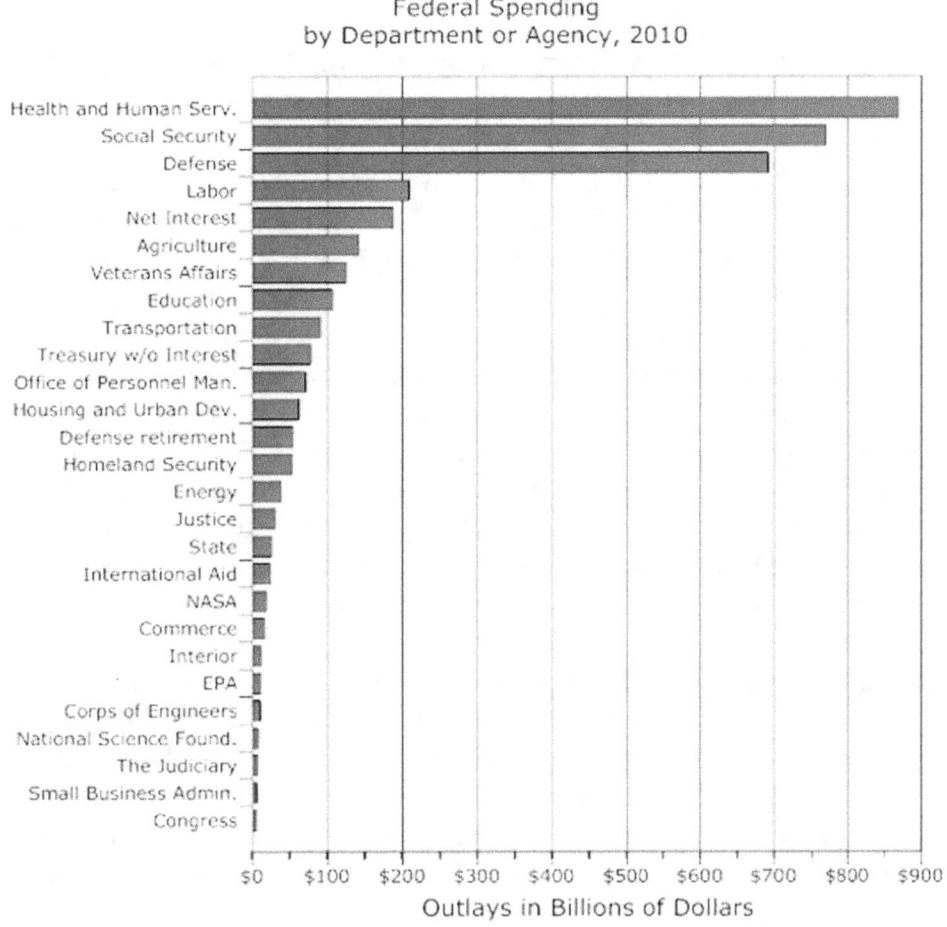

Federal Spending
by Department or Agency, 2010

Outlays in Billions of Dollars

(Source: Originally published by The Cato Institute, http://www.downsizinggovernment.org/compare-the-departments, copyright The Cato Institute, Used by Permission)

This graph shows the huge amount of money being spent on entitlement programs. HHS and Social Security alone make up $1.6 trillion in spending per year. Interesting to note that this doesn't even include *all* entitlement spending. Defense retirement spending is at least $50 billion dollars, and costs more than Homeland Security. We also spend more on International Aid than we spend on either NASA, the Commerce Department, Interior Department, or the EPA. Year after year spending continues to rise. Instead of going in the other direction, spending continues to increase. Legislation like ObamaCare will only accelerate this increase in the decade ahead. Considering our spending in 2010 led to a deficit of $1.3 trillion, can you imagine what the deficit is going to be year-over-year for the next decade (1 trillion or more per year for ten years—an extra $10 trillion to our already massive federal debt)? It's hard to imagine or comprehend, but it's going to be absolutely massive, especially since our government continues to add entitlement spending to the total every chance they get.

## *More Proof We Can't Stop Poverty by Making It More Comfortable...*

On Jan. 8, 1964, President Lyndon Johnson delivered a State of the Union address to Congress in which he declared an "unconditional war on poverty in America." Then, the poverty rate in America was around 19% and falling rapidly. It was reported that the poverty rate for 2010 is expected to be roughly 14.3%, and is climbing.

Between then and now, the federal government spent more than *$15 trillion* fighting poverty, and state and local governments added another couple of trillion. Yet the poverty rate never fell below 10.5%. The federal government now has 122 separate anti-poverty programs (defined as either means-tested programs or programs whose legislative language specifically refers to their purpose as combating poverty). These range from Medicaid, the largest and most expensive anti-poverty program, to the tiny Even Start Program for Indian Tribes and Tribal Organizations. Combined, these 122 programs spent more than $591 billion in 2009, and costed even more this year (2010). That amounts to $14,849 for every poor man, woman and child in America. Given that the poverty line is $10,830, it would have been cheaper just to mail every poor person a check for $11,000.

Welfare spending increased significantly under the Bush administration, but President Obama has thrown money at anti-poverty programs at an unprecedented rate. Just during his first two years in office, Obama's administration increased spending on Welfare programs by more than $260 billion. Some of the increase, of course, is due to the recession. But the administration has also made conscious policy choices to ease eligibility and expand caseloads. For example, the stimulus bill included a provision that created a new "emergency fund" to help states pay for added Welfare recipients, with the federal government footing 80% of the cost for the new "clients."

This was an important change because it undid many of the incentives contained in the 1996 Clinton Welfare reform for states to reduce Welfare rolls. Under the new rules, states that succeed in getting people off Welfare would lose the opportunity for increased federal funding. And states that make it easier to stay on Welfare (by, say, raising the time limit from two years to five) were rewarded with more taxpayer cash. The bill even lets states with rising Welfare rolls to still collect their "case-load reduction" bonuses. The end result is that <u>one out of every six Americans is now receiving some form of government assistance.</u>

Of course all this Welfare spending could arguably be justified, if we were actually reducing poverty. But, as the most recent numbers make clear, we're not. Clearly we are doing something wrong. Throwing money at the problem has neither reduced poverty nor made the poor self-sufficient. Instead, government Welfare programs have torn at the social fabric of the country and been a significant factor in the collapse in marriage and increasing out-of-wedlock births with all of their attendant problems. Before the War of Poverty people had to have a job in order to have a child. This usually meant getting married, and one or both parents worked to provide for their child. Now, many women can get on Welfare indefinitely just by having children, the more children they have, the more money they get. It matters not whether they are married, and penalizes them if they have a job.

There thus seems to be more incentive simply to have children (and not work) in order to collect more benefits. The program has eliminated the work ethic and actually rewards people for not working and penalizes those that do work. States that provide the most Welfare benefits, like Illinois for example become magnets for people seeking to maximize their Welfare benefits—they simply move to Illinois from all over the country and immediately sign up for Welfare. Instead of fixing this problem, politicians are "doubling down" by increasing spending for a program that doesn't work (literally).

Most tragically of all, the pathologies they engender have been passed on from parent to child, from generation to generation. In the days of the Roman Empire, rights to Welfare were hereditary—the right to get Welfare was passed from parent to child. Now, children coming out of Welfare homes are faced with working or Welfare. Many choose Welfare by having children, often times before they finish school. Since the War on Poverty was started in the sixties, there have been two and three generations of people on Welfare. In fact, the whole theory underlying our Welfare programs is wrong. We focus far too much on making poverty more comfortable, and not enough on creating the prosperity that will get people out of poverty.

Observers have known for a long time that the surest ways to stay out of poverty are to finish school, not get pregnant outside marriage and get a job, any job, and stick with it. That means that if we wish to fight poverty, we must end those government policies — high taxes and regulatory excess — that inhibit growth and job creation. We must protect capital investment and give people the opportunity to start new businesses. We must augment our education system, and we must encourage the poor to work, save and invest. The best thing for people in poverty is a stable and productive middle class—it's where those in poverty can aspire to get into. Yet, the middle class is increasingly disappearing. Instead of those in poverty working themselves into the middle class, the middle class is increasingly falling into poverty—and into the Welfare system.

More importantly, the real work of fighting poverty must come not from the government, but from the engines of civil society. An enormous amount of evidence and experience shows that private charities are far more effective than government Welfare programs. While Welfare provides incentives for counterproductive behavior, private charities can use their aid to encourage self-sufficiency, self-improvement, and independence. Private charities can individualize their approaches and target specific problems that are holding people in poverty. People have to be rewarded for working, not get paid for not working. Healthcare needs to be given to people that work and are productive rather than as an incentive to quit your job and not work.

One definition of insanity is doing the same thing over and over and expecting different results. Perhaps that's something to keep in mind the next time we hear a call for more Welfare spending.

If the Welfare system wasn't bad enough, it's also rife with fraud. Economists and observers believe fraud is rampant in HHS entitlement programs. Examples include people that are on Welfare, but work and receive income that is not reported, people that get health benefits although they work (again unreported), and people that just refuse to work and use the system to get money and other benefits. Below are some more examples of fraud.

Examples of Welfare Fraud

1.) The executive director of the Illinois Legislative Advisory Committee for Public Aid took action against Linda Taylor, a Chicago resident. It was claimed that Taylor used 14 alias names to receive an estimated $150,000 in medical coverage, cash assistance and food stamps. It was said that the woman migrated from district to district using these aliases to fraudulently obtain benefits.

2.) Dorothy Woods was jailed on 12 counts of Welfare fraud. She claimed 38 non-existent children and manipulated the system for more than $300,000. The most disturbing part about this story is that Woods was rumored to be a wealthy woman before committing the crime.

3.) Arlens Otis of Cook County, Illinois was indicted on 613 counts of fraudulently receiving $150,839 in Welfare benefits.

4.) The biggest case of Welfare fraud came when Barbara Williams was found guilty of manipulating Los Angeles County for $239,000 in benefits. The crime provoked a conviction that sentenced her to eight years in prison.

(Source: Department of Justice Website, Justice.gov)

These are just the people that got caught. Since there is no policing of Welfare recipients and the benefits they get, there is no way to determine what the actual cost of fraud is. Welfare fraudsters are usually only caught if someone reports them, and even then there are few mechanisms in place to go after the fraud. Regardless of fraud, the Welfare system is costing us so much money it's almost incomprehensible—more than $15.9 trillion dollars since its inception; and President Obama plans to spend another $10.3 trillion in the coming years, for a grand total of $26.2 trillion dollars. Instead of actually paying for it, the government simply borrows more money. There is no way of reducing our deficits and governmental spending until the Welfare problem is addressed. As with most government programs that have gotten out of control, it started out with a reasonable idea: to help the poor and now has grown to consume almost a trillion dollars a year. Instead of fixing the system, the current politicians, especially President Obama, want to pay *more* into the system. Yet, until the system is fixed, our country will be heading closer and closer to bankruptcy and insolvency.

## *"Secure the Blessings of Liberty to ourselves and our Posterity"*

The last promise of our Constitution is to secure the blessings of liberty to ourselves and our posterity. Liberty (def: the quality or state of being free: the power to do as one pleases: freedom from physical restraint: freedom from arbitrary or despotic control: the positive enjoyment of various social, political, or economic rights and privileges: the power of choice). Nowhere are the blessings of liberty more apparent than in the U.S. We really are free to do as we please. The government often times seems arbitrary and despotic, but people put up with that. We are free to enjoy social, political, and economic rights and privileges—if we have saved for them.

Retirement used to be a guarantee for everyone that worked (and those that don't work) via Social Security and pensions. Like healthcare, however, many private companies have cut out pensions and profit-sharing plans. For instance, Walmart, the largest private employer in the U.S. recently announced they were doing away with profit-sharing entirely. Many people once thought their house was a way of indirectly saving for retirement, but housing values have collapsed, and as many as 40% of people owning houses owe more on their mortgage than their house is now worth. In addition, many 401k plans invested in stocks have either remained flat or lost money for the last ten years. Clearly, many people aren't going to be able to enjoy their economic rights and privileges when they don't have enough money to retire.

Again, here are some statistics of what is happening in the retirement arena: More than 36 percent of Americans say that they don't contribute anything to retirement savings. A staggering 43 percent of Americans have less than $10,000 saved up for retirement. A total of 24 percent of American workers say that they have postponed their planned retirement age in the past year. Having a financially secure retirement is clearly not a right or privilege any longer. This all leads to more dependence on the government. Social Security will have to be a "safety net" for more and more retirees. *In Seeds of Destruction,* Hubbard and Navarro point out that Social Security was never intended to be a national pension plan, and it will likely collapse in the next twenty years unless something is done.

If you're a federal employee, however, you don't have much to worry about—you get to retire at 50 with a massive taxpayer-supported pension. As we have seen (and is presented in another chapter) the federal government will continue paying pensions and health benefits (cost what it may), but what if you are a state or local employee/retiree?

## *Another Looming Financial Catastrophe: 10 State Pension Funds that May Run Out of Money*

Everyone has heard rumblings about the massive financial problems of the states. The most immediate state pension crises aren't in New York or California. They're in Middle America. When it comes to state pensions in the most trouble, do places like New Hampshire come to mind? After all, it makes sense that the biggest, most populous members of the union, where budget follies are fairly common, would be facing the most urgently needed fixes. The truth is considerably different. Hawaii, Kansas and others made their way on to the list. Now, these pension plans aren't going to be obliterated tomorrow – New Hampshire, for instance, is estimated to see its plan run out of money in 2022, so they've got 12 years to rectify the situation.

For some other states, the matter is more pressing and no more so than for the Land of Lincoln. Illinois is just 8 years away from exhausting its pension fund and creating a yearly $14 billion hole, according to data from Joshua Ruah, an associate professor of finance at the Kellogg School of Management at Northwestern University. That's a projected 32 percent of the state's revenue going to fill a pension hole every year.

Indiana, Louisiana, Oklahoma and Colorado are among the next pension funds to fall. The rest of the union is just around the corner. But wait. Just to make sure the list is not a complete surprise, know that the New York City suburbs of Connecticut and New Jersey made it on board. They have until 2019 to sort it out.

### 10 State Pension Funds That May Run Out of Money:

**#1 Illinois**
Bill in the following year: $13.6 billion

Year pension fund runs out: 2018
Share of state revenue: 32%

**#2 Connecticut**
Bill in the following year: $4.9 billion

Year pension fund runs out: 2019
Share of state revenue: 27%

**#3 Indiana**
Bill in the following year: $3.6 billion

Year pension fund runs out: 2019
Share of state revenue: 17%

**#4 New Jersey**
Bill in the following year: $14.4 billion

Year pension fund runs out: 2019
Share of state revenue: 34%

**#5 Hawaii**
Bill in the following year: $1.7 billion

Year pension fund runs out: 2020
Share of state revenue: 24%

**#6 Louisiana**
Bill in the following year: $4.3 billion

Year pension fund runs out: 2020
Share of state revenue: 27%

**#7 Oklahoma**
Bill in the following year: $3.7 billion

Year pension fund runs out: 2020
Share of state revenue: 30%

**#8 Colorado**
Bill in the following year: $7.8 billion

Year pension fund runs out: 2022
Share of state revenue: 54%

**#9 Kansas**
Bill in the following year: $2.5 billion

Year pension fund runs out: 2022
Share of state revenue: 23%

**#10 Kentucky**
Bill in the following year: $5.3 billion

Year pension fund runs out: 2022
Share of state revenue: 35%

(Source: *10 State Pension Funds that May Run Out of Money*, by Gus Lubin, The Business Insider, October, 18, 2010. businessinsider.com)

If you live in any of these states or worked for any of these states, government pensions are going to become a big issue. Illinois, for example, has its pension protected by law, something the State Employee Union got passed. If you live in Illinois, 1/3 of tax revenue is going to pay for retired employees. States like Colorado, more than ½ of tax revenues are going to pay for pensions of people that don't work anymore. The Federal Reserve reports in *Flow of Funds Accounts of The United States: table F.119 State and Local Government Employee Retirement Funds* 2010 *second quarter,* state and local government pension liability was $30.3 billion. So, states and local government already have more than $30 billion in unfunded pension liability.

Kurt Erickson of *The Southern Illinoisan* reported on Dec. 2, 2010, that Illinois is finally starting to do something about their massive pension problems. Illinois cities eventually could see some financial relief as part of a revamp of retirement benefits for police officers and firefighters approved by the Senate. Under legislation forwarded to Gov. Pat Quinn's desk on a 46-4 vote, police and fire personnel hired after Jan. 1 would receive reduced pension benefits. Mayors and other municipal officials have pushed to reduce benefits in order to cut the amount local taxpayers must contribute to finance the pensions. Police and fire unions, however, have argued the high costs hitting cities are because of underfunding in the past. For example, a study showed that some cities overstated how much they would make in investment returns, allowing them to pay less into the system. "It had a devastating impact on the funds," said Pat Devaney of the Associated Firefighters of Illinois.

Lawmakers are trying to raise the retirement age for police and firefighters from 50 to 55. Those who retire at age 50 would see a 30 percent reduction in their benefits. Cap the maximum salary to calculate benefits at $106,800. Police and firefighters will get to retire only ten years earlier than everyone else, and will only get $106,800 a year, almost twice as much as the average American makes. Unions have inflated government employee salaries and pensions to unimaginable levels, and lowered the age of retirement to fifty. Why do taxpayers put up with this? Since union officials don't have to pay for salaries, benefits, and pensions, they have nothing to lose. The taxpayers in Illinois and the rest of the country have to pay for these outrageous salaries and benefits, for state and federal employees—public servants. I guess everyone has to make some sacrifices.

Something that has also gotten a lot of attention lately is the *amounts* of pensions that state and local government officials are getting. In an opinion piece in *Fortune Magazine*, author Nina Easton chronicles huge pensions former government employees are getting. In the California town of Bell, former chief administrative officer Robert Rizzo wrote himself a million dollar compensation agreement, including a $600,000 a year pension (he was later arrested for corruption). "It's the many legal pensions that are even more troubling." The city manager of San Ramon California is entitled to a $261,000 a year pension, and the local fire chief was to get a base pension of $284,000 per year. The article reports "Governor Schwarzenegger has blamed his state's $550 billion in retirement debt on 'huge unfunded pension and retirement healthcare promises'." In Orange County Cal., pension requirements in 2014 will consume about 84% of the counties law-enforcement payroll. "The underlying threat? Lay off current cops to pay for the vacations of retired officers."

The article goes on to explain that state pensions are underfunded nationwide. "Earlier this year (2010) the *Pew Center on States* calculated a $1 trillion shortfall between the $2.35 trillion…set aside and the $3.35 trillion committed." "Struggling states like Ohio and Illinois face the biggest crisis…with unfunded commitments totaling about half of those states' economies." This situation has already happened. "Generous retirement packages… helped sink Detroit—eventually landing GM and Chrysler at Treasury's door." How did these workers get such massive pensions that threaten to bankrupt federal and state governments (and did bankrupt GM)? The answer is unions—the UAW and American Federation of State, County and Municipal Employees (AFSCME). And, unlike pensions in the private sector, unions have lobbied and gotten government retirement packages embedded in law, meaning they can't be changed, altered, or reduced. Taxpayers are going to have to pay these massive pensions, and they aren't happy about it. In Illinois recently, the states' teachers union marched on the capital in Springfield with signs "please raise my taxes." This, of course, generated a huge anti-tax backlash, with people putting up signs in their yards across the state saying "taxed enough already." Why should federal, state and local employees get huge guaranteed pensions while workers in the private sector barely have any retirement benefits and even less in retirement savings? Many observers predict a "class war" between those guaranteed massive pensions and those who have to pay them.

(Source: *Prosperous Pensioners, the start of the next populist storm?* Nina Easton; Fortune-Opinion, Fortune Magazine, Oct. 18, 2010)

## *State and local governments have become wards of the Federal Government:*

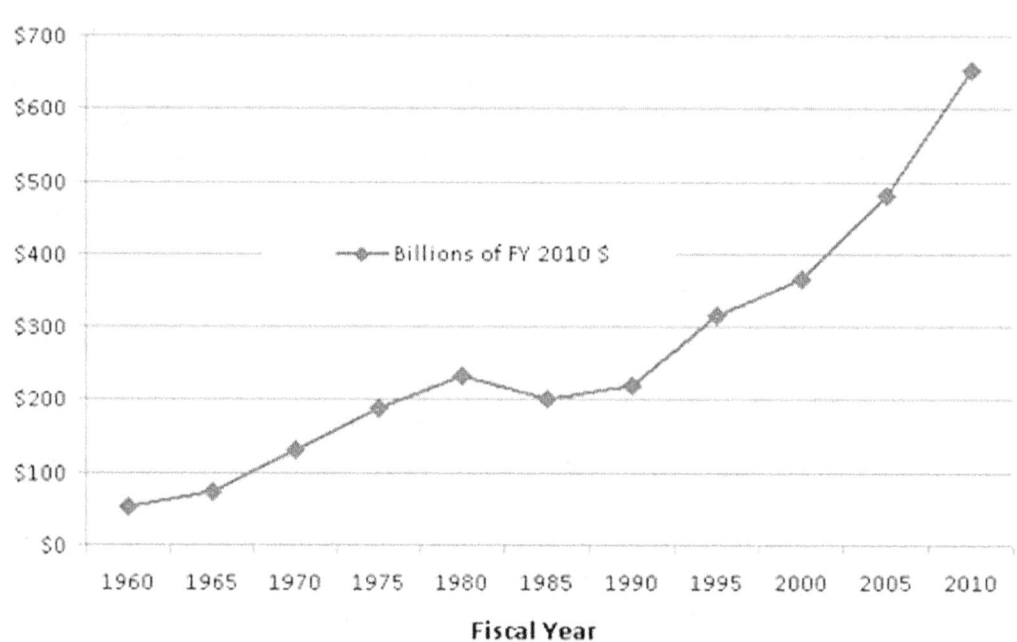

**Federal Aid to State and Local Governments**

Source: U.S. Budget, FY2010, Analytical Perspectives, Table 8-2

The Federal Government not only bails out banks and Wall Street, it also bails out state and local govern-ments. Since 1960, total federal subsidies to state and local government have increased an astounding 1,173%. State and local budgets are collapsing because of overspending and state and local employee pensions/healthcare, Medicaid and Welfare spending and have become increasingly dependent on the Federal Government. The Federal Government is transferring more than $600 billion dollars a year to state and local governments. This is a shell game however, as all federal money (like state money) comes from taxes or deficit spending. This amount doesn't include what it's going to cost when state and local pension funds run out of money. States have managed to overspend, over-commit, and over-promise hundreds of billions of dollars they don't have, and, like the Federal Government, have gone into massive debt.

## *So, how have states gotten into debt?*

While states and local governments have made huge pension promises to retirees, they have also gone into more debt than ever before. It is well-known that the federal government is amassing trillions in debt, but state and local governments are piling up debt as well. Data released by *The Federal Reserve* shows that total state and local debt was stable during the 1990s but soared from $1.19 trillion in 2000 to $1.85 trillion by 2005, an increase of 55 percent. About 39 percent of the total is state debt and 61 percent is local debt. Most state and local debt takes the form of long-term bonds ("municipal bonds"). Issues of municipal bonds raised an average $230 billion annually in new funds between 2001 and 2005, up sharply from the $152 billion average between 1996 and 2000.

How did state and local government run up almost 2 trillion in debt? By turning future revenues into piles of debt. There are two main types of municipal bonds: general obligation (GO) bonds and revenue bonds. GO bonds are backed by general taxation and are often subject to constitutional limits. Revenue bonds are backed by particular sources of revenue and are usually subject to fewer restrictions. GO bonds are about 39 percent of long term municipal debt and revenue bonds are 61 percent. Revenue bonds are financed by receipts of future taxes, fees, lease payments, federal grants, lottery earnings, or tobacco settlement payments. The idea is to securitize expected streams of cash to allow state and local officials to spend now rather than later. The trend to securitize and spend is called "innovative finance" in state budget circles. Wall Street uses many creative methods to help officials put their jurisdictions further into debt. A growing trend is to securitize future federal aid for highways, housing, and other items in "grant anticipation" debt. Federal aid has long spurred overspending by the states, but such debt innovation is exacerbating the problem. Recent federal legislation has included new ways for states to go further into debt, such as the creation of three types of municipal "tax credit bonds."

Perhaps the best reason to start reducing debt is that large financial burdens are looming over the states. Medicaid costs are growing rapidly and breaking state budgets. Pension plans for state and local employees have huge funding shortfalls. Even more costly may be the generous retirement healthcare plans promised to state and local workers. An estimate by *Mercer Human Resources* put the unfunded costs of those plans at $1 trillion. This data was gathered before the Great Recession, so debt totals are undoubtedly higher now, especially since tax receipts tend to dip during recessions. The point is, states and local governments feasted on debt during the decade, and now have debt service in addition to owing hundreds of billions of dollars in pension funds. So, if you're expecting your state or local pension to see you through old age, maybe it's time for plan B—the only problem is, most people don't have a plan B. State and local pensioners might be thrown into the same pool as people that have jobs in the private sector, almost half of which have less than $10,000 in retirement savings.

(Source: *State and Local Government Debt Is Soaring,* Tax Policy Studies, originally published by The Cato Institute, No. 37 • July 2006, CATO.org, copyright The Cato Institute, used by permission)

## *The unfortunate people that will follow us in "posterity"*

The founding fathers wanted the benefits of liberty to follow them into "posterity." Fast forward to today and what are we going to leave our descendants? For starters, more than $13.8 trillion dollars in federal debt, then add on the several trillion in state and local debt. The taxes that are going to be required just to service this debt are almost incomprehensible, not to mention paying off the principle. Instead of cutting spending in a big way, to slow the growth of U.S. debt, politicians continue to spend, and continue to *increase* spending on programs for people that don't work or produce. Add in more spending to try to provide healthcare (ObamaCare), increases in government healthcare spending for federal, state, and local employees and retirees, cost of living increases (raises) for these same federal, state, and local employees and pensioners, military spending, increases in Social Security, Welfare and Medicare spending, the list goes on ad infinitum.

Even if a balanced budget law were passed today for federal, state, and local governments, we would still have the increases in these spending programs, so cuts would have to come from somewhere. The truth is, there is nowhere to cut that much money. There was talk early after the recession "ended" that we could grow our way out of the debt we owed (by increasing business activity, thereby increasing taxes), but it's clear the chances of that happening are slim. Even worse, the Federal Reserve is now trying to inflate their way out of our problems by buying treasury bonds (quantitative easing), also known as "printing money." If you add up Medicare, Medicaid, Social Security, Disability, military, and Welfare spending (as a percentage of GDP), it would take a massive growth in GDP just to cover the increases in spending, not taking into account the debt. Just paying the interest on our debt is an incredible amount of money. And interest payments alone on the national debt will *triple* over the next six years, to approximately $600 billion annually (if interest rates remain at current levels). That's more than Congress spends on education, energy, transportation, housing, and environmental protection combined—and *over half of these payments will go to foreign investors.* Some economists believe we have already outgrown our ability to *ever* pay off federal, state, and local debt, they believe the government is already insolvent.

## *Is The U.S. Bankrupt Already?*

In a chilling report Laurence J. Kotlikoff , a professor of economics at Boston University and a research associate at the *National Bureau of Economic Research*, analyzes data from 2006: *before* the Obama administration, ObamaCare, massive increases in entitlement spending, the great recession, stimulus spending, bailout spending, and all the other increases in spending that's been done since that time. It's his findings that are important as he analyzes if the U.S. was solvent *back in 2006*, some of which are presented below:

(Introductory paragraph) "Is the United States bankrupt? Many would scoff at this notion. Others would argue that financial implosion is just around the corner. This paper explores these views from both partial and general equilibrium perspectives. It concludes that countries can go broke, that the United States is going broke, that remaining open to foreign investment can help stave off bankruptcy, but that radical reform of U.S. fiscal institutions is essential to secure the nation's economic future. The paper offers three policies to eliminate the nation's enormous fiscal gap and avert bankruptcy: a retail sales tax, personalized Social Security, and a globally budgeted universal healthcare system."

(Excerpt from page 239)

### ECONOMIC MEASUREMENT OF THE U.S. FISCAL CONDITION

"As suggested above, the proper way to consider a country's solvency is to examine the lifetime fiscal burdens facing current and future generations. If these burdens exceed the resources of those generations, get close to doing so, or simply get so high as to preclude their full collection, the country's policy will be unsustainable and can constitute or lead to national bankruptcy. Does the United States fit this bill? No one knows for sure, but there are strong reasons to believe the United States may be going broke. Consider, for starters, Gokhale and Smetters's (2005) analysis of the country's fiscal gap, which measures the present value difference between all future government expenditures, including servicing official debt, and all future receipts. In calculating the fiscal gap, Gokhale and Smetters use the federal government's arbitrarily labeled receipts and payments. Nevertheless, their calculation of the fiscal gap is label-free because alternative labeling of our nation's fiscal affairs would yield the same fiscal gap. Indeed, determining the fiscal gap is part of generational accounting; the fiscal gap measures the extra burden that would need to be imposed on current or future generations, relative to current policy, to satisfy the government's inter-temporal budget constraint. The Gokhale and Smetters measure of the fiscal gap is a stunning $65.9 trillion! This figure is *more than five times U.S. GDP and almost twice the size of national wealth.*"

"One way to wrap one's head around $65.9 trillion is to ask what fiscal adjustments are needed to eliminate this red hole. The answers are terrifying. One solution is an immediate and permanent doubling of personal and corporate income taxes. Another is an immediate and permanent two-thirds cut in Social Security and Medicare benefits. A third alternative, were it feasible, would be to immediately and permanently cut all federal discretionary spending by 143 percent. The Gokhale and Smetters study is an update of an earlier, highly detailed, and extensive U.S. Department of the Treasury fiscal gap analysis commissioned in 2002 by then Treasury Secretary Paul O'Neill. Smetters, who served as Deputy Assistant Secretary of Economic Policy at the Treasury between 2001 and 2002, recruited Gokhale, then Senior Economic Adviser to the Federal Reserve Bank of Cleveland, to work with him and other Treasury staff on the study. The study took close to a year to organize and complete. Gokhale and Smetters's $65.9 trillion fiscal gap calculation relies on the same methodology employed in the original Treasury analysis. Hence, one can legitimately view this figure as our own government's best estimate of its present-value budgetary shortfall. The $65.9 trillion gap is all the more alarming because its calculation omits the value of contingent government liabilities and relies on quite optimistic assumptions about increases over time in longevity and federal healthcare expenditures."

(Source: *Is the U.S. Bankrupt Already?* By Laurence J. Kotlikoff, Federal Reserve Bank of St. Louis Review, July/August 2006, *88*(4), pp. 235-49)

This figure ($65.9 trillion) doesn't take into account *growth* in spending for Social Security, Welfare, Medicare and Medicaid spending, nor the Medicare part D benefit, and certainly not the cost of ObamaCare, stimulus spending, bailout spending and other problems resulting from the recent recession. You can also add at least a trillion more a year in debt, each year since this paper was published, and the $65.9 trillion amount is now closer to *$70 trillion.* You can decide for yourself, but if the U.S. does have a fiscal gap more than five times GDP or twice as much as our entire national wealth, it is going to be very difficult to keep the promise in the Constitution to "Secure the Blessings of Liberty to ourselves and our Posterity."

**In conclusion,** in 1776 our founding fathers promised *"We the People of the United States, in Order to form a more perfect Union, establish Justice, insure domestic Tranquility, provide for the common defense, promote the general Welfare, and secure the Blessings of Liberty to ourselves and our Posterity, do ordain and establish this Constitution for the United States of America."* They formed a more perfect Union. Now, we have a massive justice system that puts more people in prison than any other country in the world—we have a domestic penal colony. Domestic tranquility, as measured economically, hasn't been as bad as since the Great Depression—our blessed middle class is disappearing, and more people are in poverty than in many decades. We have the best military in the world, but one that is incredibly expensive and spread across the world. We have certainly promoted the general Welfare, as we spend more money on Welfare than almost anything else. To reiterate, if Welfare spending continues unabated, a Welfare recipient-family-of-four will be (based on spending) the equivalent of millionaires within a decade. By the end of this decade, at current funding levels, the U.S. will have spent a mind-boggling total of *$26.2 trillion dollars* on Welfare since its inception in 1964. We clearly have the blessings of liberty, if we can afford them, but those that come after us are going to be crushed with taxes and debt as a result of flagrant government spending that has almost bankrupted our country. Several "wars" we engaged in that *didn't* involve the military—the War on Poverty and the War on Drugs have cost taxpayers much, much more than all the military wars we have participated in since the birth of our country. Even considering these daunting situations we now find ourselves in, our leaders, the politicians, are *increasing spending* and making a horribly bad situation even worse. Without a mandate from our Constitution or the American people, politicians have taxed, borrowed and spent our country to the brink of insolvency. How can the people that got us into this situation (the politicians) ever be trusted to get us out of this situation? Would our founding fathers be happy with what has happened to their Union?

# CHAPTER 2

# *The Federal Behemoth*

The Federal Government itself is bigger economically than the entire GDP of many countries—and is the largest employer in the U.S. It is responsible for many things, from our military, Welfare, Social Security, Medicare, Medicaid, protecting against foreign and domestic terror threats, protecting the President, occupational safety, resource management, food and drug safety, census data gathering, patents and intellectual property, foreign relations and embassies, border regulation, domestic and foreign intelligence and crime, and the list goes on and on. The costs and makeup of Federal Government employees is published in the *FEDERAL CIVILIAN WORKFORCE STATISTICS: THE FACT BOOK 2007 EDITION* (the most recent publication).

The fact book is produced annually by the U.S. Office of Personnel Management (OPM) as a "convenient reference suitable for a variety of audiences." It contains descriptive statistical information, using tables and charts, about many aspects of the Executive Branch workforce. This book is a downloadable (http://www.opm.gov/feddata/factbook/index.asp) fact repository of who works for the Federal Government, how much they make, the race and sex of federal employees, and how much of our tax money is spent on federal employee benefits. The last edition published by OPM is the 2007 version, which only shows data up until 2006. It was from this report which the following data was gleaned.

## *Total number of Federal Employees:*

The Federal Government is the largest employer in the U.S. The number of federal employees has, surprisingly, stayed relatively stable from 2000 (2.78 million) to 2006 (2.7 million). Despite the pervasive view that the Federal Government is growing, due mainly to growth in spending, the actual number of employees hasn't increased much. Or, another way of looking at it, the number of employees is stable, but the money they are spending or has been spent on them has risen significantly. Let's take a look at what they are getting.

*(Source: "Monthly Report of Federal Civilian Employment (SF 113-A)" Workforce Information and Planning Group. fedstats@opm.gov)*

## Trend of Employment, 1997 – 2006:

Despite fluctuations, average annual federal base salary jumped from $43,187 in 1997 to $66,372 in 2006. Data shown for "Annual Base Salary" represents averages for full-time permanent employees. This is a 53.7% increase in base pay in a nine year period. This represents a 6% increase in base salary, year after year. As reported elsewhere in this book, in the United States, the average federal worker now earns 60% MORE than the average worker in the private sector. Are government employees more qualified than the workers in the private sector? Are they more educated? What other industry has been able to increase base starting salaries for employees 6% a year, every year?

## Civilian Payroll for Executive Branch Agencies 1994 – 2006 Annual Payroll:

Once they have a job (at an average starting pay in 2006 of $66,372), do federal employees continue to get more than everyone else? Annual payroll for executive branch agencies rose from $83.1billion in 1994 to $115.0 billion in 2006, a 38.4% increase in twelve years. Payrolls thus increased 3.2% per year, year after year. Despite what the economy does, and what happens in the private sector, Federal employees get raises, year after year. Most of the time, they can probably give themselves raises.

(Note: Data excludes U.S. Postal Service and Postal Rate Commission.)

## Executive Branch Retirement and Insurance Payments 1998 - 2007

Unlike the private sector, federal employees are virtually guaranteed health benefits, despite rising costs. Government Payments for Annuitants Health Benefits jumped from $4.115 billion in 1998 to $8.615 billion in 2007, or more than double in nine years.

Government payments to civil service <u>Retirement and Disability Fund</u> was $21.357 billion in 1998 and jumped to $32.105 billion in 2007, a 50.3% increase in just nine years. More than $30 billion a year is paid so retired federal employees can have health benefits and retirement pensions. We pay retired federal workers more per year than the entire GDP of the following nations: Costa Rica $29B North Korea $27B, Burma $27B, Latvia $26B Yemen $25B, Panama $25B and many others.

(Budget Data for 2005, 2006 are actual. Budget. Data for 2007 are estimated. Notes: Amounts shown reflect OPM's payment of the Government's share for annuitants' health and life insurance benefits and General Fund payments to the retirement fund. These payments do not include amounts contributed by Federal agencies on behalf of their employees. GDP data from List of countries by GDP {nominal}, Wikipedia.org)

Again, in the United States, the average federal worker now earns 60% more than the average worker in the private sector. Federal employees get raises yearly, increases in payroll every year, and huge increases in health-care and retirement expenses that we are paying for. Meanwhile, in the private sector (2010), the number of **unemployed persons** (14.9 million) and the **unemployment rate** (9.6 percent) were little changed in many months. From May through August 2010, the jobless rate remained in the range of 9.5 to 9.8 percent. Among the **major worker groups**, the unemployment rate for adult men (9.8 percent), adult women (8.0 percent), teenagers (26.3 percent), whites (8.7 percent), blacks (16.3 percent), and Hispanics (12.0 percent) showed little change in recent months.

(Source: *THE EMPLOYMENT SITUATION – AUGUST 2010*, Bureau of Labor Statistics, U.S. Department of Labor, DOL.gov)

Do you remember the days when getting elected to Congress or choosing to work for the government was referred to as "public service"? The idea was that you would be making a sacrifice for the greater good of the country. Well, those days are long gone. Today, getting elected to Congress or working for the federal government is a good way to get rich. Median household income in the United States fell from $51,726 in 2008 to $50,221 in 2009, and yet the personal wealth of members of Congress and the salaries of federal workers (especially at the higher levels) continue to explode. There is certainly nothing wrong with making a lot of money, but does it seem right that so many of our "public servants" are getting rich while so many of the rest of us are barely getting by?

Members of Congress and employees of the government are supposed to work for us. We are the ones who pay their salaries. But today, they are the ones "living the American dream" while most of the rest of us scramble just to survive from month to month. Eleven more disturbing statistics:

**#1** According to an article in *the Hill*, House Speaker Nancy Pelosi's net worth soared from $13.7 million in 2008 to $21.7 million in 2009.

**#2** In 2005, 7420 federal workers were making $150,000 or more per year. In 2010, a whopping 82,034 federal workers are making $150,000 or more per year. That is more than a tenfold increase in just five years.

**#3** More than half of the members of the U.S. Congress are millionaires.

**#4** The total compensation that the U.S. government workforce is going to take in this year is approximately $447 billion dollars.

**#5** Today, all members of Congress earn at least $175,000 for 80 days of work a year (*or $2187 per day*). This is more than 3x what the average American makes.

**#6** 60 percent of the federal government workforce is represented by labor unions.

**#7** The median wealth of a U.S. Senator in 2009 was 2.38 million dollars.

**#8** In 2005, the U.S. Department of Defense had just nine civilians earning $170,000 or more. When Barack Obama took office, the U.S. Department of Defense had 214 civilians earning $170,000 or more. In June 2010, the U.S. Department of Defense had 994 civilians earning $170,000 or more, a 110-fold increase in just 5 years.

**#9** Insider trading is perfectly legal for members of the U.S. Congress - and they refuse to pass a law that would change that. Is there any wonder why government doesn't prosecute Wall Street?

**#10** According to a recent study conducted by the Heritage Foundation, federal workers earn up to 60 percent more money on average than their counterparts in the private sector.

**#11** When you factor in such things as retirement and healthcare benefits, the compensation gap between federal workers and private sector employees gets even larger. Including non-cash benefits adds to this disparity. *The average private-sector employer pays $9,882 per employee in annual benefits, while the federal government pays an average of $32,115 per employee (see graphs below).*

(Source: *12 Facts That Will Blow Your Mind – Federal Employees And Members Of Congress Are Getting Rich While Those Of Us Who Pay Their Salaries Suffer*, by Michael Snyder, 11-22-10. The Economic Collapse, theeconomiccollapseblog.com, used with permission) and (The Heritage Foundation, Heritage.org)

Meanwhile, back in the "private world" according to a survey released by the US Centers for Disease Control and Prevention (CDC), 46.3 million Americans, or about 15.4%, did not have health insurance coverage in 2009, representing a slight increase from 2008. Nearly 60 million, or one in five, had gaps in insurance coverage over the course of the year, according to the survey data. All federal employees, whether working or retired, have full health benefits. The military even has their own health service (VA hospitals), and their own insurance company (Tricare and USAA). Non-military federal employees have to choose a health plan from commercial carriers in the U.S.

Despite what federal employees get (nearly ½ a trillion dollars per year), the people they serve get food stamps. For the first time in U.S. history, more than 40 million Americans are on food stamps and the U.S. Department of Agriculture projects that number will go up to 43 million Americans in 2011. Who pays for food stamps? Yes, the taxpayers. Federal employees aren't the only government employees, however.

## UNITED STATES, **STATE GOVERNMENT EMPLOYMENT DATA**: MARCH 2009
UNITED STATES TOTALS

| | |
|---|---|
| Full Time Employees: | 3,836,544 |
| Full Time pay: | $17,516,226,809 |
| Part Time Employees: | 1,492,478 |
| Part Time pay: | $1,874,952,481 |
| | |
| Total annual state government pay: | $19,391,179,290 |

(SOURCE: 2009 Annual Survey of State and Local Government Employment and Payroll. For information on sampling and non-sampling errors and definitions, see http://www.census.gov/govs/apes/how_data_collected.html. the U.S. Census Bureau is the source of the original data)

## 2009 **Public Employment Data Local Governments**
United States Total

| | |
|---|---|
| Full time employees: | 10,980,855 |
| Full time pay: | $46,585,856,291 |
| Part time employees: | 3,246,308 |
| Part time pay: | $3,562,013,504 |
| Total local government pay: | $50,147,869,795 |

(SOURCE: 2009 Annual Survey of State and Local Government Employment and Payroll. For information on sampling and non-sampling errors and definitions, see http://www.census.gov/govs/apes/how_data_collected.html. the U.S. Census Bureau is the source of the original data.)

So, if you total up the costs of federal, state, and local government workers, you have annual expenditures of more than $250 billion dollars, and that doesn't even include benefits, or payments to pension funds. A quarter of a trillion dollars per year. Considering that federal, state, and local government officials get as much as 75% of their previous pay while retired, and get health benefits, you would easily have to double that amount, to an estimated $449 billion dollars per year or more. Many federal, state and local government employees get to retire early, many as early as 50 years old while collecting up to 2/3 of their regular pay (while retired). Unlike the real world, many government and military employees get to retire based on number of years worked, not their age. And, as always, they get subsidized health insurance in addition to generous pensions. While it's great to retire at 50, let's see what this benefit is costing taxpayers.

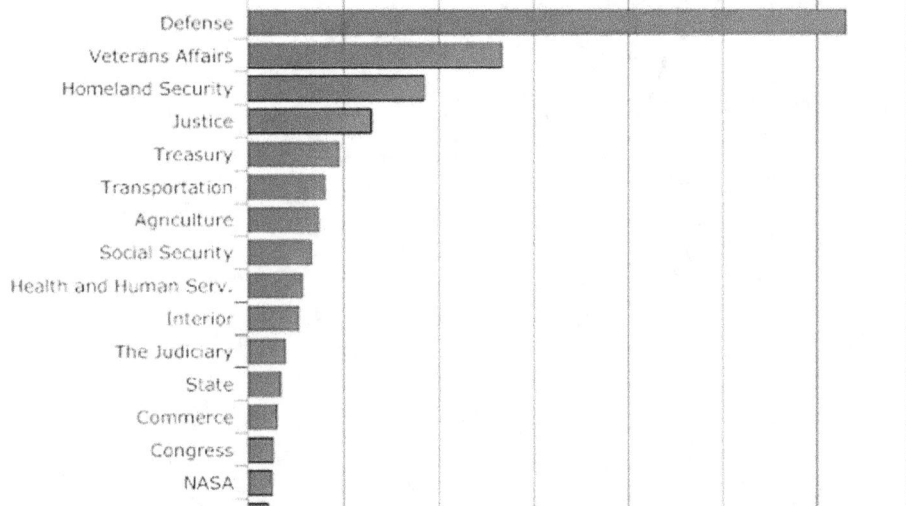

Civilian Employee Compensation Costs by Department or Agency, 2010

Billions of Dollars

(Graph: originally published by The Cato Institute, downsizinggovernment.org, copyright The Cato Institute, used by permission)

The total number of government employees: federal, state, and local, is more than 18 million. If the U.S. work-age population (eighteen and over) is about 224 million, government employees represent 8% of working/voting age adults in the U.S. *Roughly one in twelve people in the U.S. are government workers.* There is one adult government employee for every twelve adults in the U.S. private sector. (based on U.S. census data). From a tax standpoint, twelve people have to pay enough in taxes to fund each employee, their retirement, and their health benefits. Our government is indeed large and expensive, and for the angry voters and others, it has become too large and expensive. Below are the numbers of civilian employees.

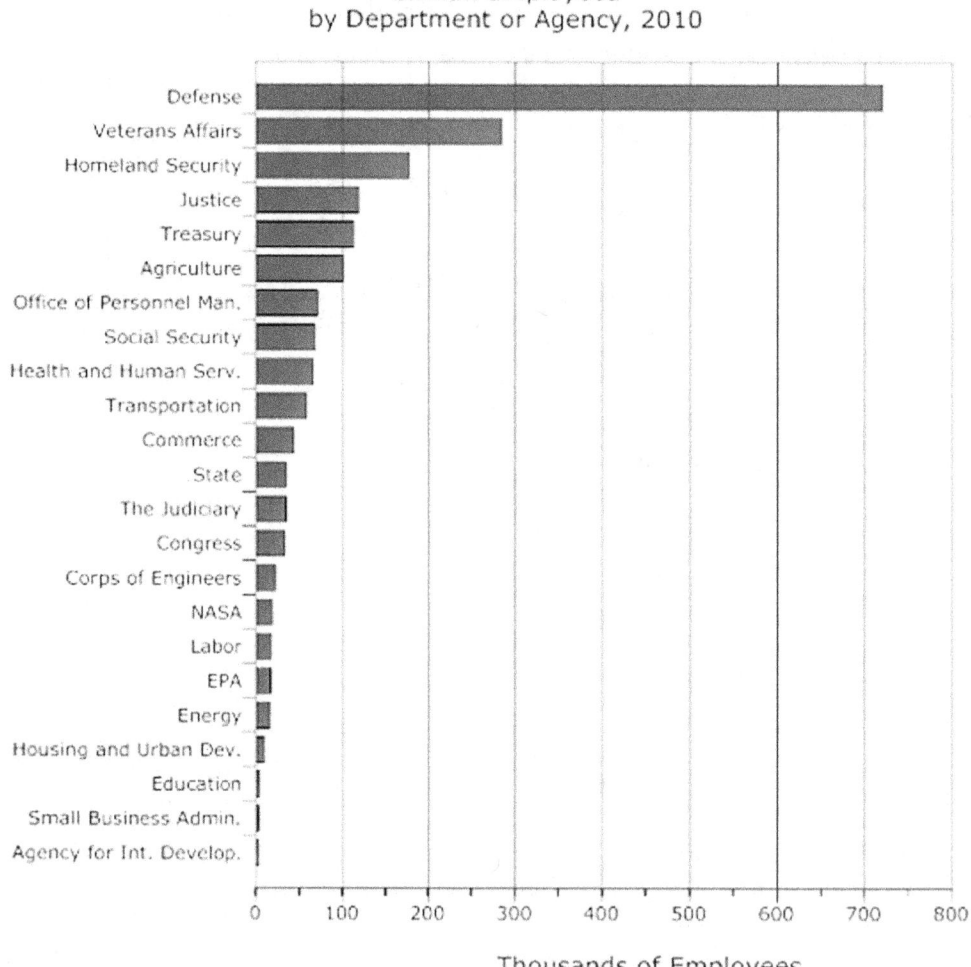

(Graph: originally published by The Cato Institute, downsizinggovernment.org, copyright The Cato Institute, used by permission)

What happens when you add in the people that are receiving unemployment benefits? When you add in the people that are unemployed (14.9 million) and may be getting government unemployment benefits, it totals about 33 million people or 14% of the population, that taxes currently support. It's no fun to be unemployed, but it becomes a benefit that has to be paid for by taxpayers. These totals, once again, don't take into consideration health benefits for the unemployed (administered through Medicaid, which currently has its highest enrollment ever). If you add in people that are unemployed to federal, state, and local employees, there are only *eight* people paying for salary (and benefits) of everyone either employed by or getting unemployment benefits from the government— and this doesn't take into account people on Welfare and Disability that don't work. The government thus supports, via taxpayers, a huge part of our population. Let's see how much it costs us per household.

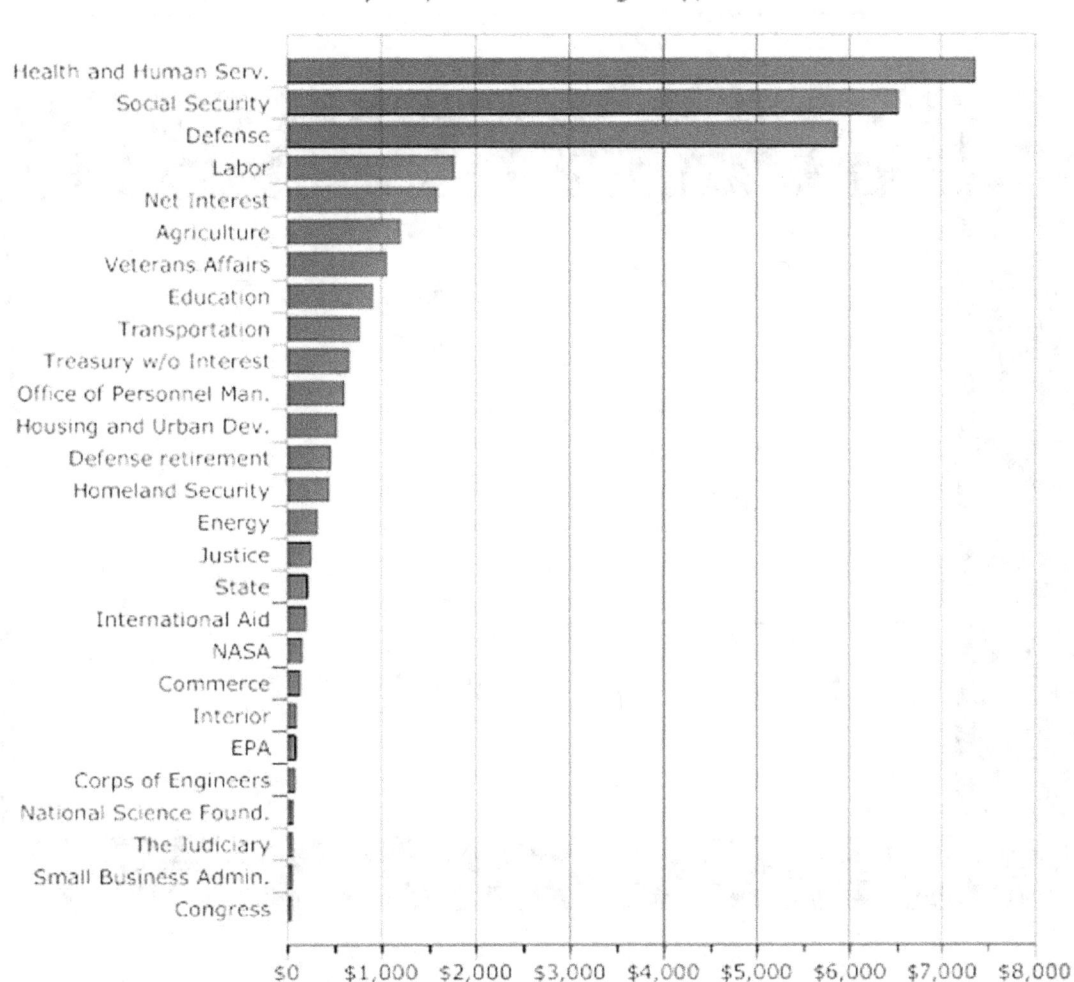

Federal Spending per U.S. Household
by Department or Agency, 2010

(Graph: originally published by The Cato Institute, downsizinggovernment.org, copyright The Cato Institute, used by permission)

Saving the best graph for last, you can see what each department of the government is costing a U.S. household. Every line on the graph is the cost of each department, and therefore must be added together if you want to figure out how much the total cost is per household. After adding the first several lines, the total becomes at least $30,000 pretty quickly. Not only are 8-12 people supporting each government worker, but it's costing each household more than $30,000 a year. It's not exactly meaningful to look at costs this way, however, since the bottom 43% of the income scale doesn't have to pay anything in income taxes. Thanks to our tax system, where you are penalized for working harder and making more money, the amount owed in taxes to fund the government increases significantly based on your tax bracket. Nowadays, however, you're lucky if you have a job.

## *Growing Federal Pay Advantage*

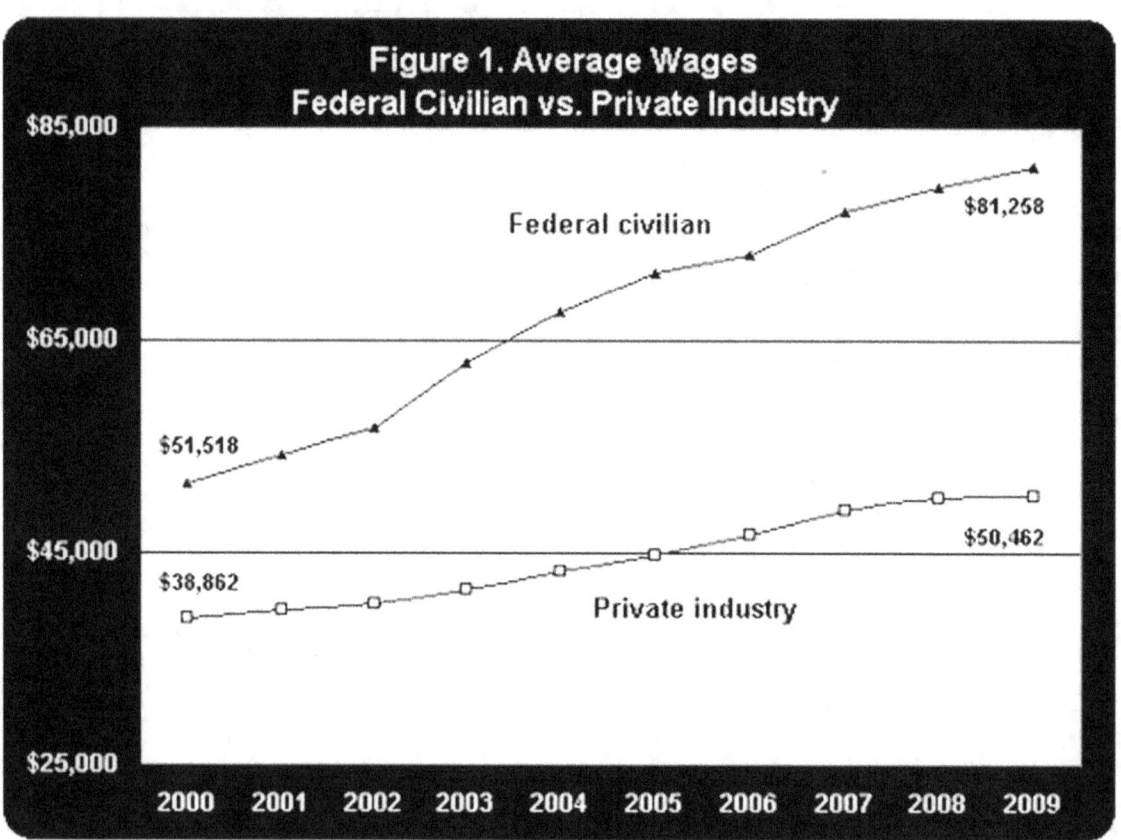

(Graph: *Overpaid Federal Workers*, Originally published by The Cato Institute, Downsizing the Government, copyright The Cato Institute, used with permission. downsizinggovernment.org)

Federal employees are indeed living the American dream, at taxpayer's expense. In 2009, federal civilian workers had an average wage of $81,258, according to data from the U.S. Bureau of Economic Analysis (BEA). By comparison, the average wage of the nation's 101 million private-sector workers was $50,462.

Figure 1 shows average federal- and private-sector wages since 2000, and it reveals that the federal pay advantage over private workers has been increasing steadily.

When benefits such as healthcare and pensions are included, the federal compensation advantage over private workers is even larger, according to the BEA data. In 2009, federal worker compensation averaged $123,049, or double the private-sector average of $61,051.

Figure 2 shows that average federal compensation has grown rapidly over the last decade.

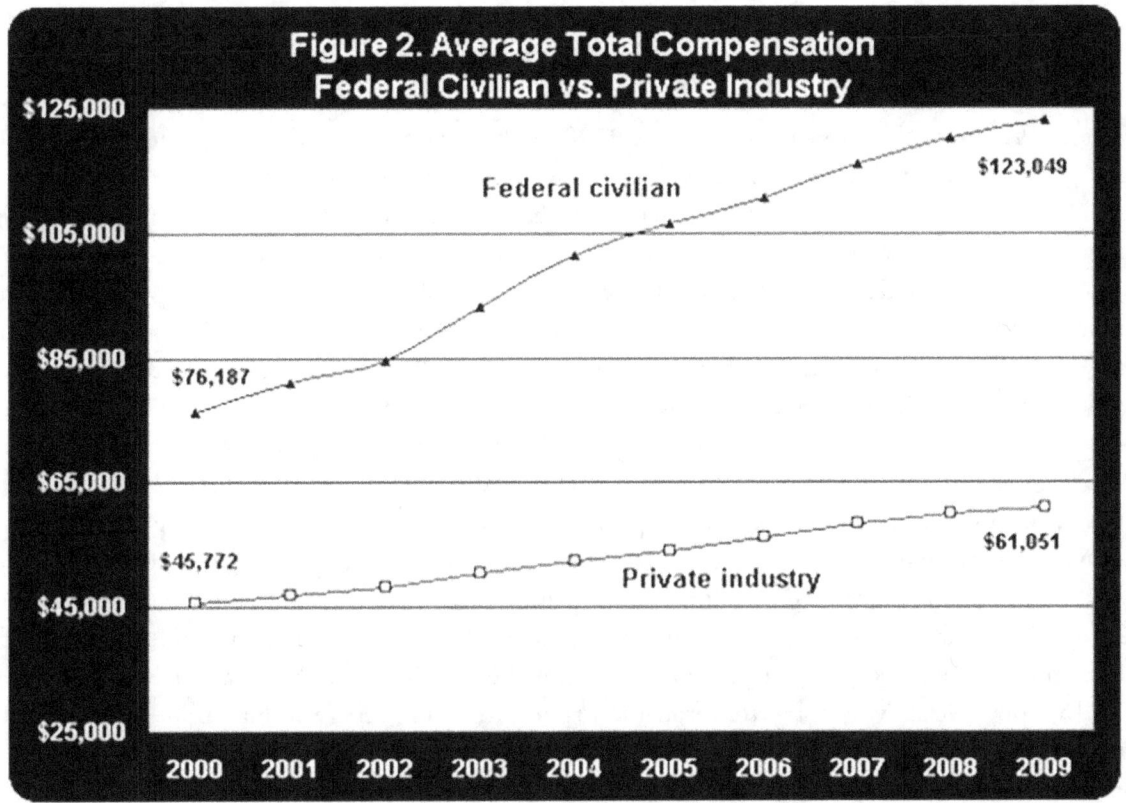

(Graph: *Overpaid Federal Workers*, Originally published by The Cato Institute, Downsizing the Government, copyright The Cato Institute, used with permission. downsizinggovernment.org)

An analysis by *USA Today* revealed particularly fast wage growth at the top end of the federal workforce in recent years. By 2009, there were 383,000 federal civilian workers with salaries of more than $100,000, 66,000 with salaries of more than $150,000, and 22,000 with salaries of more than $170,000. Between late 2007 and mid-2009, the number of federal workers earning more than $150,000 more than doubled, even as the economy fell into a deep recession during that period. Although government employees make at least 60% more than comparable workers in the private sectors, when you include benefits, it's more than double.

(Source: *Overpaid Federal Workers*, by Chris Edwards, Originally published by The Cato Institute, Downsizing the Government, copyright The Cato Institute, used with permission. downsizinggovernment.org) and (*Federal Pay Ahead of Private Industry*, by Dennis Cauchon, USA Today, March 8, 2010)

The huge number of government employees and their cost doesn't even cover the entire cost of people employed by the government. In his book *Free Lunch*, author David Cay Johnston presents data that "...the ranks of people who are hired on contract at much greater cost increases. In 2000 workers hired on contract cost our federal government $207 billion. By 2006 this had swelled to $400 billion...These contract workers typically cost twice as much as civil servants doing the same work, yet they are even less accountable." Contract workers thus add another $400 billion on top of the expenses for government workers. Added together, government workers and government contract workers may cost almost *$900 billion dollars a year*.

Associated Press and others reported On Nov. 29th 2010, President Barack Obama announced a pay freeze for 2 million federal employees and warned the American public that the move is the first of many difficult decisions that must be made to slash the nation's mounting deficits. "The hard truth is that getting this deficit under control is going to require some broad sacrifice, and that sacrifice must be shared by the employees of the federal government," Obama said. The two-year freeze would apply to all civilian federal employees, including those working at the Department of Defense, but would not affect military personnel. The freeze is expected to save more than $5 billion over two years, $28 billion over five years and more than $60 billion over 10 years, White House officials said.

The plan "saves" $5 billion over 2 years; at the same time President Obama *increased* Welfare spending by $263 billion over 2 years to almost a trillion per year. For some reason, this fact wasn't mentioned with the story. The wage freeze is meaningless in the face of increased spending on entitlements. It should be noted, however, that simply freezing pay for federal employees will not affect the deficit or spending, it only prevents spending increases in the future; so it's not savings, as the White House suggests. Not surprisingly, union leaders immediately condemned the freeze. John Gage, president of the 600,000-member American Federation of Government Employees, called the decision "a slap at working people. ..... To symbolically hit at federal employees I think is just wrong." Colleen Kelley, head of the 150,000-member National Treasury Employees Union, said union officials would try to derail the proposal in Congress. She may find some sympathy with union-friendly Democrats still in control for another month "We're going to do everything we can to make this not happen and to explore all our options," Kelley said. Despite the fact that government employees make at least 60% more than the average person, union leaders will continue to fight for higher wages, pensions and benefits until Uncle Sam files his bankruptcy papers. Again, this wage freeze will only prevent *increases* of $2 billion per year, and won't affect current deficit spending levels, now at more than $100 billion per month.

## *Can the government create more jobs?*

The government only seems adept at creating more government jobs, yet job creation was one of the most important issues in the November 2010 elections. What policies can be implemented to ensure the creation of jobs? Many people don't understand how or why we got to the high rates of unemployment. But, only with that understanding, an understanding of what happened in the competitive economic environment that has made the

U.S. uncompetitive and rocketed its unemployment rate into the stratosphere, will Congress and our economic policy makers be able to choose the correct path.

The answer is simple: It's a matter of cost. It just costs too much to produce most goods in the U.S. And, while Congress and the administration regularly demonize those private-sector companies that produce their goods in lower-cost countries, it's clear that the government itself is a huge part of the problem.

Over the past 20 years, the federal budget has grown at a compounded annual rate of 5.6%; that number is 6.8% over the past 10 years. But, disposable personal income grew at a much slower 4.8% annual rate over the 20-year period and an even slower 4.5% annual rate over the last 10 years. The implications of this data are that 1) taxes and fees have increased the costs of private-sector businesses; 2) the ever-growing government, by its nature, expands its span of control over the lives of its citizens through a rapidly expanding set of rules and regulations, all of which raise the cost of production

Over the last two decades, the growing uncompetitiveness of U.S. private-sector businesses was obvious, as production facilities moved south of the border or overseas and lower-cost countries such as China, South Korea, Mexico, and Thailand. While this was obvious, the ultimate impact on the US economy was masked by two bubbles: the dot.com bubble followed immediately by the housing bubble. Both of these bubbles were enabled by excessively easy monetary policies. And during this period, fiscal policy steadily continued toward deficits. With the false sense of prosperity caused by these bubbles, there was no sense of urgency to reverse the trends.

Nevertheless, the bursting of the bubbles has unmasked two significant economic issues:

**1. Overtaxation** – The US has one of the highest corporate tax rates in the world, and is one of a handful of countries that taxes its citizens on their worldwide incomes instead of the income made within the country. In addition, the US has relatively high income taxation coupled with state and local income, property, and sales taxes, various business fees, and a 15% payroll tax burden (not to mention the cost of other benefits paid for by many businesses). Business owners, looking for high returns on investments, move production to lower-cost areas to avoid many of these onerous costs.

**2. Overregulation** – Every Congress produces ever-increasing regulations; state and local governments are no better. And no regulations, no matter how worthless, ever go away. For example, it costs the private financial sector significantly more to administer "backup withholding" (i.e., W-9s) than the cash generated for the government. Both bubbles have in fact created more regulation. The housing bubble, at least, took place while the government stood by and did nothing. The FBI was aware of fraudulent lending practices in 2005 (see reports published on their website, FBI.gov), but was able to do nothing to stop the problem. Washington's reaction after the bubble was, of course, more regulations. Instead of enforcing regulations and preventing fraud, the government bureaucrats simply make more regulations. Let's see how much federal regulations cost U.S. businesses.

## The cost of federal regulations to business and people

Most Americans are painfully aware of the amount of taxes they pay, but explicit taxes and spending are only part of the total burden that government places on Americans. The rest comes in the form of hidden taxes imposed by government regulations. These "regulatory taxes" appear on no budget or balance sheet but are very real: They cost Americans an estimated $1 trillion or more each year, and these costs are increasing. In fiscal year 2009, new regulations costing more than $13 billion per year were adopted by the Bush and Obama Administrations, the highest annual total since 1992. Much more are in the works. Anyone who uses electricity, drives a car, has a job, visits a doctor, owns stocks, or patronizes a bank will be affected by the additional regulations passed by the Obama Administration. The effects of such a regulatory tsunami could be disastrous—destroying jobs, threatening enterprises, and deterring new investment.

**Some facts:**

- **Record-High Regulatory Page Count.** The Code of Federal Regulations, a compendium of all existing federal rules, hit a record high of 163,333 pages in 2009, an increase of some 22,000 since the beginning of the decade. In 2008, the CFR weighed in at 157,974 pages, having increased by 16,693 pages since the start of the George W. Bush Administration.

- **Ballooning Regulatory Agency Budgets.** President Obama's fiscal 2011 budget calls for direct expenditures by regulatory agencies of over $59 billion, an increase of 4.1 percent over fiscal 2010, and 8.9 percent over fiscal 2009.

- **Flood of New Rules.** This year, the Obama Administration has adopted some 25 major new regulations. That is higher than the full-year total for all but one year since 1997.

- **Trillion-Dollar Cost.** According to a 2005 study by the *Small Business Administration*, the total burden to businesses of federal regulation is some $1.1 trillion—more than Americans pay in personal income taxes each year.

- **Major New Regulatory Regimes Created.** New regulatory threats are coming from a variety of areas. Two of the biggest areas of increase have been healthcare and financial reform, both of which were the subject of massive new regulatory legislation passed in 2009 and 2010.

(Source: *Red Tape Rising: Obama's Torrent of New Regulation*," by James Gattuso , Diane Katz and Stephen Keen, originally published by The Heritage Foundation, October 26, 2010, Backgrounder #2482. Heritage.org. copyright The Heritage Foundation, used with permission)

How many months would it take to read and try to figure out 163,333 pages of federal regulations, let alone try to comply with them? Compare 163,333 pages with the number of pages of our Constitution and Declaration of Independence—how did this happen? 224 years of lawyers running things. Federal regulatory agencies cost more than $59 billion per year, yet didn't protect us from the financial collapse, sub-prime lenders, insider trading, foreclosuregate, Wall Street pyramid schemes, credit card company usury or a myriad of other problems. What do the regulatory agencies do with that $59 billion? Salaries, benefits and administration, supporting more government employees. We keep hearing about tainted meat and vegetables, and other products the government is supposed to be inspecting. Our drinking water isn't even safe: a study by the Environmental Working Group (see EWG.org) found hexavalent chromium (a carcinogen) in the tap water of 31 out of 35 cities sampled. Businesses have to spend $1.1 trillion a year on lawyers and accountants just to comply with federal regulations. Trying to comply with ever-increasing federal regulations adds tens of billions to healthcare costs, and financial regulations have failed time and again to protect investors and consumers from financial fraud.

Many people in the private sector have warned about these problems for decades. They have another word for it—red tape. Businesses have moved jobs offshore in an effort to save money and avoid onerous regulations. Ironically, businesses that produce goods overseas get U.S. tax breaks and write downs for the factories they close in the U.S. (and ship abroad). They usually often don't have to pay taxes on goods and profits made overseas, and spend money on research and development in other countries instead of the U.S. Government policy, instead of making it easier for companies to create jobs in the U.S., makes it easier to send jobs abroad, which has been the trend for many years. As they say, "that ship already left" a long time ago, those jobs are gone and aren't coming back. The politicians can talk about job creation and reducing the amount of unemployment, but until there is real structural change in how our government operates with regard to taxes and regulation, jobs will continue to be shipped out.

## The Disability Nightmare:

The Social Security system was set up by FDR as a "social safety net" and a partial reaction to the Great Depression. It was never intended to be a primary source of healthcare, pensions, or any other entitlements. It was designed to help people that had nowhere else to turn. Most importantly, back when it was started the "age of retirement" was the same as life expectancy at the time (65 years). This means most people weren't going to collect benefits since they were only expected to live to be 65. Since then, this program has grown and more and more entitlements have been added and funded. Medicare spending is massive, partially because life expectancy has gone up so much (a good thing). The U.S. Census Bureau now estimates total life expectancy for 2010 is 78.3 years. People are living 13.3 years longer than back in the 1930s when Social Security was begun. The program was never designed to handle this increase in life expectancy. Despite all that has happened in society to extend our lives, Social Security hasn't changed, only gotten bigger. More people are dependent on the government than ever before in our history as a nation.

Social Security has many facets. Most people think of Social Security is what they are entitled to when they get to be 65 years old. They then qualify for Medicare, the federally-subsidized health benefit program administered by the government (which only pays 80% of most healthcare costs). Elderly people that have been paying into Social Security (FICA) their whole life deserve what little they get from the government.

What is important to look at is the Social Security *Disability Program*. It is a huge expense, as you will see, for "people who are disabled and can't work." Of course, there are people that are blind, those that were injured in defending our country, people that were born with birth defects or are paralyzed, people that don't have the mental faculties to work. But, looking at the data, and especially that the ranks of the disabled have doubled in the last two decades, and that the cost of disabled healthcare, both Medicare and Medicaid have tripled in the same amount of time, this has become one of the costliest social benefit/entitlement programs ever. There is surely something else going on here, and it's very, very expensive to taxpayers.

## Total cost of Social Security Disability benefits, by type of beneficiary, 1970–2003

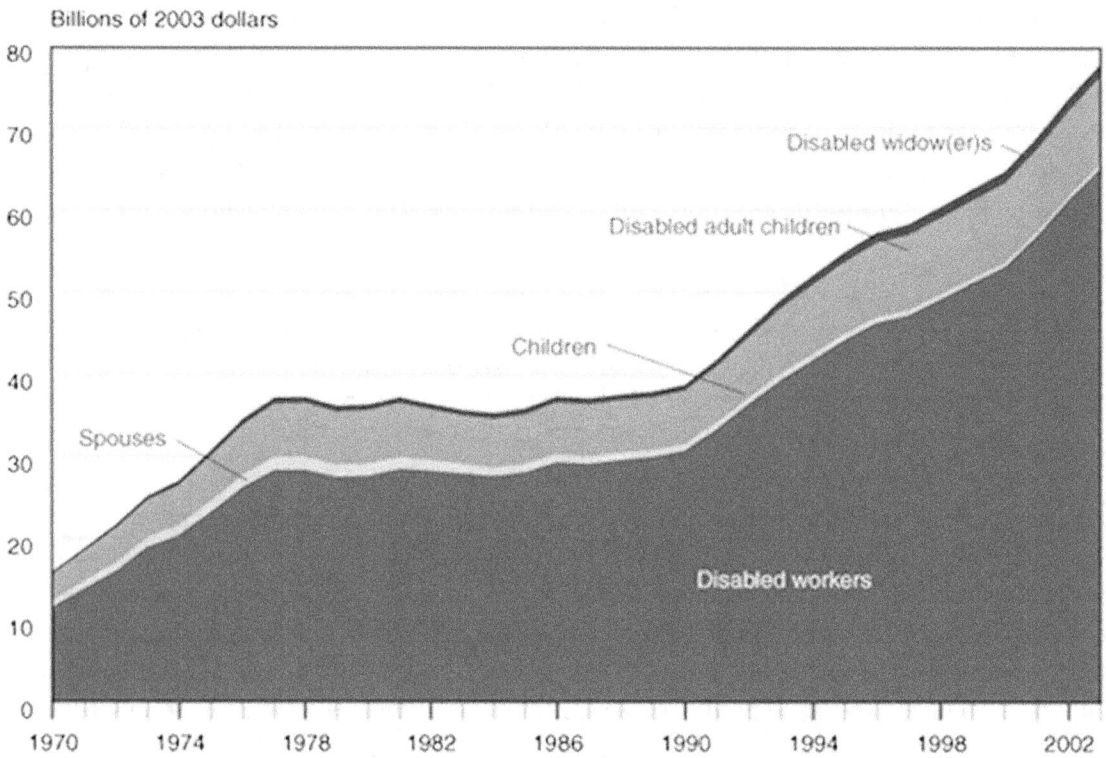

(SOURCE: *Annual Statistical Supplement to the Social Security Bulletin, 2004*, Tables 4.A6 and 5.A17 (monthly amount multiplied by 12). NOTES: This chart excludes a small number of young spouses of retired workers and mothers who are entitled solely on the basis of having a disabled adult child in their care. In 2003, there were fewer than 20,000 mothers and fewer than 12,000 young spouses, for whom the costs were $200 million and $80 million, respectively. Those costs are less than one-quarter of 1 percent of the expenditures in 2003. All dollar amounts are in constant price-adjusted 2003 dollars)

As with much of government reporting, this is the latest data available. Since 1990, the amount of money spent on disabled workers went from $30 billion to at least $80 billion per year today (or more). The numbers of spouses, children, disabled adult children, and disabled widowers remained almost constant over the measuring period. The term "disabled workers" is misleading because it represents people who used to work but now have been proclaimed "disabled" by a judge—misleading because they no longer work.

### Number of disabled Social Security beneficiaries, by type of beneficiary, December 1970–2003

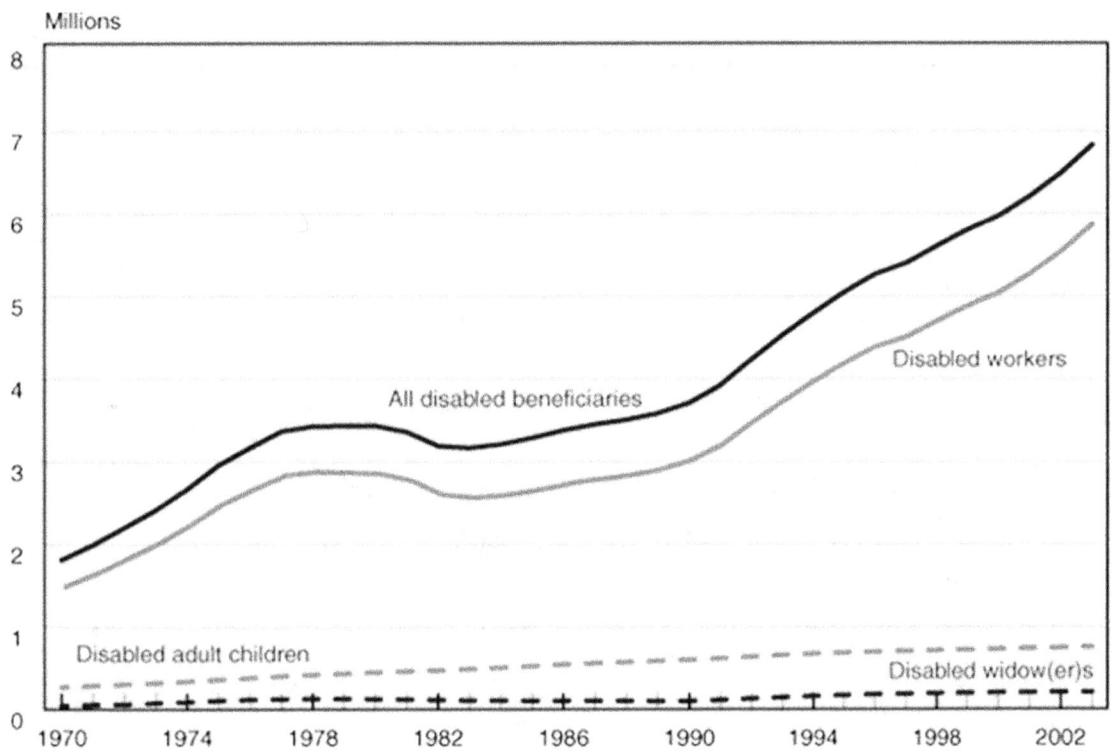

(SOURCE: *Annual Statistical Report on the Social Security Disability Insurance Program, 2004*, Table 1; *Annual Statistical Supplement to the Social Security Bulletin*)

This is the most recent data available from the government concerning number of disabled persons. But, you can easily extrapolate from the 2002 data point, and it's clear that by now there are more than <u>eight million people</u> on Disability benefits. It's easy to also see the number of people on Disability benefits has doubled since the early 1990's. If you study this graph, one thing becomes apparent—the massive increase in numbers of disable people is almost solely from increases in disabled "workers." The disabled adult children, disabled widowers, and people that have been disabled since birth has remained about the same. It's only the number of disabled workers, those that used to work but aren't anymore than has driven the massive increase in beneficiaries. To look at it another way, the number of blind people or people mentally unable to work has remained about the same, but the number of people that used to be fine and worked (but don't anymore—they collect Disability benefits) has skyrocketed since 1990.

## Number of disabled-worker beneficiaries and as a percentage of the insured population, December 1970–2003

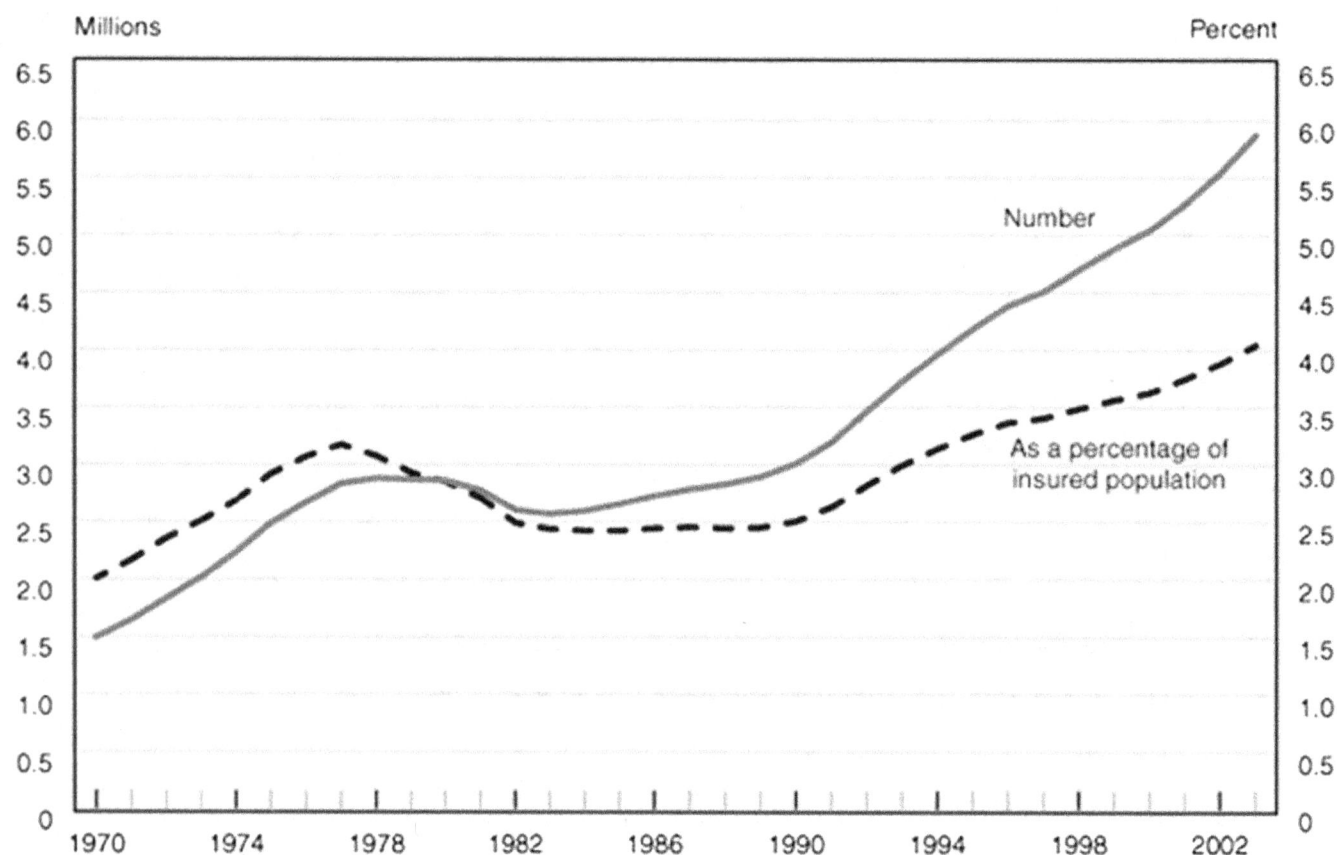

(SOURCES: *Annual Statistical Supplement to the Social Security Bulletin, 2004*, Table 4.C1; *Annual Statistical Report on the Social Security Disability Insurance Program, 2003*, Table 1)

Back in the "good old days" of the 1970's, before the advent of HMOs, more people had insurance than Disability beneficiaries. Since 1990 however, the percentage of insured population can't keep up with the disabled-worker beneficiaries. Don't forget, when you have health insurance, you have to pay part of your insurance yourself, you have co-pays at the doctor, and have deductibles and medication expenses that people on Disability don't necessarily have to pay. When Disability Medicare and Medicaid are combined, as they usually are in most states for Disability beneficiaries, they end up paying little or nothing out-of-pocket for health expenses, and have unlimited coverage. Social Security and Medicaid have tried to cut services to beneficiaries lately, but the impact has been minimal so far.

## Total cost of Medicare for the disabled, 1973–2001

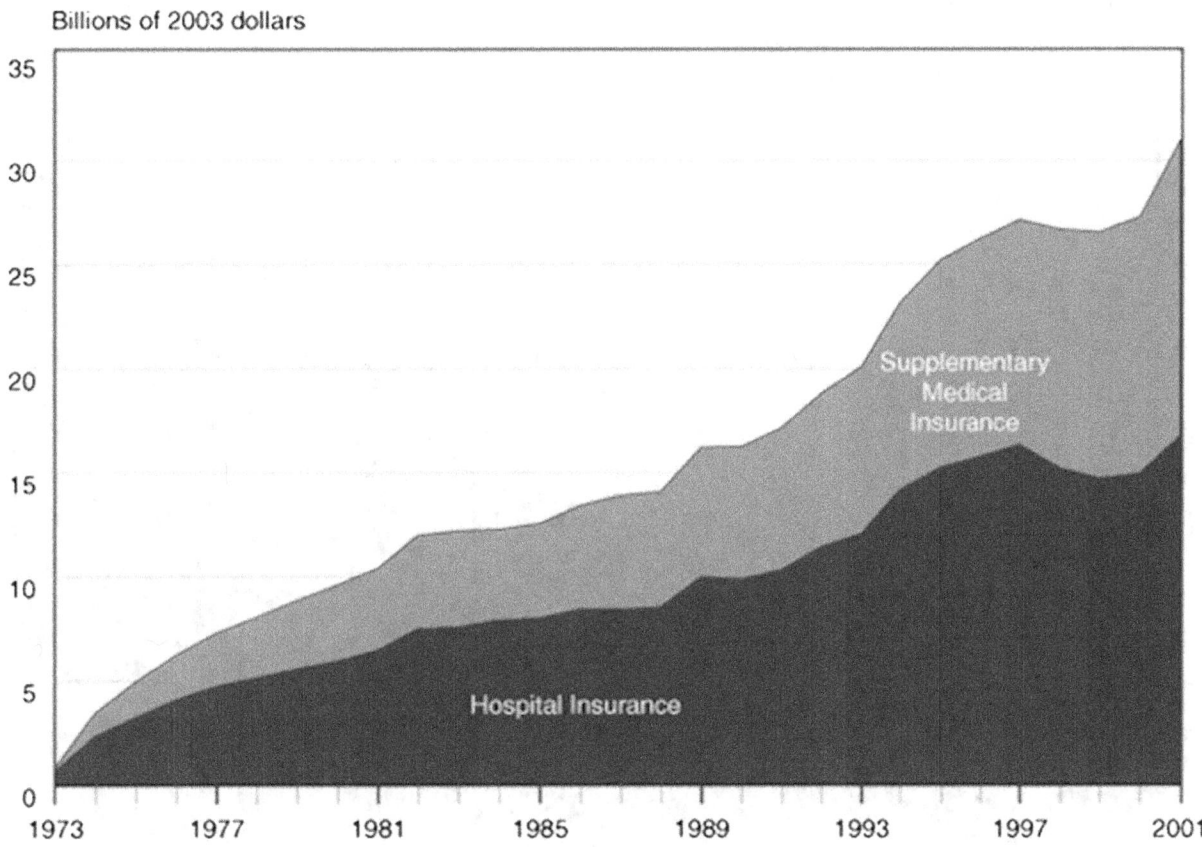

(SOURCE: Centers for Medicare & Medicaid Services, *Medicare & Medicaid Statistical Supplement*, Table 12, available at http://www.cms.hhs.gov/MedicareMedicaidStatSupp/LT/list.asp. NOTES: Medicare uses a different definition of Disability, and not all disabled Medicare beneficiaries receive cash Disability benefits from Social Security. All dollar amounts are in constant price-adjusted 2003 dollars)

This graph shows how Medicare costs for the disabled have more than tripled, just since 1990. This is an absolutely huge number, and this is just data up to 2001, not taking into consideration the last 9 years. It's not too difficult to extrapolate out another nine years, just add another five billion dollars. Again, Disability beneficiaries have little or no out-of-pocket medical expenses, they get combined Medicare and Medicaid. Even average Social Security Medicare recipients have to buy supplemental insurance to cover the 20% the Medicare doesn't pay for.

## Total cost of Medicaid for the disabled, fiscal years 1975–2001

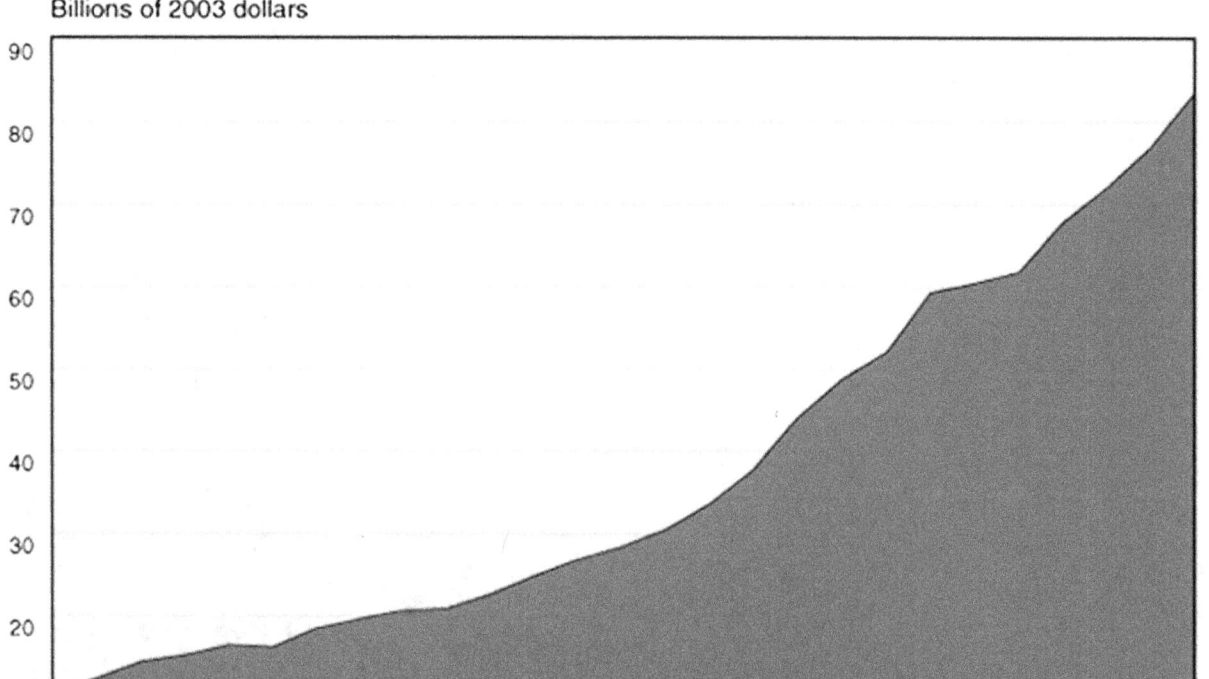

(SOURCE: Centers for Medicare & Medicaid Services, *Medicare & Medicaid Statistical Supplement, 2003*, Table 94. fiscal year data available at cms.hhs.gov/MedicareMedicaidStatSupp/LT/list.asp)

NOTES: Medicaid uses a different definition of Disability, and not all disabled Medicaid recipients receive payments from the SSI program. Also, not all SSI recipients are categorically eligible for Medicaid. All dollar amounts are in constant (price-adjusted) 2003 dollars.

When you total the cost of SSI Disability cash payments: $80 billion, Medicare benefits for the disabled: $30 billion and Medicaid benefits for the disabled $80 billion, it's more than $190 billion, and that was for 2001, the last time data was reported. The Disability ranks have continued to swell, so the total figure for today is probably closer to $250 billion (a quarter of a trillion dollars). The above graphs show that since about 1990, the cost of Disability beneficiaries that get Medicare and Medicaid health benefits has almost tripled.

---

*Cost of Disability benefits as a percentage of gross domestic product, by type of benefit, 1970–2001*

---

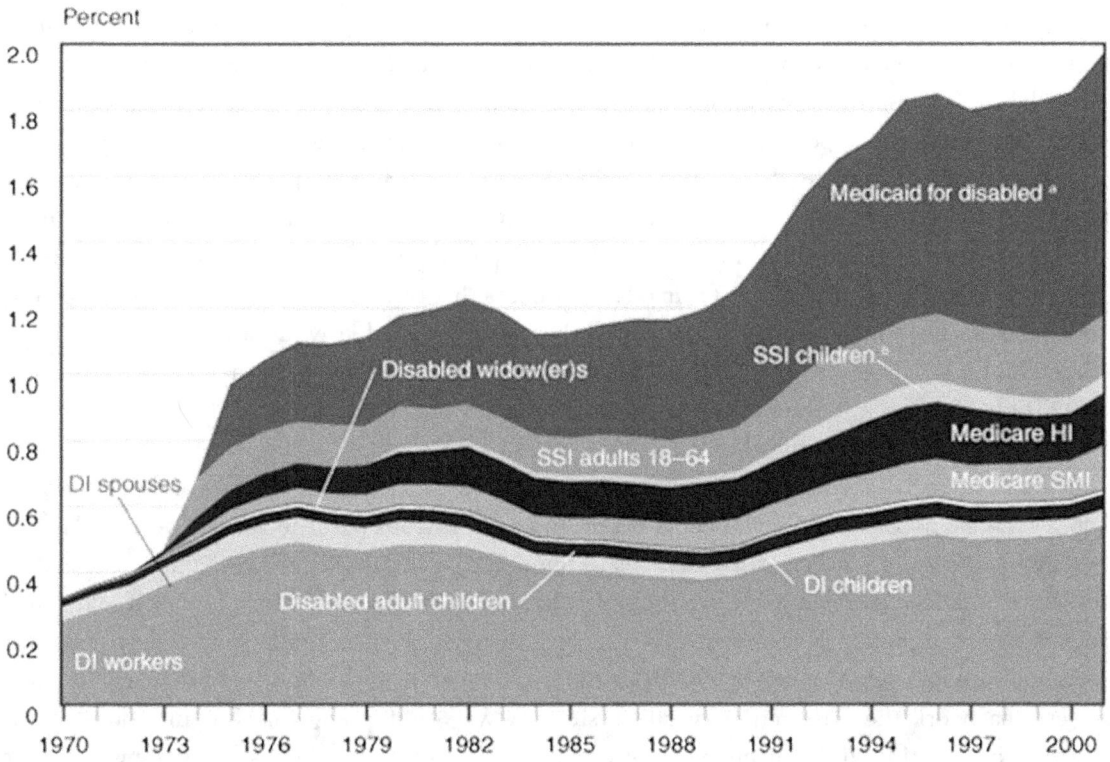

(SOURCES: Centers for Medicare & Medicaid Services, *Medicare & Medicaid Statistical Supplement, 2003*, Tables 12 and 94 (fiscal year data), available at http://www.cms.hhs.gov/MedicareMedicaidStatSupp/LT/list. asp; *2004 Annual Report of the Supplemental Security Income Program*, Table IV.C1; *Annual Statistical Supplement to the Social Security Bulletin, 2004*, Tables 4.A6 and 5.A17; Bureau of Economic Analysis, gross domestic product. NOTE: Medicaid data are for the fiscal year. All other data are for the calendar year. a. Medicaid is for disabled persons, including those aged 65 or older. b. Before 1980, SSI children were counted in the category "SSI adults 18–64.")

---

Although earlier charts showed that benefit costs have increased dramatically, nearly doubling in real terms since 1990, it is important to view these benefits relative to the size of the economy. The chart above presents the major Disability programs as a percentage of gross domestic product (GDP). Expenditures on cash and medical benefits for the disabled, as a percentage of GDP, increased 57 percent between 1990 and 2001, consuming 1.98 percent of GDP in 2001, up from 1.26 percent in 1990. Although many of the expenditures have increased over time, the most dramatic growth is seen in Medicaid expenditures for the disabled. As shown earlier, Medicaid costs have increased because of a tripling of the number of disabled individuals receiving Medicaid since 1975 and a 175% percent increase in the average cost of Medicaid benefits during the same period.

Again, a whopping 2% of GDP, gross domestic product, the output of our whole economy, just to pay for Disability benefits. How can this possibly be? The Disability system is managed, again, by the Social Security Administration, which has offices everywhere in the U.S. If you feel you are disabled, don't want to work anymore, you simply go to the Social Security office and complete the obligatory paperwork. They then send it in, and SSI requests medical records from your doctor. You can have a hearing, but most of the time, you just get automatically rejected. That's when *lawyers* come into the picture. Most won't even take a Disability case until a person is rejected first. Then starts the appeal process, which is when lawyers take over, cajole doctors, get appeal hearing after appeal hearing, and eventually the Federal Disability judge caves and the person gets considered "disabled."

Getting Disability benefits is a permanent condition, on the federal dole for the rest of their life, including cash, health benefits and even free housing. The best thing, especially for the lawyers, is that once they "win" their case the judgment is *retroactive to the date of filing*. So, a process that can take a year or two is back-paid to the date you filed your papers. So, you get a huge check, for all that time, and so does your lawyer, 1/3 to ½ of your whopping first benefit check. I have seen people that barely worked a day in their life in the first place file for Disability and get $50,000 in one check, followed by a lifetime of monthly checks, and free healthcare to boot. Many states also provide housing and a variety of other services.

Not surprisingly, Social Security Disability has become a huge windfall for lawyers and people that just don't want to work. The amount of money you get is based on your previous pay. You can get years of "back pay" from SSI once you win your case. The larger law firms have hundreds or thousands of cases going at once. In fact, as of 12/10, there are *2 million cases* pending for people that have filed for Disability. The longer it takes the better for the attorney. Once an attorney becomes involved, no matter how long the endless appeal process may go on, I haven't seen one case lose yet. The larger SSDI/Disability lawyer mills make more and regular income than many of the lawyers that work the class-action lawsuit system. A way of stopping this system would be to eliminate "back pay" from the equation. If that happened, lawyers probably wouldn't love Disability filings so much, because they would only get their hourly rates—much less than the windfall they get from back payment checks from the government.

People have a hurt knee, a sore back, are depressed, anxious or whatever it is they think prevents them from doing a job, if they are patient, can cash in on the "holy grail" of social-benefits-entitlement programs – *permanent Disability*.

Guess who makes a fortune getting people onto the Disability roles: LAWYERS. That's right,

# *"Success Stories"*

Lawyers are proud of getting people victories in their "fight" for Disability. They are also getting rich doing so. The Federal Government, who runs the Disability lottery system, is just a target. Lawyers have found interesting and creative ways of getting around the laws, filing endless appeals, and doing whatever they can to get money from the government. The famous quote of the Disability lawyer is "we don't get a dime until you win your case." Once they do win, they get $20,000 to $30,000 just for filing a few appeals and showing up in court once or twice, and its money you are paying, as taxpayers. Here are some stories designed to get people into their offices so they might also be able to get on Disability. The complete stories are not given, just the initial facts of the case.

Actual cases from Social-Security-Lawyers.net

#### SSDI benefits awarded despite limited medical records

Claimant had scant medical documents due to lack of insurance and other resources. Case considered as critical case and claimant awarded SSDI benefits for degenerative arthritis in knee and back  and for depression. .....

#### 34 year old insurance sales person gets SSDI.

SSA denied Peter, a 34 year old insurance sales agent because he was young and SSA said he could do other work despite his fractured neck. Benefits awarded after hearing......

#### Social Security thought Mary could work as an assembly line worker. Mary could not even clean her apartment, let alone work. She needed legal help.

Mary always wanted to be a nurse. She worked for 10 years as a nurse, but could no longer maintain that employment due to fatigue, pain, and poor concentration. She sought treatment from numerous specialists, none of whom.....

#### 48 year old man wins SSDI

Jeffery worked in construction and injured his back and shoulder requiring surgery. SSA denied him saying that although he could not do construction work, he could do other jobs. Testimony and records were presented which.....

#### Crohn's Disease victory-5 years of back pay awarded to 42 year old lady

It took three hearings and three different administrative law judges to secure a 42 year old lady with Crohn's Disease her benefits.The case was presented to an Administrative Law Judge for the first time in February 2006. He denied the.....

#### Psychological Disability

The Social Security Administration will grant psychological Disability which is properly documented. It is gratifying in these, as in all cases, to see the Administration working so well  in situations where people think that they don't want to work anymore because.....

#### A 55 year old dentist who lifted an X-ray machine awarded Social Security without a hearing before an ALJ.

The dentist had several surgeries after lifting an X-ray machine and pulling muscles in his back. He could not return to work but was denied twice by the SSA. His lawyer appealed his case and was able to.....

#### Montana woman awarded Social Security Disability after 4 back surgeries

A 53 year old Montana woman who had four unsuccessful back surgeries and arthritis was awarded Social Security Disability after the her law firm took her case before  an Administrative Law Judge recently and.....

<u>Woman 51 years old awarded SSDI despite a work history of sedentary work.</u>

Mary had two back surgeries, was morbidly obese and had chronic diabetes. SSA said that since she worked as a secretary, she was denied SSDI benefits. At hearing we produced a medical record and testimony that won her case......

<u>We understand the Social Security regulations that determine when pain is a disabling condition.</u>
<u>Our client explains how we helped him:</u>

"Well, I was in a lot of pain. I had already had two discs that had ruptured... They weren't touching on the nerve endings, but I was in a lot of pain. I couldn't sit. I couldn't stand. I knew I had to do something because I couldn't work.....

<u>40 Year Old, 400 lb Woman Wins SSI-Then Dies</u>

Beverly called our office one week before her hearing in June of 2008. She had never worked outside of her home. She raised two children. Her husband recently filed for divorce after 15 years of physical abuse and her morbid obesity.....

<u>Fast Track Approval For client with back injury</u>

55 Year old man was awarded benefits within 6 months of the case getting to the administrative law judge level instead of the usual 2 year wait. We developed evidence early and submitted it with a letter brief requesting a staff.....

---

## *What qualifies you for Disability?*

---

<u>Mental Disabilities</u>: <u>Anxiety</u>, <u>Bipolar Disorder</u>, <u>Depression</u>, <u>PTSD</u>, <u>Mental Retardation</u>, <u>Schizophrenia</u>
<u>Physical Disabilities</u>: <u>Asthma</u>, <u>Migraines</u>, <u>Arthritis</u>, <u>Pain</u>, <u>Back Problems</u>, <u>Cancer</u>, <u>Cerebral Palsy</u>, <u>COPD</u>, <u>Diabetes</u>

It's not hard to see, it is relatively easy to get on Disability. Politicians have eased requirements for getting into the Disability program so much that practically anyone can qualify. Those nagging health problems you've had all your life *can pay off for the rest of your life*. As a doctor for the last 13 years, I've seen many, many people get on Disability. I've also seen many people with too much pride to seek Disability who continue to work with asthma, migraines, anxiety, depression, arthritis, back problems, pain, COPD, diabetes, anxiety, depression—I've even had patients that continue to work while they had cancer and even cerebral palsy.

Yet, 90% of the people on Disability drive their cars to go bowling, to the store, to water parks with their families, hunting and fishing. They shop at the mall, eat out all the time, take road trips. Some coach little league teams, take cruises, go to Disney World, and many have jobs on the side—yes, many of the people that have been declared unable to work *are* working and making money *and* collecting Disability checks every month. And there is no mechanism to catch these people, unless a concerned taxpayer videotapes them doing something they aren't supposed to be able to do, like lifting weights at the gym or mowing their grass. Many have their own businesses (fixing cars, mowing lawns, home improvement, even roofing) and are paid "under the table"—all cash businesses that the government can't track. Even then, unless someone in the government decides to pursue the issue, they continue to get away with it. There is little or no incentive for the government to go after people that have been declared (by a judge) disabled. In fact, local offices encourage people to get on Disability whenever possible to increase their case-loads. Increased case-loads are job and budgetary security for the federal workers at these offices. It's amazing how acceptable it is to defraud the government—and why not? As long as you can get away with it. Bernie Madoff is sitting in jail because he defrauded investors for $50 billion dollars over ten years. Many people on Disability are defrauding the government and taxpayers for a large part of $250 billion *every year* and get away with it.

If someone, like the large group of Disability lawyers, lined up their clients, you usually wouldn't be able to tell who was disabled. You could easily spot the blind people, those missing limbs or otherwise disfigured, crippled or paralyzed, or those that are talking to themselves—people that really are disabled. But you can't pick most disabled people out of the population, because most of them are doing the same thing you're doing (except going to work). They have arthritis, back pain, neck pain, obesity, asthma, COPD, depression or anxiety, diabetes or migraines. Considering there are more than 8 million people getting Disability benefits, it's very likely you already know someone on Disability. Their lawyers worked the system, however, and now they have been declared by the government unable to work. People can win their case and get on Disability for almost any reason, including the ones above. Who among us hasn't had arthritis, back problems, pain, headaches, depression or anxiety? Just about anyone could qualify for Disability and collect government checks for a lifetime of idleness without much trouble. Lawyers are waiting to hear from you now!

## *What do you get?*

Calculating Benefits: If a claimant has been approved for <u>SSI</u>, the monthly amount depends on household income and assets. Social Security takes into account earned and unearned income, mortgage or rent payments, and other income amounts in the same household. SSI has a maximum monthly amount of $674. (A Cost of Living Adjustment may apply each year.)

But, if a claimant has been approved for <u>Disability</u> (Title II), the maximum monthly amount is approximately $2000. The most a family can receive for SSI and Disability combined is currently about $3300 per month – $39,500 per year, with cost of living increases, for life. Most people on Disability can live a very comfortable life collecting almost $40,000 a year without having to work. The <u>back benefits</u> (sometimes called retro benefits or past due benefits) are more difficult to calculate. The back benefits basically reimburse you for the months you waited to be approved, and in some cases can go even further back. In the case of SSI, the retro benefits can only go back to the date of filing, or the date you submitted your initial application.

## *Disability claimants willing to become violent*

*The Association of Administrative Law Judges* (AALJ.org) reports that judges who hear Social Security Disability cases are facing a growing number of violent threats from claimants angry over being denied benefits or frustrated at lengthy delays in processing claims. These judges are the only thing standing between claimants/lawyers and getting free money and healthcare for life. There were at least 80 threats to kill or harm administrative law judges or staff over the past year (2010) an 18 percent increase over the previous reporting period, according to data collected by the agency. One claimant in Albuquerque, N.M., called his congressman's office to say he was going to "take his guns and shoot employees" in the Social Security hearing office. In Eugene, Ore., a man who was denied benefits said he is "ready to join the Taliban and hurt some people." Another claimant denied benefits told a judge in Greenville, S.C., that he was a sniper in the military and "would go take care of the problem."

"I'm not sure the number is as significant as the kind of threats being made," said Randall Frye, a judge based in Charlotte, N.C., and the president of the judges' union. "There seem to be more threats of serious bodily harm, not only to the judge but to the judge's family." Fifty of the incidents came between March and August, including that of a Pittsburgh claimant who threatened to kill herself outside the hearing office or fly a plane into the building like a disgruntled tax protester did earlier this year at the Internal Revenue Service building in Austin, Texas. The more entitlements our government offers, the more people are going to feel entitled, and entitled to do whatever it takes to get into entitlement programs.

AALJ also reported nearly 2 million people are waiting to find out if they qualify for Disability benefits (as of 12/10), with many having to wait more than two years to see their first payment. Considering there are more than 8 million people already on Disability, you can see that many, many people want to get into the best entitlement program our government has to offer and never again have to work a day in their life. Apparently the word has gotten out as an incredible 20% more people are in line to get into the program (than are already on Disability), and they are more desperate than ever. Considering we are already spending $250 billion per year on Disability, this would increase spending by at least another $50 billion *per year*, for a total of $300 billion per year. And let's say "back pay" will be an average of $30,000 per beneficiary for these 2 million people (a low-ball estimate) once they get in, the back pay alone will cost taxpayers another *$60 billion dollars*—a third or half of which will go to their lawyers.

The Congressional Budget Office (CBO) recently released a report stating SSDI is "not financially sustainable" at current spending levels, and addresses ways to get people on Disability back to work and limiting the numbers of new participants into the program. Good luck with that. The report also projects growth in SSDI to almost 16 million beneficiaries by the year 2020; so Disability is expected to double again by 2020. Growth in Disability spending is accelerating, costing more than 8% of the Federal Budget.

(Source: *Social Security Disability Insurance: Participation Trends and Their Fiscal Implications,* Economic and budget issue brief, a series of issue summaries from the Congressional Budget Office, by Molly Dahl and Noah Meyerson, July 22, 2010, CBO.gov)

## Permanently unable to work?

The thing with Disability is once you get it, it's permanent. The system is completely ridiculous for people that *used* to work simply because they don't think they can do their previous job anymore, they can't do *any* job anymore? For example, say a guy hurts his knee working in the coal mines (actual story) and decides to file for Disability (his father is also on Disability). Some doctor saw him and some lawyer filed his appeals and won. So, this guy doesn't have to work again for the rest of his life. Having absolutely no trouble walking normally (without even a limp), he still drives his truck around, still hunts and fishes, still plays football and baseball with his kids and does odd jobs on the side. You get the idea. But our government says he is disabled, not able to do *any* job. No job re-training, no seated job, no job driving a truck, no nothing. Just collect your huge check every month and free unlimited healthcare, all paid for by you, the taxpayer.

**In conclusion**, the Federal Government is huge; "public servants" account for 1 in 12 people in the U.S., and they get massive salaries, retirement benefits, pensions, retire early, have health insurance, and get raises and make more money than almost anyone else in the private sector can ever hope to make. Public servants make up to 60% more than everyone else they "serve", despite getting their salaries frozen lately. Government employees are living the American dream, at the expense of the taxpayers. You would think there would be a line at the Mississippi River to Washington for people trying to get jobs with the government. And if you can't get a job with the government, just get on the "holy grail" of entitlement programs: Disability. You don't even have to work, and you collect up to $40,000 per year and have free unlimited healthcare. It seems life is good, if you happen to be in the right category (dependent on the government). If you have to get a job on your own, try to get healthcare, or even just pay your taxes (to support everyone else), you are probably out of luck.

# CHAPTER 3

# *Government Subsidies*

All a person has to do is look at the sheer number of governmental subsidy programs to understand why our government is in such poor financial shape:

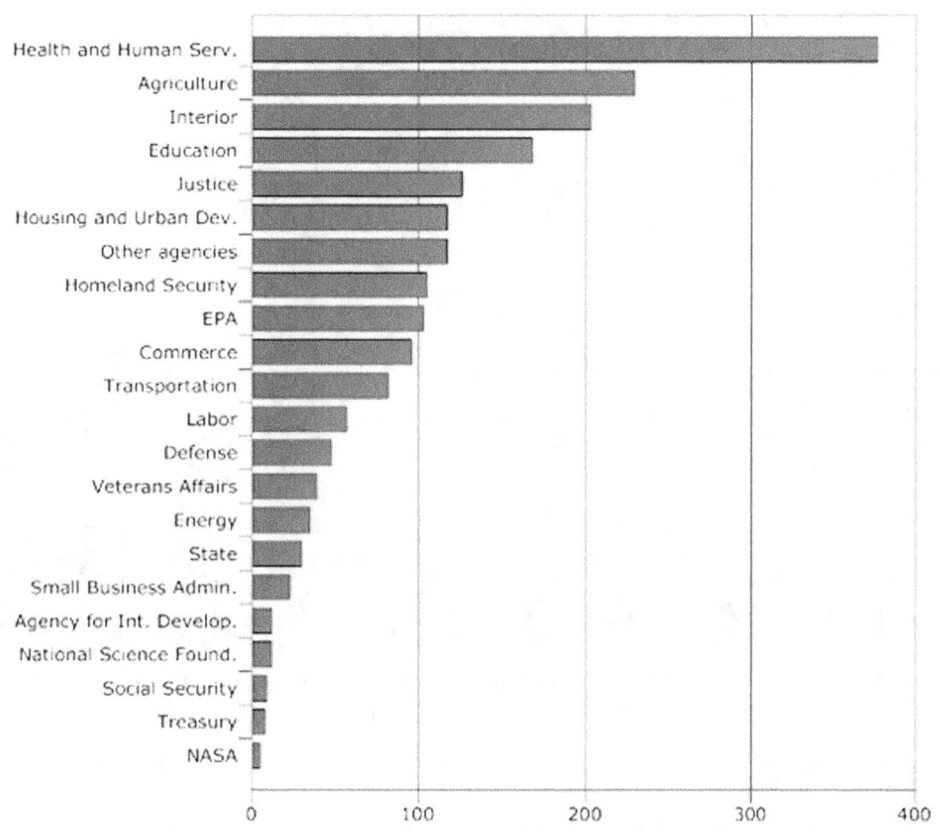

Number of Subsidy Programs Administered by Department or Agency, 2010

Number of Subsidy Programs per www.cfda.gov

(Source: Catalogue of Federal Domestic Assistance – CFDA.gov)

Subsidy programs are another way of saying the government hands out money. While some of the organizations on the following list need federal (your tax dollars) support, others are suspect. But it's the sheer number of programs that is staggering. For instance, our government has almost 400 different programs just through Health and Human Services to hand out money. Just the administration costs of trying to manage almost 400 different organizations handing out free money are staggering. And what about the second largest number: Department of Agriculture (USDA). It has about 225 separate organizations handing out free money, and the list goes on. This redundancy wastes tens of billions of dollars, and those adept at ripping off the government often take advantage of this redundancy as they extract money from multiple programs.

*The number of subsidy programs is growing:*

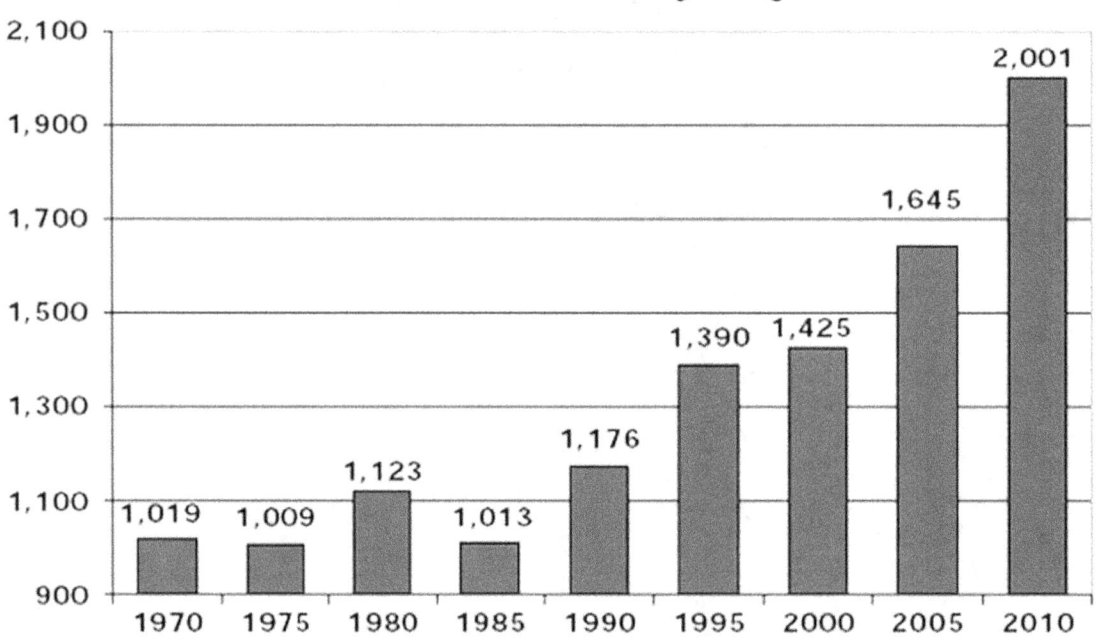

**Number of Federal Subsidy Programs**

(Graph originally published by The Cato Institute, downsizinggovernment.org, copyright The Cato Institute, used by permission)

| Year | Conservation Subsidies | Disaster Subsidies | Commodity Subsidies | Crop Insurance Premium Subsidies | Total USDA Subsidies |
|---|---|---|---|---|---|
| | Payments / Recipients | Payments / Recipients | Payments / Recipients | Subsidies / Policies | Payments / Recipients |
| 1995 | $1,904,452,900 432,904 | $657,973,426 145,206 | $4,679,764,533 1,025,820 | $889,372,304 2,454,932 | $8,131,563,163 1,336,234 |
| 1996 | $1,804,021,315 414,145 | $147,621,222 54,645 | $5,322,161,643 1,352,477 | $982,062,670 2,231,091 | $8,255,866,849 1,570,749 |
| 1997 | $1,732,828,816 387,122 | $105,935,165 55,460 | $5,616,337,125 1,338,946 | $902,794,419 1,847,715 | $8,357,895,525 1,529,392 |
| 1998 | $1,548,032,756 347,367 | $42,394,671 9,544 | $10,767,204,784 1,312,575 | $946,312,180 1,744,944 | $13,303,944,390 1,458,747 |
| 1999 | $1,584,294,106 345,573 | $2,263,991,556 370,858 | $17,723,999,810 1,372,191 | $1,391,886,240 1,798,333 | $22,964,171,712 1,634,585 |
| 2000 | $1,731,207,875 399,615 | $1,436,475,735 392,292 | $20,224,767,431 1,656,471 | $1,347,891,738 1,938,026 | $24,740,527,630 1,902,014 |
| 2001 | $1,945,843,939 415,896 | $2,405,487,177 392,840 | $18,126,966,692 1,621,781 | $1,774,055,666 1,909,850 | $24,252,355,149 1,880,274 |
| 2002 | $1,990,918,128 429,667 | $1,358,545,176 469,197 | $8,969,002,441 1,319,208 | $1,741,410,009 1,888,143 | $14,059,875,754 1,705,726 |
| 2003 | $2,021,149,009 445,068 | $2,951,001,044 492,035 | $11,102,816,553 1,556,856 | $2,042,030,619 1,922,526 | $18,116,997,224 1,836,597 |
| 2004 | $2,084,040,924 461,281 | $546,881,095 83,783 | $10,234,552,177 1,228,744 | $2,477,423,738 1,988,947 | $15,343,287,807 1,456,609 |
| 2005 | $2,634,199,434 510,963 | $3,032,173,649 356,139 | $16,226,360,490 1,266,090 | $2,343,826,824 1,969,461 | $24,238,033,030 1,540,000 |
| 2006 | $2,964,226,425 546,135 | $166,038,477 26,653 | $11,225,437,719 1,223,295 | $2,682,005,763 1,952,696 | $17,038,090,620 1,480,650 |
| 2007 | $3,014,687,659 548,816 | $461,957,503 92,064 | $6,605,277,722 1,110,553 | $3,823,591,690 1,933,745 | $13,905,866,024 1,388,585 |
| 2008 | $3,072,906,878 543,218 | $2,063,638,823 411,973 | $6,209,452,127 1,088,881 | $5,691,433,057 1,956,216 | $17,037,571,296 1,450,961 |
| 2009 | $1,955,017,326 461,955 | $243,838,571 37,997 | $7,786,459,937 1,022,231 | $5,424,581,239 2,047,839 | $15,409,905,033 1,274,433 |
| Total | $31,987,827,491 1,258,255 | $17,883,953,290 1,321,411 | $160,820,561,182 2,801,445 | $34,460,678,156 29,584,464 | $245,155,951,207 3,501,983 |

Since 1990, the number of federal subsidy programs has almost doubled. Again, subsidies are direct pecuniary aid furnished by the government—money handouts. In the U.S., aid seems to go to anyone, foreign or domestic. With deficit spending out of control, the government is making more and more subsidy programs to give away more and more money. You can thank the lobbyists for this. They persuade congress to form programs for the people or groups the lobbyists represent. Notice also from this graph that subsidy programs only dropped between 1980 to 1985, the rest of the time the number has gone up a staggering amount. In the five years between 2005 and 2010, the number of subsidy programs *went up by 356*. This means the U.S. government has added a new subsidy program (financed by taxpayers) about *every five days for five years!* The government is handing out another huge *new* pile of free money to someone or something every five days! This is in addition to the massive piles of money the government is handing out to already-established subsidy programs. Why isn't this talked about in the news?

All this waste and redundancy costs hundreds of billions of dollars a year. Since We can't possibly look at each of the 2001 subsidy programs individually, and since Health and Human Services (HHS) spending is addressed in other sections of this book, let's take a look at the other sacred cash cow that more than 60% of the voting public doesn't support—farm subsidies. Below is a chart showing the breakdown of farm subsidy spending in the last 14 years.

(Source: Environmental Working Group © 2010. Reprinted with permission. Farm.ewg.org)

## USDA Subsidies to United States by year

| Year | | Subsidy Amount |
|------|---|----------------|
| 1995 | | $8,131,563,163 |
| 1996 | | $8,255,866,849 |
| 1997 | | $8,357,895,525 |
| 1998 | | $13,303,944,390 |
| 1999 | | $22,964,171,712 |
| 2000 | | $24,740,527,630 |
| 2001 | | $24,252,355,149 |
| 2002 | | $14,059,875,754 |
| 2003 | | $18,116,997,224 |
| 2004 | | $15,343,287,807 |
| 2005 | | $24,238,033,030 |
| 2006 | | $17,038,090,620 |
| 2007 | | $13,905,866,024 |
| 2008 | | $17,037,571,296 |
| 2009 | | $15,409,905,033 |
| | | |
| 1995-2009 | | $245,155,951,207 |

| | Total USDA Subsidies in United States, 1995-2009 | | |
|---|---|---|---|
| Recipients of **Total USDA Subsidies** from farms in United States totaled **$245,156,000,000** in from 1995-2009. | | | |
| **Rank** | **Recipient** (* ownership information available) | **Location** | **Total USDA Subsidies 1995-2009** |
| 1 | Riceland Foods Inc | Stuttgart, AR 72160 | $554,343,039 |
| 2 | Producers Rice Mill Inc * | Wynne, AR 72396 | $314,028,012 |
| 3 | Farmers Rice Coop | Sacramento, CA 95851 | $146,174,314 |
| 4 | Harvest States Cooperatives | Saint Paul, MN 55164 | $49,489,434 |
| 5 | Dnrc Trust Land Management - Exem | Helena, MT 59620 | $47,207,258 |
| 6 | Tyler Farms * | Helena, AR 72342 | $37,009,744 |
| 7 | Ducks Unlimited * | Ann Arbor, MI 48103 | $33,271,517 |
| | **NOTE:** Over 80 percent of the payments listed for Ducks Unlimited are 'cost share' reimbursements for technical assistance to restore wetlands at many locations on private lands not owned by D.U. The technical assistance is provided to private landowners under contractual arrangement through USDA's Natural Resources Conservation Service. | | |
| 8 | Sd Building Authority | Sioux Falls, SD 57117 | $31,110,468 |
| 9 | Pilgrim's Pride Corporation * | Broadway, VA 22815 | $26,461,206 |
| 10 | Missouri Delta Farms * | Sikeston, MO 63801 | $25,280,578 |
| 11 | Bureau Of Indian Affairs * | Prescott, AZ 86304 | $23,841,619 |
| 12 | Montana Board Of Investments - Se | Saint Paul, MN 55170 | $23,448,121 |
| 13 | Dublin Farms * | Corcoran, CA 93212 | $22,302,288 |
| 14 | Due West * | Glendora, MS 38928 | $20,745,781 |
| 15 | Balmoral Farming Partnership * | Newellton, LA 71357 | $18,783,608 |
| 16 | Gila River Farms * | SaCaton, AZ 85247 | $18,136,605 |
| 17 | Kelley Enterprises * | Burlison, TN 38015 | $17,869,689 |
| 18 | Cargill Turkey Products | Harrisonburg, VA 22801 | $17,593,150 |
| 19 | Colorado River Indian Tribes Farm * | Parker, AZ 85344 | $17,404,643 |
| 20 | Napi * | Farmington, NM 87499 | $17,215,618 |

(Source: originally published by Environmental Working Group © 2010. Reprinted with permission. Farm.ewg.org)

## This money is subsidizing:

- Farm Programs
- Crop Insurance Premium Subsidies
- Conservation Programs
- Disaster Programs

- <u>National Summary Analysis</u>:
- $245.2 billion in subsidies 1995-2009.
- **62 percent** of farmers in United States did not collect subsidy payments - according to USDA.
- Ten percent collected **74 percent** of all subsidies.
- Spending for this ten percent amounted to **$156.2 billion** over 15 years.
- **Top 10%:** $29,675 average per year between 1995 and 2009.
- **Bottom 80%:** $579 average per year between 1995 and 2009.

(Source: Environmental Working Group © 2010. Reprinted with permission. Farm.ewg.org)

The data presented above are truly staggering. In fourteen years, the government has handed out $245.2 billion in farm subsidies, almost a quarter of a trillion dollars. Yet, from 1995-2009, 62% percent of farmers in United States did not collect subsidy payments. The top ten percent collected 74% of all subsidies, amounting to $156.2 billion over 15 years just for them. Who says being a farmer can't make you rich? In fourteen years, the #1 farm subsidy recipient, Riceland Farms, received more than ½ a billion dollars. The second leading recipient, Producers Rice Mill received almost 1/3 of a billion dollars. These amounts are just the subsidies they received, over and above what they made from actually farming. It appears that Wal Mart is not the only cash cow in Arkansas.

## *More on Agricultural Subsidies*

### Overview

The U.S. Department of Agriculture distributes between $10 billion and $30 billion in cash subsidies to farmers and owners of farmland each year. The particular amount depends on market prices for crops, the level of disaster payments, and other factors. More than 90 percent of agriculture subsidies go to farmers of five crops—wheat, corn, soybeans, rice, and cotton. More than 800,000 farmers and landowners receive subsidies, but as you can see above, the payments are heavily tilted toward the largest producers.

In addition to routine cash subsidies, the USDA provides subsidized crop insurance, marketing support, and other services to farm businesses. The USDA also performs extensive agricultural research and collects statistical data for the industry. These indirect subsidies and services cost taxpayers about $5 billion each year, putting total farm support at between $15 billion and $35 billion annually.

Agriculture has long attracted federal government support. One of the first subsidy programs for agriculture was the Morrill Act of 1862, which established the land-grant colleges. A large array of farm subsidies were enacted during the 1930s, beginning with the Agricultural Adjustment Act of 1933. New Deal programs included commodity price supports and production controls, marketing orders to limit competition, import barriers, and crop insurance. The particular features of farm programs have changed over the past seven decades, but the central planning philosophy behind them has not. While many other industries have been deregulated, agricultural policies remain stuck in the past, despite the high costs and ongoing economic damage.

Between the 1940s and the 1980s, Congress occasionally considered farm reforms, usually when commodity prices were high, but then it reverted to subsidy increases when market conditions were less favorable. In the 1980s, the Reagan administration proposed major cuts to farm subsidies, but farm finances were in bad shape at the time, which prompted Congress to increase farm support, not reduce it.

Agriculture subsidies have never made economic sense, but since the 1930s farmers have resisted reductions to subsidies, and they have generally held sway in Congress. While farmers represent a smaller share of the population today than in the 1930s, the farm lobby is as strong as ever. One reason is that farm-state legislators have co-opted the support of urban legislators, who seek increased subsidies in agriculture bills for USDA programs such as food stamps. Legislators in favor of environmental subsidies have also been co-opted as supporters of farm bills. As a result, many legislators have an interest in increasing the USDA's budget, but few come to the defense of taxpayers who foot the bills.

In 1996, Congress finally enacted some pro-market agriculture reforms under the "Freedom to Farm" law. The law allowed farmers greater flexibility in their planting decisions and moved toward greater reliance on market supply and demand. However, the law did not end up cutting farm subsidies, as Congress expanded support in a series of large supplemental farm bills in the late 1990s. When the 1996 law was passed, subsidies were expected to cost $47 billion in total from 1996 to 2002, but ended up costing $121 billion.

Sadly, federal farm policies have been a long-standing rip off of American taxpayers, which continues into the 21st century. In 2002, Congress and the George W. Bush administration agreed to farm legislation that partly reversed the reforms of 1996. The 2002 law *increased* projected subsidy payments by 74 percent over 10 years. It added new crops to the subsidy rolls, and it created a new price-guarantee scheme called the "countercyclical" program.

In 2008, Congress overrode a presidential veto to enact farm legislation that extended existing supports and created new subsidy programs. The legislation added a "permanent disaster" program for areas often hit by adverse conditions, and it added a revenue protection program designed to lock in 2008's high commodity prices. It also aided producers of specialty crops, such as fruits and vegetables, with various new programs.

The 2008 farm bill added a new sugar-to-ethanol program under which the government buys excess imported sugar that might put downward pressure on inflated domestic sugar prices. The program defends domestic sugar growers' 85 percent of the U.S. sugar market, and it provides for the government to sell excess sugar, at a loss if need be, to ethanol producers.

The extensive federal welfare system for farm businesses is costly to taxpayers and it creates distortions in the economy. Subsidies induce farmers to overproduce, which pushes down prices and creates political demands for further subsidies. Subsidies inflate land prices in rural America. And the flow of subsidies from Washington hinders farmers from innovating, cutting costs, diversifying their land use, and taking the actions needed to prosper in a competitive global economy.

The distortions caused by federal farm policies have long been recognized. In 1932, a member of Congress noted that the Agriculture Department spent "hundreds of millions a year to stimulate the production of farm products by every method, from irrigating waste lands to loaning and even giving money to the farmers, and simultaneously advising them that there is no adequate market for their crops, and that they should restrict production." The folly is the same seven decades later, except that subsidies have increased from "hundreds of millions" to tens of billions of dollars.

The cost to taxpayers of yet another subsidy subsystem, the federal crop insurance program, mushroomed from $2.7 billion in 2005 to $7.3 billion in 2009, precisely because prices were high. The cost of crop insurance goes up as crop prices increase because the government's premium subsidies, and its subsidies to crop insurance companies for administrative and operation costs, are tied to the cost of policies—and policy expenses rise with crop prices. And since it is taxpayers who pay a good portion of crop insurance claims, the costs we incur for any crop losses climb along with crop prices.

Even after the bitterly contested new health insurance reforms eventually take effect, most crops could fairly be said to have better coverage than many people in this country—and it's single-payer coverage at that (the single payer, taxpayer, being you). Taxpayer subsidized crop insurance is available to farmers if their crop is eligible for coverage in their area and provides, at *no cost*, 50 percent catastrophic coverage to farmers. (In 2008, just four crops—corn, cotton, soybeans, and wheat—accounted for more than two-thirds of total acres enrolled in crop insurance and for the vast majority of subsidies through the commodity programs).

Small wonder that since 1995, America's public option-only crop insurance program has cost taxpayers $35 billion. One thing government subsidies reliably produce, other than ingratitude and a sense of entitlement among their recipients, is a demand for more subsidies.

## *Eight Types of Farm Subsidy*

**1. Direct Payments**. Direct payments are cash subsidies for producers of 10 crops: wheat, corn, sorghum, barley, oats, cotton, rice, soybeans, minor oilseeds, and peanuts. The last three were added in the 2002 farm law. Direct payments are based on a historical measure of a farm's acres used for production and are not related to current production or prices.

Established in 1996, direct payments were intended to be transitional, a way to wean farmers from old-fashioned price guarantee programs. Unfortunately, direct payments have not been reduced over time as originally planned. In most years, direct payments are the largest source of subsidies to farmers at more than $5 billion annually.

Direct payments are decoupled from current production, which makes them less distortionary than other types of subsidies. However, a substantial amount of these payments are made to owners of land that is no longer even used for farming. *The Washington Post* estimated that between 2000 and 2006 the USDA handed out $1.3 billion in direct payments to people who don't farm. The newspaper pointed to thousands of acres of land previously used for rice growing in Texas. The land is now used for suburban housing and other purposes, but the landowners continue to receive federal farm subsidies.

**2. Marketing Loans**. The marketing loan program is a price-support program that has been part of the farm subsidy system since the New Deal. Originally it was just a short-term loan program, but today it provides large subsidies by paying guaranteed minimum prices for crops. The marketing loan program encourages overproduction by setting a floor on crop prices and by reducing the price variability that would otherwise face producers in open markets.

The marketing loan program covers the same crops as the direct subsidy program—wheat, corn, sorghum, barley, oats, cotton, rice, soybeans, minor oilseeds, and peanuts. In addition, the 2002 farm law expanded eligibility to producers of wool, mohair, honey, dry peas, lentils, and chickpeas. In recent years, payments under this program have ranged from about $1 billion to $7 billion annually. Taxpayers were stuck paying the loan costs and the costs of storing crop stockpiles. Today, most marketing loan subsidies are in the form of "loan deficiency payments," which allow farmers to bypass the loan process and simply receive a subsidy payment. Alternatively, farmers can receive "marketing loan gains," under which farmers can repay their USDA loans at preferential rates.

Farmers don't receive subsidies from the marketing loan program only when crop prices are low. They have become experts at gaming the system to maximize their subsidies every year. Farmers can lock in high government benefits when seasonal prices are low, and then sell their crops when market prices are higher. *The Washington Post* reports that "growers reap benefits even in the good years," noting that the program "has become so ingrained in farmland finances that farmers sometimes wish for market prices to drop so they can capture a larger subsidy."

**3. Countercyclical Payments**. While the 1996 farm law moved away from traditional price guarantee subsidies, the 2002 farm bill reversed course and embraced them with the addition of the countercyclical program. This program covers the same 10 commodities as the direct payments program—wheat, corn, sorghum, barley, oats, cotton, rice, soybeans, minor oilseeds, and peanuts—and the 2008 farm bill added dry peas, lentils, and chickpeas. In recent years, countercyclical payments have ranged from about $1 billion to $4 billion annually.

**4. Conservation Subsidies**. USDA conservation programs dispense about $3 billion annually to the nation's farmers. The largest conservation subsidy program is the Conservation Reserve Program, which was created in 1985 to idle millions of acres of farmland. Under CRP, *farmers are paid not to grow crops*, but to cultivate ground cover such as grass or trees on retired acres. A large share of land idled under the CRP is owned by retired farmers, thus one does not even have to be a working farmer to get these subsidies.

The USDA provides a range of other conservation subsidy programs, including the Conservation Security Program, which was added in 2002. These programs respond to the damage caused by overproduction on marginal farmland, which is exacerbated by federal subsidies. An easier and cheaper way to reduce overproduction would be to simply eliminate farm subsidies.

**5. Insurance**. The Risk Management Agency runs the USDA's farm insurance programs. Both "yield" and "revenue" insurance are available to farmers to protect against adverse weather, pests, and low market prices. The RMA describes its mission as helping farmers "manage their business risks through effective, market-based risk management solutions." The RMA has annual outlays of about $4 billion, employs about 550 people, and its activities are far from "market-based."

Federal crop insurance policies are sold and serviced by 16 private insurance companies, which receive federal subsidies for their administrative costs and insurance risks. The firms operate like a cartel, earning excess profits from the high premiums they charge. They get away with it because the government provides large subsidies for insurance premiums, such that farmers pay only about one-third the full cost of their policies. The cartel-like structure of the current system was made clear in 2005, when, under lobbying pressure from insurance companies, Congress derailed an attempt by a company to offer discount insurance policies to farmers.

In 2007, USDA crop insurance programs were criticized at a rare oversight hearing of an agriculture program by a non-agriculture committee in Congress. The then chairman of the House Oversight and Government Reform

Committee, Henry Waxman (D-CA), called USDA insurance "a textbook example of waste, fraud, and abuse in federal spending…over $8 billion in taxpayer funds have been squandered in excess payments to insurers and other middlemen."

**6. Disaster Aid**. Over the decades, Congress has repeatedly expanded crop insurance programs in order to reduce farmers' dependence on emergency bailouts. But both insurance subsidies and emergency bailouts have grown in cost. After just about any sort of crop damage, Congress jumps in to declare a "disaster" and distribute millions of dollars to farmers, whether or not particular farmers actually sustained substantial damage. A *Washington Post* analysis found that "farmers often get paid twice by the government, once in subsidized insurance and then again in disaster assistance." The 2008 farm bill has a costly new permanent disaster program, intended to reduce ad hoc emergency relief bills. And note that products not covered by federal insurance, such as aquaculture, mushrooms, Christmas trees, ginseng, and turf grasses, have a special Noninsured Crop Disaster Assistance Program.

**7. Export Subsidies**. The USDA operates a range of programs to aid farmers and food companies in their foreign sales. The *Market Access Program* hands out $200 million annually to producers in support of activities such as advertising campaigns. Recipients include the Distilled Spirits Council, the Pet Food Institute, the Association of Brewers, the Popcorn Board, the Wine Institute, and Welch's Food. Another program, the Foreign Market Development program, hands out $35 million annually to groups such as the American Peanut Council, the Cotton Council International, and the Mohair Council of America.

**8. Agricultural Research and Statistics**. Most American industries fund their own research and development programs. The agriculture industry is a notable exception. The USDA spends about $3 billion annually on agricultural research, statistical information services, and economic studies. The USDA carries out research in 108 different locations and provides subsidies to the 50 states for research and education.

(Source: *Agricultural Subsidies*, by Chris Edwards, Downsizing the Federal Government, originally published by The CATO Institute, June 2009, CATO.org, copyright The Cato Institute, used by permission)

Being a farmer has become very lucrative. Farmers don't even have to pay much for their crop insurance—taxpayers foot that bill. Despite no mandate in the Constitution for farm subsidies and a lack of support by the American people, the farm lobby continues to pressure politicians for more and more money—and get it. The system is fraught with abuses and the cost to taxpayers is enormous.

## *Farm Subsidizes Pay $1.3 Billion to People Who Don't Farm.*

The *Washington Post* series "Harvesting Cash: A Yearlong Investigation" chronicles how much money farm subsidizes cost taxpayers, and who is getting the money. "Nationwide, the federal government has paid at least $1.3 billion in subsidies for rice and other crops since 2000 to individuals *who do no farming at all*, according to an analysis of government records. Some of them collect hundreds of thousands of dollars without planting a seed. Mary

Anna Hudson, 87, from the River Oaks neighborhood in Houston, has received $191,000 over the past decade. For Houston surgeon Jimmy Frank Howell, the total was $490,709." Only the government would pay huge sums of money in farm subsidies to people that don't even farm.

Farm subsidizes began in the 1930s as a limited safety net for working farmers has swollen into a far-flung infrastructure of entitlements that has cost $172 billion over the past decade. The *Post* reported that "In 2005 alone, when pretax farm profits were at a near-record $72 billion, the federal government handed out more than $25 billion in aid. Today, even key farm-state figures believe the direct-payment program needs a major overhaul. 'This was an unintended consequence of the farm bill,' said former representative Charles W. Stenholm, the west Texas Democrat who was once the ranking member on the House Agriculture Committee. 'Instead of maintaining a rice industry in Texas, we basically contributed to its demise." "The strength of the farm lobby in this town is really unbelievable,' former Texas rep. Dick Armey said. 'I don't think there's a smaller group of constituents that has a bigger influence.'"

Farm subsidies are a huge expense to taxpayers, most of whom don't support these subsides. Farmer's collect money not to farm, and billions in farm subsidies are paid to people who don't farm. It's a typical situation in Washington. Farmers pay into funds that supply lobbyists in Washington. These lobbyists pressure politicians to increase subsides, which in turn results in more money going to farmers. Farmers, in turn, now have more money (from taxpayers) to contribute to funds that result in more lobbying. The cycle continues ad infinitum. You can substitute anyone or anything getting government money. More government hand-outs result in more money for lobbying and more hand-outs. It's a self-perpetuating cycle, where everyone makes out with billions of dollars while the taxpayer gets stuck paying the bill. And, don't forget, the bureaucrats in Washington are making a *new* government subsidy program every five days!

## Grocery Store Subsidies

The USDA also administers another program that pays massive subsidies, this time to food stores and food companies. It's the United States Supplemental Nutrition Assistance Program (SNAP), formerly known as food stamps. In 2010, the number of Americans receiving food stamps reached more than 40 million, the highest number since the SNAP program began in 1939. Average monthly benefits run from $150 to up to $2000 per person per month. This adds up to a cost of more than *$6 billion per month*. Currently one in eight Americans and one in four children are using food stamps and the program rate is growing at a rate of 20,000 people a day. While people get free food and drink, the stores where they shop collect huge government windfalls

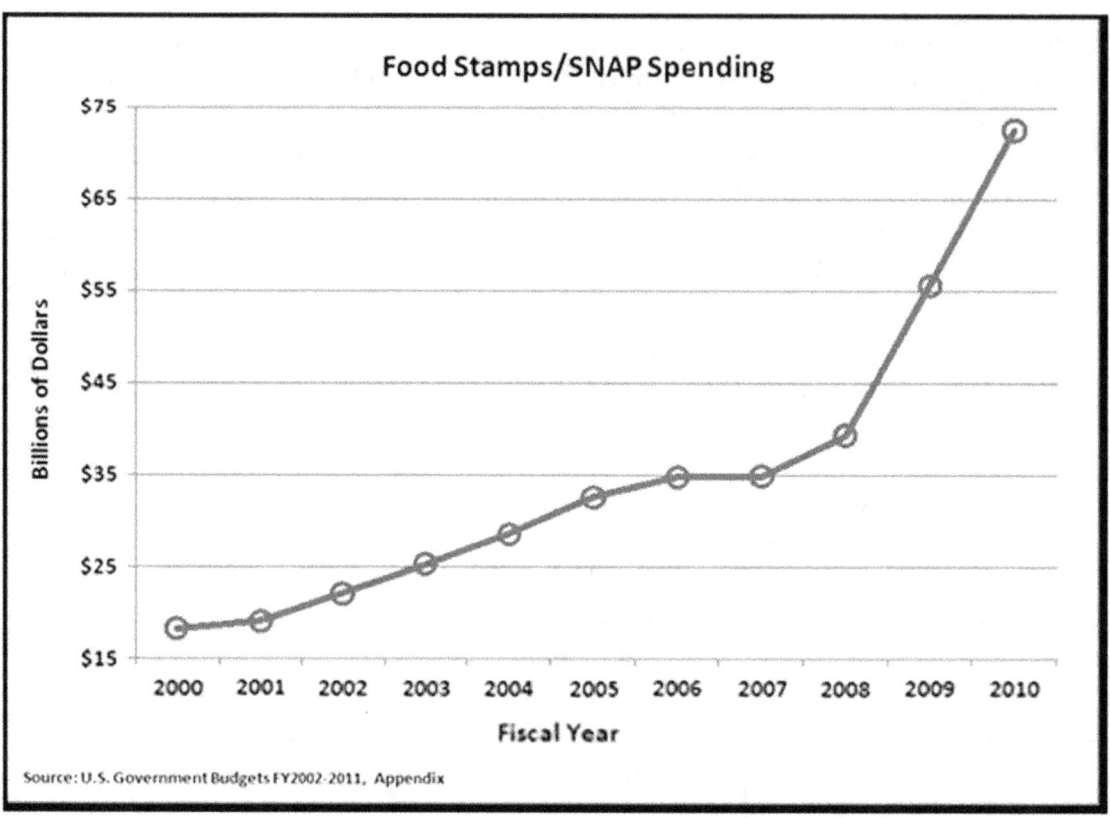

The program tops out at almost $75 billion per year (2010). But consider how much the stores where people shop are getting of this money, and the food suppliers and producers. One of the largest food chains in the country, Walmart, already the biggest company in the U.S. probably gets a whole lot of this business. While there is no way to know the margins (wholesale versus retail) of food stores, let's say it's at least 40%, especially for such a large buyer as Walmart. While retails sales equal the $75 billion, the government subsidies $30-$40 billion of profit at grocery stores across the country. The food and drink industries (the wholesale suppliers and producers) get the rest of the money—another $40 billion. And further down the food chain farmers untimely receive some of this money. It's only $75 billion, but a tidy amount of money, all paid for by taxes.

(Source: Census Bureau, census.gov)

## *Corporate Welfare Spending: Business Subsidies*

The mission of the Department of Commerce is to "foster, promote, and develop the foreign and domestic commerce" of the United States. To the extent that this mission includes promoting free trade, removing interstate trade restraints, and reducing barriers to investment, the department's mission makes economic sense. Indeed, some of the department's efforts to reduce trade barriers are laudatory.

However, a number of Commerce programs subsidize particular companies and activities, which distorts the economy and increases tax burdens. The department's business subsidies are not huge—a few hundred million dollars annually—but this "corporate welfare" should be eliminated nonetheless. The following sections describe some of the department's business subsidy programs, and concludes with a summary of the general problems with such corporate welfare.

## *Technology Innovation Program*

The Technology Innovation Program (TIP) was created by the America Competes Act of 2007. The program replaced the previous Advanced Technology Program (ATP) and it costs taxpayers about $70 million annually. TIP provides grants to small and medium-sized companies to "support, promote, and accelerate innovation in the United State through high-risk, high-reward research in areas of critical national need."

The idea that government subsidies are needed to support "high-risk, high-reward" investments does not hold water. The private sector undertakes risky projects all the time. Consider the growing interest in private space travel spurred by the 2004 launch of SpaceShipOne, the world's first private manned space flight. That flight was funded by Microsoft co-founder Paul Allen, and other wealthy entrepreneurs have launched their own space projects, including PayPal's Elon Musk, Virgin Group's Richard Branson, and hotel developer Robert Bigelow. These ventures may succeed or they may fail, but they suggest that no innovation that has a big potential payoff is too risky for private entrepreneurs to explore.

TIP's promise of investing in risky but "high reward" projects is certainly overconfident. With fast-changing technology markets, no one knows whether risky ventures will end up being "high reward" or being flops. Even the smartest venture capitalists end up investing in many duds, but at least the costs of those failures are borne by private investors. With TIP, the costs of failed investments are borne involuntarily by taxpayers.

The idea that government should act like a venture capitalist, through programs such as TIP, is fraught with contradictions. TIP is supposed to give grants to worthy companies that cannot find private funding, but why should the government fund activities that have been rejected by private investors? If a project is too risky for venture capitalists, then it is too risky for federal taxpayers as well.

Alternatively, it might be the case that programs such as TIP and ATP attract companies that have second-rate ideas and the companies know it, so they don't bother to look for private funding. A Government Accountability Office study suggested that this might often be the case, finding that most companies that applied for ATP grants had never even looked for private capital.

Another possibility might be that some companies that seek federal funding could get private funding if they looked for it. The GAO suspected that many of the projects funded by ATP might otherwise have been funded privately. In this case, federal funding is simply duplicative of private sector financing.

The ATP was created in the 1980s, when there were concerns that the United States was lagging Japan in innovation. Many pundits thought that the wave of the future was central planning of technology through agencies such as Japan's MITI. But MITI turned out to be a big failure. It's computer ventures were a flop, and it infamously provided bad business advice to Honda and Sony. Japan's industrial success until the 1980s was the result of intense domestic competition—in automobiles, motorcycles, steel, and robotics, and other industries—not a result of government planning.

Experience in the United States, Japan, and Europe has shown that government subsidization of technology does not work. The good news is that government subsidies are not needed, because U.S. venture capital and angel investors pump $50 billion or more annually into innovative young firms. And there would be even more funding of private innovation if policymakers freed U.S. capital markets from excessive tax and regulatory burdens.

## *Manufacturing Extension Partnership*

The Department of Commerce spends about $90 million annually on the Manufacturing Extension Partnership. The MEP is a nationwide network of extension centers that provide technical and managerial assistance to small and medium-sized firms. Federal funds pay for one-third of the costs of MEP centers, with the balance of costs being paid by state and local governments and the private sector. About 24 percent of federal MEP funding goes toward federal administration and about 76 percent goes to the extension centers.

Like the TIP program, MEP originated from concerns about U.S. competitiveness in the 1980s. The original MEP legislation intended federal funding to be temporary and end after six years, and more recently the George W. Bush administration argued that it was time for federal funding to end. However, federal funding for MEP survives and the Competes Act of 2007 added a new MEP grant for businesses "to solve new or emerging manufacturing problems."

MEP's strategy to disseminate ideas about new production techniques is duplicative of mechanisms already in place in private markets. For example, engineers and scientists often move back and forth between firms, which spreads knowledge of the latest techniques throughout the economy. Similarly, entrepreneurial people often leave established companies to launch their own start-up firms, and they carry technical knowledge with them.

Can the MEP do any better than such market mechanisms? A GAO survey of firms utilizing the MEP program found that the majority had a favorable view of the services provided. However, those firms that had paid fees for MEP assistance were far less likely to be as positive as those that did not. That suggests that MEP services are not particularly valuable to many users.

Those companies that do find MEP services valuable should be willing to pay for such help from private consultancies. Indeed, MEP's description of its own activities sounds like a business consultancy: "MEP will serve as business and technology advisors for manufacturers. MEP will work with manufacturers on the formation of key business strategies, development of focused business plans, and the evolution of growth initiatives that allow manufacturers to aggressively compete."

That does not sound like something that the government should be doing. It suggests that the government is unfairly arming certain companies in order to do battle with other companies in the marketplace. Rather than playing favorites, the federal government ought to create an attractive environment of low taxes and light regulation so that all American businesses can "aggressively compete" in national and international markets.

## *Minority Business Development Agency*

The Minority Business Development Agency (MBDA) was created in 1969 by an executive order issued by President Richard Nixon. The agency is supposed to provide management and technical services to minority-owned businesses, and its budget in fiscal 2008 was $29 million. It funds a nationwide network of Minority Business Development Centers, Native American Business Development Centers, and Minority Business Opportunity Centers. These centers are run by state and local governments and private organizations.

The essence of the MBDA is bureaucracy. Of the total budget in 2008 of $29 million, just $12 million went toward grants to the business centers. About $11 million went to wages and benefits for the MBDA's 100 employees, and $6 million went to headquarters administrative costs. The latter expense included large fees to Washington lobbyists and public relations experts, such as Felix R. Sanchez, who has received $1.35 million from MBDA.

MBDA grants go to groups such as the Los Angeles Urban League, the City of Birmingham, the Milken Institute, and Grijalva and Allen. The latter is a for-profit consulting firm that has received millions of dollars to manage business centers in Texas. The firm's website notes that "to be eligible for services you must be socially or economically disadvantaged. African Americans, Hispanic Americans, Asian Americans, Asian Indians, Pacific Islanders, and Native Americans automatically qualify."

A brief review of the agency's spending reveals that most goes toward sustaining the agency's Washington bureaucracy and consulting contracts, and only a fraction trickles down to small businesses, minority or not. A recent report by the Department of Commerce Inspector General found that the MBDA's claims of running successful programs that helped businesses were generally not substantiated.

Government programs are not the solution to increase minority entrepreneurship. A detailed survey by the *National Federation of Independent Business* found that most of the 10 "most severe problems" for small businesses were *caused* by government. Those included: "federal taxes," "property taxes," "tax complexity," "unreasonable regulations," "state taxes," and "workers' compensation costs." Thus, the government could greatly help all businesses, including minority businesses, if it reduced its burden on the economy—if it simply got out of the way of productive entrepreneurs.

## *General Problems with Business Subsidies*

With massive deficits facing the federal government, policymakers should be looking for areas to cut the budget. Corporate welfare spending at the Department of Commerce and other agencies should be a prime target. Following are some general reasons why business subsidies should be cut.

*Unconstitutional.* The Constitution gives Congress the power to "regulate Commerce . . . among the several States." That provides the federal government the power to remove barriers to interstate trade, not to hand out money to particular commercial interests.

*Taxpayer Cost.* Corporate welfare at Commerce is only a small portion of business subsidies in the federal budget, but it nonetheless imposes an unfair burden on taxpayers.

*Uneven Playing Field.* By aiding some businesses, corporate subsidies put other businesses that do not gain political support at a disadvantage. U.S. businesses are generally overtaxed and overregulated, thus it rubs salt in the wound when certain favored firms get special subsidies from the government. Further, when the government gives favors to some businesses, it invites a feeding frenzy of other businesses to hire lobbyists and demand their own hand-outs.

*Government Is a Poor Decision maker.* Private entrepreneurs and investors put careful thought into new ventures because they risk their own money. Many private investments don't work out, but at least they help markets figure out what will ultimately work. By contrast, government policymakers have little incentive to ensure that spending projects succeed because they are not risking their own money and they are virtually never fired.

*Corruption.* Corporate welfare generates an unhealthy relationship between businesses and the government. The more tentacles the government has into the economy, the more lobbying activity will be generated. The more subsidies it hands out, the more pressure lawmakers will be under to create new subsidies. As the ranks of lobbyists grow, more economic decisions will be made based on politics, more resources will be misallocated, and the nation's standard of living will be reduced.

*Weakening of Private Sector.* Corporate welfare draws talented people away from productive private pursuits and into wasteful political activities. When companies start chasing after hand-outs from Washington, they lose focus on generating returns in the private marketplace. Companies receiving subsidies become weaker and less efficient, and they take on riskier and more wasteful projects. Enron Corporation, for example, sought and received large federal subsidies to invest in risky and dubious foreign projects that ended up crashing to the ground.

*Duplicative of Private Activities.* Many federal subsidy programs attempt to duplicate activities that are already provided in private markets. The Commerce TIP program, for example, funds risky technology ventures, but that makes no sense because America has private investment markets that specialize in funding innovative technologies.

*Picking Winners Doesn't Work.* Over the decades, many federal initiatives have aimed to fund new technologies in energy, computers, and other industries. But the complexity of markets has made most of the government's efforts a failure. As noted, the experience of most industrial countries in trying to centrally plan innovation has been dismal.

In sum, the United States was a great economic power long before Commerce started handing out business subsidies. Its greatest economic successes, such as Silicon Valley's technology industry, were based on individual entrepreneurial achievement, not federal subsidies. Federal subsidies should be ended, and America should revive its entrepreneurial tradition by cutting taxes, regulations, and other barriers to growing businesses.

*The U.S. government is subsidizing some of the most successful businesses in our country:*

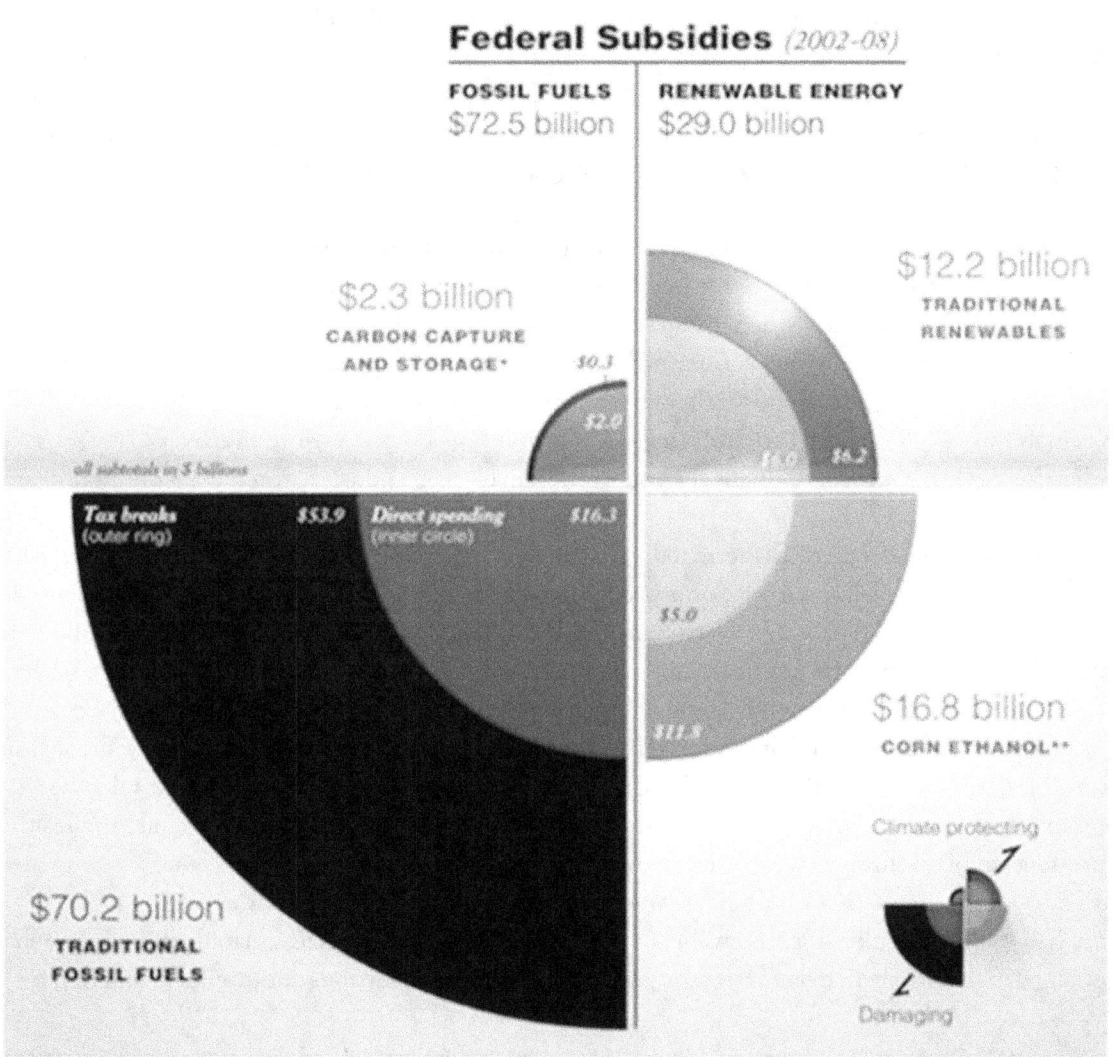

(Source of Graphic: *Estimating U.S. Government Subsidies to Energy Sources: 2002-2008*, copyright Environmental Law Institute, ELI.org. used with permission)

The above graphic is astounding on a number of levels. First, the Federal Government hands out more than $70 billion dollars of taxpayer money or tax breaks to fossil fuel producers (gas, oil, and coal). These industries are some of the most profitable of all corporations in the U.S. People use energy no matter what the economy is doing, and despite how they may want to improve our environment. Do oil, gas and coal companies really need

$70 billion dollars in government handouts and tax breaks? Exxon Mobil Corp., one of the largest oil companies in the U.S. recently reported revenues of $329 billion and profits of $125 billion. Does a company making that kind of money need a government hand-out? Obviously not, but taxpayers still had to cough up $72.5 billion in total subsidies and tax breaks for these companies.

Fossil fuels receive a tremendous amount of federal support: $70.2 billion an amount that has traditionally dwarfed the supports given to renewables like solar, wind and geothermal. And while the feds have ramped-up investment in renewables and President Obama has proposed eliminating federal subsidies for fossil fuels in his 2011 budget, the billions of dollars spent on securing and protecting our oil interests in the Middle East means that the federal energy subsidy scales will likely still tip in favor of the fossil fuel industry for the foreseeable future.

Applying a conservative approach Environmental Law Institute (ELI) found that:

- The vast majority of federal subsidies for fossil fuels and renewable energy supported energy sources that emit high levels of greenhouse gases when used as fuel.
- The federal government provided substantially larger subsidies to fossil fuels than to renewables. Subsidies to fossil fuels—a mature, developed industry that has enjoyed government support for many years—totaled approximately $72 billion over the study period, representing a direct cost to taxpayers.
- Subsidies for renewable fuels, a relatively young and developing industry, totaled $29 billion over the same period.
- Subsidies to fossil fuels generally increased over the study period (though they decreased in 2008), while funding for renewables increased but saw a precipitous drop in 2006-07 (though they increased in 2008). The largest subsidies to fossil fuels were written into the U.S. Tax Code as permanent provisions. By comparison, many subsidies for renewables are time-limited initiatives implemented through energy bills, with expiration dates that limit their usefulness to the renewables industry.
- The vast majority of subsidy dollars to fossil fuels can be attributed to just a handful of tax breaks, such as the Foreign Tax Credit ($15.3 billion) and the Credit for Production of Nonconventional Fuels ($14.1 billion, though this credit has since been phased out). The largest of these, the Foreign Tax Credit, applies to the overseas production of oil through an obscure provision of the Tax Code, which allows energy companies to claim a tax credit for payments that would normally receive less-beneficial tax treatment.
- Almost half of the subsidies for renewables are attributable to corn-based ethanol, the use of which, while decreasing American reliance on foreign oil, raises considerable questions about effects on climate.

(Source: *Estimating U.S. Government Subsidies to Energy Sources: 2002–2008*, originally published by Environmental Law Institute, PDF at http://www.elistore.org/Data/products/d19_07.pdf, copyright by Environmental Law Institute, used with permission)

## *Oil Industry Gets Tax Breaks and Government Subsidies*

When the Deepwater Horizon drilling platform set off the worst oil spill at sea in American history, it was flying the flag of the Marshall Islands. Registering there allowed the rig's owner to significantly reduce its American taxes. The owner, Transocean, moved its corporate headquarters from Houston to the Cayman Islands in 1999 and then to Switzerland in 2008, maneuvers that also helped it avoid taxes.

At the same time, BP was reaping sizable tax benefits from leasing the rig. According to a letter sent in June 2010 to the Senate Finance Committee, the company used a tax break for the oil industry to write off 70 percent of the rent for Deepwater Horizon — a deduction of more than $225,000 a day since the lease began. With federal officials now considering a new tax on petroleum production to pay for the cleanup, the industry is fighting the measure, warning that it will lead to job losses and higher gasoline prices, as well as an increased dependence on foreign oil.

But an examination of the American tax code indicates that oil production is among the most heavily subsidized businesses, with tax breaks available at virtually every stage of the exploration and extraction process. According to the most recent study by the Congressional Budget Office, released in 2005, capital investments like oil field leases and drilling equipment are taxed at an effective rate of 9 percent, significantly lower than the overall rate of 25 percent for businesses in general and lower than virtually any other industry.

And for many small and midsize oil companies, the tax on capital investments is so low that it is more than eliminated by various credits. These companies' returns on those investments are often higher after taxes than before. "The flow of revenues to oil companies is like the gusher at the bottom of the Gulf of Mexico: heavy and constant," said Senator Robert Menendez, Democrat of New Jersey, who has worked alongside the Obama administration on a bill that would cut $20 billion in oil industry tax breaks over the next decade. "There is no reason for these corporations to shortchange the American taxpayer."

Oil industry officials say that the tax breaks, which average about $4 billion a year according to various government reports, are a bargain for taxpayers. By helping producers weather market fluctuations and invest in technology, tax incentives are supporting an industry that the officials say provides 9.2 million jobs. The American Petroleum Institute, an industry advocacy group, argues that even with subsidies, oil producers paid or incurred $280 billion in American income taxes from 2006 to 2008, and pay a higher percentage of their earnings in taxes than most other American corporations.

As oil continues to spread across the Gulf of Mexico, however, the industry is being forced to defend tax breaks that some say are being abused or are outdated. The Senate Finance Committee recently announced that it was investigating whether Transocean had exploited tax laws by moving overseas to avoid paying taxes in the United States. Efforts to curtail the tax breaks are likely to face fierce opposition in Congress; the oil and natural gas industry has spent $340 million on lobbyists since 2008, according to the nonpartisan *Center for Responsive Politics*, which monitors political spending.

Jack N. Gerard, president of the American Petroleum Institute, warns that any cut in subsidies will cost jobs. "These companies evaluate costs, risks and opportunities across the globe," he said. "So if the U.S. makes changes in the tax code that discourage drilling in gulf waters, they will go elsewhere and take their jobs with them."

But some government watchdog groups say that only the industry's political muscle is preserving the tax breaks. An economist for the Treasury Department said in 2009 that a study had found that oil prices and potential profits were so high that eliminating the subsidies would decrease American output by less than half of one percent. "We're giving tax breaks to highly profitable companies to do what they would be doing anyway," said Sima J. Gandhi, a policy analyst at the Center for American Progress, a liberal research organization. "That's not an incentive; that's a giveaway."

Some of the tax breaks date back nearly a century, when they were intended to encourage exploration in an era of rudimentary technology, when costly investments frequently produced only dry holes. Because of one lingering provision from the Tariff Act of 1913, many small and midsize oil companies based in the United States can claim deductions for the lost value of tapped oil fields far beyond the amount the companies actually paid for the oil rights.

Other tax breaks were born of international politics. In an attempt to deter Soviet influence in the Middle East in the 1950s, the State Department backed a Saudi Arabian accounting maneuver that reclassified the royalties charged by foreign governments to American oil drillers. Saudi Arabia and others began to treat some of the royalties as taxes, which entitled the companies to subtract those payments from their American tax bills. Despite repeated attempts to forbid this accounting practice, companies continue to deduct the payments. The Treasury Department estimates that it will cost $8.2 billion over the next decade.

Over the last 10 years, oil companies have also been aggressive in using foreign tax havens. Many rigs, like Deepwater Horizon, are registered in Panama or in the Marshall Islands, where they are subject to lower taxes and less stringent safety and staff regulations. American producers have also aggressively exploited the tax code by opening small offices in low-tax countries. A recent study by Martin A. Sullivan, an economist for the trade publication *Tax Analysts,* found that the five oil drilling companies that had undergone these "corporate inversions" had saved themselves a total of $4 billion in taxes since 1999.

Transocean — which has approximately 18,000 employees worldwide, including 1,300 in Houston and about a dozen in Zug, Switzerland — has saved $1.8 billion in taxes since moving overseas in 1999, the study found. Transocean said it had paid more than $300 million in taxes so far for 2009, and that its move reflected its global scope, with only 15 of its 139 rigs located in the United States. "Transocean is truly a global company," it said in a statement.

Despite the public anger at the gulf spill, it is far from certain that Congress will eliminate the tax breaks. As recently as 2005, when windfall profits for energy companies prompted even President George W. Bush — a former Texas oilman himself — to publicly call for an end to incentives, the energy bill he and Congress enacted still included $2.6 billion in oil subsidies. In 2007, after Democrats took control of Congress, a move to end the tax breaks failed.

Mr. Menendez said he believed the Gulf spill was devastating enough to spur Congress into action. But one notable omission in his bill shows the vast economic reach of the industry. While the legislation would cut many incentives over the next decade, it would not touch the tax breaks for oil refineries, many of which have operations and employees in his home state, New Jersey.

Mr. Menendez's aides said the senator thought it was legitimate to allow refineries to continue claiming a manufacturing tax credit that he wants to eliminate for drillers because refining is a manufacturing business and because refineries do not benefit from high oil prices. Mr. Menendez did not consult with New Jersey refineries when writing the bill, his aides said.

(Source: *As Oil Industry Fights a Tax, It Reaps Subsidies*, By David Kocieniewski, Published: July 3, 2010, New York Times—Business Section online, NYtimes.com. Used with permission)

## *Non-American Military subsidies*

Taxpayers in the U.S. also subsidize military spending, not for the U.S., but for other countries. The U.S. gives money to foreign countries to buy our arms, train their soldiers, and set up programs that are in the interests of the U.S. By far, however, most of the money goes to these countries to by arms. These arms are manufactured and sold by U.S. private companies—often the largest military suppliers in the world. The U.S. subsidies the development of arms and arms technology as well.

The Foreign Military Financing (FMF) program provides grants and loans to help countries purchase weapons and defense equipment produced in the United States as well as acquiring defense services and military training. FMF funds purchases are made through the Foreign Military Sales (FMS) program, which manages government-to-government sales.

Total FMF spending for 2008: $ 4,536,000,000

By country:

Israel is the largest beneficiary of FMF and receives about half of all the funds distributed by the program. In 2008, Israel received $2.4 billion, a number that is expected to increase to $3.1 billion a year in 2018 by the agreement signed between the two countries in August 2007. Other countries in the Middle East and Greater Middle East (including Pakistan $300 million, Jordan $200 million, and especially Egypt $1.3 billion) are among the other major recipients of FMF funds. Countries in Central and South America also reap huge cash windfalls. From 2006 to 2011, Mexico has or will receive $428,750,000, and Columbia has or will receive $386,670,000

U.S. arms corporations promote exports to maintain their profits. (Publicly, of course, they talk about the need to maintain jobs) These corporations are among the largest in the world, and they have tremendous political influence. Arms industry executives sit on federal advisory commissions at the Commerce, Defense and State Departments dealing with arms export policy issues, ensuring that their preferences are well known to administration policymakers. In addition, the industry provides hundreds of thousands of dollars annually to Congressional campaigns, ensuring that their lobbyists have access to Members of the House and Senate. They also pump cash into Presidential campaigns (usually to both sides, just to be safe), ensuring access at the very highest levels.

Using this clout, arms exporters have arranged it so that the American public pays $6-7 billion annually to market and finance sales of their product. On top of that, the public bears the costs of researching and developing the weapons in the first place. One of the corporate lobbyists' top priorities in past years was to have Congress repeal a statute which mandated that foreign customers be charged a fee to refund U.S. taxpayers for some of the R&D costs. The arms industry claimed that this fee—which has returned several hundred million dollars annually to the Treasury—raises the price of the weapons and makes them less competitive.

Industry has (effectively, thus far) sought to paint these subsidies as a matter of national security: If taxpayers don't subsidize arms sales, the industry might lose a deal to a foreign competitor; this would lead to the shutdown of a production line, thereby endangering America's very security. Never explained is why America needs to maintain surplus arms production lines in the first place. (If U.S. forces were still buying the weapon system, loss of foreign sales would not affect the continuation of the production line.)

Some taxpayers may not mind subsidizing U.S. military spending, but we are sending billions of dollars to other countries. In addition to giving foreign governments cash to buy arms, we offer them the Defense Export Loan Guarantee Program. The U.S. government guarantees loans to foreign countries. Many of these "loans" turn into grants as most are in default and have not been repaid. The U.S. taxpayer also finances these loans in an effort to sell foreign countries more U.S. arms. Taxpayers subsidize weapons production on the front end and we give countries money to buy them. Another in a very long line of things our government subsidizes.

(Source: *U.S. Aid from Foreign Military Financing, Entire Region, 2006-2011*, Just the Facts, justf.org) and (*Foreign Military Financing Account Summary*, U.S. Department of State, June 23, 2010. State.gov)

## *Government creates another bubble: Student Loans*

Many economists believe interest rate easing by the Federal Reserve contributed to the housing bubble and sub-prime disaster. Despite this mistake, the government guarantees most student loans, and has allowed another bubble to form, and it may be about to burst. Laura Rowley of *Yahoo! Finance* reports that "just as lenders offered easy no-money-down mortgages to unqualified borrowers during the housing boom, private student loan firms offered instant online approval for up to 100 percent of college costs to students, in some cases for four consecutive years. In early 2007, half of loans made by government-controlled Sallie Mae, one of the industry's biggest players, were to students with no co-signers, according to Mark Kantrowitz, founder of informational Web site *finaid.org*. Secondly, defaults have soared amid a difficult job market. In 2008, the most recent year for which data are available, nearly 3.4 million borrowers began repayment, and more than 238,000 defaulted on their loans. The number of loans that went into forbearance or deferment (when borrowers receive temporary relief from payments) rose to 22 percent in 2007, from 10 percent a decade earlier, according to *The Chronicle of Higher Education*. Over a 15-year period, default rates range from 20 percent for federal loans to 40 percent on loans to students who attend for-profit schools, The Chronicle found."

Rowley further reports "Over the last decade, private lenders, abetted by college financial aid offices, eagerly handed young people hundreds of thousands of dollars to earn bachelor's degrees. As a result of easy credit, declining grants and soaring tuitions, more than two-thirds of students graduated with debt in 2008 — up from 45 percent in 1993. The average debt load is $24,000, according to the *Project on Student Debt*. In some respects, the student loan crisis looks remarkably like the subprime mortgage crisis. First, outstanding student loan debt has ballooned: It grew roughly four-fold in the last decade to $833 billion as of June 2010 — surpassing outstanding credit-card debt for the first time." And there couldn't be a worse time for students to be going into such massive debt. *The Cato Institute* reported that for college students graduating in spring 2010, only ¼ were able to find jobs that required a college degree. Students have to go into huge debt in the form of student loans, and colleges and universities keep raising tuition, padding their endowments and bleeding students dry.

President Obama made a grand "back to school" speech in Sept. 2010 about how he wanted the U.S. to once again have the most college graduates in the world, per capita, by 2020. While claiming that higher education was a priority, it is interesting to note the *actual* priorities of our government and President Obama: students trying to work hard, be productive and get ahead in life often have to go into massive debt, while the government spends enough in *one year* on Welfare as the total of all outstanding student loan debt – $833 billion. Or, stated another way, if one year's Welfare spending was transferred instead to student loan debt, *all student loan debt in this country would be wiped out*. And President Obama *increased* Welfare spending by $263 billion over just his first two years in office, a little less than 1/3 the amount needed to wipe out all student loan debt. Our government subsidizes the leisure of tens of millions, while those that feed our economy and productivity—those that work and students that graduate college and then get jobs, buy homes, furniture, appliances, cars and start families are strangled by debt before even finishing school. The engines of future advancement and productivity of our nation—those that have educations, are having their legs cut out from under them, economically, before they even get jobs while tens of millions of people get free money and benefits for not working; and businesses, foreign countries, farmers, oil companies and many others get hundreds of billions of dollars in free money via 2001 different government subsidy programs. Maybe students should pool their money, hire a lobbyist, and get free money from the government like everyone else. Of course, when students graduate in debt and can't find a job, they will have no choice but to default on their student loans, requiring another huge government bailout of Sallie Mae.

## *The earmark battle, or "unofficial" subsidies and pork spending*

As if having more than 2001 different subsidy programs wasn't bad enough, politicians have another way of giving away billions of taxpayer dollars. Recently, badgered by taxpayers and Tea Party members, the Senate took a vote to get rid of "earmarks," the pork projects and funding that is added to any legislation that results in billions being spent and wasted by politicians that often aren't publicized or even known by voters. Not surprisingly, by a nearly 3-2 margin, the Senate voted to let lawmakers keep sprinkling bills with home-state pet projects like roads, bridges, grants to local police departments and special interest tax breaks. Politicians get away with "secretly" spending billions on earmark projects because they are not included in the budget proposal that the President submits to Congress each year–and even Tea Party politicians aren't immune from continuing to use earmarks.

Reid Wilson of the *National Journal* ran a story on Dec. 2, 2010 that "Members of the Congressional Tea Party Caucus may tout their commitment to cutting government spending now, but they used the 111th Congress to request hundreds of earmarks that, taken cumulatively, added more than $1 billion to the federal budget. According to a review of records compiled by *Citizens Against Government Waste*, the 52 members of the caucus, which pledged to cut spending and reduce the size of government, requested a total of 764 earmarks valued at $1,049,783,150 during Fiscal Year 2010, the last year for which records are available."

"It's disturbing to see the Tea Party Caucus requested that much in earmarks. This is their time to put up or shut up, to be blunt," said David Williams, vice president for policy at *Citizens Against Government Waste*. "There's going to be a huge backlash if they continue to request earmarks."

"In founding the caucus in July 2010, Rep. Michele Bachmann (R-Minn.) said she was giving voice to Americans who were sick of government overspending. 'The American people are speaking out loud and clear. They have had enough of the spending, the bureaucracy, and the government-knows-best mentality running rampant today throughout the halls of Congress,' Bachmann said in a July 15 statement. The group, she wrote in a letter to House Administration Committee chairman Bob Brady, 'will serve as an informal group of members dedicated to promote Americans' call for fiscal responsibility, adherence to the Constitution, and limited government.'"

"Bachmann and 13 of her Tea Party Caucus colleagues did not request any earmarks in the last Fiscal Year, according to CAGW's annual Congressional Pig Book. But other caucus members have requested millions of dollars in special projects. Rep. Robert Aderholt (R-Ala.), for one, attached his name to 69 earmarks in the last fiscal year, for a total of $78,263,000. The 41 earmarks Rep. Rodney Alexander (R-La.) requested were worth $65,395,000. Rep. Todd Tiahrt (R-Kan.) wanted $63,400,000 for 39 special projects, and Rep. Rob Bishop (R-Utah) wanted $93,980,000 set aside for 47 projects. Rep. Denny Rehberg (R-Mont.) takes the prize as the tea partier with his name on the most earmarks. Rehberg's office requested funding for 88 projects, either solely or by co-signing earmark requests with Sens. Max Baucus (D) and Jon Tester (D), at a cost of $100,514,200. On his own, Rehberg requested 20 earmarks valued at more than $9.6 million." It seems that even politicians who supposedly align themselves with the Tea Party ideals of smaller government and less spending are, in fact, trying to spend hundreds of millions on earmarks and pork projects. Ms. Bachman didn't, however, and one can only wonder how many politicians jumped on the Tea Party bandwagon simply because it was popular; and have no intention of cutting spending and earmarks. Hopefully Ms. Bachmann and others *that are* serious about cutting government spending will win out. With the new Congress coming in soon, and anti-earmark GOP reinforcements, the curtain may soon come down on the wasteful and expensive practice of earmarks.

**In conclusion**, Ronald Reagan is sometimes remembered by a quote he was fond of repeating on his march to the White House. It was from an original quote by British historian Lord Woodhouselee, but was first uttered by Ronald Reagan in 1964: *"A democracy cannot exist as a permanent form of government. It can only exist until the voters discover they can vote themselves largesse out of the public treasury. From that moment on the majority...always vote(s) for the candidate promising the most benefits from the treasury with the result that democracy always collapses over a loose fiscal policy, always to be followed by a dictatorship."* There are more than 2001 different subsidy programs that receive "benefits from the treasury," and they are pushing our democracy toward collapse.

The U.S. government subsidizes a wide range of people and industries, from farmers to arms companies to foreign governments to politicians using earmarks. Our government hands out hundreds of billions of dollars from programs that have been around for decades, and *new programs that are growing at one every five days.* If this book sat on your desk for three weeks, during that time politicians created another three subsidy programs to hand out piles of free money to someone. "Free money" is not free, however, and the taxpayer gets to pay for this looting of our government. Federal spending on subsidizes continues to grow and increase at an alarming rate. Polls over the years have clearly shown the U.S. taxpayer does not support most of these programs, especially farm subsidies, yet they continue to hand out billions of dollars, many times to large corporate farmers that don't need the money or people that don't even farm. The reason, as always, is lobbyists continue to pay for influence and grow and perpetuate this gravy train year after year. The will of the people (as expressed in polls) is not taken into account, and the spending continues. Like many federal programs, subsidy programs just grow and morph into huge money black holes.

Instead of reforming, shrinking or closing these programs, which is what the people who pay for them want, politicians continue to grow and consume ever increasing amounts of tax dollars. Politicians hand out hundreds of billions of dollars; "largesse out of the public treasury" to lobbyists and those they represent. Politicians, special interests and lobbyists loot the treasury and taxpayers with the end result being the collapse of democracy "over loose fiscal policy". Wealthy people and organizations pay lawyers and lobbyists to get subsidizes and free money from politicians and the government; their greed never satisfied until democracy collapses. A fairly accurate assessment of what is happening today. Politicians will never stop spending and giving away money to special interests and lobbyists, and have always voted against any limits of their power to do so. Until this power is taken away from them, our democracy and economy will be at ever increasing risk.

# CHAPTER 4

# *Our Litigious Society*

<u>Thomas Jefferson</u> said, "If the present Congress errs in too much talking, how can it be otherwise in a body to which the people send one hundred and fifty lawyers, whose trade it is to question everything, yield nothing, and talk by the hour?"

**A countryman between two lawyers is like a fish between two cats.**

*Benjamin Franklin*

**Whenever a man has cast a longing eye on offices, a rottenness begins in his conduct.**

*Thomas Jefferson*

According to the *Statistical Abstract of the United States* "….. in 1980 there was one lawyer per 403 people in the U.S., by 1990 that number rose to one lawyer per 340, by the year 2000, the number was one lawyer per 300 people."…..today in the **U.S.A.: There is one lawyer for every 200 adult Americans."**

Brazil follows closely with one lawyer for every 326 Brazilians.

**Country Lawyers Population People/Lawyer**

| | | |
|---|---|---|
| **US:** Lawyers: 1,143,358 | **Pop:** 303MM | **P/L:** 200 |
| **Brazil:** Lawyers: 571,360 | **Pop:** 186MM | **P/L:** 326 |
| **New Zealand:** Lawyers: 10,523 | **Pop:** 4MM | **P/L** 391 |
| **Spain** Lawyers: 114,143 | **Pop:** 45MM | **P/L:** 395 |
| **Italy** Lawyers: 121,380 | **Pop:** 59MM | **P/L:** 488 |
| **UK** Lawyers: 151,043 | **Pop:** 61MM | **P/L** 401 |
| **Germany** Lawyers: 138,679 | **Pop:** 82MM | **P/L:** 593 |
| **France** Lawyers: 45,686 | **Pop:** 64MM | **P/L:** 1,403 |

Among the Top 7 "lawyerly countries" listed above, the US has about 50% of the lawyers, with 37 percent of the population of this group.

(Source: The 2010 Statistical Abstract of the United States, U.S. Census Bureau. Census.gov)

## Can We Ever Reduce the Number of Lawyers?

An article in *lawyer reform* states "there are currently 1,143,358 lawyers. And our nation's 192 accredited and government-subsidized law schools are unleashing 40,000 new lawyers each year as they have consistently for the last 20 years. In a decade we will have 1,500,000 lawyers. An almost 50% increase" and will result in there being one lawyer for every 150 adults–double the number of lawyers since 2000. "The large numbers of lawyers are like locusts" (a swarm that eats everything in its path) or cancer cells; and have "resulted in the public losing control of many of our institutions. Today they make the rules as statutes in legislatures and Congress. They make the rules as case law during trials. They make the rules with verdicts as lawyer-judges. And if at any point a citizen questions the legality or morality of any aspect of a lawyer's or judge's work in using these rules, then discipline boards made up almost entirely of lawyers will make the final ruling." It is a completely closed system with the large number of lawyers being completely in control—the ultimate definition of tyranny. Most lawyers don't care what's right or wrong, what's ethical or just or morally acceptable, they only care about what's legal and what they can get away with.

**I have accepted a seat in the House of Representatives, and thereby have consented to my own ruin, to your ruin, and to the ruin of our children. I give you this warning that you may prepare your mind for your fate.**

*John Adams*

**I love litigation**

David Boies, famous lawyer, founder and Chairman of Boies, Schiller & Flexner LLP, recent quote in *Fortune Magazine*

## Why the number of lawyers has increased so dramatically

During the 19th century, many people without formal training helped others with legal matters, in and out of court. Even most lawyers of Abraham Lincoln's time did not attend law school, pass a bar exam or hold a professional license. Rather, they studied under other lawyers and were eventually allowed to argue in court. And it was also common for people to represent themselves, often with the help of popular books such as *Every Man His Own Lawyer*, by John G. Wells.

At the end of the 19th century, the American Bar Association (ABA) set out to turn lawyering into a profession, with the idea that increased status would generate higher fees. To accomplish this, it fashioned a code of ethics and urged states to adopt minimum educational requirements and a professional entrance (bar) examination for anyone who wanted to call himself a lawyer. By the late 1920s, most states had fallen into line.

But to make the practice of law more lucrative, it wasn't enough just to raise the professional image of lawyers. It was also crucial to keep accountants, insurance companies, bankers and just plain business folk from practicing law at cheaper rates. So, soon after the 1929 stock market crash made times even tougher for attorneys, the ABA began a successful push to establish a lawyer monopoly over lawyering. But unfortunately, instead of clearly defining the practice of law in language all could understand (and competitors could resist), ABA rules gave state court judges (lawyers all) the power to enforce the new lawyer monopoly on a case-by-case basis. Non lawyers in the gray area of whether an activity was considered the practice of law could not take a chance as it was not defined.

As the Great Depression deepened, lawyers faced with dwindling legal business pressured criminal prosecutors and state judicial authorities to go to court to close down non lawyer practitioners. Judges apparently eager to support the interest of their professional brethren soon banned non lawyers from handling all matter of activities that they had performed for decades, including real estate closings, title searches, negotiating insurance settlements and providing tax advice. By the onset of World War II, lawyers had successfully carved out a legal monopoly that would remain securely and profitably in their hands for decades.

## The legal monopoly

In an article *Lawyers Try to Reestablish Their Monopoly* by Stephen R. Elias, Attorney and Ralph Warner, Attorney, the authors evaluate what has been going on in our legal system. "The legal profession is nervous. The economy is deteriorating; law firms are laying off lawyers or, in some cases, closing altogether. And even more troublesome, competition from non lawyers is nibbling away at the lawyers' market, as many consumers choose tax preparation services over tax attorneys, self-help law books over divorce lawyers and bankruptcy petition preparers over bankruptcy lawyers." Websites like "Legalzoom.com" have also made it easier for people to avoid getting a lawyer.

To reverse the trend towards self-representation and keep non lawyers off its turf, the lawyers' trade organization, the American Bar Association (ABA), has proposed a new legal rule If states adopt it, a person would be presumed to be "practicing law" (forbidden to all who aren't licensed lawyers) by doing any of the following: Giving advice about someone's legal rights or responsibilities; selecting, drafting, or completing legal documents or agreements that affect someone's legal rights of a person; Representing a person before a court or other hearing body, including preparing or filing documents; or negotiating legal rights or responsibilities on someone's behalf.

This definition is so broad that it's hard to imagine any law-related activity not covered. It would include, for example, helping a taxpayer negotiate a tax claim with the IRS, preparing a real estate contract or helping an athlete negotiate a contract. If states adopt this proposal, accountants, real estate brokers, sports agents and many others would be at risk of losing much or all of their livelihoods. Strictly applied, it could even force many law-related websites to close, and block publication of most self-help law books and software.

The legal profession's public rationale for proposing anti-competitive laws has always been "consumer protection"—only lawyers could be trusted to perform legal tasks safely. However, scholars who study this claim, including Stanford Law School Professor Deborah Rhode (*Stanford Law Review*, 1981), invariably find no evidence that non lawyer legal providers harm consumers. The profession's true motive, they conclude, is self-protection.

Why does the ABA think it can stake out so much legal turf exclusively for lawyers? Probably because ABA has done this since their inception. The first significant hole in the ABA's anti-competitive wall was drilled in 1971, when Nolo began publishing the first comprehensive line of self-help law books to surface in many years. Once again, Americans had reliable, affordable help with routine legal documents. Consumers who couldn't afford –or didn't want—to pay a lawyer quickly made the little company a success. As the number of legal self-helpers grew over the next several decades, other businesses sprang up to help them. For example, relatively low-cost legal typing services run by non lawyers, some of whom were former court clerks or paralegals, became popular in many states as an alternative to lawyers. State bar associations occasionally tried—sometimes successfully—to close down these services. But although the self-help industry's claim of First Amendment protection for its activities was often ignored by pro-bar association judges, its survival was assured by the huge demand for affordable legal help. For example, today in California an estimated 65% of all divorces are done without lawyers. Instead, consumers use either self-help legal books or hire non lawyers, known as Legal Document Assistants, to help prepare the paperwork.

Which brings us back to the present. Although consumers have found many safe ways to access high quality legal information at affordable prices, lawyer trade groups such as the ABA haven't given up on the idea that only lawyers should provide Americans with legal information and services. Just a few years ago, a committee of lawyers sponsored by the Texas Supreme Court tried and failed to ban self-help law products published by Nolo and others from Texas bookstores and libraries. And now the ABA itself is attempting to outdo even this extreme anti-competitive effort by seeking to re-impose its professional monopoly on a national basis. As the Wall Street Journal pointed out in an editorial, "The real ABA game here is to tighten its cartel so lawyers can raise prices." Sorry, but the era when the legal profession could write self-serving laws to outlaw its competition is long past. Today, American consumers are finally enjoying the right to purchase legal information in a free market. They deserve to keep it. Like the tax system, our legal system has become onerously complicated and self-serving.

## Divorce and GDP

Consider how badly the legal system has handled divorce. Sometime in the 1960's, around the same time as women started going into the work-force, the divorce rate started to rise. This was a great boon to lawyers. Many home-town lawyers make most of their income from divorces (and bankruptcies and Disability). In the old days, you needed some documented cause, some kind of proof in order to get divorced. Today, with the popularity of divorce proceedings by lawyers, you don't need any reason. Lawyers and the court system, in order to secure more income, have resulted in the breakup of more families than in any time in history. Worse still, lawyers and women's rights attorneys have made unlimited child support laws which are unfair and ridiculous. The ex-wife gets up to 30% of the income of the ex-husband, and can spend it any way she chooses. There is never any proof needed that it is actually spent on the children (despite being labeled "child support"). As these men now have an almost 30% tax added onto any income they might make, many quit working so much. Considering that ½ of marriages end in divorce, there are as many as half the formerly married men in our population who are working and earning less than they ordinarily would be making.

Since nobody has ever studied this phenomena and how it may actually reduce GDP in this country, there is no way to tell. The child support tax and the resulting production decline hurts not only the earner, but those that might work for him, and the government, which isn't going to get as much tax revenue from this earner. Instead of showing or proving how much an ex-wife might spend on the children, like a budget, they are given free reign with the money, and can go back to court (with their lawyer) an unlimited amount of times to get more child support as the ex-husbands income may rise. Most ex-husbands simply quit working so hard, try to minimize their incomes, and through their lawyer, go back to court to reduce child support payments. This system, like many other laws and governmental practices, rewards people who don't work with money, and penalizes men who do work for working harder. Again, ½ the formerly married population are now divorced, but there is no way to calculate the number of under-working men, and the amount of money lost. For ease of this argument, men as earners and women as collectors was used, but you can easily substitute women for men as earners, as is sometimes the case.

Once again, the noble idea of marriage and of providing for the welfare of their children has been bastardized by the legal profession and lawyers to effectively collapse the institution of marriage and remove any safeguards that children actually get any benefits from child support and provide an up to eighteen year tax on the productive ex-spouse in any relationship, thereby reducing work-output and income. It's interesting that lawyers call it "family law" as it results in the dissolution of families. Lawyers are always in the middle of misery situations like this; increasing conflict while collecting the proceeds on an hourly basis. Lawyers have a way of taking any simple, noble idea and turning into a contentious, lucrative quagmire.

## Lawsuits and GDP

Lawyers and lawsuits have moved some pharmaceutical research and development off-shore, along with those jobs. Pharmaceutical companies have to set aside huge amounts of money for potential lawsuits on their products and hire still more lawyers to protect themselves from lawsuits. Every business, from U.S. car makers to cement companies are at risk for litigation. There is a "lawsuit tax" on every business that produces goods in the U.S. as they too have to always be vigilant and prepared for litigation. It's safe to say that other countries, especially China, India and our other main competitors in the global market place, do not have the threat and costs of litigation that our businesses have to contend with.

As a reminder: GDP (gross domestic product) is the total of all goods and services we produce in the U.S. It is the sum total of our economic output as a nation. *Towers Perrin*, a major consultant to the insurance industry, releases a report every year on the cost of torts (lawsuits) in the U.S. Their last and latest report *2008 Update on U.S. Tort Cost Trends* reported the following:

"U.S. tort costs increased by 2.1% in 2007. The largest increase in personal tort costs since 2003 helped fuel the overall increase in costs. The increase in personal tort costs was the result of a rise in auto accident frequency, the first such rise since 1999. The U.S. tort system cost *$252 billion* in 2007, which translates to *$835 per person* or $9 per person more than in 2006. Overall economic growth in 2007 was 4.8%. As such, the ratio of tort costs to gross domestic product (GDP) shrank in 2007, marking four consecutive years of a decline in the ratio. <u>Since 1950, growth in tort costs has exceeded growth in GDP by an average of approximately two percentage points.</u> We are forecasting growth in U.S. tort costs of 4.0% in 2008, with higher growth (5.0%) in 2009 and 2010. They also report that tort costs were just 0.6% of GDP in 1950 and 1.3% of GDP in 1970."

"Growth in lawsuits (torts) since 1950 has exceeded growth in GDP by 2% (on average). The growth and cost of lawsuits has, on average, grown faster than our economy for the last 60 years. This cost comes from the fact that at least *15 million* lawsuits are filed every year." Given the fact that there are at least 1,143,358 lawyers in this country, that's an average of 13 lawsuits filed per lawyer. And in a decade the number of lawyers is expected to grow by 50%. Another way to look at this is <u>*any growth our economy has made in the last sixty years has been erased by the cost of lawsuits*</u> (less another 2%). All the productivity of our nation (as measured by GDP) for the last 60 years has been wiped out because of lawsuits.

As for jobs, there is a clear relationship - the higher the growth of real GDP, the larger the increase in employment; or conversely, a reduction of GDP (from lawsuits), the larger the loss of employment. According to data presented by Jan Hatzius in a research piece *Employment and Real GDP*, a loss of potential GDP of 2% (the amount of GDP reduction due to lawsuits) translates into a loss of 1,049,000 jobs. Were it not for lawsuits, a million people might have jobs. Lawsuits have wiped out GDP growth and jobs for more than 60 years. The cost to each person, as the report states, is $835 per year. You may not write a check to lawyers every year, but you pay for it in the form of increased costs passed on to consumers for the goods, services and insurance we buy. Considering GDP has grown at less than 2% since the recession, the cost is even higher now.

Our country and economy thus supports a large and wealthy class: lawyers; cost what it may. They use the money they extract from lawsuits to lobby Washington to make sure there are no changes to the tort laws or to decrease awards. As you will see, it's not surprising that the American Assn. for Justice (formerly the American Trial Lawyers Association) is the largest contributor to political campaigns in the U.S. (97% of which goes to the Democratic Party). They want to make sure nobody changes the system that pays them a quarter of a trillion dollars every year. A quick check of recent tort reform efforts shows that tort reform has been a "non-starter" every time the subject comes up. Why? Lobbying, political campaign contributions and the fact that most senators and congressmen at the federal and state level are lawyers, and are not going to jeopardize any future opportunities for themselves or fellow lawyers. Abraham Lincoln (a lawyer himself) had the right idea in the following quote:

**Never stir up litigation. A worse man can scarcely be found than one who does this.**

*Abraham Lincoln*

**We the people are the rightful masters of both Congress and the courts, not to overthrow the Constitution but to overthrow the men who pervert the Constitution.**

*Abraham Lincoln*

## Lawyers and our government

An article entitled *Respect the Constitution* by Vern Wuensche states "In Congress today there are good lawyers who want a smaller government, there are good lawyers who want to protect private property, and there are good lawyers who want to use common sense in solving America's problems. Those lawyers in Congress who want something else must be shown the door."

"In America today there are 1,143,358 lawyers. In our nation, 1 in every 200 adults is a lawyer. If the 535 members of Congress were truly representative of the American people, its numbers would include only three lawyers. But this is obviously not the case. Instead, today Congress has 213 lawyers. But the problem does not stop there. In our three branches of government 100% of the Judicial Branch, our Supreme Court, are lawyers; 100% of the Executive Branch, our President, is a lawyer; and 46% of the Legislative Branch, the United States House of Representatives and the United States Senate, are lawyers. So although lawyers are a surprisingly large one-half percent of our population, they are responsible for running an even more stunning 82% of our government."

James Madison, the Father of our Constitution, designed these three branches of government each to serve as a check on the other. In *Federalist No. 47* Madison stated: *"the accumulation of all powers, legislative, executive and judiciary in the same hands, whether of one, a few or many, and whether hereditary, self-appointed, or elective, may justly be pronounced the very definition of tyranny."* So today who can say otherwise than that we have a government where the accumulation of all powers is in the same hands of lawyers who are many and elected? And so, according to James Madison, we thereby now (in 2010) have the very definition of governmental tyranny.

"To make matters worse, members of Congress who have a lawyer's training, a lawyer's developed habits and a lawyer's loyalties clearly are not suited to serve the people of our nation. A lawyer is trained that there is no right and wrong behavior, but only legal and illegal behavior." Its okay to sell votes to lobbyists and special interests, give money away in pork and subsidies to these same people, and even let lobbyists write legislation—because they've made it legal. Congress actually has the ability to make whatever they are doing legal, as they write legislation that, when passed, becomes law. Right and wrong don't matter, only what is legal and what you can get away with. The declining values that follow this training and right of law are soon reflected in how we are governed—at our continued peril.

"A lawyer's developed habits in his work do not serve the people. A lawyer usually only considers what the law says, ignoring cost and common sense. As a lawyer is paid by the hour, his habit of passing laws in Congress which are complex, ambiguous, and inefficient to administer profits his profession greatly. As does his habit of *increasing* conflict among differing parties. And in focusing only on the short-term goal of winning the case before him, an attorney rarely considers the long-term consequences of what he does. Moreover, by habitually treating all factors as static as the fixed laws he deals with every day, he does not consider the multitude of non-legal effects a new law he creates has. And of course a lawyer's habit is never to admit error, because it may result in his losing a case or political standing. Ordinary people, in a contrary manner, know that admitting and correcting errors are a natural part of progress."

"And a lawyer's loyalties are only to his individual client and to the government bureaucracy of which he is a part as an Officer of the Court—not to the American public at large." Lawyers who want to grow government have been in charge for 50 years and have made a catastrophic mess of things. It's time to give someone else a chance. There is a better way.

## Lawsuits are like the lottery, only better...

Our legal system has become a lottery system. When you go to the store and buy a lottery ticket, your chances of winning those millions of dollars is pretty slim, statistically speaking. But you can increase your odds of becoming an instant millionaire by simply getting a lawyer and filing a lawsuit. Surely there is someone out there with deep pockets that has caused you harm. In recent years people have sued McDonald's because they spilled their coffee and got burned or have become obese as a result of eating there. People sue homeowners and businesses when they clumsily fall and hurt themselves. The fact is, you can sue anybody for any reason. We have the biggest tort system in the world. The bigger the business you sue, the more money you can get.

For example, a Colorado jury recently awarded $15 million to a truck driver who said she slipped and fell on ice and grease while making a delivery to a Walmart in Greeley. Wal-Mart Stores Inc. said it's considering appealing the award for 41-year-old Holly Averyt of Cheyenne, Wyo., which a jury ordered recently. Her lawyer, Gregory Gold, says it could be one of the highest such verdicts in the country. Gold presented city documents showing that some grease from the store's deli didn't get trapped in a device designed to keep it from getting into the sewer. He said Averyt had to undergo three back surgeries, was unable to return to work and lost her truck. A Wal-Mart spokesman said the company respectfully disagrees with the verdict.

These kinds of lawsuits are possible only because lawyers can get any case heard by a court, and can persuade a jury to award any amount of money. Did this person really have $15 million in damages? Since the jury didn't have to figure out where the money came from, they simply awarded the equivalent of a winning lottery ticket. Oh, and don't forget, her lawyer may get as much as half of that winning judgment. After the court case was over, her lawyer undoubtedly filed for SSI Disability for her. Fifteen million just for slipping on some ice and grease; It's great to be an American, especially if you're clumsy.

**Power always thinks it has a great soul and vast views beyond the comprehension of the weak.**

*John Adams*

**Power always thinks..... that it is doing God's service when it is violating all his laws.**

*John Adams*

America will never be destroyed from the outside. If we falter and lose our freedoms, it will be because we destroyed ourselves.

*Abraham Lincoln*

A typical vice of American politics is the avoidance of saying anything real on real issues.

*Theodore Roosevelt*

When they call the roll in the Senate, the Senators do not know whether to answer "Present" or "Not guilty."

*Theodore Roosevelt*

# Lobbyists

**There is danger from all men. The only maxim of a free government ought to be to trust no man living with power to endanger the public liberty.**

*John Adams*

**Few men have virtue to withstand the highest bidder.**

*George Washington*

Maybe John Adams was warning us about the dangers of lobbyists, who have been given the "power to endanger the public liberty" like no others in our history. The term "lobbyist" owes its origin to President Ulysses S. Grant. During Grant's first term as President, his wife disapproved of his drinking, so Grant would regularly slip out of the White House and visit the lounge at the nearby Willard Hotel in downtown Washington, D.C. Grant's visits to the Willard Hotel soon became common knowledge. Those wishing to catch a minute or two with the President to petition their causes would collect in the hotel lobby to corner Grant as he went to and from the lounge. Frustrated by the ever-growing crowd of petitioners, Grant frequently complained of the "lobbyists" who would get in his way.

Professional lobbyists are generally more effective than non-lobbyists at petitioning government for a variety of reasons. Professional lobbyists tend to represent wealthy corporate interests or well-connected associations that wield resources critical to the election and staying power of officeholders. Many lobbyists have high levels of expertise and knowledge in the legislative process of the issues of concern to legislators. *Members of Congress frequently rely on lobbyists even to draft legislation*. Yes, unelected lobbyists are writing our legislation. Lobbyists are employed full-time to follow specific legislation and hound legislators round-the-clock, an opportunity not available to most citizens. And, increasingly, some professional lobbyists greatly benefit from the phenomenon known as the "revolving door," in which former government officials cash in on their friendships, inside information and networks established earlier to exert disproportionate influence over the government's policy agenda.

The rise of the professional lobbyist has meant an incredible – and very dangerous – concentration of power over government within a small, elite cadre of persons. This concentration of power, in turn, means it is ever-so essential for legislators and the public to know who is paying the lobbyists how much to lobby whom on what. Legislators need this information to properly evaluate the political pressures to which they are being subjected. The public needs this information to evaluate the integrity of their legislators.

## Lobbying Disclosure Act of 1995
Craig Holman reports in *Origins, Evolution and Structure of the Lobbying Disclosure Act* that after decades of failed attempts to close the many loophole of the 1946 Act, Congress finally stepped up to the plate at the end of 1995

and approved the fairly sweeping Lobbying Disclosure Act (LDA) of 1995. LDA represents a comprehensive reform when compared to the earlier regulatory efforts, though it certainly was seen as falling short of a complete success by its biggest sponsors. The Lobbying Disclosure Act received unanimous approval in the Senate and was signed into law by President Bill Clinton on December 19, 1995. The new Act took effect on January 1, 1996. LDA marked the first comprehensive reform of federal lobbying laws in 50 years. Congress had been very reluctant to modify the 1946 lobbying law, despite the fact it was widely recognized as a failure in achieving the objectives of registering and disclosing to the public the swelling ranks and financial activity of federal lobbyists. Several forces came into play in the mid-1990s to compel congressional action. First and foremost, Congress had been enwrapped in a sensational case of corruption touching several members of Congress, known as the Wedtech scandal. In 1987, the Senate Subcommittee on Oversight of Government Management investigated "improper activities in the award of federal contracts to the Wedtech Corporation." The Subcommittee noted that Wedtech had hired numerous lobbyists, including some former members of Congress, to help land lucrative government contracts. All the lobbying activity went unreported, and even involved bribing government officials. The investigation highlighted inadequacies of federal lobbying laws, prompting the Subcommittee to convene hearings specifically on the lobbying registration and reporting in 1991.

The lawyers/law firms-industry encompasses a variety of law-related interests. It consists of both trade organizations that promote legislation beneficial to the industry and members of prestigious firms – including former lawmakers and high-ranking government staffers – that are highly involved in various political processes. Members of this group of politically embedded law firms frequently show up in the *Center for Responsive Politics'* Revolving Door database (Center for Responsive Politics, OpenSecrets.org).

Contributions to federal candidates and political committees by lawyers have increased during the past 10 years, and collectively, they are consistently larger during presidential election years. Each cycle, the contributions significantly favor Democrats. In the 2008 election cycle, the industry contributed a massive $234 million to federal political candidates and interests, 76 percent of which went to Democratic candidates and committees.

In the 2008 presidential election, the lawyers/law firms industry was the top source of campaign donations for both Barack Obama and Hillary Clinton – Obama received $43.2 million and Clinton received $16 million. It was the second most profitable source (behind retired individuals) for John McCain, who received $9.9 million.

The top contributor of these substantial funds is "heavy hitter" American Association for Justice, a group of plaintiff's attorneys formerly known as the Association of Trial Lawyers of America whose main political priority is fighting tort reform. In the past 20 years, the AAJ has donated $31.6 million, 91 percent of which has gone to Democrats, who also generally oppose tort reform.

Lobbying by lawyers and law firms has generally decreased during the past six years; in 2009, the industry spent $20 million on lobbying. The American Association for Justice tops the list with $4.7 million – although it's spending has steadily decreased from its peak earlier in the decade. The American Bar Association in 2009 placed second within the industry with $1.1 million in lobbying expenditures. The rest of the lobbying clients from this industry consist of a combination of specific law firms and lawyer's organizations, such as Lawyers for Civil Justice.

Significant legislation that these organizations lobbied on in 2009 includes the Medical Device Safety Act of 2009 and the Sunshine in Litigation Act. The Medical Device Safety Act would overturn a 2008 Supreme Court decision that denied patients injured by certain medical devices the right to seek compensation through state product liability lawsuits. The Sunshine in Litigation Act would prohibit courts from restricting the disclosure of information obtained through discovery or restricting access to court records in a civil case.

The lawyers/law firms industry also lobbies extensively on various arbitration reform, patent reform and access to justice legislation.

Total contributions: **$97,977,715 for 2008:**

| Rank | Organization | Amount | 🐴 Dems | 🐘 Repubs |
|------|--------------|--------|---------|-----------|
| 1 | American Assn for Justice | $2,484,100 | 97% | 3% |
| 2 | Akin, Gump et al | $1,139,288 | 72% | 28% |
| 3 | Patton Boggs LLP | $985,196 | 72% | 27% |
| 4 | DLA Piper | $930,922 | 68% | 30% |
| 5 | K&L Gates | $918,834 | 65% | 35% |
| 6 | Greenberg Traurig LLP | $868,248 | 68% | 31% |
| 7 | Holland & Knight | $822,983 | 69% | 27% |
| 8 | Brownstein, Hyatt et al | $630,305 | 74% | 25% |
| 9 | Sonnenschein, Nath & Rosenthal | $624,699 | 68% | 32% |
| 10 | Bryan Cave LLP | $616,283 | 66% | 33% |
| 11 | Thornton & Naumes | $610,569 | 97% | 3% |
| 12 | Kirkland & Ellis | $593,411 | 71% | 29% |
| 13 | Boies, Schiller & Flexner | $545,731 | 99% | 1% |
| 14 | Susman Godfrey LLP | $525,425 | 98% | 2% |
| 15 | Nix, Patterson & Roach | $520,381 | 100% | 0% |
| 16 | Skadden, Arps et al | $495,924 | 84% | 16% |
| 17 | Blank Rome LLP | $482,250 | 60% | 39% |
| 18 | Sidley Austin LLP | $477,589 | 73% | 27% |
| 19 | Simmons Cooper LLC | $468,968 | 100% | 0% |
| 20 | Waters & Kraus | $445,405 | 99% | 1% |

(Source: The Center for Responsive Politics, OpenSecrets.org, copyright The Center for Responsive Politics, used with permission)

## *Top Industries Giving to Members of Congress, 2010 Cycle*

Who's got the most juice on Capitol Hill for 2010? Here's a list of the top industries contributing to members of the 111th Congress during the 2009-2010 election cycle. The first list shows the overall 50 biggest industries. The other two highlight the top 25 industries giving to members of each of the two major parties. In all cases, the Top Recipient listed is the individual member of the 111th Congress who received the most from the industry. *Totals shown here include only the money that went to current incumbents in Congress.*

| Rank | Industry | Total | Dem Pct | GOP Pct | Top Recipient |
|------|----------|-------|---------|---------|---------------|
| 1 | Lawyers/Law Firms | $50,575,308 | 81% | 19% | Harry Reid (D-Nev) |
| 2 | Health Professionals | $30,568,099 | 58% | 42% | Harry Reid (D-Nev) |
| 3 | Retired | $28,741,670 | 53% | 47% | Scott P. Brown (R-Mass) |
| 4 | Securities/Invest | $26,344,658 | 65% | 35% | Charles E. Schumer (D-NY) |
| 5 | Real Estate | $24,507,327 | 61% | 38% | Charles E. Schumer (D-NY) |
| 6 | Insurance | $20,403,040 | 53% | 46% | Charles E. Schumer (D-NY) |
| 7 | Leadership PACs | $17,411,855 | 62% | 37% | Roy Blunt (R-Mo) |
| 8 | Lobbyists | $16,091,358 | 68% | 31% | Harry Reid (D-Nev) |
| 9 | Pharm/Health Prod | $13,350,003 | 58% | 41% | Richard Burr (R-NC) |
| 10 | Democratic/Liberal | $12,619,011 | 100% | 0% | Joseph A. Sestak, Jr (D-Pa) |
| 11 | Electric Utilities | $12,189,462 | 60% | 38% | Rick Boucher (D-Va) |
| 12 | TV/Movies/Music | $11,365,061 | 69% | 31% | Charles E. Schumer (D-NY) |
| 13 | Misc Finance | $11,091,574 | 57% | 43% | Charles E. Schumer (D-NY) |
| 14 | Public Sector Unions | $10,753,111 | 91% | 8% | Gerry Connolly (D-Va) |
| 15 | Bldg Trade Unions | $10,355,360 | 93% | 7% | Joseph A. Sestak, Jr (D-Pa) |
| 16 | Oil & Gas | $10,295,878 | 37% | 60% | Blanche Lincoln (D-Ark) |
| 17 | Business Services | $9,941,701 | 70% | 30% | Charles E. Schumer (D-NY) |
| 18 | Commercial Banks | $9,195,888 | 48% | 52% | Kirsten Gillibrand (D-NY) |
| 19 | Hospitals/Nurs Homes | $9,138,935 | 69% | 30% | Charles E. Schumer (D-NY) |
| 20 | Transport Unions | $9,101,897 | 87% | 13% | James L. Oberstar (D-Minn) |
| 21 | Misc Mfg/Distrib | $8,470,267 | 54% | 46% | Charles E. Schumer (D-NY) |
| 22 | Crop Production | $8,287,246 | 60% | 40% | Blanche Lincoln (D-Ark) |
| 23 | Computers/Internet | $8,280,544 | 66% | 34% | Charles E. Schumer (D-NY) |
| 24 | Pro-Israel | $7,570,230 | 67% | 32% | Mark Kirk (R-Ill) |
| 25 | Air Transport | $7,553,127 | 54% | 45% | John L. Mica (R-Fla) |
| 26 | Industrial Unions | $7,429,428 | 98% | 2% | Mark Critz (D-Pa) |
| 27 | General Contractors | $7,036,853 | 46% | 54% | Roy Blunt (R-Mo) |
| 28 | Accountants | $6,794,984 | 51% | 49% | Charles E. Schumer (D-NY) |
| 29 | Defense Aerospace | $6,718,259 | 58% | 41% | Howard P. (Buck) Mckeon (R-Calif) |
| 30 | Retail Sales | $6,412,715 | 52% | 47% | Blanche Lincoln (D-Ark) |
| 31 | Beer, Wine & Liquor | $6,288,983 | 59% | 41% | Mike Thompson (D-Calif) |
| 32 | Candidate Cmtes | $6,263,734 | 81% | 19% | Scott Murphy (D-NY) |
| 33 | Education | $6,225,080 | 81% | 18% | Bill Foster (D-Ill) |
| 34 | Construction Svcs | $5,982,222 | 63% | 36% | Barbara Boxer (D-Calif) |
| 35 | Health Services | $5,966,638 | 65% | 35% | Charles E. Schumer (D-NY) |

| Rank | Industry | Total | Dem Pct | GOP Pct | Top Recipient |
|------|----------|-------|---------|---------|---------------|
| 36 | Telephone Utilities | $5,349,256 | 53% | 46% | Rick Boucher (D-Va) |
| 37 | Misc Business | $5,259,679 | 63% | 37% | Barbara Boxer (D-Calif) |
| 38 | Repub/Conservative | $5,136,314 | 0% | 100% | Scott P. Brown (R-Mass) |
| 39 | Railroads | $5,047,098 | 59% | 41% | Corrine Brown (D-Fla) |
| 40 | Agricultural Svcs | $5,014,836 | 54% | 46% | Blanche Lincoln (D-Ark) |
| 41 | Food & Beverage | $4,777,995 | 47% | 51% | Roy Blunt (R-Mo) |
| 42 | Automotive | $4,675,414 | 43% | 56% | Roy Blunt (R-Mo) |
| 43 | Defense Electronics | $4,590,245 | 60% | 40% | Ike Skelton (D-Mo) |
| 44 | Misc Unions | $4,505,070 | 99% | 1% | Mark Critz (D-Pa) |
| 45 | Finance/Credit | $3,978,308 | 53% | 47% | Richard C. Shelby (R-Ala) |
| 46 | Food Process/Sales | $3,724,426 | 48% | 52% | Blanche Lincoln (D-Ark) |
| 47 | Casinos/Gambling | $3,714,765 | 74% | 26% | Harry Reid (D-Nev) |
| 48 | Misc Defense | $3,658,004 | 57% | 42% | Ike Skelton (D-Mo) |
| 49 | Chemicals | $3,429,510 | 49% | 50% | Dave Camp (R-Mich) |
| 50 | Telecom Svcs/Equip | $3,040,612 | 66% | 34% | Harry Reid (D-Nev) |

Based on data released by the FEC on Monday, October 25, 2010. (Source: originally published by The Center for Responsive Politics, OpenSecrets.org, copyright The Center for Responsive Politics, used with permission)

Once again, lawyers and law firms contributed the most money to politicians for 2010 (as in the 2008 election) by over $20 million. If you don't think lawyers control what goes on in Washington, guess again. They chipped in almost $20 million more than the second largest contributor. It's amazing the number of industries and services that buy influence in Washington. It's also amazing how many different organizations are trying to buy influence from Harry Reid (D-Nev)—a very powerful man beholden to many. Harry Reid is one of biggest spenders of taxpayer money the world has ever seen—the conduit for hundreds of billions, if not trillions of taxpayer's dollars into the pockets of his friends and supporters over the years. This influence spending is huge, but 2010 saw the Supreme Court change the rules of the game so that almost anybody, including corporations and billionaires, could contribute as much as they wanted. Lawyers and law firms spent more than $50 million dollars (81% of which went to Democrats) with the top recipient being Democrat Harry Reid, who with Nancy Pelosi, were responsible for the stimulus spending bill and massive deficit spending. One can only wonder how many of Reid's contributors got a huge chunk of the stimulus spending. Health Professionals covered their bets with $30 million in spending, split almost evenly between Democrats and Republicans. All that money buys *a lot* of influence and friends in Washington. The people back home—not so much.

**Behind the ostensible government sits enthroned an invisible government owing no allegiance and acknowledging no responsibility to the people.**

*Theodore Roosevelt*

# The Revolving Door

Although the influence powerhouses that line Washington's K Street are just a few miles from the U.S. Capitol building, the most direct path between the two doesn't necessarily involve public transportation. Instead, it's through a door—a revolving door that shuffles former federal employees into jobs as lobbyists, consultants and strategists just as the door pulls former hired guns into government careers. While officials in the executive branch, Congress and senior congressional staffers spin in and out of the private and public sectors, so too does privilege, power, access and, of course, money.

The bulk of the work that gets done in Congress can be traced back to the various committees, where members and staffers develop specialized expertise in the policy areas of education, science, the federal budget and agriculture and a host of other topics. This expertise, in addition to the committee connections they bring with them, makes these employees prime picking for lobbying firms, whose clients are seeking to shape policies that affect their industry. The most powerful committees, such as Energy & Commerce, Appropriations and Ways & Means are of special interest to lobbying firms. The committees listed here are the current record-holders for staffers-turned-lobbyists or lobbyists-turned-staffers, including former staff directors, chief counsels and aides.

Dick Armey. Tom Daschle. Tom Foley. Trent Lott. Once, these politicos ranked among Congress' most powerful members. Today, they share another distinction: They're lobbyists (or "senior advisors" performing very similar work). And they're hardly alone. Dozens of former members of Congress now receive handsome compensation from corporations and special interests as they attempt to influence the very federal government in which they used to serve.

After every election, the Revolving Door spins a little faster, as headhunters for lobbying firms and interest groups snatch up departing government officials and aides. The members of Congress shown here have the greatest number of staffers who either came to Capitol Hill after representing private interests or left the member's staff for a lobbying position. A current or former staffer may have developed a lawmaker's political strategy as chief of staff, managed his or her contact with reporters as press secretary or worked in any number of official capacities in his or her office. While some congressional staffers may instead make their way into academia, start a business or have nothing to do with government after leaving it, capitalizing on their Capitol Hill connections to represent private interests has a powerful incentive: money.

Former employees of federal agencies can often find good (and lucrative) jobs as lobbyists, capitalizing on the connections that they forged while in public service. An Environmental Protection Agency administrator may go on to lobby his former colleagues on environmental issues, and a White House staffer can tap her West Wing connections when she starts a new job on K Street. The White House is traditionally the executive branch's largest supplier of fresh lobbyists; the office of the president employs a large team of staffers of varying seniority. But public servants switching to careers as lobbyists (and back again) come from agencies as varied as the Department of Defense, NASA and the Smithsonian Institution. Agency employees strolling through the revolving door include those as powerful—and well connected—as secretaries of state and as far from Washington as Peace Corps volunteers. The agencies shown here have employed the greatest number of former lobbyists—or sent the greatest number of former employees to lobbying firms and interest groups.

When American voters discard elected officials—and their staffs—lobbying firms and interest groups are quick to snap up the unemployed. Lobbying firms—which often charge steep fees from their deep-pocketed clients—can offer former government employees salaries far greater than those proffered by Uncle Sam, as well as continued influence on Capitol Hill. In return, firms get lobbyists who already have established connections in the federal government and whose résumés can act as a powerful draw for potential clients. The lobbying firms shown here have the greatest track record of hiring former government employees.

The country's largest companies, trade associations, professional associations and trade unions often maintain their own in-house lobbyists in Washington. These organizations can—and do—also hire outside lobbying firms to press their agendas on Capitol Hill, but they rely on internal government affairs professionals to maintain a full-time presence in DC. Like lobbying firms, these organizations like to hire former government employees, whose connections and expertise can provide valuable access to lawmakers shaping policy that affects them.

While lobbying firms are generally nonpartisan and take up issues as they take up clients, the in-house lobbyists for companies, associations and unions are exclusively devoted to their organizations' legislative goals. These goals can range from the procurement of defense contracts to the championship of dental health—but all require access to lawmakers that former government employees can best provide. The organizations shown here have hired the most former government employees to work in their government affairs divisions.

The Center for Responsive Politics's Revolving Door project identifies those people whose career trajectory has taken them from Capitol Hill, the White House and Cabinet office suites to K Street, and vice versa. The Center's Revolving Door Database is the most comprehensive source to date to help the public learn who's who in the Washington influence industry, and to uncover how these people's government connections afford them privileged access to those in power.

Generally, the *Revolving Door Database* (Center for Responsive Politics.OpenSecrets.org) consists of any person with previous or current government experience who also has held, or currently holds, a professional position in the private sector where they can reasonably be expected to influence, or be seeking to influence, public policy decisions. Private sector employment certainly includes traditional lobbyists, but may also include people who lead organizations that are in a position to influence public and elite opinions, who advise clients on regulatory or political law, who counsel organizations on public affairs strategies, who publish opinions on public policy matters, or who otherwise serve in a capacity to contribute ideas to the public sphere that may ultimately affect policy decisions in Washington.

Clearly, the most observable employment that meets these qualifications is that of a registered lobbyist. Traditional lobbyists and policy advocates engage in "inside lobbying" when they communicate policy preferences to federal government policymakers on behalf of their clients. However, this commonsense understanding of lobbying, and the statutory definition of "lobbyist" under the Lobbying Disclosure Act, remains overly narrow to recognize every person employed in Washington's influence industry. The Center's practical characterization of influence includes professionals engaged in all methods of influencing policy decisions, including traditional lobbying (personal contacts with policymakers), invited testimony at public hearings, grassroots lobbying, formal comment submissions to administrative rulemakings, amicus curiae filings in federal court, legal and strategic advice on political and policy matters and any other attempts of a person to manipulate (or help their clients manipulate) the outcome of a public policy debate.

People with past government experience who use their expertise, professional networks and policy background to engage in "outside lobbying"-or efforts to mobilize the public in an effort to influence policymakers-or to engage in political consulting are just as significant for the Revolving Door as are traditional lobbyists. These professionals indirectly influence public policy through grassroots lobbying campaigns, public relations operations, coalition-building, public discourse and political strategy development, all with the ultimate goal of shaping public policy. Lobbyists have many different methods to trade their access and expertise for money.

# Lobbying Database

In addition to campaign contributions to elected officials and candidates, companies, labor unions, and other organizations spend billions of dollars each year to lobby Congress and federal agencies. Some special interests retain lobbying firms, many of them located along Washington's legendary K Street; others have lobbyists working in-house. We've got totals spent on lobbying, beginning in 1998, for everyone from AAI Corp. to Zurich Financial.

| Total Lobbying Spending | | |
|---|---|---|
| 1998 | | $1.44 Billion |
| 1999 | | $1.44 Billion |
| 2000 | | $1.56 Billion |
| 2001 | | $1.64 Billion |
| 2002 | | $1.82 Billion |
| 2003 | | $2.04 Billion |
| 2004 | | $2.17 Billion |
| 2005 | | $2.43 Billion |
| 2006 | | $2.62 Billion |
| 2007 | | $2.85 Billion |
| 2008 | | $3.30 Billion |
| 2009 | | $3.49 Billion |
| 2010 | | $1.78 Billion |

| Number of Lobbyists* | | |
|---|---|---|
| 1998 | | 10,404 |
| 1999 | | 12,944 |
| 2000 | | 12,542 |
| 2001 | | 11,845 |
| 2002 | | 12,131 |
| 2003 | | 12,923 |
| 2004 | | 13,158 |
| 2005 | | 14,071 |
| 2006 | | 14,521 |
| 2007 | | 14,873 |
| 2008 | | 14,228 |
| 2009 | | 13,694 |
| 2010 | | 11,972 |

(NOTE: Figures are on this page are calculations by the Center for Responsive Politics based on data. 2010 spending was not complete at the time of this graph)

(Source: Originally published by The Center for Responsive Politics, OpenSecrets.org, copyright The Center for Responsive Politics, used with permission)

These two small graphs should send chills down your spine. Theodore Roosevelt would not be surprised, but hopefully the American people will be. These two graphs offer direct proof that *behind the ostensible government sits enthroned an invisible government owing no allegiance and acknowledging no responsibility to the people.* The invisible government of lobbyists has increased their spending and influence more than two-fold since 2000 alone. Lobbyists now spend close to $3.5 billion dollars influencing politicians. In 2009 there were a whopping 13,694 lobbyists pressing their issues to politicians. The spending *per lobbyist* in 2009 averaged $255,000—a quarter of a million dollars. The doubling in lobbying spending says only one thing—it works. Corporations, unions, special interests and PACs that hire lobbyists wouldn't continue to spend this kind of money if it didn't pay off in a big way. $3.49 billion can buy ten to a hundred times as much in tax breaks, subsidies, government projects, contracts and earmarks for money handouts. The old adage "it takes money to make money" has certainly been true in Washington, and there is no way to calculate how many hundreds of billions of tax dollars are spent by politicians on causes influenced by these lobbyists.

# Top Spenders

| | |
|---|---|
| US Chamber of Commerce | $651,035,680 |
| American Medical Assn | $236,012,500 |
| General Electric | $214,234,000 |
| Pharmaceutical Rsrch & Mfrs of America | $185,063,920 |
| AARP | $183,922,064 |
| American Hospital Assn | $183,723,431 |
| AT&T Inc | $155,187,314 |
| Northrop Grumman | $152,085,253 |
| Blue Cross/Blue Shield | $148,091,902 |
| National Assn of Realtors | $146,697,380 |
| Exxon Mobil | $144,796,942 |
| Verizon Communications | $141,474,841 |
| Edison Electric Institute | $141,075,999 |
| Business Roundtable | $136,944,000 |
| Boeing Co | $130,558,310 |
| Lockheed Martin | $129,220,193 |
| PG&E Corp | $116,190,000 |
| General Motors | $111,112,920 |
| Southern Co | $110,710,694 |
| Pfizer Inc | $99,327,268 |

(Source: The Center for Responsive Politics, OpenSecrets.org, copyright The Center for Responsive Politics, used with permission)

Big investments by big industries to get big concessions from politicians. The biggest spender, the U.S. Chamber of Commerce represents many types of businesses that obviously contribute large sums of money for lobbying. Heatlhcare, insurance, oil and other large corporations spend huge sums to influence our politicians.

## Top Lobbying Firms

| | |
|---|---|
| Patton Boggs LLP | $373,567,000 |
| Cassidy & Assoc | $316,275,000 |
| Akin, Gump et al | $305,545,000 |
| Van Scoyoc Assoc | $246,773,000 |
| Williams & Jensen | $177,724,000 |
| Hogan & Hartson | $154,753,907 |
| Ernst & Young | $154,296,737 |
| Quinn Gillespie & Assoc | $140,783,500 |
| Barbour, Griffith & Rogers | $136,960,000 |
| Holland & Knight | $127,869,544 |
| Greenberg Traurig LLP | $119,053,249 |
| PMA Group | $115,950,578 |
| Dutko Worldwide | $112,056,766 |
| PriceWaterhouseCoopers | $102,844,084 |
| Alcalde & Fay | $102,590,660 |
| Carmen Group | $99,895,000 |
| Brownstein, Hyatt et al | $96,775,000 |
| Ferguson Group | $90,242,291 |
| Clark & Weinstock | $89,980,000 |
| Verner, Liipfert et al | $88,595,000 |

NOTE: All lobbying expenditures on this page come from the Senate Office of Public Records. Data for the most recent year was downloaded on July 26, 2010.

(Source: The Center for Responsive Politics, OpenSecrets.org, copyright The Center for Responsive Politics, used with permission)

This short list represents a consolidation of power and influence that is unimaginable. Through these lobbying law firms pass vast sums of money targeted at politicians. The success of these firms is self-evident—they get results from the politicians they influence. Considering many of the people that work as lobbyists in these firms used to work in government is not surprising. Lobbying is where the real money is, and money buys influence and results from politicians in Washington in the form of subsidizes, ear marks, tax breaks, deregulation, and line item money hand-outs to every organization or individual that hires a lobbyist. Unless you can put together an interest or trade group and/or have tens of millions to spend on lobbyists, don't expect to get much attention or anything accomplished in Washington.

## Top Industries

| | |
|---|---|
| Pharmaceuticals/Health Products | $1,956,898,643 |
| Insurance | $1,427,862,637 |
| Electric Utilities | $1,345,479,505 |
| Computers/Internet | $1,080,849,699 |
| Business Associations | $1,068,462,638 |
| Oil & Gas | $1,003,530,221 |
| Education | $916,703,543 |
| Misc Manufacturing & Distributing | $875,229,711 |
| Hospitals/Nursing Homes | $847,968,184 |
| Real Estate | $829,993,587 |
| Health Professionals | $761,595,958 |
| Securities & Investment | $760,205,758 |
| TV/Movies/Music | $755,069,734 |
| Civil Servants/Public Officials | $724,711,476 |
| Air Transport | $715,990,983 |
| Misc Issues | $645,148,729 |
| Automotive | $599,158,576 |
| Telephone Utilities | $597,709,366 |
| Telecom Services & Equipment | $574,579,915 |
| Defense Aerospace | $504,475,101 |

NOTE: All lobbying expenditures on this page come from the Senate Office of Public Records. Data for the most recent year was downloaded on July 26, 2010

(Source: The Center for Responsive Politics, OpenSecrets.org, copyright The Center for Responsive Politics, used with permission)

Once again, it takes money to make money. These organizations spend hundreds of millions or billions to buy influence for their industries or sectors. Despite public pressure and outrage, these industries protect themselves from regulations, oversight, taxes, and just about anything the government can do to help. They can also lobby to get subsidies, contracts, and new laws passed to further protect themselves and increase their bottom line.

## Ranked Sectors

Lobbying spending totals from 1998 to 2010.

| Sector | Total |
|---|---|
| Agribusiness | $1,257,707,616 |
| Communic/Electronics | $3,424,294,247 |
| Construction | $454,375,270 |
| Defense | $1,191,446,953 |
| Energy/Nat Resource | $3,024,930,630 |
| Finance/Insur/RealEst | $4,178,632,318 |
| Health | $4,111,248,510 |
| Lawyers & Lobbyists | $330,637,195 |
| Transportation | $2,196,472,792 |
| Misc Business | $4,034,591,512 |
| Labor | $417,436,640 |
| Ideology/Single-Issue | $1,446,974,674 |
| Other | $2,164,256,327 |

NOTE: All lobbying expenditures on this page come from the Senate Office of Public Records. Data for the most recent year was downloaded on July 26, 2010. (Source: The Center for Responsive Politics, OpenSecrets.org, copyright The Center for Responsive Politics, used with permission)

Not surprisingly Agribusiness heads this list. They spent $1.257 billion (1998-2010) yet received $245.2 billion (1995-2009) in government subsidies—*more than a 195-fold return* on their investment. Where else can you get this rate of return on your money? Taxpayers and Washington paid off on Agribusiness' investment in a big way. Evident from all this data is the ever increasing spiral of lobbying. Groups "invest" in lobbying, get subsidy money, use this money for more lobbying, and get ever increasing subsidies. Hence the doubling of the amount spent on lobbyists in 9 years. No other investment pays off like lobbying.

---

### *Top Contracts*

---

This provides a view into how much special interests contract with lobbying law firms to get what they want from politicians in Washington in 2010. These amounts represent investments made by these clients to get legislation passed favorable to their cause and bottom lines.

| Firm | Client | Total |
|---|---|---|
| Swidler, Berlin et al | Asbestos Study Group | $30,020,000 |
| Patton Boggs LLP | Mars Inc | $19,610,000 |
| Hogan & Hartson | Nissan North America | $16,260,000 |
| Akin, Gump et al | Gila River Indian Community | $14,760,000 |
| Canfield & Assoc | Consumer Mortgage Coalition | $13,810,000 |
| Dickstein Shapiro LLP | Loews Corp | $13,640,000 |
| Ogilvy Government Relations | Blackstone Group | $13,500,000 |
| Akin, Gump et al | AT&T Inc | $10,830,000 |
| Cassidy & Assoc | Boston University | $10,740,000 |
| Dewey & Leboeuf | Lloyd's of London | $10,600,000 |
| Federal Policy Group | General Electric | $9,665,000 |
| Williams & Jensen | Owens-Illinois | $9,470,000 |
| Akin, Gump et al | Mortgage Insurance Companies of America | $9,180,000 |
| Hogan & Hartson | FM Policy Focus | $8,920,000 |
| DLA Piper | Medicines Co | $8,800,000 |
| Mayer, Brown et al | US Chamber of Commerce | $8,688,159 |
| MLBA Services Inc | Loews Corp | $8,496,740 |
| Dickstein Shapiro LLP | Lorillard Inc | $8,450,000 |
| Deloitte & Touche | Deloitte Touche Tohmatsu | $8,305,685 |
| Akin, Gump et al | PG&E Corp | $8,140,000 |
| Sidley, Austin et al | MasterCard Inc | $7,780,000 |
| Alcalde & Fay | International Council of Cruise Lines | $7,670,660 |
| Covington & Burling | Qualcomm Inc | $7,420,000 |
| Winston & Strawn | Government of the US Virgin Islands | $7,030,000 |
| Baker & Hostetler | Major League Baseball Commissioner's Ofc | $6,930,000 |

NOTE: All lobbying expenditures on this page come from the Senate Office of Public Records. Data for the most recent year was downloaded on July 26, 2010.

For the paltry sum of ten or twenty million dollars, groups can get laws passed or changed, subsidy programs added to their industry, tax loopholes and breaks given away, earmarks or line item money, or regulations passed or changed. There is almost nothing politicians can't do in order to collect their lobbying income. The top contract, The Asbestos Study group, has made a resurgence lately. They've lobbied to get the Asbestos Trust Fund extended or increased so lawyers could continue to sue and gain awards for victims of asbestos exposure. The government currently controls this trust fund, and lawyers want the trust fund increased to $250 billion dollars. What a deal—spend $30 million to get $250 billion. That would be an 8333-1 return on their investment. Organizations that support lobbyists really get a bang for their buck in Washington—especially lawyers.

# Top Bills

Lobbying disclosure forms ask filers to disclose which "specific lobbying issues" they worked on during the period. "Specific" is up for interpretation, however, as some filers name bills by number and title while others provide vague descriptions that offer little information. Here we've counted up the number of filers that reported lobbying on a particular piece of legislation, to the extent that can be counted.

| Bill Number | Congress | Bill Title | No. of Clients |
|---|---|---|---|
| H.R.1 | 111 | Economic stimulus bill | 1,997 |
| H.R.2638 | 110 | Making appropriations for the Department of Homeland Security for the fiscal year ending September 30, 2008 | 1,326 |
| H.R.3590 | 111 | Healthcare reform bill | 1,224 |
| H.R.1105 | 111 | Afghan Allies Protection Act of 2009 | 1,052 |
| H.R.3200 | 111 | America's Affordable Health Choices Act of 2009 | 1,049 |
| H.R.2454 | 111 | American Clean Energy and Security Act of 2009 | 1,003 |
| H.R.3043 | 110 | Department of Labor Appropriations Act, 2008 | 998 |
| S.1710 | 110 | Department of Labor Appropriations Act, 2008 | 924 |
| H.R.5647 | 109 | Departments of Labor, Health and Human Services, and Education, and Related Agencies Appropriations Act, 2007 | 920 |
| H.R.5631 | 109 | Department of Defense Appropriations Act, 2007 | 913 |

(Source: The Center for Responsive Politics, OpenSecrets.org, copyright The Center for Responsive Politics, used with permission)

For the stimulus bill, almost 2,000 lobbyists registered. The stimulus bill was the kind of legislation that lobbyists can usually only dream about—totally unstructured spending on a mammoth scale—close to one trillion dollars. While the Democrats were deciding how to spend this $1 trillion dollars, they were influenced and otherwise pressured by 2000 lobbyists trying to get their share of that money. If you didn't see any of the stimulus money, maybe you should get a lobbyist (and get results). This stimulus bill will undoubtedly go down as biggest waste of taxpayer money in recorded history. Instead of handing out money, the government should be handing out indictments.

# Lobbying: Influence Inc 2000

Influence Inc. was a team effort from the staff of the *Center for Responsive Politics* requiring months of labor-intensive data collection, analysis, writing, and production (presented with permission). This project, and the data contained are a "snapshot" and deep examination of lobbying and its effects, for year 2000. The money spent on lobbying since then has doubled—the problem is twice as big now. Although we are more than ten years past the time of this exam, it is very telling of who really runs our government and is therefore worth an examination. Please keep this in mind.

## SUMMARY

At first blush, it appears that lobbyists had a down year in 1999. The roaring 13 percent growth of lobbying expenditures in 1998 slowed to a 2 percent trickle in 1999. The tobacco industry, which had accelerated the lobbying boom, slashed its spending from $67.4 million to $23.7 million. Congressional and federal authorities made headway in their corruption case against lobbyist Ann Eppard, who allegedly solicited clients from the phone at the prison where she was serving time for fraud.

Yet despite it all, at $1.45 billion K Street's economy is bigger than Mongolia's, but without the yurts. (lobbying total money spent for 2009 was 3.49 billion, almost 2 ½ times higher than in 2000) Since 1997, lobbying expenditures has grown by a robust average of 7.3 percent annually. The collapse of tobacco spending was compensated by strong growth in pharmaceutical and computer industry lobbying. Lobbying firms were still able to find 129 former members of Congress willing to lobby on everything from postal rates to defense appropriations. Former Rep. Bob Livingston (R-La.), who was once days away from becoming Speaker of the House, drummed up $1.14 million in business in his first year as an independent lobbyist.

## THE BIG PICTURE

The result is a mixed bag. The total lobbying expenditures of $1.45 billion are only a slight rise over the 1998 figure of $1.42 billion, but still a notable increase over the 1997 figure of $1.26 billion. However, the pattern of lobbying spending changed in 1999 as several large players cut back their presence in Washington while the number of smaller spenders proliferated. As a result, the falloff in big fees didn't stop Gucci Gulch from flowing along.

The number of active lobbyists rose from 11,043 in 1998 to 12,113 in 1999.(and peaked in 2007 at 14,873). The most popular issue for lobbyists was tax policy—nearly a quarter of all lobbyists spent time lobbying on taxes in 1999. On average, *there were more than 22 active lobbyists and $2.7 million in lobbying expenditures for each member of Congress in 1999.*

The biggest industries in the lobbying game remained basically the same, with the pharmaceuticals and health products industry edging out the insurance industry at the top. Only one of the top 25 spending industries in 1998 failed to make the 1999 list. However, the stability of this group's composition masks large shifts in the ordering of the top 25. Tobacco remained one of the top industries even though it's total lobbying expenditures plummeted by nearly two-thirds. This $40 million falloff is also the primary reason why agribusiness fell from the sixth largest sector to eighth. Although it moved up only two places, the health sector increased its spending by more than $30 million in 1999 after growing by less than $5 million in 1998. The jump in health spending reflected increased Congressional attention to a patient's bill of rights as well as lobbying to extend soon-to-expire copyrights for various medications. For example, Schering-Plough, a pharmaceutical firm which was attempting to extend the life of its patent on the allergy drug Claritin, leapt from the 51st spot on the top spender list in 1998 to the ninth spot in 1999, when it spent $9.2 million.

---

## MEANWHILE, ON K STREET

---

Smaller clients did not dampen the growth prospects for Washington's biggest lobbying firms. Firms reporting over $1 million in spending grew from 117 in 1998 to 130 in 1999. The number of firms with lobbying income of more than $5 million rose from 14 to 21, and for the first time, one firm (Cassidy & Associates) broke the $20 million barrier. .

For lobbying firms, the moral of the story is that diversification pays. Cassidy & Associates, which led all lobbying firms in 1999 income, has clients ranging from Adelphi University to Major League Baseball to United Space Alliance. As a result, it is well placed to ride out the booms and busts in each industry's lobbying needs.

Other firms were not as fortunate. In a year when overall lobbying expenditures grew, Verner, Liipfert, Bernhard, McPherson & Hand, Washington's third biggest lobbying firm, reported a drop of nearly 15 percent in its lobbying income. The biggest cause of Verner Liipfert's drop was a sharp reduction in its income from tobacco firms. In 1998, the firm received a total of over $7.5 million from five tobacco companies. In 1999, it received a mere $160,000 from three tobacco clients. One of its clients, Philip Morris, slashed its contract with Verner Liipfert from $3.6 million to $80,000—a whopping 98 percent reduction.

Likewise, groups with a variety of interests, such as the Chamber of Commerce of the United States, tend to remain among the top spenders year in and year out. In 1999, the Chamber was the largest spender, with 75 lobbyists working on a host of issues ranging from the Juvenile Justice Act to U.S. aid to Kyrgystan.

The gridlock that has gripped Capitol Hill over the last few years has actually been a boon for lobbyists. Many lobbyists feel that their worth actually *increases* when partisan fighting grinds Congress to a halt. Their logic is that with few bills passed each session, someone who promises to drive legislation important to a client through Congress can be extremely valuable. At the same time, there are more opportunities to kill legislation harmful to a client.

More than anything else, the changes in lobbying expenditures reflect Congress's legislative agenda. When an issue that directly affects an industry is discussed, that industry mobilizes a lobbying effort to pursue its interests. For example, when Congress was considering legislation to regulate or fine cigarette manufacturers in 1997-98, the tobacco industry was spending over $50 million a year on lobbying. In 1999, with federal tobacco legislation effectively dead, tobacco companies spent less than $25 million.

Lobbying expenditures can fluctuate wildly in a short period of time. MBNA, the nation's largest credit card firm, spent $860,000 in the last six months of 1998, $640,000 in the first six months of 1999, and $800,000 in the last six months of 1999. By and large, MBNA's lobbying followed the fortunes of legislation to deregulate the financial services industry and to change bankruptcy laws.

# *IT DEPENDS ON WHAT YOUR DEFINITION OF 'LOBBYIST' IS*

The Lobbying Disclosure Act (LDA) of 1995 requires that each registrant disclose its total expenditures or income for lobbying activity as defined by the Act. The LDA defines lobbying to include salaries for individuals who contact members of the legislative or executive branches and their staffs; overhead, support staff, and other office expenses; expenses for background preparation and coordination of lobbying; and payments to outside firms.

However, such expenditures hardly tell the whole story on lobbying. Grassroots campaigns, such as an effort by the National Rifle Association to get its members to write their members of Congress, are not covered under the LDA. Fees that are received as part of a judicial proceeding—for example, lobbying the White House for a pardon—are excluded from the Act. Money spent on preparation and presentation of testimony to Congress is excluded. Even a public relations campaign designed to pressure Congress falls outside the LDA's reporting requirements.

The LDA also requires firms to list the registered lobbyists they have hired. However, the definition of lobbying established by the LDA does not cover 'strategic advisors' and consultants who devise lobbying strategies. This class of individuals often includes former members of Congress who are prohibited from lobbying their former colleagues for a year after leaving office. For example, former Senate Majority Leader and presidential candidate Bob Dole works for the lobbying firm Verner Lipfert, but since he does not contact officials covered under the Act, he does not have to register.

Another loophole in the reporting requirements means that the lobbying expenditures reported by each organization are not strictly comparable. Filers get three options for accounting expenditures; one method laid out in the Lobbying Disclosure Act and two others defined by the Internal Revenue Code (IRC). The dissimilarities among lobbying definitions in each piece of legislation affect the quality of disclosure. For example, 1999's top two spenders—the Chamber of Commerce of the U.S. and the American Medical Association—both used the IRC definition. As a result, their disclosure forms include state, local, and grassroots lobbying. The IRC also has a far more circumscribed list of 'covered' officials, so the Chamber of Commerce and American Medical Association numbers do not include contact with a number of executive branch officials. On the other hand, Philip Morris and the American Hospital Association both used the Lobbying Disclosure Act definition. Thus, neither organization had to report state or grassroots lobbying expenditures, while they did have to report contacts with the Clinton administration.

Even with IRC definitions, lobbyists find ways to skirt the law. Pharmaceutical makers, for example, provide seed money to small activist groups around the country. In turn, these organizations tend to push the drug makers' agenda to both their members and their Congresspersons. According to the *New York Times*, in 1994 the Pharmaceutical Research and Manufacturers of America (PhRMA), a drug industry trade group, provided seed money and expertise in order to create Citizens for the Right to Know, a consumers group opposed to managed care. In turn, Citizens for the Right to Know pushed for more prescription drug benefits in managed care plans—a potential bonanza for PhRMA's members. PhRMA also contributes to a number of non-profit public policy institutions, many of which have subsequently come out against generic drugs or in favor of prescription drug benefits. None of these contributions to non-profits are included in PhRMA's lobbying disclosure forms.

## *POLITICAL POWER FLOWS FROM THE BARREL OF A CHECKBOOK*

Contributions are not limited to non-profit groups. Contributions to political campaigns constitute a parallel track to gaining influence on the Washington lobbying game. In the 1999-2000 election cycle, nearly $3 billion was spent on federal elections, or $1.5 billion per year. At $1.45 billion, lobbying expenditures in 1999 were virtually identical to the annual average for campaign expenditures.

However, industries that spend money on lobbyists do not necessarily spend on campaign contributions. The $90 million spent on lobbyists by the pharmaceuticals and health products industry in 1999 is more than the industry's combined campaign contributions for the last *decade*. By contrast, lawyers and law firms donated over $108 million in the 1999-2000 election cycle despite spending a meager $12 million on lobbyists.

Lobbyists themselves are big players in the money game. In 1999-2000, lobbyists donated over $15.5 million to federal campaigns. However, this figure masks lobbyists' true influence, since many are also key party fundraisers. For example, the Dutko Group's late chairman Daniel Dutko not only donated over $10,000 in hard and soft money to the Democrats in 1999, he also was a major fundraiser for the Democratic Party. Lobbyists deny that their campaign donations are a quid pro quo for congressional votes. Instead, they claim that contributions ensure access to congressmen—in other words, campaign contributions get a lobbyist's foot in the door to allow them to make his or her client's case.

For some groups, campaign contributions and lobbying are only peripheral extensions of political power. For example, the Christian Coalition dramatically slashed its Washington presence from $8.0 million in 1997 to just $1.3 million in 1999. Since the Christian Coalition's real power lies in its ability to get its members to the polls on election day, a decline in lobbying spending hardly reflects a drop-off in the group's political power. Similarly, labor spending remained virtually constant from 1998 to 1999 despite a series of trade measures opposed by the unions. However, labor's power is in the votes its members possess and, to a lesser extent, in its campaign contributions. Thus, its lobbying expenditures bear little relation to its real power. Groups like the American Association of Retired Persons (AARP), the American Israel Public Affairs Committee, and the Sierra Club all fall into the category of groups whose lobbying power is greatly magnified by their membership base.

The result is that there is little correlation between campaign contributions and lobbying expenditures by businesses or industries. Among the 20 industries that spent the most in 1999 on lobbying, 12 also were among the top 20 political contributors in 1999-2000. Of the 20 organizations that spent the most on lobbyists in 1999, only four were also on the top 20 list of Lobbying: Influence Inc 2000

## *Top Spenders*

The figures for spending may seem high, but they are paltry sums compared to the amount of money that hinges on congressional decisions. Members of the Chamber of Commerce of the United States stand to benefit from an investment bonanza if China is admitted to the World Trade Organization; strict environmental laws could cost them billions of dollars in pollution control equipment and clean up costs. Doctors who have seen their incomes stagnate under managed care have the American Medical Association on Capitol Hill pushing for regulation of HMOs. Businesses are rarely known for spending money frivolously—they do not spend money on lobbyists if they don't think the potential benefits outweigh the costs.

Among the broad economic sectors, finance, insurance and real estate remains the top spender on lobbying, although its margin over the next largest sector has been significantly reduced. In 1998, miscellaneous business was the second largest sector, with $30 million less in lobbying expenditures than finance. In 1999, health was the second ranking sector, just $15 million behind. Every economic sector grew in 1999 except for agribusiness, which fell over 30 percent, and lawyers and lobbyists, which fell 7 percent.

At the industry level, the pharmaceuticals and health products industry reclaimed its title as the largest spender on the strength of a 23 percent surge in spending. Insurance, which was 1998's largest spending industry, fell to second despite an 11 percent hike in lobbying spending. The big story, though, was the explosive growth in the computer industry's lobbying expenditures, which have grown an average of 42 percent each of the last two years. In 1999, the computer equipment and services industry was the sixth largest spender at $50.4 million. The big loser was tobacco, which fell from $67.4 million in 1998 to $23.7 million in 1999.

In 1999, nearly a quarter of all lobbyists in Washington — 2,945 to be exact — spent at least some time lobbying on tax policy, making it the most heavily lobbied issue. More than 2,000 lobbyists also worked on budget/appropriations issues, healthcare, and domestic and international trade. The least attention was paid to unemployment, which was lobbied on by a mere 16 lobbyists out of 12,113 who were active in 1999.

## THE GOLDEN PARACHUTE

Every two years, a buzz normally associated with the NBA draft circulates around K Street. A new batch of elected officials leaves office to enjoy the lucrative contracts that the world of lobbying has to offer. *The Center* identified 129 former members of Congress who worked as lobbyists in 1999. Among them was former House Appropriations Committee Chairman and almost-Speaker of the House Bob Livingston, who set up Livingston Associates. After his one-year 'cooling off' period expired, he was able to earn $1.14 million in fees for lobbying his former colleagues.

Former lawmakers like Livingston are especially valuable as lobbyists because they know the legislative process and because of their personal connections to members of Congress. Former legislators have the kind of connections that it would take an outsider hundreds of hours in schmoozing and thousands of dollars in campaign contributions to develop. Thus, the true crown jewels of the lobbying world are popular former Congress people who retain the ability to donate to congressional candidates through their fundraising committees.

Ethics rules prohibit members of Congress and officials in the executive branch from lobbying their former colleagues for a year after leaving office. However, this does not prevent some individuals from reaching agreements with lobbying firms before they are even out of office. The logic for lobbying firms is twofold. First, former Congress members know the ins and outs of the legislative process and often have a grip on complex issues. Thus, hiring them as lobbying strategists is worthwhile even if they themselves can't lobby for a year. Second, reeling in a big-name Congressperson such as former Democratic Congressional Campaign Committee Chairman Vic Fazio (D-Calif.) gives a lobbying firm luster that can attract potential clients.

Lawmakers view lobbyists as key players in the legislative process. For legislators and their aides, lobbyists are sources of ideas on legislation or information about arcane issues. At times, *lobbyists even write proposed bills and amendments* that lawmakers introduce as their own. At a minimum, lawmakers get feedback from lobbyists on legislation to prevent objections late in the legislative process. It is not unheard of for a congressional committee to request that lobbyists appear to comment on proposed legislative action or upcoming government reports. Congressmen hoping to get legislation passed or defeated often coordinate their activities with K Street in order to fully mobilize the relevant constituency.

Lobbying is also making a move into the twenty-first century by going on-line. Tony Podesta, the brother of the former White House Chief of Staff, renamed his lobbying firm podesta.com. Lobbyists are creating Web sites with password-only chat rooms where lobbyists and legislators can get together to discuss pending bills and amendments. Moreover, lobbyists are turning to the Web to build grassroots support for or opposition to legislation that can pressure key Congressmen.

## TOP ISSUE AREAS

The lobbying disclosure forms lobbyists file with the House and Senate have a section that requires lobbyists to list the subjects on which they are lobbying. The House and Senate have developed 76 "issue area codes" that are used to identify the general issue on which lobbying occurs. Registrants must identify the names of each individual lobbyist working on each issue area. Ranging from accounting to welfare, the issue area codes are the most consistent indiCator of what the hot-button issues were in 1999.

The table below contains the number of individual lobbyists, clients, and registrants that lobbied on each issue area code. Not surprisingly, tax policy was the biggest issue, with nearly a quarter of Washington's 12,113 active lobbyists attempting to weigh in on some aspect of the tax code. Similarly, 1,053 of 3,587 registrants lobbied on tax issues. However, the budget was the issue in which the highest number of clients were interested; 1,800 of 8,145 active clients lobbied on appropriations or the budget.

Note that many lobbyists, clients, and registrants lobby on more than one issue. Therefore, the sum of the lobbyists column is far higher than the 12,113 lobbyists who were active in 1999.

| Rank | Issue Code | Issue Name | Lobbyists | Clients | Registrants |
|------|-----------|-----------|-----------|---------|-------------|
| 1 | TAX | Taxation/Internal Revenue Code | 2,945 | 1,411 | 1,053 |
| 2 | BUD | Budget/Appropriations | 2,689 | 1,800 | 880 |
| 3 | HCR | Health Issues | 2,444 | 1,137 | 853 |
| 4 | TRD | Trade (Domestic & Foreign) | 2,047 | 824 | 682 |
| 5 | ENV | Enviromental/Superfund | 1,878 | 865 | 655 |
| 6 | DEF | Defense | 1,358 | 921 | 505 |
| 7 | MMM | Medicare/Medicaid | 1,332 | 666 | 422 |
| 8 | TRA | Transportation | 1,266 | 810 | 491 |
| 9 | TEC | Telecommunications | 1,247 | 414 | 394 |
| 10 | LBR | Labor Issues/Antitrust/Workplace | 1,234 | 484 | 478 |
| 11 | GOV | Government Issues | 1,105 | 484 | 402 |
| 12 | ENG | Energy/Nuclear | 1,013 | 468 | 383 |
| 13 | EDU | Education | 1,008 | 505 | 377 |
| 14 | BAN | Banking | 890 | 379 | 316 |
| 15 | FIN | Financial Institutions/Investments/Securities | 770 | 294 | 283 |
| 16 | CPT | Copyright/Patent/Trademark | 755 | 298 | 290 |
| 17 | CAW | Clean Air & Water (Quality) | 754 | 360 | 293 |
| 18 | AGR | Agriculture | 733 | 434 | 321 |
| 19 | AVI | Aviation/Aircraft/Airlines | 727 | 291 | 237 |
| 20 | UTI | Utilities | 702 | 265 | 272 |
| 21 | NAT | Natural Resources | 689 | 387 | 246 |
| 22 | CPI | Computer Industry | 642 | 209 | 200 |
| 23 | FOR | Foreign Relations | 631 | 265 | 215 |
| 24 | LAW | Law Enforcement/Crime/Criminal Justice | 617 | 273 | 228 |
| 25 | BNK | Bankruptcy | 593 | 183 | 197 |
| 26 | SCI | Science/Technology | 592 | 307 | 262 |
| 27 | INS | Insurance | 572 | 212 | 213 |
| 28 | COM | Communications/Broadcasting/Radio/TV | 563 | 222 | 197 |
| 29 | CSP | Consumer Issues/Safety/Protection | 523 | 205 | 191 |
| 30 | MED | Medical/Disease Research/Clinical Labs | 523 | 240 | 181 |
| 31 | HOU | Housing | 513 | 224 | 175 |
| 32 | IMM | Immigration | 499 | 220 | 195 |
| 33 | WAS | Waste (hazardous/solid/interstate/nuclear) | 456 | 203 | 191 |
| 34 | FOO | Food Industry (Safety, Labeling, etc.) | 440 | 168 | 152 |
| 35 | MAR | Marine/Maritime/Boating/Fisheries | 429 | 242 | 175 |
| 36 | RET | Retirement | 403 | 142 | 147 |
| 37 | FUE | Fuel/Gas/Oil | 400 | 140 | 132 |
| 38 | TOB | Tobacco | 367 | 96 | 131 |
| 39 | SMB | Small Business | 353 | 122 | 122 |
| 40 | ECN | Economics/Economic Development | 341 | 217 | 133 |

| Rank | Issue Code | Issue Name | Lobbyists | Clients | Registrants |
|---|---|---|---|---|---|
| 41 | PHA | Pharmacy | 333 | 105 | 108 |
| 42 | RES | Real Estate/Land Use/Conservation | 333 | 159 | 116 |
| 43 | RRR | Railroads | 323 | 100 | 131 |
| 44 | IND | Indian/Native American Affairs | 305 | 197 | 111 |
| 45 | POS | Postal | 287 | 86 | 105 |
| 46 | CIV | Civil Rights/Civil Liberties | 273 | 94 | 93 |
| 47 | TOR | Torts | 260 | 100 | 107 |
| 48 | DIS | Disaster Planning/Emergencies | 228 | 104 | 95 |
| 49 | AER | Aerospace | 223 | 92 | 83 |
| 50 | ROD | Roads/Highway | 215 | 110 | 84 |
| 51 | ALC | Alcohol & Drug Abuse | 205 | 72 | 68 |
| 52 | WEL | Welfare | 205 | 108 | 90 |
| 53 | VET | Veterans | 203 | 74 | 68 |
| 54 | ART | Arts/Entertainment | 201 | 99 | 71 |
| 55 | MAN | Manufacturing | 200 | 126 | 113 |
| 56 | AUT | Automotive Industry | 197 | 65 | 80 |
| 57 | GAM | Gaming/Gambling/Casino | 196 | 90 | 76 |
| 58 | FAM | Family Issues/Abortion/Adoption | 194 | 65 | 68 |
| 59 | CHM | Chemicals/Chemical Industry | 179 | 71 | 75 |
| 60 | URB | Urban Development/Municipalities | 177 | 120 | 76 |
| 61 | TRU | Trucking/Shipping | 155 | 60 | 63 |
| 62 | CON | Constitution | 141 | 49 | 53 |
| 63 | ANI | Animals | 134 | 58 | 55 |
| 64 | BEV | Beverage Industry | 125 | 30 | 47 |
| 65 | FIR | Firearms/Guns/Ammunition | 114 | 46 | 43 |
| 66 | TOU | Travel/Tourism | 101 | 49 | 40 |
| 67 | ADV | Advertising | 91 | 36 | 30 |
| 68 | APP | Apparel/Clothing Industry/Textiles | 75 | 41 | 34 |
| 69 | MIA | Media (Information/Publishing) | 67 | 30 | 27 |
| 70 | MON | Minting/Money/Gold Standard | 58 | 27 | 27 |
| 71 | CDT | Commodities (Big Ticket) | 55 | 19 | 17 |
| 72 | REL | Religion | 54 | 18 | 18 |
| 73 | SPO | Sports/Athletics | 52 | 30 | 28 |
| 74 | DOC | District of Columbia | 51 | 20 | 20 |
| 75 | ACC | Accounting | 38 | 17 | 15 |
| 76 | UNM | Unemployment | 16 | 10 | 10 |
| Total | | Unique Lobbyists, Clients, or Registrants | 12,113 | 8,145 | 3,587 |

Note: Lobbying figures are for calendar year 1999; campaign contributions figures are for the 1999-2000 election cycle and reflect data released by the Federal Election Commission by April 1, 2001.

(Source: *Lobbying: Influence Inc 2000*, by Larry Makinson and Sheila Krumholz et. al., The Center for Responsive Politics, opensecrets. org/lobby/lobby00/summary.php, copyright The Center for Responsive Politics, used with permission)

Looking at this long list, one thing becomes evident: the government reaches into almost every aspect of our lives. It's also obvious that every industry and group in America is reaching into the pockets of the government. Our treasury is indeed being looted by lobbyists, politicians and special interests. Behind the government of politicians lies a shadow government of at least 12,000 lobbyists pushing their case for themselves and their clients. One has to wonder, looking at how much influence lobbyists have with congressmen, if there is anyone in Washington lobbying for the American people? Obviously not. The power behind our government—the lobbyists—are well funded and well connected. Our government, elected to represent the people, is listening not to the people, but the 12,000 lobbyists. Lobbyists even influence grass-roots movements—nothing is sacred in politics except money and influence.

Not surprising, taxation and tax code was the most lobbied issue. More lobbyists, clients, and registrants signed up to get changes made in the tax code than any other issue. In his best-selling book *Perfectly Legal* Pulitzer prize-winning author David Cay Johnston profiles "the covert campaign to rig our tax system to benefit the super rich—and cheat everybody else." He further states "whether your family makes $30,000 or $300,000 a year, you are being robbed because the IRS and other institutions have been systematically corrupted—under both Republican and Democratic administrations—to serve the needs of people making millions…how the tax code and many other laws have been twisted over the past three decades to subsidize the richest and most powerful fraction of 1 percent of our country." The rich hire lobbyists, who corrupt politicians and get favorable tax policies for themselves. Politicians can easily change language in the tax code to favor lobbyists, or can simply enact tax breaks or tax holidays for specific groups represented by lobbyists. Nowhere else except in Washington is it possible to get such political favors (except state governments, which are also lobbied). With the proper amount of money and hiring a lobbyist, you can get whatever you want.

Our government has become an open access system, not to the people our country, but to lobbyists, unions, special interests, political action committees. Yet, it is a closed access system to everyone except those hired lobbyists that have access to our politicians. Anyone can play this system, however, if they have enough money. All you have to do is form a special interest group, collect a pile of money, hire some lawyers/lobbyists, and decide how you want the government to *work for you*. Removed from all these proceedings are silly ideas like "right and wrong," "just or unjust," "moral or immoral" "corrupt or not corrupt" and "good or bad." These things don't matter to lawyers, lobbyists and politicians, only how much money and influence you can afford to pay. This is not democracy at work; our government has become something much different.

# House Appropriations Committee 111th Congress (2010 cycle): Overview

*Rep. David R. Obey (D-Wis), Chair*

*Rep. Jerry Lewis (R-Calif), Ranking Member*

When Congress sets the budgets for all the federal agencies every summer, there is no committee busier or more lobbied than House Appropriations. The committee does not just provide funding for lucrative government contracts, but is also famous for inserting last-minute industry-backed provisions riders blocking regulatory actions interest groups oppose. Since the committee deals with funding for agencies that regulate a variety of interests, members attract donations from a variety of interests including health professionals, defense contractors, and oil and gas companies.

| Sectors Contributing to Members of this Committee, 2010 Election Cycle |
| --- |

| ▓ FROM PACS ░ FROM INDIVIDUALS |
| --- |

| Agribusiness | |
| --- | --- |
| Communic/Electronics | |
| Construction | |
| Defense | |
| Energy/Nat Resource | |
| Finance/Insur/RealEst | |
| Health | |
| Lawyers & Lobbyists | |
| Transportation | |
| Misc Business | |
| Labor | |
| Ideology/Single-Issue | |
| Other | |

Figures are based on Federal Election Commission data released electronically on August 22, 2010. Numbers are taken from PAC donations and individual contributions of more than $200

(Source: Originally published by The Center for Responsive Politics, OpenSecrets.org, copyright The Center for Responsive Politics, used with permission)

# House Financial Services Committee 111th Congress (2010 cycle): Overview

*Rep. Barney Frank (D-Mass), Chair*

*Rep. Spencer Bachus (R-Ala), Ranking Member*

This committee, formerly known as the Banking Committee, has long been considered a "big money" panel, with jurisdiction over commercial banks and savings and loans that traditionally have been very generous with their campaign contributions to committee members. That trend has continued with the addition of two cash-rich industries to the committee's portfolio: insurance and securities. Look for the giant financial sector, which includes banks, insurance companies, and securities firms, to continue its robust giving to committee members.

| Sectors Contributing to Members of this Committee, 2010 Election Cycle | |
|---|---|
| ▮ FROM PACS ▮ FROM INDIVIDUALS | |
| Agribusiness | ▮ |
| Communic/Electronics | ▮▮ |
| Construction | ▮ |
| Defense | ▮ |
| Energy/Nat Resource | ▮ |
| Finance/Insur/RealEst | ▮▮▮▮▮▮▮▮▮▮▮▮ |
| Health | ▮▮ |
| Lawyers & Lobbyists | ▮▮ |
| Transportation | ▮ |
| Misc Business | ▮▮ |
| Labor | ▮▮▮ |
| Ideology/Single-Issue | ▮▮ |
| Other | ▮▮ |

Figures are based on Federal Election Commission data released electronically on August 22, 2010. Numbers are taken from PAC donations and individual contributions of more than $200.

This committee has jurisdiction over a few select, identifiable groups: Accountants, Commercial Banks, Credit Unions, Finance/Credit companies, home builders, insurance, real estate, savings and loans, and securities and investments.

(Source: Originally published by The Center for Responsive Politics, OpenSecrets.org, copyright The Center for Responsive Politics, used with permission)

# House Ways and Means Committee 111th Congress (2010 cycle): Overview

*Rep. Sander Levin (D-Mich), Chair*

*Rep. Dave Camp (R-Mich), Ranking Member*

When Congress is drafting tax legislation, there is no committee busier and more popular than House Ways and Means. Lobbyists often pay people to stand in the corridors of Congress watching every move. Because when it comes to this type of complex legislation, every detail counts for something. Special interests often use these behemoth bills as vehicles for their legislative wish lists, hoping the sheer size of the proposals will divert attention from their sought-after provisions. Since tax bills affect so many industries' bottom lines, its little surprise that members should attract generous donations from a variety of sources, including health professionals and insurance companies.

| Sectors Contributing to Members of this Committee, 2010 Election Cycle | |
|---|---|
| | FROM PACS    FROM INDIVIDUALS |
| Agribusiness | |
| Communic/Electronics | |
| Construction | |
| Defense | |
| Energy/Nat Resource | |
| Finance/Insur/RealEst | |
| Health | |
| Lawyers & Lobbyists | |
| Transportation | |
| Misc Business | |
| Labor | |
| Ideology/Single-Issue | |
| Other | |

Figures are based on Federal Election Commission data released electronically on August 22, 2010. Numbers are taken from PAC donations and individual contributions of more than $200

You get the idea pretty quickly after looking at these charts—pay money to the politician-members and get legislation drafted the way *you* want. Why look at committees?

When the President signs a major piece of legislation into law, what Americans see are the much-hyped and well-attended ceremonies. What they don't see is the road the bill traveled. That road starts in the committees and subcommittees of Congress where members hold hearings, draft, debate, and revise legislation — and where each word is carefully crafted. It is during these meetings — usually held behind closed doors — that the real action takes place and special interests and consumer groups pay closest attention. Because it is at this point during the legislative process that they can change America's public policies. In short, congressional committees are the legislative trenches — and the bigger the bill, the higher the stakes, the more generous the campaign donations to members of the committee with jurisdiction over the issue.

That's one reason these congressional committee assignments are so important and competitive. Lawmakers who win seats on the lucrative banking, tax-writing, or commerce committees quite often enhance their campaign war chests from industries seeking to influence legislative outcomes. Many newly elected members tend to start getting donations from special interests based on their new appointments. Lobbyists and special interests have almost unlimited access to our legislative processes and money, and pay politicians to get what they want—all in back room, closed door deals away from the eyes of the American public.

## *Congressional Members' Personal Wealth Expands Despite Sour National Economy: Members of Congress are enjoying their own financial stimulus*

Despite a stubbornly sour national economy congressional members' personal wealth collectively increased by more than 16 percent between 2008 and 2009, according to a new study by *the Center for Responsive Politics* of federal financial disclosures released earlier this year.

And while some members' financial portfolios lost value, no need to bemoan most lawmakers' financial lot: Nearly half of them — 261 — are millionaires, a slight increase from the previous year, the Center's study finds. That compares to about 1 percent of Americans who lay claim to the same lofty fiscal status. And of these congressional millionaires, 55 have an average calculated wealth in 2009 of $10 million or more, with eight in the $100 million-plus range.

"Few federal lawmakers must grapple with the financial ills — unemployment, loss of housing, wiped out savings — that have befallen millions of Americans," said Sheila Krumholz, the Center for Responsive Politics' executive director. "Congressional representatives on balance rank among the wealthiest of wealthy Americans and boast financial portfolios that are all but unattainable for most of their constituents."

In 2009, the median wealth of a U.S. House member stood at $765,010, up from $645,503 in 2008. The median wealth of a U.S. senator was nearly $2.38 million, up from $2.27 million in 2008. For all members of Congress regardless of chamber, median wealth in 2009 reached $911,510, up from $785,515 in 2008. This spike in personal wealth represents a notable rebound from the period between 2007 and 2008, when overall congressional wealth slipped by more than 5 percent. Federal lawmakers' personal wealth climaxed in 2007 — the pinnacle of nearly a decade's worth of steady asset value expansion.

## MANY CONGRESSIONAL HAVES, BUT A FEW HAVE-NOTS, TOO

When averaging lawmakers' minimum and maximum potential wealth for 2009, Rep. Darrell Issa (R-Calif.) tops the list with holdings exceeding $303.5 million. Issa is followed by a fellow Californian, Rep. Jane Harman (D-Calif.), with $293.4 million. Sen. John Kerry (D-Mass.) places third at $238.8 million.

Issa, Harman and Kerry realized wealth gains of nearly 21 percent, 19.8 percent and 14.3 percent respectively. Sen. Mark Warner (D-Va.), Rep. Jared Polis (D-Colo.), Sen. Herb Kohl (D-Wis.), Rep. Vernon Buchanan (R-Fla.) and Rep. Michael McCaul (R-Texas) round the list of lawmakers who in 2009 recorded an average wealth of at least $100 million.

In the House, there are five Democrats and five Republicans among the 10 wealthiest members. On the Senate side, six Democrats and four Republicans rank among the top 10 wealthiest. On the other end of the wealth spectrum is Rep. Alcee Hastings (D-Fla.), whose average calculated wealth for 2009 is a bank-busting -$4.73 million. But because of the broad ranges lawmakers may use to report their assets and liabilities, Hastings could be even deeper in the red — -$7.35 million at worst — or a more minor anti-millionaire at -$2.11 million in the hole.

Meanwhile, Rep. Charles Rangel (D-N.Y.), who a House Ethics Committee panel convicted on 11 counts of ethics violations — including improper disclosure of his personal finances — reported assets of $872,006 in 2009. That's above the median amount for a House member.

## POWERFUL POLITICAL PLAYERS AMONG MOST POPULAR INVESTMENTS

The most popular investments among congressional members reads as a who's who list of the most powerful corporate political forces in Washington, D.C. — companies that each spend millions, if not tens of millions of dollars each year lobbying federal officials. Many of them likewise donate millions of dollars to federal candidates each election cycle through their top employees and political action committees. With 82 current members of Congress invested, General Electric tops this list. It's followed by Bank of America (63), Cisco Systems (61), Proctor & Gamble (61) and Microsoft (54).

Apple, with 42 current congressional investors, edges IBM, with 41. Coca-Cola's 39 congressional investors pop it a notch above PepsiCo, with 36. And at least 20 current members of Congress were also last year invested in companies that found themselves the subject of congressional or federal agency inquiries, including Goldman Sachs and BP.

Furthermore, the companies behind a number of lawmakers' favorite investments played key roles in lobbying Congress on two of the most critical legislative initiatives of the past two years: healthcare reform and financial regulatory reform. Among healthcare-related companies, at least 20 current lawmakers reported owning stakes in Pfizer (49), Johnson & Johnson (39), Merck (27), Abbott Laboratories (25), CVS/Caremark (23), Bristol-Myers Squibb (22) and Amgen (20). As for financial firms, Bank of American and Goldman Sachs are joined by Wells Fargo (45), JPMorgan Chase (38) and Citigroup (24). In all, there were 50 separate stocks or investment funds in which at least 20 current members of Congress invested during 2009. Most of these financial firms received government bailouts, and are some of the favorite investments of those giving them the bailouts – politicians.

(Source: *Congressional Members' Personal Wealth Expands Despite Sour National Economy*, opensecretsblog: Investigating money in politics. Contact: Dave Levinthal. By Communications on November 17, 2010, opensecrets.org. Used with permission)

Politicians are in bed with lobbyists, banks, Wall Street and big corporations in more ways than you can imagine. Owning stock is the same as owning a piece of the company. David Weidner reports in his story *Banks to Taxpayers: Get Over It* for Yahoo! Finance/MarketWatch that after the bank/Wall Street bailout was passed by politicians "The Federal Reserve unveiled…the final tally – $3.3 trillion…Morgan Stanley borrowed $61 billion in one overnight loan. Goldman Sachs Group Inc. hit up the Fed 81 times for a combined $600 billion. Citigroup Inc. and Bank of America Corp. borrowed a combined $2.6 trillion under the Fed's primary dealer facility. Even J.P. Morgan Chase & Co used the central bank's term auction facility seven times." Despite Americans clearly not wanting bank and Wall Street bailouts, politicians allowed Citibank and Bank of America to receive $2.6 trillion from the government in bailouts/loans because at least 60 congressmen may have owned stock in these companies; and at least 40 congressmen may have owned Goldman Sachs and JPMorgan Chase stock while giving them $600 billion from the treasury. Maybe this clears up their motivation—they were looking after the interests of their stock portfolios, not the interests of the American people. Politicians are even allowed to "insider trade," use information they may have gotten from a business or client that is illegal to everyone else. If a politician has big stock holdings in a company, they will almost surely give the company any financial, tax, bailout, loan, or subsidy help they may require—it would only be prudent to do so—to protect their investment. This quickly becomes the *very definition* of "conflict of interest" and corruption. It's not surprising that politicians hold stocks in the companies that spend the most on lobbying; it's just another way they can cash in on their positions in government.

**In conclusion**, it's easy to see the record of wreckage that has been wrought by lawyers, and lawyers turned politicians (and politicians turned lobbyists). Lobbyists compose a system of "shadow government," or as Theodore Roosevelt stated *"Behind the ostensible government sits enthroned an invisible government owing no allegiance and acknowledging no responsibility to the people."* In this chapter, again with special thanks to *The Center for Responsive Politics* (opensecrets.org), you can see who is really running our government—and it's not the people of the U.S. The politicians—mostly lawyers and mostly millionaires—don't reflect or represent the people of the U.S. You can also see that politics is a huge business. In the year 2000 study there were almost 13,000 lobbyists. Considering the amount of money spent on lobbying more than doubled by 2009, it's reasonable to assume the number of lobbyists in action today is even higher. There is also the 10-1 rule: for every dollar spent on lobbying, you can get $10 of pork, ear marks, deregulation, tax breaks, subsidies, special consideration, or line-item rewards, all courtesy of the taxpayer's bank of the U.S. Oh, wait, there isn't such a bank, it's just money from taxes, your money, money you worked hard for, sent to Washington and *given away* by politicians in many multiples of what they receive from lobbyists. The 10-1 rule is probably too conservative—Agribusiness and the farm lobby got 195-1 return on their money spent on lobbyists.

With the vast sums of money the government is spending, especially on things like stimulus, which is completely untargeted pork spending, it's easy to "follow the money" out of Washington and into the pockets of firms and companies that hired the lobbyists. Not to be outdone, politicians own stock in some of the very companies they are giving political favors to. Anyone who still believes we have a real Democracy doesn't have to look any further than this lobbying data to find out they are wrong.

Politicians don't want to get elected to represent the "people back home," they want to get elected to have a chance at cashing in on the billions of dollars that are up for grabs from lobbyists and special interests. At any given time, there are 12,000 to 14,000 registered lobbyists pressing their case to politicians that are supposed to be running our government *for us*. It's government of the highest bidder, not a democracy. It's better than the lottery, and all you have to do to get your ticket punched is to win an election. Even if you lose an election, or get driven out as an incumbent, you can open up a lobbying business and start making millions of dollars a year (instead of the paltry sum you get paid as a congressman or senator). You simply go back to where you used to work (the government) and start handing out money and contributions to those you used to work with.

And it's apparent from data released since the "too big to fail" bank and Wall Street bailouts that politicians may have approved these bailouts/loans despite what the American people wanted because they owned stock in the same companies that got $3.3 trillion dollars from the Federal Reserve and Treasury. Already-wealthy politicians may vote and pass massive spending bills and bailouts based on their stock portfolios, not the will of the American people.

Corruption is (as defined by Merriam-Webster): a: *impairment of integrity, virtue, or moral principle : depravity* b : *decay, decomposition* c : *inducement to wrong by improper or unlawful means (as bribery)* d : *a departure from the original or from what is pure or correct*. Yes, that definition pretty well nails what is going on in Washington. People may wonder how things got this bad—but how could it be otherwise? We elect and send mostly lawyers to Washington, where they have unlimited access to the biggest checking account in the U.S. (a checking account you fund), with free reign to tax, spend, and borrow as much money as they want. They control lawmaking, so they passed laws that allowed lobbyists, special interests, unions, and political action committees to spend billions to loot our government and get what they want from politicians with little or no oversight.

Remember the saying "power and money corrupt, and absolute power and money corrupt absolutely?" It was an observation (slightly changed) by Lord Acton, a British historian that a person's sense of morality lessens as his or her power and wealth increases. We have a powerful ruling political class that is not concerned with morality, just or unjust, right or wrong, only what's legal; and the same ruling class that has *empowered itself to determine what is legal*. It's the ultimate form of corruption; and may turn out to be the superlative and most expensive example of corruption the world has ever seen. How can the will of the people ever be heard in a system that accepts this kind of money and influence from special interests and lobbyists? It can't and it won't be heard—and some people are starting to finally wake up to this fact. There is a better way.

# CHAPTER 5

---

# Healthcare

**The care of human life and happiness, and not their destruction, is the first and only object of good government.**

*Thomas Jefferson*

Healthcare costs in the U.S. and health insurance has been a hot topic for several decades. Since the mid 1990's, the health insurance industry has taken over healthcare in the U.S. and has taken over ever larger portions of our tax dollars that are supposed to be spent on healthcare. With some swift lobbying and pressure, the health insurance companies even managed to get control of the prescription drug market during the Bush Administration with the passage of Medicare Part D (remember that?). Any talk of wasteful government and government spending must deal with healthcare and health insurance companies first and foremost.

It is simply staggering how much money is spent by the government every year for Medicaid and Medicare. The thing is, the government doesn't really want to have to administer healthcare benefits, they want people to have healthcare, and they are willing to pay hundreds of billions for it. There was even a provision in the original ObamaCare bill were the government would administer health benefits, as an option to the health insurers. But guess what, lobbyists had that taken out of the bill. Almost all the money that's going to be spent on healthcare under the ObamaCare bill (if it's not repealed) is going to go to health insurers, one way or another. It has to, they already control everything. This couldn't be better news for the health insurance companies, who say, in essence, "We'll cover people, just show us the money." The government has shown them the money. The cost of ObamaCare is going to be more than anyone can imagine as various agencies and think tanks try and come to terms with future costs and spending. Instead of fixing a broken system to provide healthcare, it "doubles down" on a system that doesn't work. (If Obamacare is repealed or voted "unconstitutional" or is otherwise voided, you will have to disregard several of the sections).

## First, a little history...

In 1929, the first modern group health insurance plan was formed. A group of teachers in Dallas, Texas, contracted with Baylor Hospital for room, board, and medical services in exchange for a monthly fee. Several large life insurance companies entered the health insurance field in the 1930's and 1940's as the popularity of health insurance increased. In 1932 nonprofit organizations called Blue Cross or Blue Shield first offered group health plans. Blue Cross and Blue Shield Plans were successful because they involved discounted contracts negotiated with doctors and hospitals. In return for promises of increased volume and prompt payment, providers gave discounts to the Blue Cross and Shield plans. The third party payer system was born. Keep in mind, the original group health plan was "nonprofit" (more on this later).

Employee benefit plans proliferated in the 1940's and 1950's. Strong unions bargained for better benefit packages, including tax-free, employer-sponsored health insurance. Wartime (1939-1945) wage freezes imposed by the government actually accelerated the spread of group healthcare. Unable by law to attract workers by paying more, employers instead improved their benefit packages, adding healthcare.

Government programs to cover healthcare costs began to expand during the 1950s and 1960s. Disability benefits were included in Social Security coverage for the first time in 1954. When the government created Medicare and Medicaid programs in 1965, private sources still paid 75 percent of all the healthcare costs. By 1995, individuals and companies only paid for about half of the healthcare with the government responsible for the other half.

During the 1980's and 1990's, the cost of healthcare rose rapidly and the majority of employer-sponsored group insurance plans switched from "fee-for-service" plans to the cheaper "managed care plans." As a result, most Americans with health insurance were enrolled in managed care plans by the mid-1990s. Since then, there has been massive consolidation, with five major health plans (United Healthcare, Wellpoint, Humana, Cigna, Aetna) owning the market.

For some reason, in the U.S., people equate having health insurance with actually having healthcare goods and services paid for. This is a pathological and often fatal mistake. People fail to see the link in the middle, the health insurance company. People need healthcare, not health insurance, but to a man they equate having health insurance with actually getting healthcare. On the other hand, you have the healthcare system; the doctors, hospitals, nurses, imaging and lab services in the U.S., arguably the best healthcare system in the world. We are always there, 24/7, ready and willing to save lives, promote health, and treat illness. On the one hand people that need to use the healthcare system, and on the other, the best healthcare system in the world. But look at what has happened, a middleman has stepped into the equation—the health insurance companies. People that want healthcare are more than willing to give their money for health insurance, and the healthcare system wants to get paid for their work. People that *want* healthcare instead *get* health insurance (not healthcare). Let's hope you can see the difference. The result is *for-profit corporations* that collect money and ration out healthcare.

The people with health insurance and the healthcare system are being held hostage by an industry that doesn't actually make or produce anything, doesn't actually function in any healthcare capacity at all, except to make profit. Profit, the ever increasing insurance premiums for health insurance, and the rationing or withholding of care (to keep profits) works great for the health insurance companies and their stock-holders, but doesn't work for either of the parties they are supposed to be serving (people that need healthcare, and the healthcare providers).

In fact, health insurance has become a massive black-hole, sucking hundreds of billions of dollars out of healthcare every year, and resulting in fewer and fewer people actually getting any healthcare. Even the people that have coverage have deductibles, co pays, and denial of service, that add untold billions to the cost of simply obtaining healthcare. Who do we look to for protection against this black hole? The government – which buckles to health insurance lobbyists at every turn. Instead of just being a black hole for businesses and people that work, now tax dollars are thrown into the health insurance black hole.

## Government Subsidies for health insurance

It's bad enough that government and politicians are going to force millions of people to get health insurance (or pay a fine). The government already subsidies health insurance companies in a big way. Way back during WWII, wage caps wouldn't allow businesses to give raises, but they were allowed to pay for health insurance for their employees. The U.S. government allowed this money spent on health insurance to become a tax break. It later became law, that money spent by businesses and employees would come out pre-tax. By allowing the purchase of health insurance to come out pre-tax, it was a tax-break, and therefore a government subsidy. It remains so today.

Businesses that want to provide health benefits are forced to buy health insurance, and more than 175 million Americans are benefitting from this government subsidy (that's the number of people that have health insurance from their job). The health insurance companies are also benefitting from this subsidy. It results in people buying more health insurance than they may need, and paying larger premiums since it all comes out of pay that isn't yet taxed. Health Insurers have been able to get away with just about anything because employers and workers feel they are getting something for nothing, thanks to the tax break. Also thanks to this tax break, businesses and people tolerate up to 30-40% increases in premiums every year. While businesses and employees seem happy with this set-up, it's not until they try to use their insurance that they find out what they really have. People that have to buy health insurance on the "open market" get no such tax break, and are forced to take what they can get.

## The big lie, the big scam: assuming health insurance will actually cover your medical bills

People still think that their healthcare will magically be paid for if they have health insurance. Again, this is the big lie, the big scam. Want proof? Let's say you are lucky enough to have a job, and lucky enough again that your job has health benefits. So, maybe you have to pay a few hundred dollars a month yourself for health insurance, at least you're covered, right? So, maybe you budget. You make allowances for food, clothes, car, whatever. But do you have an allowance for medical costs? No, not the hundreds of dollars you pay for health insurance at work, money for medical costs. Here's why you should: The No. 1 cause of bankruptcy in the U.S. is medical bills. Harvard Law Professor and co-director of the *Bankruptcy Database Project at Harvard* Elizabeth Warren and her colleagues found that 62 percent of all bankruptcies are caused by medical bills. Even more disturbing: <u>78 percent of those were people who *had* health insurance</u>. In 2009, 1.4 million people declared bankruptcy. Doing the math, roughly 677,000 of the people that declared bankruptcy in 2009 because of medical bills *had health insurance*. A whopping 677,000 declared bankruptcy because of medical bills *even though they thought they were covered* for healthcare costs by having health insurance. Obviously, they were wrong and found out about "the big lie" too late.

In the law review article *Beyond Hospital Misbehavior: An alternative account of medical related financial distress* (by Melissa B. Jacoby & Elizabeth Warren,, Northwestern University Law Review 2006; Vol. 100, No. 2, pgs. 536-580) "Almost seven out of ten (67.4%) medical filers (for bankruptcy) said all family members had insurance at the time of the filing. Among the telephone survey medical (bankruptcy) sample, more than three-quarters reported that the ill or injured person(s) had insurance at illness onset. *More than eight out of ten (82.7%) of the ill or injured person(s) in the telephone survey medical bankruptcy sample were insured* at the time of the telephone interview. Yet, medical debt caused financial difficulty for the insured (that filed for bankruptcy). Indeed, those with private insurance at illness onset reported higher out-of-pocket costs on average ($13,460) than those *uninsured* at illness onset ($10,893)."

People *with* health insurance actually paid more money out-of-pocket for health expenses than people that had *no* health insurance. Having health insurance doesn't really guarantee anything, except that you are going to have to pay health insurance premiums. The health insurance companies have tens of thousands of people whose job it is to figure out ways not to pay claims, to stick the consumer with some or all the cost of getting healthcare, and make sure that insurance premiums continue to rise year after year no matter what. Ask one of the 677,000 people that had health insurance why they had to declare bankruptcy because of medical bills how it happened. They had health insurance, but still had such overwhelming healthcare bills that they were forced to declare bankruptcy? How can that be? Isn't health insurance supposed to cover healthcare costs? Appearently not. So, while the government continues to give more money and control to health insurance companies, they will continue to hire more people to figure out ways not to pay for healthcare and put more money into their own pocket (all with the government's blessing).

## Why so many people with health insurance have to declare bankruptcy...

Health insurers often times pay whatever they want, not what is billed. How they get away with this is simple. They have created a system called UCR (usual, customary, and reasonable rates). This is insurance-speak for health insurance companies paying whatever *they* think they should pay. Using complicated formulas, questionable data, and simple lies, *they* set prices for what they will pay in any given area. For example (actual case), a woman has breast cancer, has surgery, chemo, and is eventually cured. The total bill for these services is $90,000. Most people with health insurance don't have full coverage anyway, but in this case a 70/30 policy, where they must pay 30% right off the top (plus deductible).

The first health insurance scam kicks in—partial coverage. You felt magically secure, because you had health insurance, but then you get sick, and suddenly realize 70/30 means you have to pay 30% yourself (plus deductible), and the security of having health insurance evaporates. So, the person is already stuck paying $31,000 out-of-pocket. Then the second health insurance scam kicks in: the doctors send in their bills, and the hospital sends in their bill. The insurance company calculates a UCR rate, which is all they are going to pay. This UCR rate is typically 30% lower than the bills they receive. Most doctors will accept 70% of what they billed, knowing otherwise they will be fighting with the insurer for years. Hospitals, however, do not accept 30% less, and send a bill to the person that had breast cancer (instead of going after the health insurance company). So, the person gets an additional bill for close to $20,000. Now the "insured person" has to pay more than $51,000 out of pocket even though they had health insurance. Most people don't have this much laying around and soon present themselves to the bankruptcy attorney. After getting home from declaring bankruptcy, the third insurance scam comes in the mail; a letter saying "we're dropping your health insurance."

## *Further strategies health insurers use not to pay:*

As a means of further reducing costs, many carriers are now routinely offering products that reimburse members based on a scheduled fee basis rather than UCR. Most common is to set their schedule of reimbursement as a percentage of Medicare reimbursements, or RVRBS (Resource Based Relative Value Studies). These schedules can pay providers approximately 30-50% less than the average UCR reimbursements.

- A class action suit filed against United Healthcare and Metropolitan Life Insurance challenging the method of calculating usual, customary and reasonable charges (UCR) has been in progress since March 15, 2000. Although other lawsuits have been filed and won by both defendants and plaintiffs, this is arguably the most significant lawsuit of its kind.
- In February 2008, New York Attorney General Andrew Cuomo announced intentions to sue UnitedHealth Group, including its subsidiary Ingenix. Cuomo and the AMA maintain the data Ingenix uses to determine usual, customary and reasonable charges is manipulated and does not accurately represent the "going rates" for services.

(Source: *Usual, Customary and Reasonable, Benefits Factsheet*, 3/28/08, Arlen Group Employee Benefits, arlengroup.com/facts/fact_ucr.pdf)

Not satisfied with just paying 30 percent less for a bill via UCR, insurers are now using creative accounting to set their rates even lower—30 to 50% lower than UCR rates, so people with health insurance get stuck paying up to 80% of the bill themselves, even though they have health insurance. Not surprisingly, people are trying to sue health insurers over these rates. Health insurers simply make up payment schemes to stick the consumer with some or all healthcare costs, even though they have insurance. And instead of fighting legal battles in court, most health insurers simply lobby politicians in Washington to get laws enacted that protect them from lawsuits. It may be awhile until you see a United Healthcare commercial "you may feel safe because you have health insurance, and your policy may say we're going to pay 70% of your healthcare costs, but really, we're only going to pay 20%, if that, so make sure you keep sending us those premiums."

## *Data Mining*

Data mining is a term used to describe the using of data, much of it personal, for benefit of people or organizations that have access to it. Health Insurers employ data mining services to figure out ways not to pay for your healthcare. For example, your friendly home-town pharmacy and all the largest retailers (except Walmart) sell your data to drug companies and health insurers. After mining this data, they can determine that someone is not taking their medication as prescribed or someone has a "pre-existing condition" that they didn't report on their health insurance application. The insured is then sent a letter. Say you aren't taking your generic Zocor, for high cholesterol, as prescribed, because you didn't get it refilled one month, they send you a letter saying that you are "non-compliant" with treatment, and if you have a heart attack or stroke, they aren't responsible and therefore won't pay that claim. The same goes for your diabetes medicine, blood-pressure medicine, and the rest.

You also leave a medical history footprint vis-à-vis the medications you've taken in the past—a footprint the health insurers can find out about to deny you insurance or deny claims. You suddenly aren't covered for a major and catastrophic illness even though you still pay your premium and "have health insurance." And this is only the tip of the iceberg. As health insurance companies become better at data mining, and when all medical records are digital, they will have unlimited access to data from the time you were a baby. They will also be able to data mine your parents and their medical problems, and use that data to deny insurance and care because of possible genetic problems you may be blessed with. For instance, if your mom had breast cancer, you (as a woman) are at higher risk for getting breast cancer yourself. Once the insurance company runs the data, you will be denied insurance, or denied treatment for breast cancer since it is yet another "pre-existing" condition. Despite those glossy happy T.V. commercials, there is almost no limit to what health insurance companies will do not to pay for your health-care. And with few regulations or anybody complaining loud enough, they will continue to get away with murder.

## Something good from ObamaCare?

Kathleen Sebelius, the U.S. secretary of Health and Human Services, wrote a piece in the online *Wall Street Journal* opinion section. It chronicles some of the positive things to come from Obamacare as well as her anger with the health insurance lobby. "In the past, health insurance companies ran wild with no accountability. Health insurance companies have been screaming lately. Why? They are being told that, as required by law, the government will review large premium increases. The health insurance lobby seems to believe that any oversight of the insurance industry is too much, and that consumers would be better off in a system where they have few rights or protections."

Over the past decade, Americans have seen what happens when insurance companies have free rein. The cost of health insurance has more than doubled, while millions of hard-working Americans lost their coverage or drained their savings to keep up with premiums. Employers—big and small—have struggled mightily to absorb these cost increases and have been losing the fight.

"Insurance premiums have gotten out of control. There are families who watched their insurance go up 20%, 30%, even 40% a year without explanation. Many small business owners have stopped offering health insurance to their employees because they couldn't afford the annual double-digit premium increases. Self-employed people, who contribute significantly to our economy, have no good options for health coverage. Yet even as our insurance markets have failed Americans time and time again, special interests successfully blocked reform."

Ms Sebelius goes on to say "That's supposed to change with the new health insurance law. Under the Affordable Care Act (ObamaCare), 46 states have already received grants to beef up their premium-review and oversight capabilities. As the state-based exchanges decide what plans to include, they must include recommendations from states about whether particular health insurance issuers should be excluded based on a pattern of excessive or unjustified premium increases."

"This already appears to be paying off. North Carolina's largest insurer announced a "one-time refund that will return $155.8 million to more than 215,000 individual Blue Cross Blue Shield customers as a result of the Affordable Care Act." This rebate will put an average of $720 back into the pockets of each of those policyholders. In addition, thanks to diligent work by North Carolina's insurance commissioner, they'll see their premiums rise by less than 6% in 2011—the smallest rate increase in four years. It's understandable that some insurance companies and their allies don't welcome this change. They've made large profits from the status quo." Instead of going after health insurance companies, which is what the Secretary of HHS should be doing, Obamacare will ultimately give more power and money to health insurers.

## *Unlike Law Schools, Medical Schools Can't Keep Up*

As the ranks of insured expand, our nation faces a shortage of 150,000 doctors in 15 years. The new federal healthcare law has raised the stakes for hospitals and schools already scrambling to train more doctors. Experts warn there won't be enough doctors to treat the millions of people newly insured under the ObamaCare. At current graduation and training rates, the nation could face a shortage of as many as 150,000 doctors in the next 15 years, according to the Association of American Medical Colleges (AAMC). That shortfall is predicted despite a push by teaching hospitals and medical schools to boost the number of U.S. doctors, which now totals about 954,000.

The greatest demand will be for primary-care physicians. These general practitioners, internists, family physicians and pediatricians will have a larger role under the new law, coordinating care for each patient. The U.S. has 352,908 primary-care doctors now, and the college association estimates that 45,000 more will be needed by 2020. But the number of medical-school students entering family medicine fell more than a quarter between 2002 and 2007.

A shortage of primary-care and other physicians could mean more-limited access to healthcare and longer wait times for patients. Proponents of the new healthcare law say it does attempt to address the physician shortage. The law offers sweeteners to encourage more people to enter medical professions, and a 10% Medicare pay boost for primary-care doctors.

Meanwhile, a number of new medical schools have opened around the country recently. As of last October, four new medical schools enrolled a total of about 190 students, and 12 medical schools raised the enrollment of first-year students by a total of 150 slots, according to the AAMC. Some 18,000 students entered U.S. medical schools in the fall of 2009, the AAMC says.

But medical colleges and hospitals warn that these efforts will hit a big bottleneck: There is a shortage of medical resident positions. The residency is the minimum three-year period when medical-school graduates train in hospitals and clinics. There are about 110,000 resident positions in the U.S., according to the AAMC. Teaching hospitals rely heavily on Medicare funding to pay for these slots. In 1997, Congress imposed a cap on funding for medical residencies, which hospitals say has increasingly hurt their ability to expand the number of positions.

Medicare pays $9.1 billion a year to teaching hospitals, which goes toward resident salaries and direct teaching costs, as well as the higher operating costs associated with teaching hospitals, which tend to see the sickest and most costly patients. Doctors' groups and medical schools had hoped that the new healthcare law, passed in March, would increase the number of funded residency slots, but such a provision didn't make it into the final bill.

"It will probably take 10 years to even make a dent into the number of doctors that we need out there," said Mr. Grover, the AAMC's chief advocacy officer. While doctors trained in other countries could theoretically help the primary-care shortage, they hit the same bottleneck with resident slots, because they must still complete a U.S. residency in order to get a license to practice medicine independently in the U.S. In the 2010 class of residents, some 13% of slots are filled by non-U.S. citizens who completed medical school outside the U.S.

One provision in the law attempts to address residencies. Since some residency slots go unfilled each year, the law will pool the funding for unused slots and redistribute it to other institutions, with the majority of these slots going to primary-care or general-surgery residencies. The slot redistribution, in effect, will create additional residencies, because previously unfilled positions will now be used, according to the Centers for Medicare and Medicaid Services.

Efforts by educators are focused on boosting the number of primary-care doctors. The University of Arkansas for Medical Sciences anticipates the state will need 350 more primary-care doctors in the next five years. So it raised its class size by 24 students last year, beyond the 150 previous annual admissions. In addition, the university opened a satellite medical campus in Fayetteville to give six third-year students additional clinical-training opportunities, said Richard Wheeler, executive associate dean for academic affairs. The school asks students to commit to entering rural medicine, and the school has 73 people in the program.

It's also tough when many doctors (already practicing) want to retire and/or get out of medicine altogether. The constant threat of lawsuits and the problems of dealing with the rules and regulations of HMOs, Medicaid and Medicare have lead many doctors into disillusionment and disgust. A survey of doctors some time ago in the magazine *Medical Economics* found almost half of doctors surveyed were unhappy with the current state of medicine, and almost half would not recommend being a doctor to their children. Most of the surveyed doctors planned to retire early or get out of medicine altogether. People assume doctors are happy in their work, but many aren't—and usually for reasons unrelated to the actual practice of medicine, like HMO's, bureaucracy and lawyers. If some doctors don't want their own children to follow in their footsteps, what does that say about our healthcare system?

(Source: Association of American Medical Colleges, AAMC.org)

## *US doctors' incomes are falling, survey finds*

According to The British Medical Journal (BMJ) the average income of doctors in the United States fell by 7% from 1995 to 2003, a new report says. The report is from the *Center for Studying Health System Change*, a non-profit research group in Washington, DC. Worst affected were primary care doctors, whose income—after expenses such as malpractice insurance but before taxes were deducted—fell by 10% over the period, while surgeons' income fell by 8%. Medical specialists' income remained relatively unchanged.

The incomes of lawyers and other professionals rose by 7% during the same period. The average reported income for a primary care doctor in 2003 was $146,405 after expenses but *before* tax. The highest paid doctors were surgeons, who had an average income of $271,652. Total taxes for this income level are close to 50%. Lawyers and government employees make more every year while doctors make less.

In 2003 the average income of all doctors who looked after patients was approximately $203,000. Static or declining fees from both public and private sources seem to be a major factor in doctors' lower incomes. For example, the increase in Medicare payment rates from 1995 to 2003 was 13%, lagging substantially behind inflation, which totaled 21% over these eight years.

Private insurance payments for doctors have lagged even more. In 1995 commercial fees were, on average, 1.43 times Medicare fees; by 2003 this fee ratio had fallen to 1.23. Although insurance payments to doctors have been constrained, says the report, the volume of services provided by doctors increased substantially, largely because of the growth in the number of tests and procedures (defensive medicine). This partly explains why medical specialists have seen their income falling at a slower pace than that of primary care doctors, who rely more on services such as diagnosis and management of patients.

Cecil Wilson, chairman of the board of the *American Medical Association*, said that the survey "confirms what they [doctors] already know from their own practices: payments are not keeping up with inflation."

The report also concludes that the downward trend in real incomes since the mid-1990s is probably an important factor in doctors being less willing to undertake pro bono work, whether providing free care for patients or volunteering to serve on hospital committees.

Doctors devote their lives to medicine and helping people. From when they are in high school until they finish residency, doctors spend more time in school and training than any other profession. They "don't have a life" for much of this time as school and training demands almost all of their time. When they are done, they are integrated into the healthcare system that is always there, 24/7 to save lives and help the sick and dying. On call for 24 hours at a time, they truly devote their life to help others. Yet, they have to fight just to get paid, and always be vigilant for frivolous lawsuits.

(Source: *US doctors' incomes are falling, new survey finds*, Fred Charatan, BMJ. 2006 July 1; 333(7557): 11, Pubmed Central, http://www.ncbi.nlm.nih.gov/pmc/articles/PMC1488748/)

---

## *Another "unintended" result of ObamaCare: Lose employer health insurance at work...*

---

The new healthcare law wasn't supposed to undercut employer plans that have provided most people in the U.S. with coverage for generations. But last week a leading manufacturer told workers their costs will jump partly because of the law. Also, a Democratic governor laid out a scheme for employers to get out of healthcare by shifting workers into taxpayer-subsidized insurance markets that open in 2014.

While it's too early to proclaim the demise of job-based coverage, corporate number crunchers are looking at options that could lead to major changes. "The economics of dropping existing coverage is about to become very attractive to many employers, both public and private," said Gov. Phil Bredesen, D-Tenn.

That's just not going to happen, White House officials say. "The absolute certainty about the Affordable Care Act is that for many, many employers who cover millions of people, it increases the incentives for them to offer coverage," said Jason Furman, an economic adviser to President Obama. Yet at least one major employer has shifted a greater share of plan costs to workers, and others are weighing the pros and cons of eventually forcing employees to strike out on their own.

"I don't think you are going to hear anybody publicly say 'We've made a decision to drop insurance,' " said Paul Keckley, executive director of the *Deloitte Center for Health Solutions*. "What we are hearing in our meetings is, 'We don't want to be the first one to drop benefits, but we would be the fast second.' We are hearing that a lot." Deloitte is a major accounting and consulting firm.

"My conclusion on all of this is that it is a huge roll of the dice," said James Klein, president of the *American Benefits Council*, which represents big company benefits administrators. "It could work out well and build on the employer-based system, or it could begin to dismantle the employer-based system." Employer health benefits have been a middle-class mainstay since World War II. About 150 million workers and family members are now covered.

When lawmakers debated the legislation, the nonpartisan Congressional Budget Office projected it would only have minimal impact on employer plans. About 3 million fewer people would be covered through the job, but they'd be able to get insurance elsewhere. Two provisions in the new law are leading companies to look at their plans in a different light. One is a hefty tax on high-cost health insurance aimed at the most generous coverage. Although the "Cadillac tax" doesn't hit until 2018, companies may have to disclose their exposure to investors well before that. A Boeing spokeswoman said concerns about the tax were partly behind a 50 percent increase in insurance deductibles the company just announced.

The tax is 40 percent of the value of a plan above $10,200 for individual coverage and $27,500 for a family plan. Family coverage now averages about $13,800. White House adviser Furman said blaming a cost increase next year on a tax that won't take effect for eight years "stretches credibility very far past the breaking point." Bigger questions loom over the new insurance markets that will be set up under the law. They're called exchanges, and every state will have one in a few years. Consumers will be able to shop for coverage among a range of plans in the exchange, with a guarantee they can't be turned down because of an existing medical problem. To help make premiums affordable, the law provides tax credits for households making up to four times the federal poverty level, about $88,000 for a family of four. It's more government subsidies, which will turn into more entitlement obligation. And how many people want to trust the government (the states in this case) to manage the fairness and equity of insurance exchanges?

Not surprisingly, politicians love the idea. Tennessee Gov. Bredesen said last week that employers could save big money by dropping their health plans and sending workers to buy coverage in the exchange. They'd face a fine of $2,000 per worker, but that's still way less than the cost of providing health insurance. Employers could even afford to give workers a raise and still come out ahead, Bredesen wrote in a Wall Street Journal opinion piece.

Employers are actively looking at that. "I don't know if the intent was to find an exit strategy for providing benefits, but the bill as written provides the mechanism," said Deloitte's Keckley, the consultant. A spokeswoman for the senators who wrote that part of the law says she's confident that when companies do the math, they'll decide to keep offering coverage. That's because employers get to deduct the cost of workers' healthcare from the company's taxes. Take away the health plan and two things happen: Employers lose the deduction and they'll probably have to pay workers more to get them to accept the benefit cut. Not only will the company's income taxes go up, but the employer will also face a bigger bill for Social Security and Medicare payroll taxes. So it's not as simple as paying $2,000 and walking away.

"It is clearly cheaper for employers to continue providing coverage," said Erin Shields, spokesman for the Senate Finance Committee. Another wrinkle: the health insurance tax credits available through the law are keyed to relatively spartan insurance plans, not as generous as most big employers provide. Send your workers into the insurance exchange, and valuable employees might jump to a competitor that still offers healthcare.

MIT economist Jon Gruber says it's impossible to create new government benefits without some unintended consequences, but he doesn't see a big drop in employer coverage. "This is a brave new world with uncertainties," said Gruber. But "the best available evidence suggests a small erosion. It's not going to go down wildly." More government benefits means more spending and more dependence on the government. It's not surprising politicians like the plan.

(Source: *Employers looking at health insurance options,* by Ricardo Alonso-Zaldiva; Associated Press, Sun Oct 24, ap.org. Used with permission)

## *Medicaid enrollment spikes to 48M in weak economy*

Swelling in the Medicaid health benefits program that already doesn't work has been severe. Several news sources recently reported a record number of Americans signed up for Medicaid last year, as the recession wiped out jobs and workplace health coverage. A report released by the nonprofit *Kaiser Family Foundation* found that enrollment in the safety-net medical insurance program jumped to more than 48 million — a record 15.7 percent share of the U.S. population. With the economy barely improving, states are forecasting a 6 percent increase in the rolls next year, meaning another strain on their cash-depleted budgets.

The Medicaid numbers are the latest piece to emerge in a grim statistical picture of the recession's toll. The ranks of the working-age poor climbed to the highest level since the 1960s last year, according to a recent Census report. Nearly 12 million households (over 40 million total) received food stamps, a record. Rising Medicaid enrollment also underscores the growing role of the government in healthcare, a polarizing issue in this year's midterm congressional elections after President Barack Obama and Democrats pushed through a massive overhaul of the nation's healthcare system.

Since the start of the recession in December 2007, nearly 6 million people have signed up for Medicaid, according to Kaiser. That period includes the biggest 12-month increase since the program's early days: 3.7 million new enrollees from December 2008 to December 2009. "There seems to be no end in sight to the fiscal pressure on the Medicaid program," said Vernon Smith, who co-authored the Kaiser report.

Starting in the fall of 2008, the federal government provided more than *$100 billion* in additional Medicaid funding to help states cover growing numbers of people in need. The last of that money will run out in June of next year, and states will face a jump of 25 percent or more in their share of costs, although they are still likely to be financially strapped. If Republicans win control of Congress, they may find it difficult to turn down requests for more aid from the states.

With or without Obama's overhaul, government is becoming the dominant player in healthcare. Federal, state and local government spending will overtake private sources in 2011, three years before the new law's major coverage expansion, Medicare economists said in a recent report. Medicaid is a federal-state partnership created with Medicare in 1965 under President Lyndon Johnson. It covers low-income families and many elderly in nursing homes, with Washington paying about 60 percent of the cost on average. Medicaid has also been assigned a major role under the new healthcare law, which expands the program to cover an estimated 18 million additional low-income adults starting in 2014. Projections thus show Medicaid will swell to almost 70 million people by 2014, all financed mostly with deficit spending. If this comes to pass, it will represent more cost than anyone can imagine, possibly more than Social Security and Medicare.

For now, states are cutting Medicaid to try to curb costs. Nearly every state — 48 in all — took some action to limit Medicaid spending this year, and most plan more cuts next year. Although they didn't reduce eligibility, Kaiser found that states took steps to restrict the scope of coverage: A record 20 states placed restrictions on benefits, and 14 plan new restrictions next year. Arizona, California, Hawaii and Massachusetts eliminated some or all dental coverage. Other states limited medical imaging, therapies, supplies and personal care. Thirty-nine states cut or froze payments to hospitals, doctors and other service providers, and most plan another round next year.

Medicaid payment rates are already so low that in many states it's hard to find doctors who will accept the coverage. Yet 20 states lowered payments to doctors this year, and 12 plan to do so next year. Eighteen states placed limits on long-term care services, and 10 plan additional limits next year. The recession officially ended in mid-2009, but the Kaiser study indicates its ill effects will take a while longer to wear off. Meanwhile, states will have to gear up for the major Medicaid expansion under the healthcare law. By not paying doctors enough to break even and denying claims, Medicaid has taken the HMO playbook and run with it.

(Source: "Medicaid Enrollment: December 2009 Data Snapshot", (#8050-02). Originally published by The Henry J. Kaiser Family Foundation, September 2010, used with permission)

## *ObamaCare's Medicaid Policy: Doubling down on a system that already doesn't work*

ObamaCare increases enrollment in the troubled Medicaid program by over 18 million persons (on top of the 48 million people already enrolled in Medicaid). However, providers are already limiting the amount of Medicaid patients they accept because of low payment rates. To entice providers to accept more Medicaid recipients, ObamaCare requires that states—with federal dollars—raise primary care physician (PCP) payment rates for Medicaid to parity with Medicare rates for 2013 and 2014.

Based on estimates from the Congressional Budget Office (CBO) and the Office of the Actuary at the Centers for Medicare and Medicaid Services (CMS), the 10-year cost of raising PCP rates to Medicare levels would be between $37 billion and $68 billion. *The Heritage Foundation* estimates that the 10-year cost could rise to $350 billion if state reimbursement rates were to rise proportionally for all physician and clinical services.

These ObamaCare provisions raise potent issues for providers and policymakers: Will states raise provider rates across the board to match the PCP increase? What actions will states take when the federal funding expires and how will those actions impact doctors? Will Congress adopt a different model for Medicare payment rates than the current one, which requires temporary fixes about once a year?

## *Medicaid's Numerous Problems*

Medicaid—the joint federal–state health insurance program for numerous categories of the poor—has significant problems. Medicaid spending growth is unsustainable, increasing over 6 percent annually (in inflation-adjusted dollars) during the past two decades. Medicaid growth has resulted in three federal bailouts in the past decade, and its growth is crowding out other state priorities, such as education, transportation, and law enforcement. And many states only pay claims and medical bills twice a year—when they get their federal matching money. Some hospitals, pharmacies and physicians have to wait almost six months to get paid for work they did.

At the same time, several states reimburse providers at extremely low rates. This causes many providers to refuse to treat Medicaid patients, effectively forcing Medicaid recipients to use emergency rooms for basic care. According to the Texas Health and Human Services Commission, less than a third of the state's practicing doctors are active in Medicaid. In many states, it's even less. Once the doctors that do take Medicaid "fill up" with all the new beneficiaries, even they won't be able to see anymore Medicaid patients. Because of these problems inherent in Medicaid, people will have "coverage" but won't be able to see a doctor.

To make matters worse, virtually all specialists don't take Medicaid patients, period. If a Medicaid patient needs to see a nephrologist, neurologist, orthopedic surgeon, plastic surgeon, vascular surgeon, general surgeon, cardiologist, pulmonologist, dentist, oral surgeon, rheumatologist, allergist, endocrinologist or all the rest they are out of luck—they won't even be accepted for an appointment because they have Medicaid. So, the primary care doctors that do accept Medicaid have nobody to refer patients to that need specialized care and thereby raise their liability and risk of a lawsuit.

## *ObamaCare Substantially Increases Medicaid*

Despite Medicaid's enormous problems, ObamaCare expands it dramatically. Beginning in 2014, states are required to cover all individuals below 138 percent of the federal poverty line with Medicaid. The CMS estimates that this will increase enrollment in Medicaid by 23 million individuals in 2014 at an added annual cost of over $70 billion.

ObamaCare requires that states increase Medicaid reimbursement rates for PCPs to applicable Medicare payment rates for 2013 and 2014 to encourage PCPs to treat Medicaid patients. However, on January 1, 2015, both the mandate and the federal funding paying for it expire.

Many Medicaid providers, who are paid on average about half of commercial rates, are skeptical of this expansion. Medicaid requires an enormous amount of paperwork, the lag time between date of service and the date of reimbursement is more than twice as long as Medicare or commercial insurance reimbursement times, and the *denial rate for Medicaid claims is three times larger than for both Medicare and commercial insurance*. Indeed, only 10 percent of PCPs believe that new Medicaid enrollees in their area will find a suitable PCP. So, while many millions of people will be dumped into the Medicaid system, few if any will be able to find a doctor, a dentist, and certainly will have limited or no access to specialists.

## What Happens to Doctors and States When the Federal Funding Disappears?

The end of federal assistance will leave states and doctors in a precarious position. If states keep the elevated PCP reimbursement rates, they will have to make up the difference with their own funds, further adding to state Medicaid costs. But if states reduce Medicaid PCP payment rates to their previous levels when the federal funding disappears, Medicaid beneficiaries' access to providers would be further compromised. Medicaid reimbursement rates are already very low, particularly in states such as New York, New Jersey, and California that pay providers approximately one-third of commercial rates.

Moreover, reducing physician payment rates is typically one of the primary ways state officials control Medicaid spending. It's a strategy where states don't pay their bills, so doctors quit seeing Medicaid patients. For example, 41 states and the District of Columbia cut provider reimbursements rates in 2009 or 2010, and 29 states and the District did so in both years. The mandated Medicaid expansion would strip states of the ability to reduce enrollment as a cost-controlling mechanism, so reductions in Medicaid reimbursement rates seem likely to continue, especially during difficult economic periods.

In addition, setting provider rates even lower will not necessarily reduce the aggregate costs of state Medicaid programs. More Medicaid enrollees will likely seek care in hospital emergency rooms because they cannot find doctors willing to accept them. A doctor's time is better spent serving his or her patients than lobbying politicians for payment increases. And the heavy administrative burden of Medicaid is another cost inflicted on physicians and their practices, which considerably reduces their levels of job satisfaction and the likelihood they will accept new Medicaid patients.

## Fundamental Reform, Not More Money

When a federal program is hemorrhaging taxpayer dollars and delivering poor results, policymakers should reform it. Fundamental Medicaid reform is desperately needed. It doesn't work now, how could it possibly work with more enrollees? The government is making more promises it can't keep—with taxpayer money. Instead of addressing the many problems of Medicaid, ObamaCare doubles down on the broken program and greatly adds to its rolls. Most doctors believe ObamaCare will "explode" Medicaid, as people will be unable to actually get any healthcare even though they have their Medicaid insurance card. Emergency rooms, however, are forced by law to see anyone who presents themselves. As of now, Medicaid barely pays for ER visits, and often times denies ER claims outright. So, a battle looms when almost 20 million additional people are added to Medicaid—they won't be able to find a doctor, can't see a specialist, and ER's may start to refuse service because Medicaid won't pay.

Based on recent experience, many states will cut provider rates when they are faced with tough budgetary decisions and the federal money goes away. Doctors will be left to rely on "fixes" at the state-level similar to what Congress does continually with Medicare rates. A better approach: Repeal the Medicaid expansion and stop these temporary fixes that produce uncertainty, division, and socially wasteful lobbying efforts and focus instead on how to best provide a social safety net within an affordable budget.

The Medicaid system we have now clearly doesn't work—just ask any doctor or hospital administrator. Making a system that doesn't work bigger is a joke, and it's not going to work. Tens of millions of people will have Medicaid cards, but won't even be able to see a doctor. It will cost taxpayers hundreds of billions or even trillions of dollars, and in the future, like now, it just won't work. There is a better way, but it is nothing to do with increasing the Medicaid system.

(Source: *ObamaCare's Medicaid Policy: Putting the Doctors in Another "Fix,"* by Brian Blase, The Heritage Foundation; *October 4, 2010,* WebMemo #3031, Heritage.org, copyright The Heritage Foundation, used with permission)

## *Healthcare law may eliminate limited insurance plans*

Yet another controversy about the new healthcare law has erupted. The new law could make it difficult for companies like McDonald's to continue offering limited insurance coverage to their low-wage workers. The world's largest hamburger chain provides its hourly workers with low-cost plans known as "mini-meds" or limited benefits plans. These plans typically cover things like doctor's office visits and prescription drugs. But they don't provide comprehensive coverage, and they often come with a cap on how much the insurer pays in annual benefits that is much lower than a major medical insurance plan.

Next year, the healthcare law passed by Congress will require insurers to pay minimum percentages of 80 percent and 85 percent of the premiums they collect toward medical care, figures that may be hard to meet for some of these limited plans. McDonald's denied a report that it's considering dropping healthcare coverage for some employees because they won't meet those limits.

*The Wall Street Journal* reported that McDonald's has warned regulators it could drop its plan for some 30,000 workers unless the government waives a new requirement in the healthcare overhaul. McDonald's said in a statement it has been speaking with federal agencies to understand the law, but the company called reports that it planned to drop healthcare coverage for employees "completely false."

Limited benefits plans have grown popular the past few years as healthcare costs have climbed, said Steve Wojcik, vice president of public policy for the *National Business Group on Health*. *Employers* in the retail or hotel industries offer this basic coverage as a way to keep workers and improve employee productivity by cutting health-related absences. About 1.4 million workers have group healthcare coverage through limited benefits plans, according to the *National Restaurant Association*, which doesn't track growth of the plans. *Fox News* reported on Dec. 8th, 2010 that more than 220 waivers from Obamacare regulations have already been granted, mostly from big corporations and lobbyists. McDonald's has been granted a waiver. Waivers protect businesses so they don't have to comply with Obamacare or face a fine. Businesses and lobbyists have already figured out ways around Obamacare, most of which hasn't even been implemented yet.

The limited coverage means patients can be stuck with big bills if something serious happens, but they also can get insurer-negotiated payment rates for that care instead of paying full price. "Compared to nothing they're a really good deal," said Robert Laszewski, a former insurance executive who's now a consultant. "Compared to comprehensive health insurance, they're a terrible deal." Limited coverage plans also clearly don't work. They are better than nothing, but they don't work. There is a better way, but it has nothing to do with limited coverage health insurance.

## Big Insurance monopolies are only going to get bigger under ObamaCare

ObamaCare's current and future harms have been well chronicled, but the major effects so far are less obvious and arguably more important: A wave of consolidation is washing over the health markets, and not surprisingly, the result is going to be higher costs.

The turn toward consolidation among insurance companies is not new, and neither is it among doctors, hospitals and other providers. Yet the health bill has accelerated these trends, as all sides race to anticipate and manage political risk and regulatory uncertainty. This dynamic is leading to much larger hospital systems and physician groups, and fewer insurers dominated by a handful of national conglomerates. ObamaCare was sold using the language of choice and competition, but it is actually reducing both.

The first surge will come among the 1,200 insurers doing business in the U.S., given that a major goal of ObamaCare is to convert these companies into "public utilities." Those regulations are now being written—and once they're up and running some medium-sized carriers will collapse under the new mandates and higher overhead. State insurance commissioners warned the administration this month that "improper or overly strident application . . . could threaten the solvency of insurers or significantly reduce competition in some insurance markets." They also implied that bankruptcies are likely.

With these headwinds, investors and Wall Street analysts are now predicting a lost decade for health insurance stocks. But it may be more accurate to say that there will be a lot of losers and some very big winners. Mergers and acquisitions will increase dramatically once companies get a better look at the regulation and figure out the valuation of M&A targets. Larger carriers will swallow smaller ones quietly before they fail.

Both publicly traded and nonprofit insurers have been heading in this direction for years, as in any industry where there are returns to scale. But scale is far more central now, because ObamaCare standardizes benefits.

Once insurers lose the freedom to design their own products, they'll essentially be selling commodities, and survival will depend on enrollment volume and market share.

The same thing will happen to stand-alone and community hospitals—always a precarious business. Nearly a third of U.S. hospitals are currently operating in the red and will get steaMr.olled by ObamaCare, and many of them will be annexed by national chains and larger local systems. This trend got a preview two weeks ago when Mercy Health Partners announced that it was seeking buyers for three Catholic hospitals in northeast Pennsylvania. CEO Kevin Cook told local media that ObamaCare was "absolutely" a factor in the decision to sell.

Though it received little attention over a year of debate, ObamaCare actively promotes provider consolidation. Writing this summer in the *Annals of Internal Medicine*, Nancy-Ann DeParle and other White House health advisers argued that "The economic forces put in motion by the Act are likely to lead to vertical organization of providers and accelerate physician employment by hospitals and aggregation into larger physician groups." Across the country, providers are building giant hospital systems and much tighter doctor alliances like multi-specialty groups to get out ahead of a concept known as "accountable care organizations," or ACOs. To modernize the delivery of medical services, ACOs would encourage doctors to work in teams to use resources more efficiently, streamline treatment and improve quality. The model is the Mayo Clinic and other large integrated systems.

At the moment ACOs are only a gleam in some bureaucrat's eye, and no one has a clue how they'll operate in practice until the government releases a working regulatory definition next year. Yet the percussive effects are already being felt across medicine. Hospitals are now on a buying spree of private physician practices in the rush to build something that will qualify as an ACO. Some 65% of doctors who changed jobs in 2009 moved into a hospital-owned practice, while 49% of doctors out of residency were hired by hospitals, according to the *Medical Group Management Association*. In its 2010 census, the *American College of Cardiology* reports that nearly 40% of private cardiology groups are currently integrating with hospitals or merging with other practices.

Doctors are selling because complying with the ever-growing list of mandates has become more cumbersome; and while staff physicians on salary do gain predictability, they also lose the autonomy of independent practice. The other problem is price controls in Medicare, which are about 20% below private payments for doctors and 30% lower for hospitals. Hospitals are also scooping up practices to lock in referral sources and make up for ObamaCare's Medicare cuts. As it is, two-thirds of hospitals lose money today on Medicare inpatient services, according to Medicare.

ACOs are also driving consolidation among hospitals. Anecdotally, Marquette General Hospital and Bell Hospital formed a strategic ACO partnership in July that will dominate Michigan's upper peninsula. In Omaha, Methodist Health System and the Nebraska Medical Center recently followed suit. Similar alliances are underway in Detroit, Baltimore, Chicago, greater Boston, Roanoke and southwest Virginia—even Youngstown, Ohio.

The accountable care movement could do some good if it spreads best practices. But no one should entertain the illusion that it will reduce costs. In fact, the most concrete effect of this wave of consolidation may be to increase private health spending significantly. Unlike Medicare and Medicaid, private reimbursement rates are determined by negotiations, often highly antagonistic. Insurers always attribute premium increases to the underlying cost of care, while doctors and hospitals always argue that there isn't enough competition among health plans. Both claims are "true," some of the time—but it depends on which side has more market power.

Insurers extract lower rates by steering patients and revenue to certain providers through their networks. Providers gain bargaining leverage when health plans can't credibly threaten to exclude them, whether because their share of the market is too large or due to public demand for "must have" hospitals. Consolidation will increasingly feed off itself as providers and insurers vie to get the upper hand in rate negotiations.

Accountable care organizations may become little more than a pretext for building up market power and fixing prices. The *American Medical Association* wants the government to stop insurers from individual contracting in favor of "exclusive dealing arrangements" with ACOs. In effect, the AMA wants a mandatory collective bargaining tool that would convert ACOs into unions. "In a lot of states, the problem is just you don't have competition at all," President Obama said in February at his health summit. "We want competition."

Yet the consolidation wave is churning the insurance markets and reshaping clinical medicine with almost no public scrutiny. A rational system would give consumers an incentive to reward those businesses that innovate and deliver higher quality at lower cost, whether they are providers or insurers. ObamaCare is already moving the U.S. even further from the rational world, and this forced retreat will continue the longer it is left in place.

(Source: *Big Insurance, Big Medicine*, WSJ-Online: Opinion Journal, review and outlook: October 26, 2010, WSJ.com. Used with permission)

## *Is there nothing that works?*

No matter how you slice it, the new healthcare plan will not work—especially the Medicaid provisions. The fact is, commercial health insurance doesn't work either. If it did, there would have been no need for the government to try to come up with a solution. If it did work, 2/3 of the people filing for bankruptcy (78% of which had health insurance) because of healthcare costs wouldn't have had to go bankrupt (677,000 in 2009 alone). The health insurance industry in the U.S. hasn't worked for more than thirty years. Most people don't remember back to the early 1970's, before the advent of HMO's, but things worked relatively well back then. Most people had health insurance, and businesses could provide health insurance for their employees. Then, HMO's came along, but more importantly, the profit motive came along. Health insurance became yet another producer of profits, not health. Thirty years later, we are all in worse shape than ever, and things are so bad that people are relying on the government to fix it. Since the government isn't good at fixing anything (only subsidizing problems), we are in a bigger mess than ever.

So, let's take a look at one of the biggest health insurance companies in the U.S. today—United Healthcare. William McGuire, United Health CEO for 12 years extracted almost $2 billion for himself from money paid for healthcare. They make so much money that they can run commercials on T.V. all day long and employ more than 80,000 people. The United Health Group Corporation was started in 1974, and you can almost hear the sucking sound starting from the day they filed their corporate charter. Make no mistake, they, like all corporations, are in business to make profits, grow and expand, and take over as much market share as they can. The way they make profits is by "providing" health insurance, that magical idea that people will get healthcare paid for by their insurance company.

Based on company financial reports for 2009 filed with the Securities and Exchange Commission, a recent report found health insurers WellPoint Inc., UnitedHealth Group, Cigna Corp., Aetna Inc. and Humana Inc. covered 2.7 million *fewer* people than they did the year before. The five biggest companies covered 2.7 million fewer people last year (2009) but earned 56% more, says the report by *Healthcare for America Now*. As the nation struggled last year with rising healthcare costs and a recession, the five largest health insurance companies racked up combined profits of $12.2 billion − up 56% over 2008.

The report also said some of the five insurers *cut the proportion of premiums they spent on their customers' medical care*, committing relatively more to <u>salaries, administrative expenses and profit</u>. Imagine that, health insurers keeping more money for salaries, administrative expenses, and profits. How can they get away with it? Why do people continue to pay money to these companies? Let's look a little deeper into United Healthcare, and maybe find out why our healthcare system has gotten so bad.

# United Healthcare

United Healthcare (United HealthGroup Inc., stock ticker: UNH), one of the nation's biggest health insurers, must file a 10-K Annual Report with the Securities and Exchange Commission (SEC). This information is public knowledge, and indeed it offers transparency into what they are doing with money paid to them for healthcare. Their 10-K annual report for 2009 shows they had revenues of $87,138,000,000 for 2009 (Premiums, Services, Products, Investment income), and paid out $65,289,000,000 in medical costs. So, United Healthcare only paid out 74.9% of the money they made for actual health coverage. This means they kept $21,849,000,000 for themselves, in one year.

They kept almost $22 billion dollars in profit that was paid to them to provide health coverage of the people that paid them (businesses, government employees, individuals, groups etc.). The money they kept (profit) is actually 33.4% of the money they spent on medical costs. In essence, they extracted almost $22 billion dollars OUT of the healthcare system. Of course, they don't report a $22 billion profit, most of the money went to "operating costs" and "costs of products sold." Yet, they go on to report that "Operating costs for 2009 decreased due to certain expenses incurred in 2008 as discussed below and disciplined operating cost management (denying claims), which were partially offset by increased costs due to acquired and organic business growth and from an increase in state insurance assessments levied against premiums, a portion of which was in lieu of state income taxes in one of the states in which we operate."

This is the whole crux of our healthcare problem. In order to make huge profits, United Healthcare and the like must spend billions on administrative costs. UNH reports that it employs 80,000 full time employees. What on earth do they need 80k full time employees for? The answer, of course, is to make sure people pay their premiums, and to make sure that people aren't able to use their insurance when they need it. There is no way to determine how many people they have reviewing and denying claims, but it must be massive. Their job is *not* to pay out money, and to keep as much as they can in profits. Their stock holders expect nothing less.

They also have massive "medical approval" departments. If your doctor wants to get an xray or CT scan, you have to call them for approval (an RQI number is given). If you have the test done and didn't get an RQI then you have to pay yourself. Considering health insurance companies are nothing more than *middlemen*, they collect money then pay some out. They are providing a service, but are not actually doing any healthcare. People and businesses, on the one hand, and healthcare providers, on the other, are separated by middle-men: health insurance companies (the 3rd party payer). Health insurance companies do nothing but administration, and collect huge profits that are removed from the healthcare system. And what did United Healthcare they do with some of their profits? Acquire more companies.

### ACQUISITIONS *(from page 36, 10-K 2009)*

*AIM Healthcare Services, Inc.* On June 1, 2009, we acquired all of the outstanding shares of AIM Healthcare Services, Inc. (AIM) for approximately $440 million in cash. AIM is a leading provider of payment accuracy solutions for healthcare payer and hospital clients in all 50 states. This acquisition strengthened our capabilities to simplify and improve administration in the healthcare industry. The results of operations and financial condition of AIM have been included in our consolidated results and the results of the Ingenix reporting segment since the acquisition date.

*Unison Health Plans.* On May 30, 2008, we acquired all of the outstanding shares of Unison Health Plans (Unison) for approximately $930 million in cash. Unison provides government-sponsored health plan coverage to people in Pennsylvania, Ohio, Tennessee, Delaware, South Carolina and Washington, D.C. through a network of independent healthcare professionals. This acquisition strengthened our resources and capabilities in these areas. The results of operations and financial condition of Unison have been included in our consolidated results and the results of our Health Benefits reporting segment since the acquisition date.34

*Sierra Health Services, Inc.* On February 25, 2008, we acquired all of the outstanding shares of Sierra Health Services, Inc. (Sierra), a diversified healthcare services company based in Las Vegas, Nevada, for approximately $2.6 billion in cash, representing a price of $43.50 per share of Sierra common stock. This acquisition strengthened our position in the southwest region of the United States. The U.S. Department of Justice approved the acquisition conditioned upon the divestiture of our individual Medicare Advantage HMO plans in Clark and Nye Counties, Nevada, which represented approximately 30,000 members. The divestiture was completed on April 30, 2008. We received proceeds of $185 million for this transaction, which were recorded as a reduction to Operating Costs. Group Medicare Advantage plans offered through commercial contracts were excluded from the divestiture. Also, we retained Sierra's Medicare Advantage HMO plans in Nevada. The results of operations and financial condition of Sierra have been included in our consolidated results and the results of the Health Benefits, OptumHealth and Prescription Solutions reporting segments since the acquisition date.

*Fiserv Health, Inc.* On January 10, 2008, we acquired all of the outstanding shares of Fiserv Health, Inc. (Fiserv Health), a subsidiary of Fiserv, Inc., for approximately $740 million in cash. Fiserv Health is a leading administrator of medical benefits and also provides care facilitation services, specialty health solutions and pharmacy benefit management (PBM) services. This transaction allows us to expand the capacity of our existing benefits administration businesses and enables existing and new customers to leverage our full range of assets, including ancillary services, our national network and technology tools. The results of operations and financial condition of

Fiserv Health have been included in our consolidated results and the results of the Health Benefits, OptumHealth, Ingenix and Prescription Solutions reporting segments since the acquisition date.

The first acquisition is interesting, and shows a point in healthcare that most people aren't aware of. UNH's description of this acquisition is "AIM is a leading provider of payment accuracy solutions for healthcare payer and hospital clients in all 50 states." Payment accuracy solutions is another word for claims processing. Billions of dollars are extracted from the healthcare system every year just for claims processing. Doctors send in claims to get paid for work they've done, and the claim has to be processed. Piles of paperwork result, as claims are checked and rechecked. Letters are mailed to the doctor, the policy holder, and whoever else is connected with the claim. The company checks and rechecks the claim amount, then compares it what they think should be paid, and after being reviewed by many people and computer programs, a check is finally generated. Payment accuracy is another way of rejecting claims also. If a claim is "bad," something is missing, an "i" is not dotted, then the claim is rejected.

Health Insurance companies save billions of dollars a year by rejecting claims, delaying payment, or underpaying claims. So, getting this company would add money to their bottom line in a big way. Billions of dollars are spent and wasted on the other end as well, as doctors and hospitals have to spend up to 10% of their income to hire billing companies, buy billing software, and be compliant with insurance company regulations for claims. This is money that is not spent on healthcare, but money that has to be spent none-the-less just to get paid. Health insurance companies know they have the money, and they try to do anything possible not to have to pay out that money for healthcare.

The second acquisition, Unison Health Plans, administers government health plans. Health insurance companies are getting their hands on more and more companies that provide health benefits to government employees. As has been shown, government employees have built-in health coverage and built-in increases in rates. Companies like United Health would like to get the entire government healthcare business if they could, but will have to be content to acquire as many of these companies as they can. The third acquisition was for Sierra Health, a Medicare advantage provider (more government money for health benefits). Guess who is getting a large part of your tax dollars? Corporations like United Health.

The last acquisition was Fiserv: "Fiserv Health is a leading administrator of medical benefits and also provides care facilitation services, specialty health solutions and pharmacy benefit management (PBM) services." UNH paid $740 million for more administration services, including pharmacy benefit management. When you hear or read about administration, you should think of thousands of people sitting at computers in an office figuring out ways to deny claims, withhold care, and mining data and actuarial tables to save money for the company. You or someone you know has probably talked with these people as you tried to find out why something you needed "wasn't covered" by your health insurance. Fiserv must be very good at it to garner a buyout of $740 million dollars. United Healthcare spent almost $5 billion dollars to acquire these companies that was paid to them by policyholders for healthcare ($5 billion that wasn't spent on healthcare).

By completing these acquisitions, United Healthcare has beefed up its administration and gotten an ever increasing share of government healthcare dollars (that you, the taxpayer, are paying for). Instead of spending that money on healthcare, which is what policy holders pay them for, they are ever increasing the size and scope of their business to ever increase profits and be able to extract even more money/profits in the future. As the previous section showed, there is going to be more consolidation and acquisition than ever in the next few years thanks to ObamaCare. United Healthcare and the others in the "big five" club are going to have more power than ever thanks to our politicians.

## *Do you believe the hype?*

### 1. Description of Business (from page 59, 10-K 2009)

"UnitedHealth Group Incorporated (also referred to as "UnitedHealth Group" and "the Company") is a diversified health and well-being company dedicated to making healthcare work better. The Company emphasizes enhancing the performance of the health system and improving the overall health and well-being of the people it serves and their communities. The Company helps people get the care they need at an affordable cost; supports the physician/patient relationship; and empowers people with the information, guidance and tools they need to make personal health choices and decisions. The Company's primary focus is on improving the healthcare system by simplifying the administrative components of healthcare delivery, promoting evidence-based medicine as the standard for care, and providing relevant, actionable data that physicians, healthcare professionals, consumers, employers and other participants in healthcare can use to make better, more informed decisions. Through its diversified family of businesses, the Company leverages core competencies in advanced technology based transactional capabilities; healthcare data, knowledge and information; and healthcare resource organization and care facilitation to improve access to health and well-being services, simplify the healthcare experience, promote quality and make healthcare more affordable."

This sounds really great doesn't it? "Promote quality and make healthcare more affordable, The Company helps people get the care they need at an affordable cost…dedicated to making healthcare work better" I didn't read the part in their description of business were they extract $22 billion in profit, I guess they forgot to mention that part. This glad-handling is nothing more than lies to justify what they are doing—extracting tens of billions from healthcare. Make no mistake, they are not in business to promote quality and make healthcare more affordable, they are in business to make profit, and they are making a *huge* profit—at the expense of people who paid them for healthcare. They "make healthcare more affordable" by raising rates every year. The sad part is, since the passage of Medicare part D, they and other large health insurers are ripping off the government (read—the taxpayers) for many more billions of dollars. They are also ripping off businesses and business owners who are simply trying to provide health benefits for their employees. There is no mention in their business description of raising rates year after year by up to 40% per year—while spending less on healthcare costs. How can the government or even business for that matter let them get away with keeping $22 billion dollars of money that should be going for healthcare, but isn't? Think Lobbyists. The health insurance companies lobby and bribe government officials, run positive publicity campaigns and commercials, and crush any opposition to what they are doing. And instead of taking on the health insurance companies, politicians reward them with ever increasing doses of money.

United Heatlhcare is just one of the big five (Wellpoint, Humana, Cigna, Aetna), all of which are taking hundreds of billions of dollars of profits out of the healthcare system. The health insurance business has become a monopoly, and their power is only growing. They are buying up many of the largest pharmacy companies, and further consolidating their control. Now, with ObamaCare pending and starting to take effect, these giant health insurers are licking their chops. ObamaCare has essentially mandated that millions of people will have to get health insurance by 1014. And instead of developing a health insurance system that actually works, the government and politicians are simply going to shove more and more money over to the health insurance companies. This system hasn't worked, and it's not going to change itself. There is a better way.

## *Let's look a little closer at United Healthcare: It's Business Summary*

### Business Summary

UnitedHealth Group Incorporated provides healthcare services in the United States. The company's Health Benefits segment offers consumer-oriented health benefit plans and services; administrative and other management services; and non-employer based insurance options for purchase by individuals. It also provides health and well-being services for individuals aged 50 and older, as well as to large national employers, public sector employers, mid-sized employers, small businesses, and individuals; health insurance products and services; and network-based health and well-being services to beneficiaries and other government-sponsored healthcare programs. As of December 31, 2009, this segment offers its services through approximately 700,000 physicians and other healthcare professionals, and 5,200 hospitals. Its OptumHealth segment provides health, financial, and ancillary services and products that assist consumers through personalized health management solutions; benefit administration, and clinical and network management; health-based financial services; behavioral solutions; and specialty benefits, such as dental, vision, life, critical illness, short-term Disability, and stop-loss product offerings (1). The company's Ingenix segment offers database and data management services, software products, publications, consulting and actuarial services, business process outsourcing services, and pharmaceutical data consulting and research services (2). Its Prescription Solutions segment provides integrated pharmacy benefit management services comprising retail network pharmacy management, mail order pharmacy, specialty pharmacy, benefit design consultation, drug utilization review, formulary management programs, disease therapy management, and adherence programs to employer groups, union trusts, managed care organizations, Medicare-contracted plans, Medicaid plans and third party administrators (3). UnitedHealth Group was founded in 1974 and is based in Minnetonka, Minnesota.

A dissection and translation of their "Business Summary" yields some interesting information:

(1)   OptumHealth provides financial services? Benefits administration (read: denying benefits and red tape), clinical and network management? What are they managing? What are "health-based financial services?" Do they loan people money so they can buy more health insurance? How do these benefit people needing healthcare?

(2)   Ingenix offers database and data management services (read: data mining to cut or reduce care). United Health offers software products? To whom and for what? Publications, consulting and actuarial services? They use these to determine where they lose the most money, and take measures to cut or reduce these

medical expenses. Pharmaceutical data consulting and research services (read: data mining to reduce costs of frequently prescribed medications and denying claims for medication non-compliance). Ingenix is currently being sued by several organizations because of low payment rates.

(3)    Prescription Solutions provides retail, mail order, and "specialty" pharmacy management. Drug utilization review (read: limiting the most utilized drugs to save costs), formulary management (read: only paying for generic medication, telling doctors what they can prescribe), and adherence programs (read: not paying for healthcare if patient doesn't take meds as prescribed).

It's plain to see, just from their business summary, that they are very involved in managing data at least as much or more than simply paying for healthcare. It is by managing their data that they can figure out where they are losing money, and can quickly change their rules, networks, plans, and benefits so that they wring out the maximum amount of profit. And this is only just getting going.

It won't be long until the big health insurance companies get access to your digital medical records. The Federal Government, via Medicare and Medicaid, is requiring an all-digital medical records system. Once your medical records are completely digitized, they will be 100% available to whoever has the lobbying power to gain access to them. You can bet the lobbyists for the health insurers are already figuring out ways to get access to your medical records. Once they have that, you will find those letters coming in the mail from your health insurance company saying "you didn't tell us you hurt your knee in high school, that is a pre-existing condition, and we aren't paying for your X-ray, medicines, or surgery that you had. Or, you complained of abdominal pain when you were eight, so we aren't paying for your appendectomy now that your twenty-five, because it may have been a pre-existing condition.

It's actually not possible to figure out all the ways your health insurance company will use data and your medical records to withhold care. But rest assured, they are working on ways to withhold care that people can't even imagine. If they can monitor when and where you refill your medication, then withhold care because you were "non-compliant" with taking your medication (because you picked it up a week late), there is probably no limit to which they won't go to use data and your medical records against you.

## Health Insurance Employees: How many is really enough?

(Employee numbers taken from each company's 2009 10-K and business summaries)

**Humana**: 26,900 employees

**Cigna**: 29,300 employees

**Aetna**: 35,000 employees

**Wellpoint**: 40,500 employees

**United Healthcare**: 80,000 employees

**Total**: 211,700 health insurance employees (just in the "big five")

<u>**Number of doctors in the U.S.**</u>: 954,000

So, If you divide the number of doctors by the number of people working for health insurance companies (just the "big five"), there is one health insurance company employee for every 4.5 doctors (this number is low as there are many more health insurers than just the big five—it's probably closer to 3 doctors per health insurance employee). This makes absolutely no sense at all. If the job of health insurance was, in fact, to provide healthcare, would they need one employee for every 4.5 doctors? This doesn't take into consideration the private-sector employees that work in the billing department at clinics and hospitals. Some clinics, for instance, have people working that do nothing but file paperwork for HMO's (for the patients at their clinic). Hospitals also have to pay employees whose only job is to fight with the HMO's to get a test, CT scan, hospital stay, or surgery approved. This again increases healthcare costs.

HMO's, and Medicaid and Medicare for that matter, have another way of saving money: denying claims. Claims are what doctors and hospitals submit for payment, much like bills. One way of not paying a medical claim is to simply reject the claim. Clinics and hospitals have tried for years to figure out ways not to have claims rejected, including going to seminars, buying expensive billing software, hiring billing companies and consultants to fight for claims, or even hiring a lawyer to go after health insurance companies that just won't pay. This of course costs piles of money, just trying to get paid for something that was already done. Imagine taking your car to get fixed. The mechanic does the work, and agrees to send you the bill. Although this is unlikely, just imagine what would happen if you send the bill back to the mechanic, saying "you didn't cross your "T" and didn't dot the "i." He would probably come after you, or refuse to fix your car again. So, he sends you another bill, and you send it back again, because he didn't put the code for diagnosis that you think he should have. This goes on and on, until the mechanic finally gives up and writes off your charges. Does this sound ridiculous? It is, but that's what health insurers get away with every day.

The health insurance company has thousands of people reviewing and rejecting claims. Or, many health insurance companies simply pay what they feel like (via the UCR scam). You send them a bill for $75 for an office visit, and they send you a check for $45. Or, if you are a surgeon and you perform surgery on a patient, and you send the insurance company a bill for $500, and they send you a check for $200. This happens every day in the health world. Many doctors and hospitals simply don't have the time and resources to fight every single claim, just to get paid (the insurance companies know this). Imagine again, you take your car to get fixed, and get the bill. Say the bill says $200, and you send the mechanic $100, with a note "paid in full." It's a joke, it would never happen. In the real world, no business operates this way, but for some reason health insurance companies/HMO's get away with it. Sometimes it just happens outright via UCR or other schemes, and sometimes it's included in the 300 page contract you signed with them, in fine print, that even your lawyer missed. It's a nightmare.

One way health insurance companies save money is by requiring massive amounts of paperwork to be completed just to cover an X-ray or a medication. Doctors that don't have staff to fight the HMO's simply give up trying to order a test for their patient after several rounds of paperwork fail to get the test approved. For things like stress-tests and MRI's, the HMO plays even harder, requiring the ordering physician to discuss the need for the test with a physician at the HMO. Yes, health insurance companies employ physicians as a way of denying services, many of whom get bonuses for denying more claims.

Health insurance companies have also used *evidence based medicine*, the common practice used by doctors, *against doctors*. Evidence based medicine, like it sounds, uses actual research to support medical practice. While doctors are supposed to be practicing evidence based medicine, it is not without limitations. There is so much medical research being done that there are often conflicting studies about the same medical practice—one says it's useful to, say, achieve a diagnosis or treatment, and another study contradicts that study. It's only over time that a cohesive analysis from many studies emerges that directs doctors on which path to take. Health insurance companies/HMO's, usually using their own doctors, cite studies that show no benefit to getting a test or following a treatment pattern, even though it is standard practice already. HMO's have become masters at using evidence based medicine as a reason to deny testing, medicine, and treatments for patients, despite what has become common practice. They are masters at using obscure research to support their case for refusing medicine, testing and treatment, thereby saving money for the HMO.

So, through the myriad of ways of to save money, health insurers like United Health and all the rest dictate not only what happens in medicine today, they dictate what it will cost. Health insurers pay so little, especially to hospitals, that hospitals have to charge three or four times the cost of a service or hospital stay just to make up for the short-fall. The people that are uninsured and are taken care of often pay three or four times what a comparable insurance patient would pay for some services. The hapless uninsured then have injury and insult laid on them as they have to pay huge medical bills that are inflated because of health insurance companies.

Our politicians have once again stood by and watched this system for decades, and done nothing. Well, they have done something – they have decided to give the health insurance companies even more money. Maybe the next time you get your pay stub, or have to write a check to your health insurance company, you attach a note asking why they have an employee for every 4.5 doctors. The doctors actually provide healthcare, not the insurance employees, but 1/3 of your check is going to pay the health insurance employee and to pay for acquisitions made by the corporation. This system doesn't work, but there is something better possible.

## Health insurers pour money into GOP campaigns

Who is responsible for bringing you our nightmare health insurance industry? Politicians; and how have health insurance companies managed to get away with it for so long? They pay vast sums of your money to lobbyists. A recent article in the *Chicago Tribune—Washington Bureau* investigated recent lobbying activity by big health insurers. Like they have for decades, the health insurance companies are using lobbying in Washington to get what they want. Writer Noam Levey reports "The insurance industry is pouring money into Republican campaign coffers in hopes of scaling back wide-ranging regulations in the new healthcare law but preserving the mandate that Americans buy coverage. Sensing a Republican take-over, the lobbyists have been busy. Since January, the nation's five largest insurers and the industry's Washington-based lobbying arm have given three times more money to Republican lawmakers and political action committees than to Democratic politicians and organizations."

"That is a marked change from 2009, when the industry largely split its political donations between the parties, according to federal election filings. The largest insurers are also paying hundreds of thousands of dollars to lobbyists with close ties to Republican lawmakers who could shape health policy in January, records show. "The industry would love to have a Republican Congress," said Wendell Potter, a former executive at Cigna Corp., one of the country's biggest insurers. "They were very, very successful during the years of Republican domination in Washington." The health insurance lobbyists got their wish.

Many Republican leaders have enthusiastically embraced the call to revise the healthcare legislation, vowing to "repeal and replace" the law in the next congressional session. But that call to repeal poses a delicate issue for the budding GOP/insurance industry partnership. The Republican Party thinks it has a winning position in denouncing the unpopular mandate that will require Americans to get health insurance starting in 2014, while insurers and independent healthcare experts see the requirement as crucial to controlling costs for everyone by spreading the risk.

The healthcare law will penalize Americans $95 in 2014 if they fail to get insurance. The penalty rises to $695 in 2016." The one thing that insurance companies would love to see are penalties that are actually stronger," said Jeff Fusile, a partner at consulting giant *PricewaterhouseCoopers*. The insurance industry, attracted by the prospect of millions of new customers as a result of the coverage mandate, initially backed President Obama's campaign to overhaul the healthcare system. And insurers scored a key victory when Democrats abandoned plans to create a government insurance plan, or "public option."

Levey goes on to explain "But insurers are increasingly balking at the myriad new directives in the healthcare law. Among other things, the law prohibits insurance companies from denying coverage to sick children and canceling policies when customers become ill. The law bars insurers from placing lifetime caps on how much they will pay when their customers get sick. Many consumers will also get new rights to appeal denied claims and win access to preventive care without being asked for co-pays. 'The health reform law did not deliver the uninsured in the way that insurers wanted,' said veteran healthcare analyst Sheryl Skolnick, senior vice president at *CRT Capital Group*."

Some insurers have said recently they will stop selling some policies rather than comply with the mandate to insure sick children. Insurers are also fighting efforts by the Obama administration to expand federal oversight of premiums. And many industry leaders worry about new regulations that will set minimum standards for the scope of benefits they offer.

Cigna's head lobbyist, G. William Hoagland, a former senior Republican Senate aide, said the company hoped to get a more receptive hearing next year. "This is all political now," he said. "Once we get beyond the election, maybe cooler heads will prevail." Insurers in the past have been able to count on the GOP, which often helped shape the market to the industry's specifications.

In another scam of the century, Republicans expanded Medicare's use of commercial insurance companies to administer benefits, which has been very profitable for insurers. With the help of GOP legislation, insurers also have increasingly shifted costs to consumers through high-deductible plans. And Republicans have pushed to allow insurance companies to sell their plans across state lines, avoiding state regulations. Party leaders have made that a centerpiece of their 2011 healthcare agenda.

"We generally support candidates whose views align with our business and healthcare interests," said Aetna Inc. spokeswoman Anjie Coplin. Hartford, Conn.-based Aetna, which gave more to Democrats in 2009, has given nearly three times more to Republicans this year. Louisville, Ky.-based Humana Inc. has done the same. And Indianapolis-based WellPoint Inc., which was vilified by Democrats for proposing huge rate increases in California, has given nearly nine times as much to Republicans this year.

Levey goes on "WellPoint's lobbying team includes a former senior aide to Wyoming Sen. Michael B. Enzi, who would chair the Senate health panel should Republicans take the chamber. Enzi is a leading proponent of less state regulation of health plans. Aetna and Humana have hired former Republican aides to the Senate Finance Committee, which would also play an important role in modifying the healthcare law. Cigna's team includes the former Republican chairman of the House Energy and Commerce Committee, another key health-care panel." Doesn't this all sound familiar? Former government aides and a former chairman of the House Energy and Commerce committee now lobbying politicians on behalf of health insurance companies to get laws and regulations enacted that favor health insurance companies. Who is lobbying for people that need healthcare?

Healthcare lobbyists are going to make sure they get what they want enacted into law, and your tax dollars are going to be spent, or maybe diverted is a better word, into the pockets of the health insurance companies. It's important for health insurance companies not to pay for sick children, and to be able to drop someone's insurance when they become sick. The interesting (and sickening) thing is that the health insurers are using money for lobbyists and paying politicians that, once again, *was paid to them by people needing healthcare*. Washington and our politicians are supposed to be protecting us from the abuses of the health insurance industry, but they are getting too much money from them to complain. It doesn't work, but there is a better way.

## *Your life versus the medical-loss ratio*

Health insurance companies have a simple way to measure how much money they are "losing" by actually paying for health care—it's called the medical-loss ratio (MLR). In his book *Deadly Spin: An insurance company insider speaks out on how corporate PR is killing health care and deceiving Americans* author and former PR agent for CIGNA health insurance Wendell Potter describes the many horrors perpetrated by health insurance companies. "By jacking up premiums and shifting more and more cost to their policyholders, insurers are able to manipulate an obscure ratio that is especially important to their shareholders: the medical-loss ratio. It is telling that insurers consider the amount of money paid out in medical claims to be a loss...(the decline) in such a report is considered very good news by investors and analysts—who want the MLR to decline every quarter...Rescinding individual policies, purging small-business customers, denying claims, cheating doctors, pushing new mothers and breast cancer patients out of the hospital prematurely, and shifting costs to consumers are the ways health insurance companies cut their medical expenses and keep their MLRs from inching up."

Health insurance companies are not concerned with your life or health; they are concerned with spending as little as possible of the money you gave them for health care. Health insurers need to keep stockholders and Wall Street happy; whether you live or die makes no difference, only how much you cost them. They will literally do anything to prevent spending money on your health care.

Potter goes on "health insurers make promises they have no intention of keeping, flout regulations designed to protect consumers, and they skew political debate with multimillion-dollar public relations campaigns created to spread disinformation...he (Potter) could no longer abide the routine practices of an industry where the needs of sick and suffering Americans take a backseat to the bottom line...how a huge share of American's health care premiums bankrolls relentless propaganda and lobbying efforts focused on protecting one thing: profits." A very telling book in total, and proof that people continue to believe in *the big lie, the big scam* that having health insurance will actually cover your medical costs—regardless of all the evidence to the contrary—a mistake which can result in your death or bankruptcy.

## Is having health insurance a death sentence?

The job of every health insurance company is to make money, not provide healthcare. By withholding care, they make more money. The people that pay for health insurance may die because insurers deny coverage for procedures and treatments, but you can't sue health insurers for causing death and disability. They made sure of that with a lobbying effort a long time ago. If your health insurance company denies you life saving treatment (which they often do, because it costs them money), and you die, you have no legal recourse against the insurance company. You can't sue the health insurance company, even though it may be their fault.

Every doctor in the U.S. has stories of how one or many of their patients died as a result of their health insurance. I remember a patient that I diagnosed with prostate cancer after an ultrasound showed a tumor still localized in his prostate gland. This diagnosis was confirmed by an urologist I sent him to a week later. The Urologist was in Kentucky, but the patient lived in Illinois (right near the border with Kentucky). In fact, this urologist was the closest urologist to the patient, and he set up surgery for this man a week after diagnosis. Then his insurance called, and said they would not pay for the appointment he already had with this urologist, and would not pay for the surgery. They gave us the names of urologists that they would pay for, all of which were in St. Louis, over a two hour drive away. It took more than three weeks to get my patient into to see a "covered" urologist, who ordered more tests and several follow-up appointments. As the months passed, the cancer spread out of his prostate and into his intestines and pelvic area. By the time he actually had surgery, they had to do a radical prostectomy, orchectomy (removal of his testicles), and a huge lymph node dissection. The cancer had spread beyond his lymph nodes and was now late stage. He underwent chemo and radiation, and died within four months. If he would have had the original surgery, two weeks after the tumor was discovered, he would only have had a prostectomy, would have retained his testicles, and wouldn't have died from metastatic disease.

The irony of the whole situation is it would have cost his insurance ¼ of the cost of what they eventually spent if he would have had it done promptly in Kentucky, and he would have lived. Their refusal to pay, their refusal to cover the doctor I referred him to, cost them at least 4x more and resulted in his death. And who decided they wouldn't cover the referral to Kentucky? Someone sitting at a computer, in some office someplace who was "just doing their job," following the dictates of someone higher up the food chain. It cost a very nice man his life. These are the kinds of people we are turning our healthcare over to more and more, and if they have their way, they will get more and more of the healthcare pie and our tax dollars regardless of who may die as a result. Health insurance companies should have to place a warning (like cigarettes) on their products "having health insurance and getting sick can result in your death or bankruptcy."

## *Tort Reform Necessary to Cutting Healthcare Costs*

A trade group representing medical professional liability insurance companies pointed to a new study indicating that physicians practicing defensive medicine cost the U.S. health system $45 billion annually.

*The Physician Insurers Association of America* (all data was taken from their website: PIAA.US) said the study in the September 2010 issue of *Health Affairs* also found that total costs related to medical liability account for more than $55 billion, and the practice of defense medicine constituted 80 percent of that cost.

"This study supports our contention that reformation of the medical liability system would result in notable savings for Americans," said Lawrence E. Smarr, president of the PIAA. Mr. Smarr brought up the study in urging that Congress take up tort reform as a means of curbing the current soaring cost of medical care. "The Congressional Budget Office studied tort reform legislation last year and reported similar findings in terms of cost savings for federal healthcare programs," he said.

"Given the continued escalation of expenses related to the provision of healthcare at both the public and private level—especially as these costs relate to the practice of defensive medicine—we believe it would be prudent for the government to reexamine the impact of medical liability reform on healthcare costs," he said. "Opponents of medical liability reform continue to trivialize these savings—but the fact is that a potential $55 billion a year in cost reductions is far from insignificant," he noted.

Mr. Smarr said that the vast majority of lawsuits against healthcare providers—while rampant—are found to be meritless. For example, he said, recent PIAA data shows that 65 percent of medical professional liability claims were dropped, dismissed, or withdrawn—and the defense prevailed in 90 percent of the cases that were resolved by trial.

However, it still costs nearly *$120,000 per claim* to defend each of these meritless cases, Mr. Smarr said. "This money could be better used to improve patient safety practices or compensate patients who have suffered actual damages," he said. "The bottom line is that the current litigious climate limits patient access to care and has led to a significant increase in the overall cost of healthcare," he said.

## *The Federal Government doesn't allow their doctors to be sued...*

If you are a physician and you work for the Federal Government, guess what—you are immune from medical malpractice lawsuits (if you are a federal doctor, you already know this, or may have become a federal doctor because of this). From military doctors to family physicians working in federally-supported rural health clinics, you cannot be sued. The Federal Government knows well about ridiculous lawsuits against doctors, and they protect their own doctors from these lawsuits. But, if you don't work for the government, you have a target on your back. In Illinois, for example, trial lawyers have deep lobbying power in Springfield, the state capital. In Illinois, a physician must provide, by law, malpractice insurance coverage of $1million/$3million (single claim/multiple claims). It's one of the highest in the country.

When I was in school in Florida, by contrast, doctors were only required to provide $100,000/300,000 in coverage for themselves. With a million dollars in coverage, lawyers can file the most ridiculous lawsuits, and will settle most for $50-$100k so that the case doesn't go to court, where a judgment may result in a million dollar award or more. President Bush actually made a speech in Belleville, Illinois at the beginning of his second term, which was televised. Belleville had one of the worst tort problems in Illinois (one of the worst medical-tort states in America), and doctors were leaving in droves, especially OB/GYN's. There has been, in general, a mass exodus of doctors from Illinois, but Belleville was "ground zero" at the time. President Bush had promised to work for tort reform, to keep doctors in Illinois, but alas, nothing was ever done. The American and Illinois Chamber of Commerce, however, poured money into unseating the incumbent judge in Belleville, and won, thereby resulting is less frivolous lawsuits in the county. The problem has never been resolved, and the insurance required by law to practice medicine in Illinois remains at $1M/$3M. Unless you work for the Federal Government in Illinois, in which case you don't need *any* malpractice insurance, because you can't be sued!

The Federal Government doesn't allow their own doctors to be sued, but for everyone else defensive medicine costs as much as $55 billion a year. There is clearly a problem here, but don't expect the politicians to do anything about it (at least Democrats). As already presented, the American Association for Justice (formerly the American Trial Lawyers Association) gives almost $20 million in political contributions, 97% of which go to Democrats. It is only by a grass-roots campaign by the people that medical tort reform is going to change. The ironic thing, and what is so utterly wrong with our political system, is that the $20 *million* (plus lobbying expenses) spent by trial lawyers is preventing the possible savings of $55 *billion* in healthcare costs via defensive medicine. In addition, doctors have to pay huge premiums for malpractice coverage, which they have to pass along to the consumer in the form of increased office charges and expenses.

## Lawsuits cost consumers in more ways than one

The cost of medical lawsuits doesn't only cost you at your doctor's office it costs you at the pharmacy. Medications cost more and more as drug companies have to set aside huge amounts of money to fight lawsuits against their medicines. It also results in fewer medicines being brought to market, as each new drug presents the possibility of a massive lawsuit down the road. Given the fact that health insurance companies don't pay for newly released medications, and almost never pay for branded medications, its amazing drug companies are doing any research and development at all. So, who is going to produce the next life-saving medicine? Lawsuits against drug companies and the money they have to pay are simply passed along to the consumer in the form of higher drug prices. Medicine in third world countries and Canada cost less because drug companies don't have to worry about fighting billion dollar lawsuits in those countries. The next time you scream when you go to the pharmacy to pick up your medicine, be sure to thank all the lawyers that made that huge price possible.

## *Now is the time for change...*

We can't wait for the politicians and Washington to fix the health insurance system and the medical malpractice system. It's never going to happen. Politicians are simply getting too much money from the lobbyists of the health insurance companies and the trial lawyers. Politicians reward people that don't work with unlimited health coverage, and do nothing for people that do work. If we have to take back our government, we also have to take back our healthcare system. If the people stand by and continue with business as usual, we are going to continue to get what we've been getting: screwed; and we'll bankrupt our government, and people still won't get healthcare. People don't have health insurance, and if they do, they still don't get many of their health expenses paid for. Doctors have to practice defensive medicine, and waste tens of billions of dollars just to cover themselves from a potential lawsuit.

The system doesn't work. Patients are angry at doctors. Doctors are angry at patients. Everyone is angry at the politicians, government and health insurance companies. The people of this country want and need healthcare, and doctors have dedicated their lives to providing the best healthcare. But in the middle is the health insurance companies and lawyers. The myth and lie of having health insurance as opposed to getting healthcare has to be smashed. Doctors have to be allowed to practice medicine instead of avoiding lawsuits or fighting with HMOs. Just because healthcare is expensive doesn't mean everyone and everything related to it have the right to siphon hundreds of billions from the system. There is a better way.

As has been presented over and over, there is a better way. It's so simple that it would take about a week to implement, and it's fool-proof. Back in the old days, health insurers started out as "not for profit" enterprises. They performed a useful task, of grouping people together to get better rates for health coverage. This model may be the only way to fix our healthcare system. It was when companies like United Healthcare came along that things started to go very wrong. Health insurers are extracting hundreds of billions of dollars out of our healthcare system, and the problems this is causing are obvious to everyone (except the health insurers). Our politicians get so much money from lobbyists for the health insurers and lawyers that they will never change the system, we are going to have to do it ourselves.

## *The fix is in...*

The way to fix our healthcare system is to make it "not for profit." This means not allowing the health insurers to extract more than the minimum needed to provide for health coverage for their insured. If health insurers were limited to 5% overhead/administrative/salary costs, it would pump hundreds of billions back into healthcare. United Health, for example, would only be allowed expenses of $1.1 billion instead of $22 billion using this system. Does anyone not believe they could easily do their job with $1 billion? Do they even need that much? This would put almost $21 billion back into the healthcare system from UNH alone.

The profit motive has to be removed. Sick kids could get healthcare. People wouldn't be dropped if they got sick. The system would work, and there would be no need for all the waste and money extraction that the health insurance companies get away with now. Over time, health insurers would understand their job is to actually provide healthcare, not withhold it in order to make more money. The profit motive of health insurers is how our system got to be the way it is today, and the only way to fix it is to once again *remove* the profit motive.

The same goes for hospitals. Many big "hospital systems" today extract money from healthcare. They also have become profit machines—they run T.V. ads all day, build huge, nice administrative buildings, and have huge administrative staffs, none of whom are actually providing healthcare. They grow and buy up other hospitals and clinics, maximize profits, and behave the same way as all other corporations behave. Hospitals and hospital systems have to be made "not for profit," limiting their spending on administration and other costs (and profits).

Yes, even drug companies have to become "not for profit." Drug companies perform valuable research and development, but they also extract tens of billions of dollars from the healthcare system. Taxpayers unwittingly subsidize drug companies in that they pay for government-administered research grants. Much of the research that the government funds ultimately benefits drug companies with their research. If the two systems were combined (which is now frowned on by the media and other observers), we could continue the vital research and development pipeline that continues to produce medications that we need now and into the future. If drug companies worked closely with research hospitals, universities, and other publically funded research institutions, we could use tax dollars to fund research, and get medications at "not for profit" prices that people could actually afford. Drug companies also have to be protected from massive lawsuits.

Medicine and drug development are not perfect, but paying out billions to lawyers solves nothing. People in other countries are happy to have medicines that improve their health and lives, and thank drug companies for these medicines—they aren't allowed to sue because of an unintended outcome with no malice involved. Medicine is an art and a science. Doctors and drug companies are doing their best, but aren't perfect. Should they be sued as a result? Consumers are the ones stuck with the costs of these lawsuits, whether they realize in or not.

Our entire healthcare system has to be made "not for profit," or else it will always be doomed to failure. You cannot extract money from the system for profit, at any level, and hope that it will survive. The more money that is extracted by health insurers, lawyers, drug companies, and hospital systems, the less money actually goes to healthcare. As these companies get bigger and bigger, they need and want to extract more and more money. The consumers are the ones stuck paying more and more money, and getting less and less healthcare. Until these entities are forced to part with profit and focus on actually providing healthcare, we are headed off a cliff. It's a solution that will work.

In addition, the entire medical tort system has to be changed. Doctors shouldn't have to run tests just to protect themselves from lawsuits. Doctors shouldn't have to view each of their patients as a potential lawsuit. Why does the government protect their doctors from lawsuits while allowing all the others to get sued? The protection from lawsuits by federal doctors should be extended to all doctors. Having a dual system is unfair, ridiculous and should be illegal. Medical boards should decide if a doctor has been negligent, not a lawyer. Funds can be set up to compensate people that have been affected by negligence, not compensate their lawyers.

With just these changes, many hundreds of billions of dollars can be put back into the healthcare system. The government is willing to put hundreds of billions of dollars into healthcare, but how much of that is actually going to healthcare? Nobody knows, but unless things are changed, you can bet most of it will go into the pockets of health insurers. If the profit margin were set, by law, at 5%, we would know exactly how much is being extracted out of healthcare, and we would be able to use the money saved to actually provide healthcare. The middlemen have to be removed as a factor in healthcare. People need healthcare, and we have an excellent, though flawed, system to provide it. Money that taxpayers, businesses, and people pay for healthcare actually needs to be used for healthcare, not for profits, acquisitions, and share-holder value. The biggest mistake ever made in healthcare was letting it be run by corporations. But that can change. We can't afford to let things continue as they are. People are literally dying as a result; those that have coverage and those that do not.

## The "Not for Profit" Cure

The solution is simple, and although may not solve all the problems in healthcare, can solve most of them. What other idea has been able to make that claim? Certainly not Obamacare or any other plan put forth by politicians. What do health insurance, hospital systems, and drug companies do with your healthcare dollars? Buy tens of thousands of T.V. commercials (with your money) so you feel better about spending so much of your cash on their services. It's not until you try to use those services that you realize you aren't getting what you were promised, and that you are paying a lot more than you bargained for. It's got to stop. How many more people with health insurance have to go bankrupt because of medical costs in 2010 and beyond? Again, and this cannot be overemphasized, for 2009, 1.4 million people declared bankruptcy, of which 62% was because of medical bills. Of these, you will remember, 78% *had health insurance* for a total of 677,000 people. Yes, *677,000 of the people that declared bankruptcy in 2009 because of healthcare bills had health insurance.* This startling fact should be talked about all day long on CNN, but it isn't, and it's not an accident. There is no other statistic that shows how much our health insurance companies are ripping us off—and of our need to reform the health insurance industry (and hospital systems and drug companies). Americans shouldn't have to buy their medications from Mexico or Canada just to afford them. We have to save the $55 billion we spend on defensive medicine every year by reforming the medical tort system—the feds already did, they don't allow their doctors to be sued. This protection needs to spread to all doctors.

As one of the top expenses of government and the private sectors, the need for real change in healthcare couldn't be greater. We have to quit waiting around for the government to solve the problem because *they are part of the problem*. People that have jobs and work for a living want and need healthcare. We have to remove the profit motive, or *they* will win the battle, but *we* will all lose the war.

# CHAPTER 6

# *The Natives are Restless...*

**To compel a man to furnish funds for the propagation of ideas he disbelieves and abhors is sinful and tyrannical.**

*Thomas Jefferson*

**The spirit of resistance to government is so valuable on certain occasions that I wish it to be always kept alive.**

*Thomas Jefferson*

**The marvel of all history is the patience with which men and women submit to burdens unnecessarily laid upon them by their governments.**

*George Washington*

## *The Boston Tea Party, as old-school rebellion*

Back in the old days, we were colonists, under the rule of the British Government. A series of actions including the Stamp Act (1765), the Townsend Acts (1767) and the Boston Massacre (1770) agitated the colonists, straining relations with the mother country. But it was the Crown's attempt to tax tea that spurred the colonists to action and laid the groundwork for the American Revolution. The colonies refused to pay the levies required by the Townsend Acts claiming they had no obligation to pay taxes imposed by a Parliament in which they had no representation. In response, Parliament retracted the taxes with the exception of a duty on tea - a demonstration of Parliament's ability and right to tax the colonies. In May of 1773 Parliament concocted a clever plan. They gave the struggling East India Company a monopoly on the importation of tea to America. Additionally, Parliament reduced the duty the colonies would have to pay for the imported tea. The Americans would now get their tea at a cheaper price than ever before. However, if the colonies paid the duty tax on the imported tea they would be acknowledging Parliament's right to tax them. Tea was a staple of colonial life - it was assumed that the colonists would rather pay the tax than deny themselves the pleasure of a cup of tea.

The colonists were not fooled by Parliament's ploy. When the East India Company sent shipments of tea to Philadelphia and New York the ships were not allowed to land. In Charleston the tea-laden ships were permitted to dock but their cargo was consigned to a warehouse where it remained for three years until it was sold by patriots in order to help finance the revolution.

In Boston, the arrival of three tea ships ignited a furious reaction. The crisis came to a head on December 16, 1773 when as many as 7,000 agitated locals milled about the wharf where the ships were docked. A mass meeting at the Old South Meeting House that morning resolved that the tea ships should leave the harbor without payment of any duty. The Collector of Customs refused to allow the ships to leave without payment of the duty. The committee reported back to the mass meeting and a howl erupted from the meeting hall. It was now early evening and a group of about 200 men, some disguised as Indians, assembled on a near-by hill. Whopping war chants, the crowd marched two-by-two to the wharf, descended upon the three ships and dumped their offending cargos of tea into the harbor waters.

Most colonists applauded the action while the reaction in London was swift and vehement. In March 1774 Parliament passed the Intolerable Acts which among other measures closed the Port of Boston. So started the American Revolution.

The original Tea Party, the dumping of tea into the harbor in Boston, was a statement. It was a statement to the British that we weren't going to put up with taxation without representation anymore. We weren't going to pay taxes to the British any longer. We had no input into how much we paid in taxes, and had no input into what the British were doing with our tax dollars. Fast forward to today. *Tax freedom day*, the day when we stop paying taxes and actually start earning money for ourselves, is April 9th. We work 99 days just to pay our tax bills. We now have no input into how our tax dollars are spent, and no input into how much we actually pay in taxes. Are we now in the same situation as the people who fought for independence of our country? Do we again have taxation without representation? Do our politicians represent us, or do they represent someone else?

It seems that every time the people speak, it falls on deaf ears. Politicians enact laws and bills that serve their party or their financial supporters, or from some vague sense of what they feel needs to be done in this country. Politicians spend money they don't have, increasing our already huge national debt. The people that send politicians to Washington often make their opinions known, through polls, emails, faxes, or letter writing, but the politicians enact laws and pass huge spending bills regardless of the opinions of the people. We acknowledge the politicians right to tax us (for fear of going to jail), but we are powerless to direct where that money goes and how much we are going to pay. And it's only going to get worse with our total national debt at over $13.8 trillion dollars, taxpayers are going to have a burden that is infinitely larger than what the colonists were facing. Colonists tarred and feathered British Tax collectors. What are an armed and angry American people going to do?

# The Tea Party

**Every reform movement has a lunatic fringe.**

*Theodore Roosevelt*

**To sin by silence when they should protest makes cowards of men.**

*Abraham Lincoln*

The Tea Party has emerged as a potent force in American politics, with a nucleus in the Republican Party, with a large majority of Republicans showing an affinity for the movement. The Democrats, by contrast, consider the Tea Party as lunatics or bigots, and routinely make jokes and criticize them in the media.

The tea-party movement has emerged as a potent force in American politics and the center of gravity within the GOP. Yet some Tea Party members are essentially conservative Republicans who are very ticked-off people. They aren't even happy with some Republican candidates, especially the ones that voted for the stimulus bill or ObamaCare.

Republicans will retain major advantages even after the election. A widely publicized poll before the November 2010 election found two-thirds of GOP voters say they are intensely interested in the election, compared with about half of Democrats, suggesting that Republican voters are more likely to turn out at the polls (they did). The Tea Party is a major driver of the so-called enthusiasm gap, with three-quarters of supporters saying they are intensely interested in the election. President Barack Obama's ratings remain low, with 46% of Americans approving of his job performance. Half of Americans have a negative view of House Speaker Nancy Pelosi, compared with 22% taking a positive view.

The findings show how the tea-party movement has grown over the past two years from a loose confederation of activist groups into a bona fide brand. The survey showed that Tea Party supporters are interested in protesting "business as usual" in Washington. The most popular issue motivating them is cutting government spending and debt, followed by reducing the size of government.

When did the Tea Party start? There are many theories, but some believe it started when the government overruled the people, and passed the Wall Street/Bank bailouts. That was followed by President Obama's healthcare bill, which sparked unrest last year at congressional town-hall meetings and helped propel the movement to prominence, yet ObamaCare ranked only fourth on the list of issues among tea-party supporters.

Republicans seem to welcome the change within the party. Yet, Tea Party members are not always backing Republicans in elections. Any Republican that doesn't back the Tea Party agenda of less spending and smaller government is an enemy, not an ally. It would seem a mistake to the Republican Party to assume that the Tea Party movement is in their corner, because they aren't. "The Tea Party has to a certain extent scared the Republican Party," said one poll respondent, Tim Bahmer. He believed it would help both parties understand that people are more or less frustrated and they want to know where politicians are on issues. Mr. McInturff (the Republican pollster) said the tea-party movement had not necessarily drawn new people into the GOP.

Rather, he said, "a substantial chunk of the Republican Party is rebranding themselves." Many people saw the 2006 election as having a lack of leadership, even with a politician like John McCain. This resulted in massive Democratic victories.

The movement's greater strength could be significant beyond 2010, as the party looks toward choosing a nominee in 2012 to challenge Mr. Obama. One of the "poster girls" for the Tea Party is Alaska Gov. Sarah Palin, who is viewed positively by about two-thirds of tea-party supporters, making her more popular in the movement than other potential presidential candidates. A recent poll also showed a Tea Party members are interested in and feel positively about former Arkansas Gov. Mike Huckabee and former House Speaker Newt Gingrich, with even less enthusiasm for former Massachusetts Gov. Mitt Romney. Gingrich campaigned for Tea Party and GOP candidates in the 2010 elections, calling Democrats "the party of food stamps" and the GOP "the party of paychecks."

While the Tea Party movement's power is still emerging and being felt, Mr. Obama and top Democrats are trying to mobilize their base by portraying tea-party-backed candidates as an extreme force within the Republican Party. President Obama even called Tea Party members "Bigots." Despite the perceived affiliation with the GOP, more than a third of independents in the survey expressed an affinity for the tea-party movement. Yet 59% of independents said they were not tea-party supporters.

# Just who is the Tea Party?

In spring of 2010 CBS News and the New York Times surveyed 1,580 adults, including 881 self-identified Tea Party supporters, to see just who is the Tea Party movement. A total of eighteen percent of Americans identify themselves as Tea Party supporters. The vast majority of them — 89 percent – are white. Just one percent is black. No mention of what the other 10% are in the survey. They tend to be older: Seventy five percent are 45 years old or older, including 29 percent who are 65 plus. They are also more likely to be men (59 percent) than women (41 percent). More than one in three (36 percent) hails from the South, far more than any other region. Twenty-five percent come from the West, 22 percent from the Midwest, and 18 percent from the northeast. The South will rise again?

They are better educated than most Americans: 37 percent are college graduates, compared to 25 percent of Americans overall. They also have a higher-than-average household income, with 56 percent making more than $50,000 per year. More than half (54 percent) identify as Republicans, and another 41 percent say they are independents. Just five percent call themselves Democrats, compared to 31 percent of adults nationwide. Seventy five percent describe themselves as conservative, and 39 percent call themselves very conservative. Sixty percent say they always or usually vote Republican. Forty percent say the United States needs a third party, while 52 percent say it does not.

They are more likely than American adults overall to attend religious services weekly (38 percent do so) and to call themselves evangelical (39 percent). Sixty-one percent are Protestant, and another 22 percent are Catholic. More than half — 58 percent — keep a gun in the household. More than three in four Tea Party supporters (78 percent) have never attended a rally or donated to a group; most have also not visited a Tea Party Web site.

For the purposes of the poll, those who have attended a rally or donated to a group have been deemed Tea Party "activists." Four percent of Americans fall into this category. Tea Party activists tend to be even angrier, more pessimistic about the country and more negative about President Obama than other Americans who they identify as against the Tea Party movement.

From this data, it's pretty obvious that most Tea Party members are from the middle class, a middle class that if fighting to stay middle class in the face of the middle class being wiped out. They seem to be mainly from political origins (Republican), but have found the need to go outside the regular political establishment to get their agenda across. Far from being unaware, they consider themselves Tea Party activists despite the fact they haven't attended a rally or even visited a Tea Party website.

## *What They Believe*

Fifty-three percent of Tea Party supporters describe themselves as "angry" about the way things are going in Washington, compared to 19 percent of Americans overall who say they are angry. Asked what they are most angry about, the top four answers among Tea Party supporters who identify as angry were the healthcare reform bill (16 percent), the government not representing the people (14 percent), government spending (11 percent) and unemployment and the economy (8 percent). The Tea Party Patriots, on their website, has been trying to get petitions signed to repeal the healthcare reform bill.

At least 92 percent say America is on the wrong track, while just six percent say the country is headed in the right direction. Fifty-nine percent of Americans overall say the country is on the wrong track. Eighty-eight percent disapprove of President Obama's performance on the job, compared to 40 percent of Americans overall. While half of Americans approve of Mr. Obama's job performance, just seven percent of Tea Party supporters say he is doing a good job.

Asked to volunteer what they don't like about Mr. Obama, the top answer, offered by 19 percent of Tea Party supporters, was that they just don't like him. Eleven percent said he is turning the country more toward socialism, ten percent cited his healthcare reform efforts, and nine percent said he is dishonest. Seventy-seven percent describe Mr. Obama as "very liberal," compared to 31 percent of Americans overall. Fifty-six percent say the president's policies favor the poor, compared to 27 percent of Americans overall.

Sixty-four percent believe that the president has increased taxes for most Americans, despite the fact that the vast majority of Americans got a tax cut under the Obama administration. Thirty-four percent of the general public says the president has raised taxes on most Americans. While most Americans (58 percent) say the president understands their needs and problems, just 24 percent of Tea Party supporters agree. Just one in five say the president shares the values of most Americans.

Only one percent of Tea Party supporters approve of the job Congress is doing, compared to 17 percent of Americans overall. Twenty-four percent of Tea Party supporters say it is sometimes justified to take violent action against the government. That compares to 16 percent of Americans overall who say violence against the government is sometimes justified.

# MAIN GOAL OF TEA PARTY MOVEMENT?

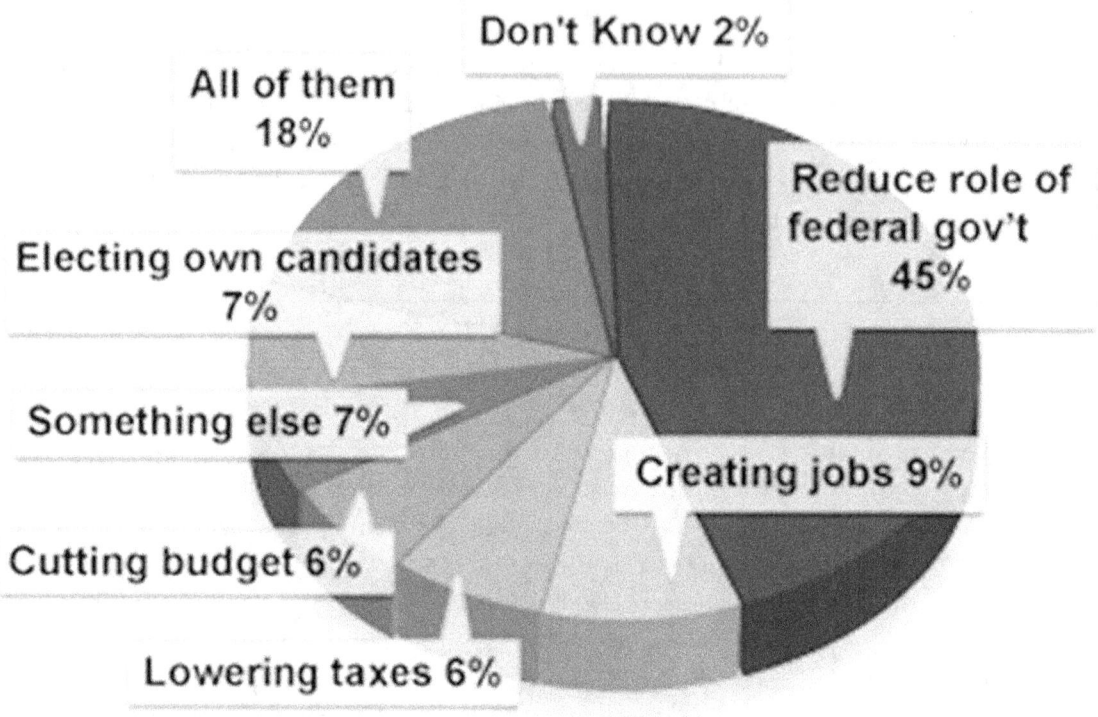

(Credit: CBS online, used with permission)

Sixty-three percent say they get the majority of their political and current events news on television from the Fox News Channel, compared to 23 percent of Americans overall. Forty-seven percent say television is their main source of Tea Party information, the top source; another 24 percent say they get Tea Party information from the internet. Nearly half say the main goal of the movement is to reduce the role of the federal government, far outdistancing any other consideration. Just seven percent say the goal of the movement is to elect Tea Party candidates.

An overwhelming majority of Tea Party supporters, 84 percent, say the views of the Tea Party movement reflect the views of most Americans. But Americans overall disagree: Just 25 percent say the Tea Party movement reflects their beliefs, while 36 percent say it does not.

## Socialism and Tea Party Leaders

Ninety-two percent of Tea Party supporters believe President Obama's policies are moving the country toward socialism (def; *any of various economic and political theories advocating collective or governmental ownership and administration of the means of production and distribution of goods: a system of society or group living in which there is no private property: system or condition of society in which the means of production are owned and controlled by the state).* Fifty-two percent of Americans overall share that belief. Asked what socialism means, roughly half of Tea Party supporters volunteered government ownership or control, far more than any other answer. Eleven percent cited taking away rights or limiting freedom, and eight percent said it means the redistribution of wealth.

Thirty percent of Tea Party supporters believe Mr. Obama was born in another country, despite ample evidence to the contrary. Another 29 percent say they don't know. Twenty percent of Americans overall, one in five believes the president was not born in the United States.

Tea Party supporters were asked in the poll what they thought of a few notable figures. The most popular was Sarah Palin, who is viewed favorably by 66 percent of people in the movement. Only 40 percent, however, believe she would be an effective president, a smaller percentage than Republicans overall. Fifty-nine percent of Tea Party supporters have a favorable impression of Glenn Beck. Nearly as many, 57 percent, have a favorable impression of former President George W. Bush, despite his role in raising the deficit and overseeing TARP bailout of the financial sector. Just 35 percent view John McCain favorably, and 28 percent view Ron Paul favorably.

## Tea Party Supporters on the Issues

Tea Party supporters are more concerned with economic than social issues. Seventy-eight percent say economic issues are a bigger concern, while 14 percent point to social issues. They are more likely than Republicans and Americans overall to see illegal immigration as a serious problem (82 percent), doubt the impact of global warming (66 percent) and call the bank bailout unnecessary (74 percent).

Ninety-three percent describe the economy as at least somewhat bad, and 42 percent say it is getting worse. Fifty-eight percent believe America's best years are behind us when it comes to good jobs, compared to 45 percent of Americans overall. Just ten percent say the stimulus package had a positive effect on the economy (compared to 32 percent of Americans overall), while 36 percent say it actually made things worse. More than half say it had no impact. Eighty-nine percent say the president has expanded the role of government too much. More than three in four say lowering the federal government is more important than government spending to create jobs.

And while the vast majority opposes the healthcare reform bill, 62 percent say programs like Social Security and Medicare are worth the costs to taxpayers. (The figure is even higher among Americans overall, at 76 percent.)

(Source and graph: *Tea Party Supporters: Who They Are and What They Believe,* by Brian Montopoli, CBS News-Politics/CBSNews.com; April 14, 2010, copyright CBSNews.com. Used with permission)

However you measure or try to quantify the Tea Party, one thing is for sure, they are becoming a force in American Politics. It's not hard to see why, with everything the government has done over the last several decades, that people have finally had enough of "politics as usual" are trying to work on something better. Does the Tea Party work outside of the political system, or is it going to try to effect change within the system? What they do with their anger is what is going to matter.

## *"It's the economy, stupid"*

Remember the campaign rallying cry that propelled Bill Clinton into office? While President Obama and the Democrats tried to rally their troops, the economy, or at least the perceived economy, is still the issue. Despite what economists say, seven in 10 adults feel the country remains in recession. And among people who said the recession had a major impact on them and their family, more said they preferred a GOP-controlled Congress to a Democratic-run Congress. This translated to a big Republican victory after the 2010 elections. One in four adults think the economy would get worse over the next 12 months. Of that group, two-thirds were people with an affinity for the Tea-Party movement. The survey did a fairly good job of classifying people in the Tea Party, and it's not hard to imagine that many are middle-class conservatives that have seen their incomes and standards of living dropping out, watched their home value and retirement savings get wiped out, and watched as the government spends hundreds of billions of dollars with little or no result.

The Tea Party seems to be more than a radical branch of the Republican Party, they see themselves as patriots, trying to take back the government for the spendthrift politicians, especially the tax-and-spend Democrats. Many people have watched as the government has spent trillions of dollars on programs people don't support, and have waited for the day when their taxes were going to start going up—the day when the government reaches deeper and deeper into their pockets. The Tea Party has watched the federal government grow and consume ever increasing amounts of money, while ignoring the polls and the will of the people. They see the government, and especially the federal government as "out of control," like a car that is heading for a cliff. The middle class is being wiped out, and they aren't happy about it, and they don't see the government as fixing anything, they are only making it worse.

Let's take a look at one candidate that the Tea Party supports, although he is not as popular as some of their other front-runners. Kentucky Senate candidate Rand Paul sees economic doom possibly on the horizon for the U.S. using one of the most spectacular collapses in history to illustrate his point. Paul says there's a similarity between America's current economic situation and the fall of the Roman Empire. In a speech given by Paul at a Tea Party rally, he compared recent U.S. government assistance programs – such as the stimulus package – to Roman emperors giving away food and entertainment as the Roman economy collapsed. "In the latter days of Rome, the economy was crumbling, the emperor…would placate the mob with bread and circus - food and entertainment to placate them since the economy was in shambles and dwindling around them. Now in our country, as our economy is in shambles, they give us cash for clunkers, food stamps and a stimulus check and they tell us to go to the mall and spend your money and everything will be OK."

Paul campaign spokesman Jesse Benton told news reporters that the candidate was simply using a metaphor to make a serious point. "He uses it as a metaphor to illustrate that great nations can fall if they're not respectful of their great traditions," Benton said. "If we don't avert ourselves from our path of unsustainable debt…we are going to see some cataclysmic consequences. Benton was asked if Paul's "metaphor" means the candidate believes the U.S. government is doling out something akin to "bread and circus – food and entertainment" simply to satisfy angry mobs of Americans. "People are scared and they very much want action," Benton told CNN. "So the government is trying to placate people by showing them they're taking action. But it's the wrong action." The economy has gotten so bad that now more people are in poverty, and more people are on food stamps than in any time in recent memory. The government spends hundreds of billions, and the people get food stamps. Rand Paul won the election in 2010.

The main concern of the Tea Party, once again, is economic. The Democrats have spent close to $1 trillion dollars on stimulus, yet most Tea Party members, and most Americans for that matter, aren't any better off. This $1 trillion dollar stimulus was *deficit spending*, which raised the national deficit to $1.37 trillion dollars for 2010 alone. People are scared, and they would be even more scared if they knew that 1,997 lobbyists were registered and lobbied for the stimulus bill. I'm sure those lobbyists know where the $1 trillion went. The average American doesn't, and neither does the average Tea Party member.

## Americans ARE Painfully Aware of the Deficit

The deficit and government spending, as a measure of the size of the government, are often mentioned as the primary source of anger among Americans. They should be concerned. An opinion piece in *Fortune Magazine* by Becky Quick presents some sobering numbers. "The federal government is currently spending $3 for every $2 it collects in revenue. We're now ratcheting up a deficit that's growing at the breakneck speed of about $100 billion a month. Our national debt as a percentage of the economy is more than 61%, breaching the 60% line for only the second time in the nation's history (the last time was during World War II). In 10 years, the Congressional Budget Office estimates, we will be spending more on interest payments to service that debt than we will for all nondefense discretionary spending…and that's assuming interest rates don't go up… Consider another set of numbers: from 1948-2008, the federal government spent about 19.6% of our GDP, while taking in tax revenues of about 17.9%. But now we are spending a whopping 25% of GDP and taking in closer to 15% in revenue."

Despite the national debt being at its highest level since World War II, *The CATO Institute* reports fewer people are actually paying taxes. In 1962, the first year measured, the percentage of people who didn't pay federal income taxes themselves (and who were not claimed as dependants by someone who paid federal income taxes) stood at 23.7 percent. By 2000, the percentage was 34.1 percent. By 2008, it was 43.6 percent. The country may be rapidly approaching a point where *one-half of taxpayers do not pay taxes,* while receiving generous federal benefits and entitlements. Is just taxing the rich going to work? Not really: According to Congressman Issa (R-CA) if there was a 100% tax on people making more than $250,000 per year (the government took all the money they earned), it would only generate close to $900 billion per year, which is *less* than annual federal government deficit spending alone. Of course you can't tax anyone 100%, but politicians would like to get their hands on at least 98% of rich people's money.

Economists interested in averting a crisis recommend either huge increases in taxes or drastic cuts in spending, neither of which our politicians are willing to tackle. Just look at the results of President Obama's deficit commission: The panel couldn't even get enough support to forward its recommendation to Congress. The politicians created this problem, and we're going to trust them to fix it?

## *How much is government spending going to cost you and your family?*

The Obama Administration has used the recession as an excuse for a historic and permanent expansion of government and deficits. Only during the height of World War II has Washington matched current levels of spending (25% of GDP) and deficits (10% of GDP). Even after the recession, runaway spending is expected to keep annual budget deficits over $1 trillion a year, which could result in sharply higher interest rates, painful tax increases, and even a Ireland or Greece-like economic crisis. The Greek economy collapsed due to debt default of around $250 billion. The U.S. racks up that much debt *every 2 ½ months*. Beyond our own economic consequences, dumping this staggering debt on future generations is absolutely wrong.

**Some facts:**

- **Soaring Spending. Federal spending per household, which has already surged from $25,000 to $31,000 since 2008, would reach $36,000 by 2020 under President Obama's budget (adjusted for inflation). If spending rises $11,000 per household, taxes will eventually have to follow.**
- **Debt and Taxes. Even with $3 trillion in tax increases over the next decade, the President's budget would double the national debt to more than $20 trillion ($138,000 per household) by 2020.**
- **Spending Is Driving Long-Term Deficits. Even if all of the tax cuts are extended, revenues will exceed their 18% of GDP historical average by the end of the decade. The reason the budget deficit is projected to rise by 6% of GDP over its historical average by 2020 is that spending will exceed its historical average by 6% of GDP. Nearly all of this growth will occur in Social Security, Medicare, Medicaid, and net interest. And deficits will expand even further if lawmakers repeat the past decade's 79% growth (adjusted for inflation) in discretionary spending.**

The people that pay taxes are going to get hammered. President Obama is planning to increase taxes by $3 trillion dollars over the next decade. Considering only 56.4% of people in the U.S. pay taxes (and 43.6% pay no taxes), they are going to have a huge tax bill before long. Despite this coming tax nightmare, politicians continue to spend and grow government at light speed. Instead of shrinking the government, Obama is spending as much as we did during World War II and much of it is deficit/debt spending. This will leave us with a national debt of $20 trillion dollars by 2020. More taxes, more spending, and bigger government.

Cutting spending obviously has to be a higher priority. Yet, politicians are utterly unable to cut spending. No politician wants to be responsible for cutting Social Security, Welfare, Disability, Medicare or Medicaid—it's political suicide. Yet, what beneficiaries of these entitlement programs don't seem to understand is that if the U.S. becomes insolvent as a result of these programs and over-spending, then they will get *nothing* anymore, our national security will be threatened, and our economy and way of life will utterly collapse.

*What will your share be?  Have a look....*

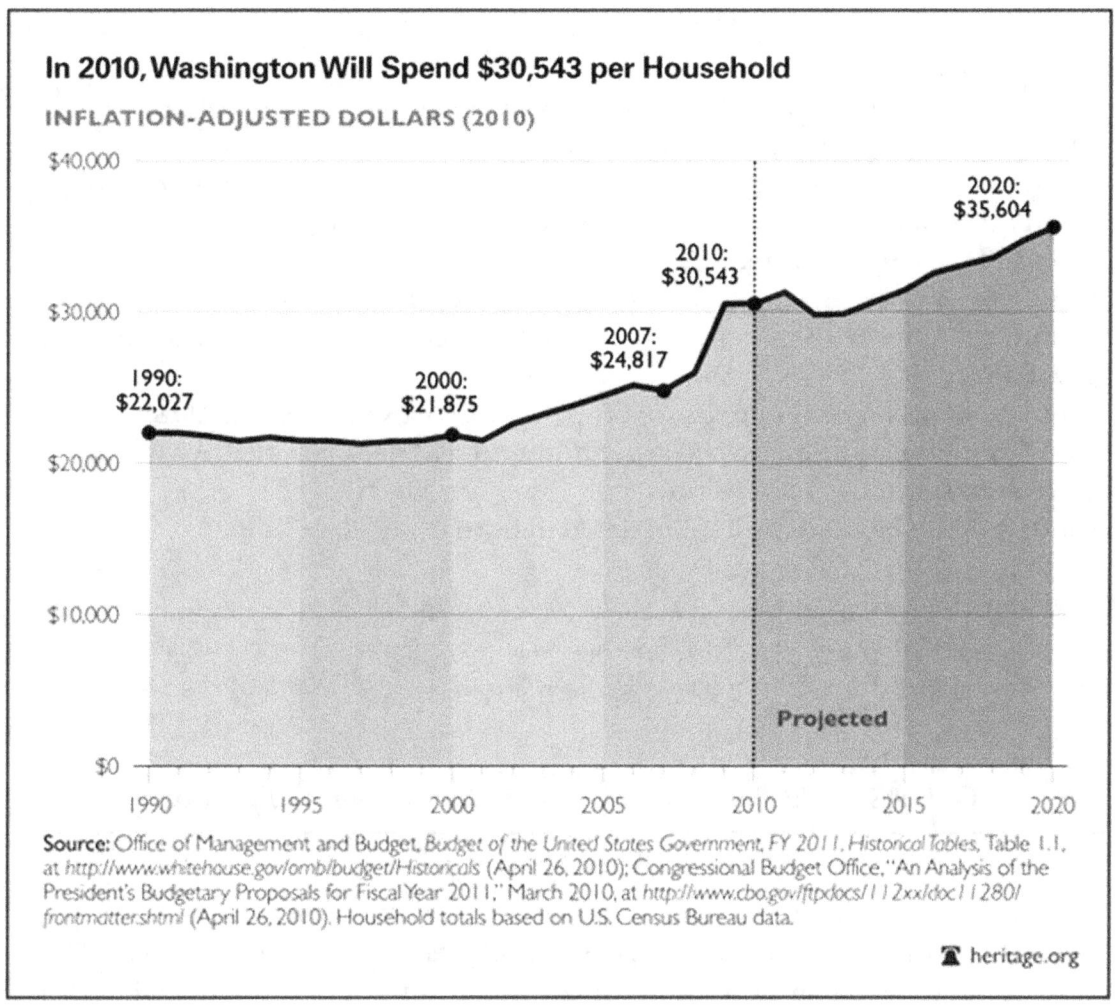

**In 2010, Washington Will Spend $30,543 per Household**

INFLATION-ADJUSTED DOLLARS (2010)

1990:
$22,027

2000:
$21,875

2007:
$24,817

2010:
$30,543

2020:
$35,604

Projected

Source: Office of Management and Budget, *Budget of the United States Government, FY 2011, Historical Tables,* Table 1.1, at *http://www.whitehouse.gov/omb/budget/Historicals* (April 26, 2010); Congressional Budget Office, "An Analysis of the President's Budgetary Proposals for Fiscal Year 2011," March 2010, at *http://www.cbo.gov/ftpdocs/112xx/doc11280/ frontmatter.shtml* (April 26, 2010). Household totals based on U.S. Census Bureau data.

☎ heritage.org

(Graph: Originally published at Heritage.org, copyright by The Heritage Foundation, used with permission)

The government is going to spend $30,000 per household this year (2010) and increase spending to over $35,000 per household by 2020. Somebody has to pay for all this spending, so let's take a look at how spending will reach these levels.

When he released his new budget proposal on February 1, 2010 President Obama asserted that the government "simply cannot continue to spend as if deficits don't have consequences; as if waste doesn't matter; as if the hard-earned tax dollars of the American people can be treated like Monopoly money; as if we can ignore this challenge for another generation."

Yet the President's new budget does exactly that – raising taxes by $3 trillion and federal spending by $1.6 trillion a year over the next ten years. If enacted, this budget would increase the 2010 deficit to more than $1.5 trillion, and leave a deficit of more than $1 trillion a year even after an assumed return to peace, prosperity and economic recovery. Overall, the President's budget would double the national debt over the next decade.

**President Obama's Budget**
- **Would permanently expand the federal government by 3 percent of gross domestic product (GDP) over 2007 pre-recession levels;**
- **Would raise taxes on all Americans by nearly $3 trillion over the next decade;**
- **Would raise taxes for 3.2 million small businesses and upper-income taxpayers by an average of $300,000 over the next decade;**
- **Would borrow 42 cents for each dollar spent in 2010;**
- **Would run a $1.6 trillion deficit in 2010 – $143 billion higher than the recession-driven 2009 deficit;**
- **Would leave permanent deficits that top $1 trillion a year as late as 2020;**
- **Would dump an additional $74,000 per household of debt into the laps of our children and grandchildren; and**
- **Would double the publicly held national debt to over $20 trillion.**

(Source: U.S. Office of Management and Budget, *Budget of the United States Government, Fiscal Year 2011* {Washington, D.C.: U.S. Government Printing Office, 2010}, pp. 146-179, Tables S-1 through S-14. Also includes the cost of House-passed cap-and-trade bill, which President Obama endorsed yet excluded from his budget tables. Based on calculations by The Heritage Foundation, Heritage.org)

---

*You can blame Congress, and Presidents Bush or Obama, for our perilous fiscal situation.*

---

Not everything can be blamed on President Obama, however. With the financial situation in the country such as it is, and many Americans angry, there is no shortage of blame to go around. President Bush walked into office with a government surplus, and walked out with a huge deficit. Although this is a problem, it has gotten worse, and the worse it gets, the more politicians start hurling blame around. During a recent press conference, President Obama blamed George W. Bush for the nation's fiscal condition. "When I walked in," he declared, "wrapped in a nice bow was a $1.3 trillion deficit sitting right there on my doorstep." Earlier this year he asserted that "we came in with $8 trillion worth of debt over the next decade."

Neither statement is correct, according to the Congressional Budget Office (CBO). The outgoing Bush administration did leave big deficits to Mr. Obama. The expected 2009 deficit was $1.19 trillion, not $1.3 trillion, however—and the actual deficit for 2009 came in at $1.41 trillion, meaning that the new president added some $220 billion to the total (this data is available online from the CBO at CBO.gov). Far more significant, however, was the president's misstatement that Mr. Bush and the Republicans left the country with $8 trillion of debt over the next 10 years. The CBO's projected 10-year deficit when Mr. Obama took office was actually $4.09 trillion. Now, after 20 months of his presidency, the expected deficit has almost doubled, to $7.68 trillion.

A strong case can be made that the people most responsible for the gigantic deficits we face today are neither George W. Bush nor Barack Obama, although they oversaw what was going on. The real culprits are Speaker of the House Nancy Pelosi and Senate Majority Leader Harry Reid. One of the biggest mistakes of the Obama administration was his handing over the stimulus spending to Pelosi and Reid. President Obama was seen just after his victory in 2008 with his new economic team, and held several press conferences with them. Then, he delegated spending to Congress instead of his economic team. When Mrs. Pelosi and Mr. Reid rose to their present jobs in January 2007, the deficit was $161 billion. It had been on a downward trajectory from $413 billion in 2004. Three years later, the Pelosi-Reid Congress had added $1.2 trillion to the deficit.

Of course, Mr. Bush sponsored or signed into law many of these deficit-raising bills, such as the bank bailouts and effective tax rebates of 2008. But the Democratic Congress passed them. Long forgotten is the promise Mrs. Pelosi made on the day she became speaker: "Our new America will provide unlimited opportunity for future generations, not burden them with mountains of debt." Congress has, in fact, leveraged our future and buried us under mountains of debt.

Today, Mr. Obama and Democrats in Congress love to talk about how Mr. Bush turned a $200 billion Clinton surplus into a $1 trillion deficit. Indeed he did, though they ignore the 9/11 terrorist attacks that happened less than a year after Mr. Bush became president. Those attacks were fiscal game-changers, forcing the economy to a temporary standstill and requiring unplanned spending for homeland security and antiterrorism efforts. For the sake of comparison, let's look at the Pelosi-Reid fiscal record over 10 years. In January 2007, the CBO projected a $379 billion surplus over the next decade. Now, after four years under Mrs. Pelosi and Mr. Reid, and two years of Mr. Obama in the White House, the 2007-2016 projection is a deficit of $7.16 trillion. One of the biggest spenders of taxpayer's money in history (Mr. Reid) is also one of the biggest recipients of special-interest campaign contributions and lobbying dollars in Washington. Is it a coincidence? Not hardly.

This deterioration of the nation's fiscal situation is arguably the worst in United States history, and it was brought to us courtesy of a congressional leadership that pledged "pay as you go," but more and more people are asking: who got paid, and where did it go?

(Source: Congressional Budget Office, CBO.gov)

---

## *More anger over bank bailouts and TARP money*

---

For years, and especially during the time of the government bailout, the media made a big deal out of the battle of "Main Street" versus Wall Street. Ground zero for the bailout and the "battle of Main Street versus Wall Street" was the huge government bailout of American International Group (AIG). It was touted by President Bush and Treasury Secretary Paulson as essential in keeping the U.S. financial system afloat. Now, several years later, AIG plans to exit the federal bailout. Some see a political motivation in the plan to exit the biggest of the Wall Street bailouts a month before midterm elections. But much as embattled Democrats might wish otherwise, the book on Troubled Assets Recovery Program (TARP) won't close anytime soon. With TARP, banks and investment houses dumped all their failed financial bets and toxic assets onto the taxpayers, and then stared minting money again.

There's no guarantee taxpayers who gave AIG a $182 billion bailout will be repaid under the plan the company announced. Under the deal, Treasury will swap its majority stake in AIG for common stock and then sell those shares over time. Although the ability to use TARP is now closed, close to $190 billion in TARP money remains unpaid, and the Congressional Budget Office estimates that taxpayers will never get back about $66 billion of it. The public remains angry about the bailouts. Americans have been particularly furious over the huge bonuses that bailed-out firms paid to executives. TARP, which Obama administration officials say helped stabilize the financial system, has been targeted by the Tea Party movement as a wasteful giveaway that rescued Wall Street while ordinary Americans suffered the effects of the Great Recession. Democratic and Republican lawmakers who voted for the bailout have become targets of voter anger.

Treasury's work on the bailouts is hardly finished. As of Aug. 31, 2010, Treasury had tapped $460 billion from TARP for banks, auto makers and mortgage companies. Of that, $386 billion was disbursed, and $187 billion had not been repaid. AIG and automakers GM and Chrysler held the bulk of that money. AIG was one of the financial companies hit hardest by the credit crisis and received the largest bailout the government handed out. AIG also drew criticism for continuing to pay out bonuses to employees after it received the bailout. GM paid back most of its money with a recent IPO which was successful.

Just how much did the government give big banks in the Wall Street bailout? Much more than anyone realized. David Weidner reports in his story *Banks to Taxpayers: Get Over It* for Yahoo! Finance/MarketWatch that "In the throes of an investor panic in the fall of 2008, U.S. financial institutions stuck to their story: We're fine, trust us. In December 2010, more than two years later, the Federal Reserve unveiled how those same financial institutions tapped emergency lending programs to survive. The final tally — $3.3 trillion in loans — exceeded even the most skeptical analyst expectations. The Fed had been hesitant to release the data for fear it could rattle the markets."

"The disclosure tells us a lot about how dire the situation was in the darkest days of the credit crisis, but it also tells us some important things about today's banking landscape: It's fragile, it's built on faith — and a lot of extraordinary backing. The phrase "zombie" banks comes to mind when the numbers are laid bare: Morgan Stanley borrowed $61 billion in one overnight loan. Goldman Sachs Group Inc. hit up the Fed 81 times for a combined $600 billion. Citigroup Inc. and Bank of America Corp. borrowed a combined $2.6 trillion under the Fed's primary dealer facility. Even J.P. Morgan Chase & Co used the central bank's term auction facility seven times. These amounts make AIG look like a cake-walk. Oh, and the banks' way of saying thanks for all of this: Get over it." If we indeed lived in a capitalistic society, the government would have let these banks fail, but instead rewarded them with trillions of taxpayer dollars.

Meanwhile, Wall Street bankers and gamblers are making more money than ever (after having gotten almost $3.3 trillion in taxpayer bail-out money/loans). Aaron Task of *Tech Ticker* and John Cassidy, a staff writer at *The New Yorker* and author of *How Markets Fail* reported "As 2010 comes to a close, it looks like another banner year for Wall Street: the top six 'too big to fail' firms booked $35 billion of profits in the first nine months of the year and year-end bonuses are forecast to be $144 billion, which would be a new record for the industry. Meanwhile, financial institutions continue to benefit from the Fed's zero interest rate policies, which amounts to a 'disguised bailout' for banks, says Cassidy. Meanwhile, consumers are 'getting screwed on our savings accounts,' where anything above 0% seemingly counts as 'high-yield' these days. So after trillions of bailouts for the banks, the question remains: *What's in it for the rest of us — other than a very large bill?*" Wall Street, big banks and investment firms are like unlimited casinos, but with very different rules — when they lose and the economy collapses, they transfer their losses, debts and "toxic assets" to the Federal Reserve and taxpayers, and when they win, they pay themselves bonuses of $144 billion dollars.

And the problem is that, even after bringing about an almost-collapse of our entire financial system, and requiring trillions of taxpayer dollars to survive, not much has changed. Consider Cassidy's finding that "in the first 9 months of this year, sales and trading accounted for 36% of Morgan Stanley's revenues and a much higher proportion of profits." The example is even more dramatic in the case of Goldman Sachs — the envy of all Wall Street — where, as Cassidy writes, "trading accounted for 63% of its revenue and corporate finance just 13%" between July and September. In short, bankers "have done very well for themselves," he says, but "not very much for the rest of the country."

## *The Federal Debt Ceiling*

The *Dallas Morning News* reported on Nov. 21, 2010 "The federal government will run out of money next spring. Tapped out. Credit line depleted. Nothing to do but borrow more — or let the government screech to a halt, with all the damage that would inflict on the economy. Only the U.S. government can raise its own credit limit. States can't do it, or homeowners, or businesses. But here's the rub: The tea partiers are in no mood to spill more red ink. Scores of freshman lawmakers elected in 2010 ran on anti-spending platforms."

"Politicians voted in February 2010 to raise the debt limit from $12.4 trillion to $14.2 trillion, yet even this limit will soon be exceeded. That will make for some interesting political contortions in a few months. 'We have a debt limit issue. The United States must pay its bills,' said Rep. Pete Sessions, a Dallas Republican who led the party's stunning return to a majority in the midterm elections. Many of the 85 or so GOP freshmen who take office in January thundered against that February debt-ceiling vote. Now, with Republicans in charge of the House, they would be blamed for a government shutdown. But with so many freshmen on record opposing a higher debt ceiling, the GOP leadership has a problem. 'The bloodbath will be extraordinary,' Alan Simpson, the former GOP senator from Wyoming who co-chairs the White House deficit commission, predicted." Our government will run out of money in the spring because the deficit is currently $13.8 trillion and deficit spending is $100 billion per month, and so will reach the debt ceiling this spring. Some economists warn further raising of the debt ceiling is dangerous because people and entities that hold our federal debt/treasury bills are waiting for a "signal" that the U.S. owes more than it can repay and/or default on its debt; and the continued raising of the debt ceiling may be that signal. Either way, politicians are going to have to come to terms with the reality of their massive spending this spring, and it's not going to be pretty.

## *Lame-duck congress sets deficit spending record in earmark orgy*

After the elections of 2010, the Democrat-controlled Congress became "lame-duck" because they won't be in control after the first of the year. Just because they call it "lame-duck" doesn't mean politicians can't continue to spend massive amounts of money they don't have. It's been presented repeatedly that our government has been deficit spending $100 billion per month it doesn't have. Well, it turns out this is low—politicians are accelerating their deficit spending in a big, record-setting way. Martin Crutsinger of Associated Press reported Dec. 10ᵗʰ, 2010 that "the monthly federal budget deficit rose to $150.4 billion in Nov. 2010, the largest November gap on record." In Nov. 2010, the government spent $5 billion *per day* it didn't have. "And the government's deficits are set to climb higher when Congress passes a tax-cut plan that's estimated to cost $855 billion over two years. The Treasury Department says November's budget gap was 25 percent more than the deficit in November 2009."

Despite an almost $14 trillion dollar deficit and our government running out of money, politicians voted another huge spending bill into effect in Dec. 2010 which added yet another estimated $855 billion to our deficit. It included extending unemployment benefits and tax-cuts. "But analysts say the tax deal President Barack Obama reached with Republicans will give the 2011 budget year the largest deficit in history – $1.5 trillion, according to economists at JPMorgan Chase. It would mark the third straight year of trillion-dollar-plus deficits. Under the tax-cut plan, JPMorgan economist Michael Feroli said he expects a $1.5 trillion deficit this year to be followed by a $1.2 trillion gap in 2012." Add this to our current $13.8 trillion dollar deficit, and we'll be up to at least $16.5 trillion by the end of 2012. Politicians are going to have to raise the debt ceiling much more than they thought after massively increasing deficit spending. Economists keep making deficit projections, and politicians amazingly keep surpassing them. At current increasing spending levels, we will see a $20 trillion dollar deficit long before the predicted date of 2020.

Not to be outdone by the tax cut bill, Democrats (and some Republicans) went wild before losing control of Congress in December 2010. *Associated Press* reported in an article titled *Earmarkers feast on pork one last time before diet* that "The spending barons on Capitol Hill, long used to muscling past opponents of bills larded with pet projects, are seeking one last victory before tea party-backed GOP insurgents storm Congress intent on ending the good old days of pork-barrel politics. You might call it the last running of the old bulls in Congress. In the waning days of the lame duck congressional session, Democrats controlling the Senate — in collaboration with a handful of old school Republicans — are pushing to wrap $1.27 trillion worth of unfinished budget work into a single "omnibus" appropriations bill. Their 1,900-plus-page bill comes to the floor stuffed with provisions sought by lawmakers. It contains thousands of pet projects, known as earmarks, pushed by Democratic and GOP senators alike — despite a pledge by Republicans to give up such projects next year."

"That omnibus bill will be loaded down with earmarks and pork-barrel spending, which is a direct — a direct — betrayal of the majority of voters on Nov. 2 who said 'Stop the earmarking, stop the spending, stop the pork-barrel projects,' protested Sen. John McCain, R-Ariz. Incoming House Speaker John Boehner, R-Ohio, is a long-standing opponent of doling out federal dollars for pork. Boehner will become the single most powerful member of Congress next year, and he has laid down the law, promising to cut as much as $100 billion from 2011 agency budgets and ban earmarks. He signed a letter last week asking Obama to veto the omnibus bill because of its earmarks, and issued a statement calling the legislation a 'disgrace' and 'a smack in the face to taxpayers.'" On their way out of town, politicians led by Harry Reid tried to pass out another $1.27 trillion to their friends and supporters. Mr. Reid even went on T.V. telling viewers how necessary this bill was. Is it time to add yet another $1.27 trillion to the deficit? At least John McCain had some recollection of what the voters wanted in the last election.

## *The Federal Deficit and National Security*

Elizabeth MacDonald of *Fox Business* reported the following quotes Oct. 10th, 2010 in the article "U.S. Debt a National Security Issue:"

"Our rising debt levels (pose) a national security threat."—U.S. Secretary of State <u>Hillary Clinton</u> to Council on Foreign Relations, Sept. 2010.

"The biggest threat we have to our national security is our debt...the interest on our debt is $571 billion in 2012 and that's notionally about the size of the Defense Department budget. It's not sustainable."—<u>Admiral Michael Mullen</u>, Chairman of the Joint Chiefs of Staff, June 2010.

"We've reached a point now where there's an intimate link between our solvency and our national security."—<u>Richard Haass</u>, President, Council on Foreign Relations.

"Several months ago, a group of logistics officers at the Industrial College of the Armed Forces developed a national security strategy as a class exercise. Their No. 1 recommendation for maintaining U.S. global leadership was 'restore fiscal responsibility.'"—<u>Washington Post</u>, May 2010.

"The Pentagon sponsored a first-of-its-kind war game...on how hostile nations might seek to cripple the U.S. economy," with the weapons being stocks, bonds and currencies..."it was the first time the Pentagon hosted a purely economic war game."—<u>Politico.com</u>, 2009.

"The United States cannot force foreign governments to increase their holdings of Treasuries...The world does not have so much money to buy more U.S. Treasuries." – <u>Zhu Min</u>, Deputy Governor of the People's Bank of China, December 2009.

With this kind of unimaginable spending by politicians, at what point does the concept of treason come to mind? Flagrant political spending is jeopardizing our national security. The most powerful military figure in the nation (besides the President and Defense Secretary)—The Chairman of the Joint Chiefs of Staff thinks "<u>the biggest threat we have to our national security is our debt</u>"—bigger than terrorism, Iran, North Korea or other nuclear threats, *our debt is the biggest threat to our sovereignty*.  Imagine he stated, for example, that Aruba was "the biggest threat we have to our national security," we would use all the resources we had to subdue Aruba. Maybe a silly example, but what are we doing to stop the *real* biggest threat to our national security—spending by politicians? Nothing. The biggest threat to our country isn't from somewhere else, it's from Washington and politicians. We should be using all our resources to stop the spending, as it is the biggest threat to our national security. Politicians are destroying our country from within – they are pouring gasoline on the fire as our country burns economically. Fortunately, Senate Majority Leader Harry Reid decided to drop the omnibus bill before passage.

## *According to Senator Coburn, Wasteful spending highlights the list of U.S. stimulus projects*

U.S. Sen. Tom Coburn (R-Oklahoma) wants to shed light on the wasteful spending in the federal stimulus and his list includes projects in his home state of Oklahoma. One of the 100 examples Coburn has compiled is $1.5 million in "free" stimulus money for a new wastewater treatment plant that results in higher utility costs for residents of Perkins, Okla. Another is $1.15 million for installation of a new guardrail for the non-existent Optima Lake in Oklahoma. There is no lake - it's a dry hole.

Coburn's report, *100 Stimulus Projects: A Second Opinion* is available in its entirety on his website (coburn.senate.gov). "Why is the federal government wasting your tax dollars on a guardrail for a 'lake' that doesn't even contain any water?" Coburn asked. The 100 projects he lists- worth $5.5 billion - range from Maine to California. "The American people have a right to know how their stimulus dollars are being spent. In too many cases stimulus projects are wasting money we don't have on things we don't need," Dr. Coburn said. "Rather than growing our economy, the overall impact of stimulus spending may prove to be harmful to our economy. For example, Washington's efforts to 'stimulate' the economy are increasing utility costs, repairing bridges nobody uses, building tunnels for turtles, and renovating extravagant train stations in remote areas while widely-used bridges and roads in poor shape are passed over."

Coburn said he opposed the bill because it just wouldn't stimulate the economy. "I opposed the stimulus bill because I was concerned that 80 to 90 percent of the spending would not be true stimulus," Coburn said. "I hope I am proven wrong. Yet, our initial findings continue to show that taxpayers are not getting the value they deserve and need." Dr. Coburn said Earl Devaney, head of the Recovery Act Accountability and Transparency (RAAT) Board, estimates that at least $55 billion of stimulus funds may be lost to waste, fraud and abuse. However, the final number will likely be much higher. If stimulus funds do not promote economic growth, history may indicate that the vast majority of stimulate dollars would have been better off staying in taxpayers' pockets, Coburn said.

Besides the two Oklahoma projects, Coburn emphasized the following eight projects: $1 billion for FutureGen in Mattoon, Illinois is the "biggest earmark of all time" for a power plant that may never work. $15 million for "shovel-ready" repairs to little-used bridges in rural Wisconsin are given priority over widely used bridges that are structurally deficient. $800,000 for little-used John Murtha Airport in Johnstown, Pennsylvania to repave a back-up runway; the "airport for nobody" has already received tens of millions in taxpayer dollars. $3.4 million for a wildlife "eco-passage" in Florida to take animals safely under a busy roadway. A Nevada non-profit gets a $2 million weatherization contract after recently being fired for the same type of work. Nearly $10 million to renovate an abandoned train station that hasn't been used in 30 years. Ten thousand dead people will get stimulus checks, but the Social Security Administration blames a tough deadline. The town of Union, New York, were encouraged to spend a $578,000 grant it did not request for a homelessness problem it claims it does not have.

"There's no question that our economic situation required bold action when Congress rushed to pass the American Recovery and Reinvestment Act (ARRA) - more commonly known as the stimulus bill," Coburn said. "Unfortunately, the stimulus has yet to really stimulate anything at all. Our nation's unemployment rate has continued to increase every month since the passage of the bill and now President Obama expects it to hit 10 percent. The unemployment rate has stayed around 9.6 for more than a year, but the Bureau of Labor and Statistics reports that true unemployment could be as high as 16.4 percent when adjusted for discouraged workers - those who would like to work full time but are discouraged from doing so.

"In my estimation, Congress chose the wrong approach to stimulating the economy by spending money we don't have on things we don't need," Coburn said. "Real stimulus includes lowering the tax and regulatory burden on hardworking families and businesses, which creates good jobs for the long term. "Now more than ever, it is imperative that we keep fighting against wasteful government spending and instead focus on implementing legislation that will actually help grow our economy and create jobs for out of work Americans."

## Some projects funded by the President Obama's Stimulus Package:

Midwestern Region: An Illinois county spent $173,824 from a weatherization grant on eight pickup trucks. A Wisconsin nursing home received $2.8 million in stimulus money it didn't need or request. Road signs costing $300 each are being placed at construction sites to alert motorists that the project is being paid for by stimulus money. In Illinois alone, the signs are expected to cost $150,000, according to the Illinois Department of Transportation (IDOT). IDOT spent millions of stimulus money in Harrisburg, Illinois for a two lane highway around the town that nobody will use and directs traffic away from an already decimated downtown. In Macomb, Illinois, $643, 945 was spent on a Prairie view public housing parking lot that no one wants. Illinois will spend $350,000 to build a four-person bunkhouse at Crab Orchard National Wildlife Refuge. The median price for a home in Marion, Illinois, the site of the park, is currently $71,000.

Akron, Ohio used up to $1.5 million to erect a suicide-prevention fence to keep people from jumping off the All-American Bridge despite concerns such a project would be wasteful, ineffective and ugly. Rather than help welfare recipients obtain jobs and escape poverty, $1 million will be used to study whether 300 people in Chicago are healthier when living in "green" public housing facilities. The National Institute of Health gave an Indiana University professor $356,000 to study how kids perceive foreign accents.

The Tallgrass Prairie National Preserve's new visitor's center and a pedestrian and bike project over U.S. Highway 75 in Kansas were some of the first projects approved for stimulus funds in the state. Failing to cite an economic benefit from the projects, officials noted that they chose "projects that strengthen the cultural, aesthetic or environmental value of our transportation system." A National Forest in Missouri will receive $462,000 to replace toilets.

The Southern Region: Memphis, Tennessee spent $1.5 million to redevelop fairgrounds and $250,000 to rehabilitate a dilapidated laundromat. Stimulus money paid for housing used by Soyono the Sumatran tiger and Luke the Lion at the National Zoo in Washington, D.C. Despite federal law that prohibits spending federal funds on local zoos, money will go to the National Zoo. The Smithsonian, which runs the zoo, is spending $11.4 of its $25 million in stimulus funds on the National Zoo and its Zoo research center in Virginia. Washington, North Carolina is using stimulus funds to pay for a "project-funding manager" whose job it is to secure even more stimulus funds. Lexington, Kentucky, spent $4.7 million on a trail connecting downtown with a horse farm. Virginia spent $340,000 on a rural bridge that carries only 20 cars a day. The South Carolina Department of Natural Resources spent $1.7 million to grow oysters.

Western Region: Washington State University (Vancouver) is receiving $148,438 to analyze the use of marijuana in conjunction with medications like morphine. According to local reports, this is the first ARRA funding received by WSU. The project is uniquely qualified to receive these funds because of its potential to stimulate the economy and create or retain jobs within the community. "Microsoft Bridge" in Seattle received $11 million in stimulus funds. Despite having nearly $20 billion in cash reserves, Microsoft will be the prime beneficiary of $11 million for construction of a bridge to connect the two campuses of its headquarters. Oregon spent $4.2 million to raise railroad track 18 inches. In Scappoose, Oregon (pop. 6,200), drivers are tired of taking a detour to get past railroad tracks that are not level with the main road. Portland, Oregon, spent $1 million in stimulus funds for bike lockers. Tualatin, Oregon, plans to spend $2.5 million on a "train-horn-free" zone. A Utah sheriff's office has plans to purchase a Harley-Davidson motorcycle. Montana's state-run liquor warehouse will receive $2.2 million in stimulus cash to install skylights. A California skate park will get a $620,000 "facelift." The Bureau of Land Management is using stimulus funds to study the impact wind farms have on the sage grouse population in Oregon.

Northeastern Region: Pawtucket, Rhode Island is spending $550,000 on a skateboard park. Yale and the University of Connecticut are receiving $850,000 in stimulus for research "to study how paying attention improves performance of difficult tasks." Maine to spend over $1.3 million on "government arts jobs," including $30,000 for basket makers, $20,000 for story telling, and $12,500 for a music festival. The National Institutes of Health is giving Yale University $680,100 in stimulus funds to study the effectiveness of diet and exercise at reducing obesity. Altoona, Pennsylvania is getting $819,000 for a homelessness prevention program despite local reports that the town may not have enough of a homeless problem to use it. Nantucket, Massachusetts, will spend $5.6 million in stimulus cash to resurface 6.4 miles of road and bike path, or roughly $875,000 a mile.

(Source: *100 Stimulus Projects: A Second Opinion*, Sen. Tom Coburn, 111th Congress, June 2009, Coburn.senate.gov. Used with permission)

## Dr. Coburn Introduces Bills to Prevent Lawmakers, Staff and Federal Employees from Cheating on their Taxes

In a press release on Senator Coburn's website (Coburn.senate.gov) U.S. Senator Tom Coburn, M.D. (R-OK) released the following statement today, September 16th, 2010, regarding two bills he has introduced that will crack down on federal employees and members of Congress and staff who are *cheating on their taxes*. S. 3790 will make federal employees who have seriously delinquent tax debts ineligible for federal employment. S. 3791 will require Members of Congress to disclose delinquent tax liability, require an ethics inquiry, and garnish the wages of a Member with federal tax liability.

"Taxpayers are fed up with those in Washington living under a different set of rules than the rest of America. At a time when Congress may allow taxes to increase on some or even all Americans, Congress should not expect other Americans to pay more taxes when they are not even paying the taxes they owe under the rates they set themselves," Dr. Coburn said.

In 2009, the Internal Revenue Service (IRS) found nearly 100,000 civilian federal employees were delinquent on their federal income taxes, owing over $1 billion in unpaid federal income taxes. When considering retirees and military, more than 282,000 federal employees owed $3.3 billion in taxes. Meanwhile, the Washington Post has reported that congressional staff, and possibly lawmakers, had tax delinquency totaling at least $9.3 million last year. Not only do government employees make 60-100% more than the average American, they apparently don't think they have to pay taxes like everyone else.

"Legislators and government employees should not be exempt from the laws they write and enforce. The very nature of 'public service' demands those being paid by taxpayers contribute their fair share of taxes. They should lead by example or be held accountable if they believe they are above the law," Dr. Coburn said. It seems at least Dr. Coburn is keeping an eye on what's going on in Washington. It also seems that government employees don't have to pay their taxes like everyone else. The total of 282,000 is not just a statistical error, it means there is a mass disregard of tax laws and responsibility by federal employees, retirees, and military workers, most of whom make 60-100 percent more than the average American.

## Ten More Reasons to be angry about Government Waste, Fraud and Abuse

The first place to trim runaway federal spending is in waste, fraud, and abuse. Congress, however, has largely abandoned its constitutional duty of overseeing the executive branch and has steadfastly refused to address the waste littered across government programs.

With all the information available on government websites, and in an era of tight budgets, why are lawmakers so resistant to reducing waste? One reason is that they see it as a thankless job that would go unnoticed back home. With Congress in session just 80 days annually, reducing waste would take precious time away from most lawmakers' higher priorities of increasing spending on popular programs and bringing pork-barrel projects home.

A second reason is that some of the most wasteful programs are also the most popular (e.g., Medicare), and lawmakers fear that opponents would portray them as "attacking" popular programs. Consequently, waste and inefficiencies continue to build up, costing taxpayers more while providing beneficiaries with less.

A real war on government waste could easily save over $100 billion annually without harming the legitimate operations and benefits of government programs. As a first step, lawmakers should address the 10 following examples of waste.

### 1. The Missing $25 Billion

Buried in the Department of the Treasury's *2003 Financial Report of the United States Government* is a short section titled "Unreconciled Transactions Affecting the Change in Net Position," which explains that these unreconciled transactions totaled $24.5 billion in 2003. http://www.heritage.org/research/reports/2005/04/top-10-examples-of-government-waste - _ftn2 By 2005, according to the Department of the Treasury's *2005 Financial Report of the United States Government* the situation had improved greatly, the government only had $4.5 billion dollars it couldn't account for. The unreconciled transactions are funds for which auditors cannot account: The government knows that $25 billion was spent by someone, somewhere, on something, but auditors do not know *who* spent it, *where* it was spent, or on *what* it was spent. Can you imagine a corporation losing $25 billion or even $4.5 billion dollars? It would be headline grabbing news, but how many people know the government lost that much? And, who would be surprised?

## 2. Unused Flight Tickets Totaling $100 Million

A recent audit revealed that between 1997 and 2003, the Defense Department purchased and then left unused approximately 270,000 commercial airline tickets at a total cost of $100 million. Even worse, the Pentagon never bothered to get a refund for these fully refundable tickets. The GAO blamed a system that relied on department personnel to notify the travel office when purchased tickets went unused. Auditors also found 27,000 transactions between 2001 and 2002 in which the Pentagon paid twice for the same ticket. The department would purchase the ticket directly and then inexplicably reimburse the employee for the cost of the ticket. (In one case, an employee who allegedly made seven false claims for airline tickets professed not to have noticed that $9,700 was deposited into his/her account). These additional transactions cost taxpayers $8 million.

## 3. Embezzled Funds at the Department of Agriculture

Federal employee credit card programs were designed to save money. Rather than weaving through a lengthy procurement process to acquire basic supplies, federal employees could purchase job-related products with credit cards that would be paid by their agency. What began as a smart way to streamline government has since been corrupted by some federal employees who have abused the public trust. A recent audit revealed that employees of the Department of Agriculture (USDA) diverted millions of dollars to personal purchases through their government-issued credit cards. Sampling 300 employees' purchases over six months, investigators estimated that 15 percent abused their government credit cards at a cost of $5.8 million. Taxpayer-funded purchases included Ozzy Osbourne concert tickets, tattoos, lingerie, bartender school tuition, car payments, and cash advances. The USDA has pledged a thorough investigation, but it will have a huge task: 55,000 USDA credit cards are in circulation, including 1,549 that are still held by people who no longer work at the USDA.

## 4. Credit Card Abuse at the Department of Defense

The Defense Department has uncovered its own credit card scandal. Over one recent 18-month period, Air Force and Navy personnel used government-funded credit cards to charge at least $102,400 for admission to entertainment events, $48,250 for gambling, $69,300 for cruises, and $73,950 for exotic dance clubs and prostitutes.

## 5. Medicare Overspending

Medicare wastes more money than any other federal program, yet its strong public support leaves lawmakers hesitant to address program efficiencies, which cost taxpayers and Medicare recipients billions of dollars annually. For example, Medicare pays as much as eight times what other federal agencies pay for the same drugs and medical supplies. The Department of Health and Human Services (HHS) recently compared the prices paid by Medicare and the Department of Veterans Affairs (VA) healthcare program for 16 types of medical equipment and supplies, which account for one-quarter of Medicare's equipment and supplies purchases. The evidence showed that Medicare paid an average of more than double what the VA paid for the same items. The largest difference was for saline solution, with Medicare paying $8.26 per liter compared to the $1.02 paid by the VA.

These higher prices not only cost the program more money, but also take more money out of the pockets of Medicare beneficiaries. In 2002, senior citizens' co-payments accounted for 20 percent of the $9.4 billion in allowed claims for medical equipment and supplies. Higher prices mean higher co-payments. Medicare also over-pays for drugs. In 2000, Medicare's payments for 24 leading drugs were $1.9 billion higher than they would have been under the prices paid by the VA or other federal agencies. Although Medicare is supposed to pay wholesale prices for drugs, it relies on drug manufacturers to define the prices, and manufacturers have strong incentives to inflate their prices.

Nor are inflated prices for drugs and supplies the most expensive examples of Medicare's inefficiencies. Basic payment errors-the results of deliberate fraud and administrative errors-cost $12.3 billion annually. As much as $7 billion owed to the program has gone uncollected or has been written off. Finally, while Medicare contracts claims processing and administration to several private companies, 19 cases of contractor fraud have been settled in recent years, with a maximum settlement of $76 million. Putting it all together, Medicare re-form could save taxpayers and program beneficiaries $20 billion to $30 billion annually without reducing ben-efits. That would be enough to fund a $3,000 refundable healthcare tax credit for nearly 10 million uninsured low-income households.

## 6. Funding Fictitious Colleges and Students

In 2002, the Department of Education received an application to certify the student loan participation of the Y'Hica Institute in London, England. After approving the certification, the department received and approved student loan applications from three Y'Hica students and disbursed $55,000.

The Education Department administrators overlooked one problem: Neither the Y'Hica Institute nor the three students who received the $55,000 existed. The fictitious college and students were created (on paper) by congressional investigators to test the Department of Education's verification procedures. All of the documents were faked, right down to naming one of the fictional loan student applicants "Susan M. Collins," after the Senator requesting the investigation.

Such carelessness helps to explain why federal student loan programs routinely receive poor management re-views from government auditors. At last count, $21.8 billion worth of student loans are in default, and too many cases of fraud are left undetected. Tracking students across federal programs, verifying loan application data with IRS income data, and implementing controls to prevent the disbursement of loans to fraudulent applicants could save taxpayers billions of dollars.

## 7. Manipulating Data to Encourage Spending

The Army Corps of Engineers spends $5 billion annually constructing dams and other water projects. Yet, in a massive conflict of interest, it is also charged with evaluating the science and economics of each proposed water project. The Corps' "strategic vision" calls on managers to increase their budgets as rapidly as possible, which re-quires approving as many proposed projects as possible. Consequently, the Corps has repeatedly been accused of deliberately manipulating its economic studies to justify unworthy projects.

Investigations by the GAO, *The Washington Post*, and several private organizations have found that Corps studies routinely contain dozens of basic arithmetic errors, computer errors, and ridiculous economic assumptions that artificially inflate the benefits of water projects by as much as 300 percent. In one case, a study's authors inflated a project's benefits by using a 2.5 percent interest rate that dated back to 1954. In many cases in which the Corps calculated that a project would be a net benefit, arithmetic corrections revealed that the costs would be many times greater than the benefits. By that point, of course, the unnecessary and wasteful project is often underway and cannot be stopped.

These errors appear to reflect more deception than sloppiness. A *Washington Post* investigation uncovered managers ordering analysts to "get creative," to "look for ways to get to yes as fast as possible," and "not to take no for an answer." After a public outcry, in 2002, the Corps suspended work on 150 projects to review the economics used to justify them. However, given the combination of Congress's thirst for pork-barrel projects and the Corps' built-in incentives to approve projects that will increase its budget, real reforms seem unlikely.

### 8. State Abuse of Medicaid Funding Formulas

Significant waste, fraud, and abuse pervade Medicaid, which provides health services to tens of millions low-income Americans. While states run their own Medicaid programs, the federal government reimburses an average of 57 percent of each state's costs.

This system gives states an incentive to over report their Medicaid expenditures in order to receive larger federal reimbursements. Not surprisingly, the GAO has identified state schemes that shift money between state accounts to create an illusion of higher Medicaid expenditures. Similarly, some states have spent their federal Medicaid dollars on non-Medicaid purposes. Tight state budgets like those experienced by most states today have increased the pressure to use such deceptive tactics.

The GAO and the HHS Inspector General have also uncovered some states' practice of recovering improper payments, retaining the funds, and then spending them on unrelated programs-a practice that costs the federal government well over $2 billion per year.

### 9. Earned Income Tax Credit Overpayments

The earned income tax credit (EITC) provides $31 billion in refundable tax credits to 19 million low-income families. The IRS estimates that $8.5 billion to $9.9 billion of this amount-nearly one-third is wasted in overpayments. The complexity of the EITC law leads to many of these mistakes. Calculating the credits is more complex than calculating regular income taxes. While the credit amount depends on the number of children in a household, the tax code does not clearly define how a child qualifies for the credit. In addition, fraud and underreporting of income are common, and the IRS lacks the resources to verify the qualifications of all EITC claimants. More fraud occurs as filers claim children they don't have, or "make up" children to get more money.

### 10. Redundancy Piled on Redundancy

Government's layering of new programs on top of old ones inherently creates duplication. Having several agencies perform similar duties is wasteful and confuses program beneficiaries who must navigate each program's distinct rules and requirements (or take advantage of the confusion to rip off the government).

Some overlap is inevitable because some agencies are defined by *whom* they serve (e.g., veterans, Native Americans, urbanites, and rural families), while others are defined by *what* they provide (e.g., housing, education, healthcare, and economic development). When these agencies' constituencies overlap, each relevant agency will often have its own program. With 342 separate economic development programs, the federal government needs to make consolidation a priority.

Consolidating duplicative programs will save money and improve government service. In addition to those programs that should be eliminated completely, Congress should consolidate the following sets of programs:

- **342 economic development programs;**
- **130 programs serving the disabled;**
- **130 programs serving at-risk youth;**
- **90 early childhood development programs;**
- **75 programs funding international education, cultural, and training exchange activities;**
- **72 federal programs dedicated to assuring safe water;**
- **50 homeless assistance programs;**
- **45 federal agencies conducting federal criminal investigations;**
- **40 separate employment and training programs;**
- **28 rural development programs;**
- **27 teen pregnancy programs;**
- **26 small, extraneous K-12 school grant programs;**
- **23 agencies providing aid to the former Soviet republics;**
- **19 programs fighting substance abuse;**
- **17 rural water and waste-water programs in eight agencies;**
- **17 trade agencies monitoring 400 international trade agreements;**
- **12 food safety agencies;**
- **11 principal statistics agencies; and**
- **Four overlapping land management agencies.**

(Source: *10 More Examples of Government Waste*, by Brian Riedl, The Heritage Foundation; *April 4, 2005*, Backgrounder #1840, Heritage. org, copyright The Heritage Foundation, used with permission)

## *The Avalanche of Post 9/11 Government Spending*

In their amazing in-depth analysis and reporting of government spending after the attacks of 9/11, Dana Priest and William Arkin of *The Washington Post* found out what has happened to all the money spent. The report *The top-secret world the government created in response to the terrorist attacks of Sept. 11, 2001*, states that "the top secret world that has become so large, so unwieldy and so secretive that no one knows how much money it costs, how many people it employs, how many programs exist within it or exactly how many agencies do the same work." These are some of the findings of a two-year investigation by *The Washington Post* that discovered "what amounts to an alternative geography of the United States, a Top Secret America hidden from public view and lacking in thorough oversight. After nine years of unprecedented spending and growth, the result is that the system put in place to keep the United States safe is so massive that its effectiveness is impossible to determine."

The Washington Post investigation's findings include:

* Some 1,271 government organizations and 1,931 private companies work on programs related to counter-terrorism, homeland security and intelligence in about 10,000 locations across the United States.

* An estimated 854,000 people, nearly 1.5 times as many people as live in Washington, D.C., hold top-secret security clearances.

* In Washington and the surrounding area, 33 building complexes for top-secret intelligence work are under construction or have been built since September 2001. Together they occupy the equivalent of *almost three Pentagons* or 22 U.S. Capitol buildings - about 17 million square feet of space.

Priest and Arkin report "Many security and intelligence agencies do the same work, creating redundancy and waste. For example, 51 federal organizations and military commands, operating in 15 U.S. cities, track the flow of money to and from terrorist networks."

The growth of counterterrorism spending since 9/11 has been sharp and dramatic. "With the quick infusion of money," write Priest and Arkin, "military and intelligence agencies multiplied. Twenty-four organizations were created by the end of 2001, including the Office of Homeland Security and the Foreign Terrorist Asset Tracking Task Force. In 2002, 37 more were created to track weapons of mass destruction, collect threat tips and coordinate the new focus on counterterrorism. That was followed the next year by 36 new organizations; and 26 after that; and 31 more; and 32 more; and 20 or more each in 2007, 2008 and 2009."

"These analysts and agents produce an estimated 50,000 reports per year — most of which are never read. Since there is little or no oversight, and everything is 'top secret', there is no way to determine what is being spent." Clearly, we need counterintelligence against terrorism, but 1,271 more government organizations? And 1,931 private companies? The equivalent of three pentagons worth of building space to house these organizations? Only the federal government could create such a situation. Someday we will find out the cost, and it will undoubtedly be in the hundreds of billions.

## 72,000 stimulus payments went to dead people

People have little faith that the government knows what they are doing when it comes to spending money. When the government isn't wasting money, it's giving it to dead people. A government investigator says 89,000 stimulus payments of $250 each went to people who were either dead or in prison.

The Social Security Administration's inspector general said in a report that $18 million went to 72,000 people who were dead. The report estimates that a little more than half the payments were returned. The report said $4.3 million went to a little more than 17,000 prison inmates. The payments were part of the government's massive economic recovery package enacted in February 2009. Under the law, the $250 payments were sent to about 52 million Social Security recipients and federal retirees. It wasn't a huge loss, but a loss nonetheless, that taxpayers will have to pay for. It seems like we hear reports like this every day. The government is unable to figure out payments to 89,000 people? Prior to the stimulus checks, has the government also been sending the dead people Social Security checks every month?

(Source: Social Security Online, Office of the Inspector General, ssa.gov/oig)

## Cost of students dropping out of college

Dropping out of college after a year can mean lost time, burdensome debt and an uncertain future for students. Now there's an estimate of what it costs taxpayers. And it runs in the billions. States appropriated almost $6.2 billion for four-year colleges and universities between 2003 and 2008 to help pay for the education of students who did not return for year two, a report released recently says. Over a five year period, $6.2 billion dollars were spent for students who weren't there. What did the colleges do with the money?

In addition, the federal government spent $1.5 billion and states spent $1.4 billion on grants for students who didn't start their sophomore years, according to *Finishing the First Lap: The Cost of First-Year Student Attrition in America's Four-Year Colleges and Universities.* The dollar figures, based on government data and gathered by the nonprofit *American Institutes for Research*, are yet another example of how the government wastes billions of dollars. As is usually the case, this waste and fraud was found out by a nonprofit organization, not by the government itself.

## Mutual fund, hedge fund, and pension fund managers fear government

Yahoo! Business and CNBC reported in October 2010 that Wall Street seems more concerned about what the government is going to do than anything else. According to a 2010 published survey of 100 mutual fund, hedge fund and pension fund managers by *Citigroup Global Markets,* Institutional investors fear a government policy mistake far more than inflation, terrorism, a housing double dip, a weak dollar, poor earnings or any other potential risk to the economy,

"Government Policy Missteps" garnered more than a third of the participants' votes as their biggest fears in the quarterly survey, ahead of the more than 15 percent who cited "Protectionism," which is also strongly-tied to the actions of the Administration and Congress.

But these very same investors are bullish on the market and plan to buy stocks this quarter because they believe the chances of that policy error will decrease after Republicans took back the House of Representatives in November.

"While political polls suggest that changes are likely in Washington, a staggering number of professional investors think that the Republicans will win back the House of Representatives in November and that may be adding to their sense of a better business environment going forward," said Tobias Levkovich, Citigroup's U.S. equity strategist, in a note. Republicans did win back the House of Representatives in 2010.

## More Regulation: "Great for Lawyers and Accountants," Bad For Business

More and bigger government results in more regulation. According to a recent Wall Street Journal op-ed by Nicole and Mark Crain titled *The Regulation Tax Keeps Growing*, "the annual cost of federal regulations in the United States increased to more than $1.75 trillion in 2008, a 3% real increase over five years, to about 14% of U.S. national income." And that's before Congress passed the sweeping healthcare law and the new 2,300 page Dodd-Frank financial overhaul.

"Small businesses suffer the most from the regulatory costs...small businesses—those with fewer than 20 employees—incur regulatory costs 42% greater than firms with between 20 and 499 employees, and 36% greater than firms with more than 500 employees. The regulatory cost per employee for small businesses was $10,585, compared to $7,454 for medium firms and $7,755 for large firm."

Sarbanes-Oxley and other recent regulations have added bureaucracy and failed to improve business conditions, in Holmes' opinion. It's "great for lawyers and accountants," but does little to improve competitiveness, he says. "You don't have to have a gazillion regulations in every part of the economy." If government were serious about protecting the economy, they would simply limit leverage. From the 1994 Mexican peso crisis to the 1997 Asian financial crisis and Russia's 1998 debt default, as well as America's recent housing and banking meltdown, "leverage is the one single pattern" at the center of it all, says Holmes. Instead of clogging the system with more laws, existing regulators need to monitor leverage and off balance sheet activity.

## What the Angry People Already Know: Government Spending Does Not Stimulate Economic Growth

A report by Brian Riedl of the *Heritage Foundation* shows why government spending does not stimulate economic growth. In a throwback to the 1930s and 1970s, Democratic lawmakers have bet that America's economic ills could be cured by an extraordinary expansion of government. This tired approach has already failed repeatedly in the past year, in which Congress and the President spent close to a trillion dollars, yet every one of these policies failed to increase economic growth. Now, in addition to passing a $700 billion financial sector rescue package, lawmakers decided to double down on these failed spending policies by passing a $900 billion economic stimulus bill. Even though the last $455 billion in Keynesian deficit spending failed to help the economy, lawmakers convinced themselves that the next $900 billion would succeed.

This is not the first time government expansions have failed to produce economic growth. Massive spending hikes in the 1930s, 1960s, and 1970s all failed to increase economic growth rates. Yet in the 1980s and 1990s-when the federal government shrank by one-fifth as a percentage of gross domestic product (GDP)-the U.S. economy enjoyed its greatest expansion to date.

Despite the decades and mountains of data that a smaller government leads economic expansion, politicians couldn't resist spending almost a trillion dollars on stimulus. Below is a graph showing an expected drop in the unemployment rate with stimulus spending. Instead, the actual unemployment rate is higher than projections of "without recovery plan." One has to wonder, based on economic history, if the stimulus spending actually increased the unemployment rate. It certainly didn't create more jobs for people.

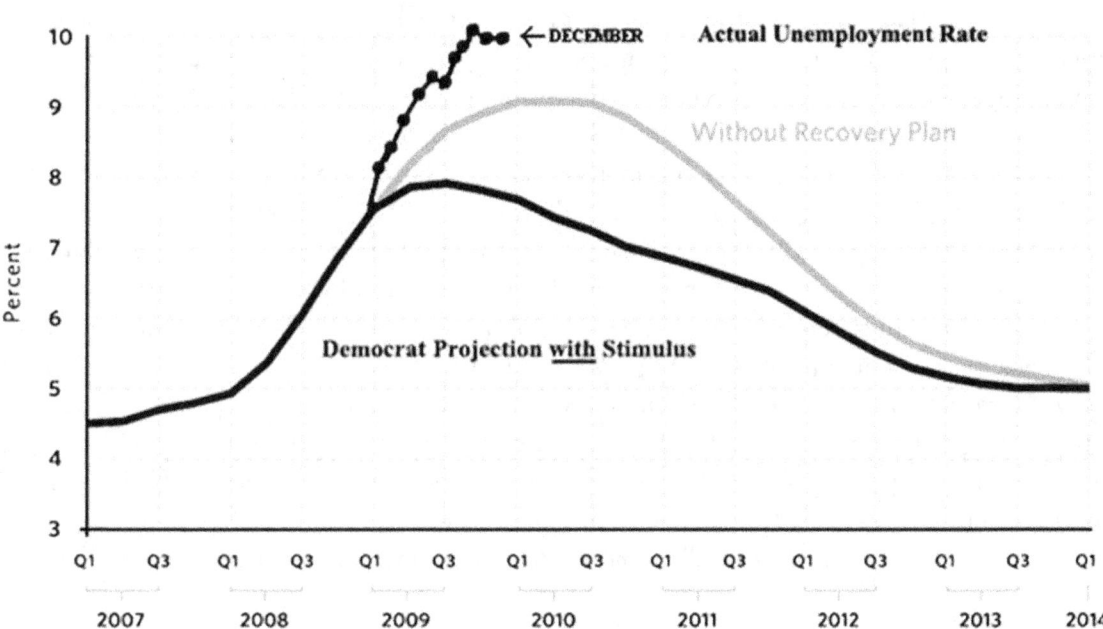

**Democrat Projection of Unemployment Rate with Stimulus vs. Actual Unemployment Rate**

(Source: Originally published by The Cato Institute, downsizinggovernment.org, copyright The Cato Institute, used by permission)

Government spending fails to stimulate economic growth because every dollar Congress injects into the economy must first be taxed or borrowed out of the economy. Thus, government spending stimulus merely redistributes existing income, doing nothing to increase productivity or employment, and therefore nothing to create additional income. Witness how the unemployment rate has barely budged, despite almost a trillion dollars of stimulus spending. Even worse, many federal expenditures weaken the private sector by directing resources toward less productive uses and thus impede income growth.

## The Myth of Spending as "Stimulus"

Spending-stimulus advocates claim that government can "inject" new money into the economy, increasing demand and therefore production. This raises the obvious question: Where does the government get the money it pumps into the economy? Every dollar Congress "injects" into the economy must first be taxed or borrowed out of the economy. No new spending power is created. It has simply been deficit spending, borrowing money and adding to the federal debt.

Government cannot create new purchasing power out of thin air. If Congress funds new spending with taxes, it is simply redistributing existing income. If Congress instead borrows the money from domestic or foreign investors via treasury bills, those investors will have to be paid back some day, plus interest. Every dollar Congress spends must first come from somewhere else.

This does not mean that government spending has no economic impact at all. Government spending tries to increase total demand, such as increasing consumption, but comes at the expense of investment. More importantly, government spending can alter future economic growth. Real economic growth results from producing more goods and services (not from redistributing existing income or from borrowing and spending), and that requires productivity growth and growth in the labor demand. The almost trillion dollar stimulus package passed by congress has done nothing to increase production and has done nothing to grow the labor market.

In the private sector, productivity growth requires increasing the amount of capital available to grow and produce more goods. The only time government spending results in productivity in the private sector is when public money is spent on education, job training, physical infrastructure, and research and development. This can increase long-term productivity rates-but only if government spending does not crowd out similar private spending, and only if government spends the money more competently than businesses, nonprofit organizations, and private citizens. The government has failed miserably in spending money competently. As much of the research on the effects of the stimulus spending show, it has caused more damage than it has to grow jobs. Even the infrastructure stimulus spending is a very long term benefit to private business.

Most government spending has historically *reduced* productivity and long-term economic growth due to:

1. <u>Taxes</u>. **Most government spending is financed by taxes or borrowing, and high tax rates reduce incentives to work, save, and invest-resulting in a less motivated workforce as well as less business investment in new capital and technology. Few government expenditures raise productivity enough to offset the productivity lost due to taxes and increased debt loads;**

2. <u>Incentives</u>. **Social spending often reduces incentives for productivity by subsidizing unemployment. This is what we are seeing today. As more and more people slip below the poverty level, more and more people qualify for welfare. People are rewarded for not working, and are penalized (get less government money) if they do work. Combined with taxes, it is clear that taxing Peter to subsidize Paul reduces both of their incentives to be productive, since productivity no longer determines one's income. People that do work have to pay for spending on people that don't have to work;**

3. <u>Displacement</u>. **Every dollar spent by politicians means one dollar less to be allocated by private industry, that creates jobs and markets. For example, rather than allowing private industry allocate investment money, politicians seize that money and earmark it for favored organizations, lobbyists, and pet programs with little regard for improvements to economic efficiency;**

4. <u>Inefficiencies</u>. **Government supported housing, education, and postal operations are often much less efficient than the private sector. Government also distorts existing healthcare services by promoting third-party payers, resulting in over-consumption and insensitivity to prices and outcomes. The government pays more than twice for items through Medicare than it spents for supplies at the VA hospitals. Another example of inefficiency is**

when politicians earmark highway money for wasteful pork projects rather than expanding highway capacity where it is most needed.

Mountains of academic studies show how government expansions reduce economic growth:

- *Public Finance Review* reported that "higher total government expenditure, no matter how financed, is associated with a lower growth rate of real per capita gross state product."
- The *Quarterly Journal of Economics* reported that "the ratio of real government consumption expenditure to real GDP had a negative association with growth and investment," and "growth is inversely related to the share of government consumption in GDP, but insignificantly related to the share of public investment."
- A *Journal of Macroeconomics* study discovered that "the coefficient of the additive terms of the government-size variable indicates that a 1% increase in government size decreases the rate of economic growth by 0.143%."
- *Public Choice* reported that "a one percent increase in government spending as a percent of GDP (from, say, 30 to 31%) would raise the unemployment rate by approximately .36 of one percent (from, say, 8 to 8.36 percent)."

Economic growth is driven by individuals and entrepreneurs operating in free markets, not by Washington spending and regulations. The outdated idea that transferring spending power from the private sector to Washington will expand the economy has been thoroughly discredited, yet lawmakers continue to return to this strategy. The U.S. economy has soared highest when the federal government was shrinking, and it has stagnated at times of government expansion. A strong private sector provides the nation with strong economic growth and benefits for all Americans.

---

## *Two More Reason Government Spending Hasn't Worked*

---

### 1) Highway Spending: The Myth of the 47,576 New Jobs

Nowhere is the government spending stimulus myth more widespread than in highway spending. Congress has already spent billions on highway spending in the stimulus package. Over the years, lawmakers have repeatedly supported their errant claim that highway spending is an immediate economic gain by citing a Department of Transportation (DOT) study. This study supposedly states that every $1 billion spent on highways adds 47,576 new jobs to the economy.

The problem: The DOT study made no such claim. It stated that spending $1 billion on highways would *require* 47,576 workers (or more precisely, it would require 26,524 workers, who then spend their income elsewhere, supporting an additional 21,052 workers). But before the government can spend $1 billion hiring road builders and purchasing asphalt, it must first tax or borrow $1 billion from other sectors of the economy-which would then lose a similar number of jobs. In other words, highway spending merely transfers jobs and income from one part of the economy to another. As The Heritage Foundation's Ronald Utt has explained, "The only way that $1 billion of new highway spending can create 47,576 new jobs is if the $1 billion appears out of nowhere as if it were manna from heaven." The DOT report acknowledged this point by referring to the transportation jobs as "employment benefits" within the transportation sector, rather than as new jobs for the total economy.

An April 2008 DOT update to its previous study reduced the employment figure to 34,779 jobs supported by each $1 billion spent on highways, and explicitly stated that the figure "refers to jobs *supported* by highway investments, not jobs *created*." Similarly, a Congressional Research Service study calculated similar numbers as the DOT study, but stated: To the extent that financing new highways by reducing expenditures on other programs or by deficit finance and its impact on private consumption and investment, the net impact on the economy of highway construction in terms of both output and employment could be nullified or even negative. By taxing or borrowing for highway spending, the government could actually make the economy worse.

Not surprisingly, highway spending has a record of stimulating the economy. The Emergency Jobs Appropriations Act of 1983 appropriated billions of dollars in highway spending (among other programs) in hopes of pushing the double-digit unemployment rate downward. Years later, an audit by the Government Accounting Office (GAO) found that highway spending generally failed to create a significant number of new jobs. The bottom line is that there is no reason that additional highway spending boosted economic growth or created new jobs. There is simply no data to suggest that the billions spent on highway projects went to jobs, or even that the building that was done was actually needed or was spent of projects that would improve our highway system. Many such projects were of the "make work" type, where the money had to be spent on something, not on anything that actually needed to be done.

As an aside, I talked with a friend of mine who is a highway worker for a big private contractor in Southern Illinois. His company lays off most of their workers after the fall season, so they all sign up for unemployment benefits (saving the company a fortune). He mentioned that he and hundreds of his co-workers won't be going back to work on the highways in the spring because their unemployment benefits were extended for the entire year. He also mentioned that after the unemployment extension was passed in December, 2010, many of his friends went out and bought cars, trucks, T.V.'s, 4-wheelers, and various other items since their "income" was secure for at least a year via unemployment. Extending unemployment will actually create jobs, as those that are unemployed no longer have to go back to work in the spring—people will get their jobs. I was told a similar story by someone who used to work at Walmart. She and some of her friends used to work at Walmart, but got themselves laid-off so they could collect unemployment benefits (and not have to work). They don't plan on going back to work anywhere for at least another year as their unemployment benefits have been extended.

## 2) State Bailouts Merely Shift Money Around

Congress has repeatedly (three times so far) used stimulus funding to bail out states dealing with their own budget nightmares. This accomplishes nothing since state spending does not suddenly become stimulative because it is funded by Washington instead of state governments. Like every other type of spending by the government, the money must first be taxed or borrowed. It does not matter which level of government is doing the taxing, borrowing, or spending.

Giving federal aid to states would not save taxpayers a dime because state taxpayers are also federal taxpayers. Increasing federal borrowing to keep state taxes from rising is again like borrowing from Peter to pay Paul. The overall costs do not change, only the people receiving the money, and those that have to come up with the money.

Governors typically love federal bailout money because it can be funded with deficits rather than new taxes. This is especially important to the 49 states with balanced-budget requirements. It is licentious for a state to enact a balanced-budget amendment, and then over spend and over commit to funding and pensions. Then again comes the demand that Washington bail it out of the consequences of its own policies.

Congress already sends more than $500 billion to state and local government every year-up 30 percent after inflation since 2000. The Federal government gives this much money because it mandates the states perform certain functions, like Medicaid and Welfare. The number of federal mandates hasn't increased more than a few percent in years, yet funding to states continues to increase. State health, education, and transportation programs remain heavily subsidized by Washington.

The effect is magnified in time of economic slowdown (less tax receipts). For example, during the 2002-2003 economic slowdown instead of sufficiently paring back their bloated budgets, the states demanded and received a $30 billion bailout from Washington. As a result of the great recession recently, states asked for and got three separate bailouts from the Federal government. When government bails out irresponsible behavior, it only encourages more irresponsibility. How will states learn to budget responsibly if they know they can keep returning to the federal checkbook?

The biggest losers from the federal bailout are the taxpayers who live in fiscally responsible states. They played by the rules and resisted extravagant new spending programs-and will be "rewarded" with higher federal taxes to bail out neighboring states that went on a spending spree they could not afford. That is simply unfair. And it encourages responsible states to be less responsible next time-better to be the bailout recipient than the bailout payer.

## A Better Way

Government spending has a terrible record of stimulating the economy. However, these repeated failures have not stopped lawmakers from proposing and enacting a seemingly endless string of stimulus bills. Rather than redistributing money, lawmakers should focus on improving long-term productivity. This means reducing tax rates to encourage working, saving, and investing. It also means streamlining wasteful spending that weakens the private sector's ability to generate income and create wealth. The government has to quit wasting hundreds of billions of dollars on spending that actually makes the economy *worse*, and encourage the private sector to grow and flourish. The additional trillions the government gave banks has failed to stimulate lending, despite record low interest rates, and has resulted in bankers and investment houses paying themselves more than $140 billion in bonuses for 2010. There haven't been any jobs created, and business is on the sidelines, holding onto money they might otherwise use to grow and improve. Investors and people that provide investment dollars fear a government misstep, because they know the government is ruining the economy, not making it better, and as the deficit looms large in everyone's mind, fear decides how "Main Street" and businesses will act until something is done in Washington.

(Source: *Why Government Spending Does Not Stimulate Economic Growth*, by Brian Riedl, The Heritage Foundation; November 12, 2008, Backgrounder #2208, Heritage.org, Copyright The Heritage Foundation, used with permission)

## *What the People Want: Smaller Government and Less Spending—and Why this is the Only Thing That Will Work*

Advocates of bigger government argue that government programs provide valuable "public goods" such as education and infrastructure. They also claim that increases in government spending can bolster economic growth by putting money into people's pockets. Proponents of smaller government have the opposite view. They explain that government is too big and that higher spending undermines economic growth by transferring additional resources from the productive sector of the economy to wasteful government, which uses them less efficiently. They also warn that an expanding government complicates efforts to implement pro-growth policies-such as fundamental tax reform and personal retirement accounts- because critics can use the existence of budget deficits as a reason to oppose policies that would strengthen the economy.

Which side is right? It's clear: A large and growing government is not conducive to better economic performance. Indeed, reducing the size of government would lead to higher incomes and improve America's competitiveness.

## *Economics of Government Spending*

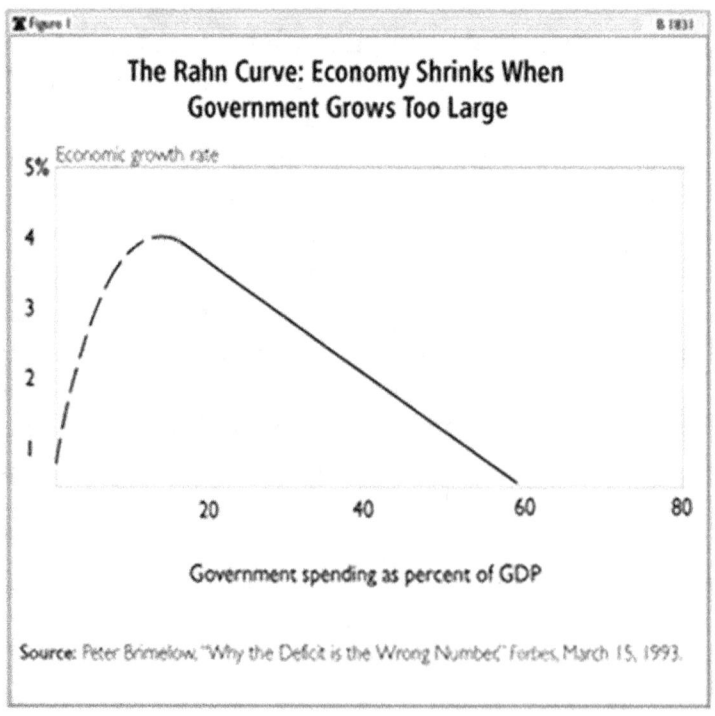

**figure 1**

**The Rahn Curve: Economy Shrinks When Government Grows Too Large**

Economic growth rate

Government spending as percent of GDP

**Source:** Peter Brimelow, "Why the Deficit is the Wrong Number," Forbes, March 15, 1993.

If government spending is zero, presumably there will be very little economic growth because enforcing contracts, protecting property, and developing an infrastructure would be very difficult if there were no government at all. In other words, some government spending is necessary for the successful operation of the rule of law. The Rahn curve illustrates this point. Economic activity is very low or nonexistent in the absence of government, but it jumps dramatically as core functions of government are financed. This does not mean that government costs nothing, but that the benefits outweigh the costs. As reported above, we are now at more than 60%, which, using the graph above, would result in an almost zero economic growth rate. While our economic growth rate is not zero, it's currently very low, and is unlikely to rise unless the government is downsized.

**Costs vs. Benefits.** Economists will generally agree that government spending becomes a burden at some point, either because government becomes too large or because outlays are misallocated. In such cases, the cost of government exceeds the benefit. The downward sloping portion of the Rahn curve can exist for a number of reasons, including:

- **The extraction cost.** Government spending requires costly financing choices. The federal government cannot spend money without first taking that money from someone. All of the options used to finance government spending have adverse consequences. Taxes discourage productive behavior, particularly in the current U.S. tax system, which imposes high tax rates on work, saving, investment, and other forms of productive behavior. Borrowing consumes capital that otherwise would be available for private investment and, in extreme cases, may lead to higher interest rates. Inflation debases a nation's currency, causing widespread economic distortion.
- **The displacement cost.** Government spending displaces private-sector activity. Every dollar that the government spends necessarily means one less dollar in the productive sector of the economy. This dampens growth since economic forces guide the allocation of resources in the private sector, whereas political forces dominate when politicians and bureaucrats decide how money is spent. Some government spending, such as maintaining a well-functioning legal system, can have a high "rate-of-return." In general, however, governments do not use resources efficiently, resulting in less economic output.
- **The negative multiplier cost.** Government spending finances harmful intervention. Portions of the federal budget are used to finance activities that generate a distinctly negative effect on economic activity. For instance, many regulatory agencies have comparatively small budgets, but they impose large costs on the economy's productive sector. Outlays for international organizations are another good example. The direct expense to taxpayers of membership in organizations such as the International Monetary Fund (IMF) and Organization for Economic Co-operation and Development (OECD) is often trivial compared to the economic damage resulting from the anti-growth policies advocated by these multinational bureaucracies.
- **The behavioral subsidy cost.** Government spending encourages destructive choices. Many government programs subsidize economically undesirable decisions. Welfare programs encourage people to choose leisure over work. Unemployment insurance programs

197

provide an incentive to remain unemployed. Flood insurance programs encourage construction in flood plains. These are all examples of government programs that reduce economic growth and diminish national output because they promote misallocation or underutilization of resources.

- The behavioral penalty cost. Government spending discourages productive choices. Government programs often discourage economically desirable decisions. Saving is important to help provide capital for new investment, yet the incentive to save has been undermined by government programs that subsidize retirement, housing, and education. Why should a person set aside income if government programs finance these big-ticket expenses? Other government spending programs-Medicaid is a good example-generate a negative economic impact because of eligibility rules that encourage individuals to depress their incomes artificially and misallocate their wealth.

- The market distortion cost. Government spending distorts resource allocation. Buyers and sellers in competitive markets determine prices in a process that ensures the most efficient allocation of resources, but some government programs interfere with competitive markets. In both healthcare and education, government subsidies to reduce out-of-pocket expenses have created a "third-party payer" problem. When individuals use other people's money, they become less concerned about price. This undermines the critical role of competitive markets, causing significant inefficiency in sectors such as healthcare and education. Government programs also lead to resource misallocation because individuals, organizations, and companies spend time, energy, and money seeking either to obtain special government favors or to minimize their share of the cost of government.

- The inefficiency cost. Government spending is a less effective way to deliver services. Government directly provides many services and activities such as education, airports, and postal operations. However, there is evidence that the private sector could provide these important services at a higher quality and lower cost. In some cases, such as airports and postal services, the improvement would take place because of privatization. In other cases, such as education, the economic benefits would accrue by shifting to a model based on competition and choice.

- The stagnation cost. Government spending inhibits innovation. Because of competition and the desire to increase income and wealth, individuals and entities in the private sector constantly search for new options and opportunities. Economic growth is greatly enhanced by this discovery process of "creative destruction." Government programs, however, are inherently inflexible, both because of centralization and because of bureaucracy. Reducing government-or devolving federal programs to the state and local levels-can eliminate or mitigate this effect.

In the United States, there is good reason to believe that government is too large. Scholarly research indicates that America is on the downward sloping portion of the Rahn Curve — as are most other industrialized nations. In other words, policymakers could enhance economic performance by reducing the size and scope of government.

## *Spending Control Success Stories*

Both economic theory and empirical evidence suggest that government should be smaller. Yet is it possible to translate good economics into public policy? Even though many policymakers understand that government spending undermines economic performance, some think that special-interest groups are too politically powerful and that reducing the size of government is an impossible task. Since the burden of government has relentlessly increased during the post-World War II era, this is a reasonable assumption.

There are examples of leaders that have successfully reduced the burden of government during peacetime. They show that it is possible to reduce government spending-sometimes by dramatic amounts. In these examples, policymakers enjoyed political and economic success. For instance:

- **<u>Ronald Reagan</u> dramatically reversed the direction of public policy in the United States. Government-especially domestic spending-was growing rapidly when he took office. Measured as a share of national output, President Reagan reduced domestic discretionary spending by almost 33 percent, down from 4.5 percent of GDP in 1981 to 3.1 percent of GDP in 1989.**

Reagan's track record on entitlements was also impressive. When he took office, entitlement spending was on a sharp upward trajectory, peaking at 11.6 percent of GDP in 1983. By the time he left office, entitlement spending consumed 9.8 percent of economic output. As a result of these dramatic improvements, Reagan was able to reduce the total burden of government spending as a share of economic output during his presidency while still restoring the nation's military strength.

- **<u>Bill Clinton</u> was surprisingly successful in controlling the burden of government, particularly during his first term. His record was greatly inferior to Ronald Reagan's, and some of the credit probably belongs to the Republicans in Congress, but Clinton managed to preside over the second most frugal record of any President in the post-World War II era. Domestic discretionary spending fell from 3.4 percent of GDP to 3.1 percent of GDP, and entitlement spending dropped from 10.8 percent of GDP to 10.5 percent of GDP.**

These were modest reductions compared to Ronald Reagan, and many of them evaporated during Clinton's second term once a budget surplus materialized and undermined fiscal discipline. Nonetheless, when combined with reasonable economic growth and the "peace dividend" made possible by President Reagan's victory in the Cold War, the total burden of federal spending fell as low as 18.4 percent of GDP in 2000, the lowest level since 1966.

## Is There Still Time?

Government spending must be significantly reduced now. It has grown far too quickly in recent years. Combined with rising entitlement costs associated with the looming retirement of the baby-boom generation, America is heading in the wrong direction. To avoid becoming an uncompetitive European-style welfare state like France or Germany, the United States must adopt a responsible fiscal policy based on smaller government.

Simply stated, *most government spending has a negative economic impact*. There is overwhelming evidence that government spending is too high and that America's economy could grow much faster if the burden of government was reduced. The key is the size of government, and how it is financed. Taxes and deficits are both harmful, but the real problem is that government is taking money from the private sector and spending it in ways that are often counterproductive. Fiscal policy should focus on reducing the level of government spending, with particular emphasis on those programs that yield the lowest benefits and/or impose the highest costs—especially entitlement spending.

In the *2010 Index of Economic Freedom*, the United States fell from the ranks of "economically free" nations, due primarily to excessive debt, spending, and taxation. How dire is our fiscal situation? In May 2010, the International Monetary Fund took the extraordinary step of placing the U.S. on its *watch list of nations* overextended by debt. The IMF called on U.S. lawmakers to reduce government debt by hundreds of billions annually or face certain economic catastrophe.

Controlling federal spending is particularly important because of globalization. Today, it is becoming increasingly easy for jobs and capital to migrate from one nation to another. This means that the reward for good policy is greater than ever before, but it also means that the penalty for bad policy is greater than ever before.

This may be cause for optimism. A study published by the IMF, which certainly is not a free-market institution, has stated:

"As the international economy becomes more competitive, and as capital and labor become more mobile, countries with big and especially inefficient governments risk falling behind in terms of growth and welfare. When voters and industries realize the long-term benefits of reform in such an environment, they and their representatives may push their governments toward reform. In these circumstances, policymakers find it easier to overcome the resistance of special-interest groups."

(Source: International Monetary Fund, IMF.org)

For most of America's history, the aggregate burden of government was below 10 percent of GDP. This level of government was consistent with the beliefs of the America's founders. As the IMF has explained, "classical economists and political philosophers generally advocated the minimal state-they saw the government's role as limited to national defense, police, and administration." America's policy of limited government certainly was conducive to economic expansion. In the days before income tax and excessive government, America moved from agricultural poverty to middle-class prosperity. Reducing government to 10 percent of GDP might be a very optimistic target, but shrinking the size of government should be a major goal for policymakers. The economy certainly would perform better, and this would boost prosperity and make America more competitive.

(Source and graph: *The Impact of Government Spending on Economic Growth*, by Daniel Mitchell, Ph.D., The Heritage Foundation; March 15, 2005 Backgrounder #1831, Heritage.org, Copyright The Heritage Foundation, used with permission)

## What is China saying about the U.S. Debt situation?

Zhou Xin, Simon Rabinovitch and Kevin Yao of *Reuters* reported in Yahoo! Finance 12/10 that U.S. fiscal health is worse than Europe's: "'The U.S. dollar will be a safe investment for the next six to 12 months because global markets are focused on the euro zone's troubles but America's fiscal health is worse than Europe's,' an adviser to the Chinese central bank said on Wednesday. Li Daokui, an academic member of the central bank's monetary policy committee, said that U.S. bond prices and the dollar would fall when the European economic situation stabilized. 'For now, market attention is still on Europe and for the coming 6-12 months, it will not shift to the United States,' Li said, when asked about U.S. President Barack Obama's plan to extend tax cuts for all Americans 'But we should be clear in our minds that the fiscal situation in the United States is much worse than in Europe. In one or two years, when the European debt situation stabilizes, attention of financial markets will definitely shift to the United States. At that time, U.S. Treasury bonds and the dollar will experience considerable declines.'"

"U.S. Treasury prices fell sharply in early December, 2010 as the proposed tax deal sparked concerns over the government's ability to service its massive debt burden. Moody's Investors Service said it is worried the tax cuts could become permanent, hurting U.S. finances and credit ratings in the long run. China has a big stake in the performance of dollar assets. The country holds the world's biggest stock pile of foreign exchange reserves at $2.64 trillion and an estimated two-thirds of that is invested in dollar assets, including U.S. Treasuries." It's important to watch what China is saying about our debt and economic situation, because they hold a vast amount of our Federal debt/Treasury bills. If they decide to quit investing in treasury bills, or worse, start selling their holdings, our government might not be able to borrow any more money, might shut down, or may default on its debt. Holding our debt buys China and other countries influence, our politicians have sold influence on our government to foreigners with massive debt-fueled deficit spending. Outsiders aren't shy about describing our dire financial situation, but nobody in Washington seems to care very much as the deficit spending continues unabated, now at $5 billion *per day*, added to the $14 trillion debt.

**In conclusion**, the angry people are right. Unless we reduce spending, fraud and abuse in government, and shrink government, we are going to not only have decreasing prosperity, but also be less competitive in the global marketplace. Even military leaders are concerned about our national debt and its effects on national security. The government cannot tax-and-spend its way to prosperity by spending $150 billion per month more than it has. Federal budgets and spending will far outstrip increased taxes and further increase deficits and debt. The government cannot continue to hand out money and healthcare to people that don't work. Somehow, several good ideas from decades past have turned into trillion dollar entitlement programs that are running our country into bankruptcy. The government sends out stimulus checks to dead people, spends hundreds of thousands of dollars on stimulus toilets, and more than 282,000 government employees think it's okay not to pay their taxes.

Economists have rung the bell of concern for years, but nobody in Washington is listening. Observers of our economy and government, like the IMF and China are wondering whether our government can overcome the lobbyists and special interests, downsize our government and repay our debt, or else proceed into economic collapse. The people of this country have every right to be angry. Americans aren't buffoons or bigots like some politicians would have us believe. The angry populous can clearly see what is happening in our country, especially what is happening in Washington. Apparently, the politicians are too myopic to see what is going on during their watch. Let's hope the yelling will wake them up before it's too late. There is a better way of doing things.

# CHAPTER 7

# *Voting*

**When a man assumes a public trust he should consider himself a public property.**

*Thomas Jefferson*

**The people will save their government, if the government itself will allow them.**

*Abraham Lincoln*

Voting is the only control the people of this country seem to have over what goes on in Washington. The amazing thing is people believe that having the power to vote actually affects what goes on in Washington. Politicians will do whatever type of popular glad-handling they need to get themselves elected, and once they are off to Washington, they do exactly what they want (not what the people who elected them wanted). Voting for the Democrats will achieve the following: Increased government, more entitlement spending, increased taxes—especially for the rich, increased power to unions, minorities, lawyers, immigrants, the idea that government can manage all our problems, alternative energy, more governmental regulations and laws, increased minimum wage, and all the rest. Voting for a Republican will produce the exact opposite: decreased government, less entitlement spending, decreased taxes—especially for the rich, decreased power to unions, minorities, lawyers, immigrants, the idea the corporations can manage all our problems, traditional energy, less government regulations and decreased minimum wage, and all the rest.

The fact that they seem to be polar opposites is not surprising. Anyone can predict what each party is going to do before they do it. Once they are in office, one party obstructs the other, and it's amazing that anything gets accomplished in Washington at all (besides spending). It is rare indeed when one party controls both the White House and the House and Senate. The results, at least lately, have been catastrophic. The perfect storm of banking and financial deregulation, followed by the sub-prime lending disaster resulted in the worst economic collapse since the Great Depression. In response, and under the guise of "change," the Democrats took almost complete control. And, as expected by their agenda, spent money like there was no tomorrow. When it's all done, and the debt becomes due, there may be no tomorrow. For the people that actually have to *pay* for ObamaCare, the $870 billion dollars of stimulus spending, the bank and Wall Street bailouts, and massive increases in spending for entitlement programs, and a $13.8 trillion national debt, the future looks bleak. As this book has shown, we, the voters and people, are looking at the possibility of financial insolvency of our government. Many state and local governments are already insolvent, and have multi-billion dollar deficits for which the Federal Government has to bail them out for just to stay afloat.

Anger may have been the topic of the 2010 elections, but what is going to change? Are we going to get out of this mess by voting for the same politicians (Republicans or Democrats) that got us into this mess? Are voters going to be able to over-rule the special interests and lobbyists in Washington? Does voting for change ever mean we are actually going to get change? How can we ever get change in a system that doesn't work in the first place? Time and again, politicians vote and enact legislation that the people don't support. They know better than the people they represent, right? They represent themselves, their party, and whoever is paying them the most. The voters are pawns in a game that increasingly doesn't need them any longer, just their taxes. And when everything goes wrong, and the debts pile up and the economy collapses, the politicians don't blame themselves or the lobbyists or special interests they serve, they blame the voters. It's the voters fault for electing them, right?

## The voters are idiots

**America is like a dog, I'm sorry, but it is. It cannot understand actual words. It understands infection. It understands fear, but you can't actually explain issues to a dog.**

*Bill Maher, Democrat & star of HBO's "Real Time with Bill Maher" episode 197, November 12, 2010.*

## *With a big loss pending, Democrats Blame the Voters*

The Wall Street Journal-online ran an article in Sept. 2010, just before the election. Fearing a loss, politicians struck back at voters. Massachusetts Senator John Kerry seems to have little respect for voters. Before the election in 2010, Mr. Kerry said "We have an electorate that doesn't always pay that much attention to what's going on so people are influenced by a simple slogan rather than the facts or the truth or what's happening." He should know, he's a politician, and as all politicians, is a master at producing simple slogans to get votes (remember "can we do it? Yes we can"). Democratic pundits like Bill Maher think American voters are idiots and dogs.

In a September 2010 interview in *Rolling Stone Magazine* President Obama chimed in with another uplifting message about the American electorate. Mr. Obama told Rolling Stone that the Tea Party movement is financed and directed by "powerful, special-interest lobbies." But this doesn't mean that Tea Party groups are composed entirely of corporate puppets. Mr. Obama graciously implied that a small subset of the movement is simply motivated by bigotry. Another telling set of statements. The Democrats, of which he is a member, gets most of their money from powerful, special-interest lobbyists, the number one being the former American Trial Lawyers Association.

The President said "there are probably some aspects of the Tea Party that are a little darker, that have to do with anti-immigrant sentiment or are troubled by what I represent as the President." Maybe they just don't like spending and deficits not seen since WWII. The Tea Party is now supported by a third of the country in some polls. Perhaps advocates for smaller government shouldn't take Mr. Obama's comments personally. In the new Democratic attacks on the voting public, not even Democrats are spared. Vice President Joe Biden recently urged the party's base to "stop whining" and "buck up," a message echoed by Mr. Obama in his Rolling Stone interview. The President demanded that his supporters "shake off this lethargy," warning that it would be "inexcusable" for liberals to stay home on Election Day.

Mr. Obama added that "if people now want to take their ball and go home, that tells me folks weren't serious in the first place." Making the case for left-wing voters to show up in November, Mr. Obama told Rolling Stone that he is presiding over "the most successful administration in a generation in moving progressive agendas forward." The only problem is that most Americans don't support that agenda. He "rammed through" his agenda, without support of the people, and despite polls that said most Americans didn't support what he was doing.

It's always amazing what happens during the election cycle. Politicians, like President Obama, build a consensus among voters, offering them hope of change and progress, and doing things differently. Then, they win, they get elected, and it's back to business as usual. President Obama, being a Democrat, pushed through their agenda (especially since they controlled the House and Senate) without considering what the people that voted them into office wanted. This is typical of politicians. They feel they have a "mandate," which means the voters support them no matter what they want to do simply because they won the election. Politicians and pundits alike have nothing but disdain and disregard for the voters of this country, the people they are supposed to be representing. This undoubtedly helps them sleep at night after selling out our government to lobbyists and special interests, the people they *actually* represent.

## *Where do candidates come from anyway?*

Except for local elections, and some elections to state government, candidates come from two places: The Democratic National Committee and the Republican National Committee (and their state and local chapters). Without the support of these two organizations, nobody gets on the ballot. These national organizations and similar organizations of the states decide who will run from each party. Voters then get to elect those presented to them, both in primaries and then in for-office elections. Somewhere along the line of our fine political history, voters got taken out of the equation of who gets to run for office. Without the support of these powerful organizations, political funding, first and foremost, is withheld. Without political funding (unless the candidate is independently wealthy), running for election is a non-starter.

The only way into the political system is to win a local election for a state senate seat. Once at the capital of the state, the politician can gain influence and acceptance into the political circles of power. If a state politician has ambition, they can run for higher office (state comptroller, state treasurer, lieutenant governor or governor etc.). Once in a higher position, and with enough backing from the power brokers within the party, they can make the jump to Washington. But, alas, nothing happens without the support and blessing of the DNC or the RNC, who decides who will be supported and who will run.

The voters, on the other hand, have no say in who is going to run for office. They are back at home, waiting to see who will be selected to run for office. It's a democracy of the political power brokers. The only time chance happens into the equation is on election day. The fickle and foolish voters can always wreck the plans of the power brokers. Through clever campaigning and hundreds of millions of dollars, the tenor and direction of an election can be manipulated and directed, so it's probably not as random and fickle as it might appear. The hapless voters are subject to campaign commercial after campaign commercial. In 2010, the truth didn't even seem to matter. Commercials run by the unions (which were illegal last election) on the one side, and the Chamber of Commerce on the other, have dispensed stories and facts that are wrong and suspect, but still run on T.V. anyway. Internet ads were far worse, with fear mongering at an all-time high. The impressionable voters have to try to decide what is fact and fiction—good luck with that.

At least one good thing has happened lately—more people are voting. Voter apathy used to be a frequently used catch-word, especially in the 90's. The data presented here (from U.S. census data) show that more people are voting – which is always a good thing.

| Reported Voting and Registration, by Race, Hispanic Origin, Sex, and Age, for the United States: November 2008 | | | | |
|---|---|---|---|---|
| (In thousands) | | | | |
| | | US Citizen | Total Population | |
| Race, Hispanic origin, sex, and age | Total Population | Total Citizen Population | Reported Registered Percent | Reported Voted Percent |
| ALL RACES | | | | |
| | | | | |
| BOTH SEXES | | | | |
| Total 18 years and over | 225,499 | 206,072 | 64.9 | 58.2 |
| 18 to 24 years | 28,263 | 25,791 | 53.4 | 44.3 |
| 25 to 44 years | 81,701 | 70,615 | 59.0 | 51.9 |
| 45 to 64 years | 78,078 | 73,372 | 70.4 | 65.0 |
| 65 to 74 years | 20,227 | 19,571 | 75.6 | 70.1 |
| 75 years and over | 17,231 | 16,724 | 74.3 | 65.8 |
| MALE | | | | |
| Total 18 years and over | 108,974 | 98,818 | 62.6 | 55.7 |
| 18 to 24 years | 14,274 | 12,967 | 50.2 | 41.0 |
| 25 to 44 years | 40,603 | 34,597 | 56.0 | 48.4 |
| 45 to 64 years | 37,957 | 35,555 | 68.6 | 63.0 |
| 65 to 74 years | 9,290 | 9,028 | 75.8 | 70.1 |
| 75 years and over | 6,850 | 6,671 | 76.7 | 70.3 |
| FEMALE | | | | |
| Total 18 years and over | 116,525 | 107,255 | 67.0 | 60.4 |
| 18 to 24 years | 13,990 | 12,823 | 56.6 | 47.7 |
| 25 to 44 years | 41,097 | 36,018 | 62.0 | 55.3 |
| 45 to 64 years | 40,121 | 37,818 | 72.0 | 66.9 |
| 65 to 74 years | 10,936 | 10,543 | 75.4 | 70.0 |
| 75 years and over | 10,381 | 10,053 | 72.8 | 62.9 |

Note: 'Not registered' includes 'did not register to vote,' 'do not know,' and 'not reported.' 'Did not vote' includes 'did not vote,' 'do not know,' and 'not reported.'

(Source: U.S. Census Bureau, Current Population Survey, November 2008. Internet release date: July, 2009)

## Data Show Significant Increases Among Hispanic, Black and Young Voters for the 2006 Presidential Election

About 131 million people reported voting in the 2008 U.S. presidential election, an increase of 5 million from 2004, according to a new table package released today by the U.S. Census Bureau. The increase included about 2 million more black voters, 2 million more Hispanic voters and about 600,000 more Asian voters, while the number of non-Hispanic white voters remained statistically unchanged.

Additionally, voters 18 to 24 were the only age group to show a statistically significant increase in turnout, reaching 49 percent in 2008 compared with 47 percent in 2004. Blacks had the highest turnout rate among 18- to 24-year-old voters — 55 percent, an 8 percent increase from 2004. The increased turnout among certain demographic groups was offset by stagnant or decreased turnout among other groups, causing overall 2008 voter turnout to remain statistically unchanged — at 64 percent — from 2004.

"The 2008 presidential election saw a significant increase in voter turnout among young people, blacks and Hispanics," said Thom File, a voting analyst with the Census Bureau's Housing and Household Economic Statistics Division. "But as turnout among some other demographic groups either decreased or remained unchanged, the overall 2008 voter turnout rate was not statistically different from 2004." Although the youngest voters were the only age group to show a statistically significant increase in turnout, voting did tend to increase with age. In 2008, younger citizens (18-24) had the lowest voting rate (49 percent), while citizens who fell into older age groups (45-64 and 65-plus) had the highest voting rates (69 percent and 70 percent, respectively).

Looking at voter turnout by race and Hispanic origin, non-Hispanic whites (66 percent) and blacks (65 percent) had the highest levels in the November 2008 election. Voting rates for Asians and Hispanics were not statistically different from one another at about 49 percent. Relative to the presidential election of 2004, the voting rates for blacks, Asians and Hispanics each increased by about 4 percentage points. The voting rate for non-Hispanic whites decreased by 1 percentage point.

The voting rate was highest in the Midwest (66 percent), while the rates in the West, Northeast and South were about 63 percent each. Among states, voting rates varied widely. Among states and state-equivalents with the highest voter turnout were Minnesota and the District of Columbia, each with voting rates of about 75 percent. Hawaii and Utah were among the states with the lowest turnouts, each with approximately 52 percent.

The overall voting age (18 and older) citizen population in the United States in 2008 was 206 million compared with 197 million in 2004. Of that total, 146 million, or 71 percent, reported being registered to vote. That's slightly lower than the 72 percent who reported being registered to vote in the 2004 presidential election, but does represent an increase of approximately 4 million registered voters. The percentage of those registered to vote that actually did so was slightly higher in the 2008 election (90 percent) than in 2004 (89 percent)

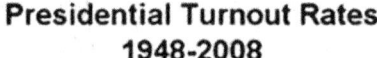

VEP: Voting Eligible Population

VAP: Voting Age Population

(Graph: U.S. Census data, census.gov)

Voter turnout rates presented here show that the much-lamented decline in voter participation is an artifact of poor measurement. Previously, turnout rates were calculated by dividing the number of votes by what is called the "voting-age population" which consists of everyone age 18 and older residing in the United States (the yellow line to the right). This includes persons ineligible to vote, mainly non-citizens and ineligible felons, and excludes overseas eligible voters. When turnout rates are calculated for those eligible to vote, a new picture of turnout emerges, which exhibits no decline since 1972 (the green line to the right). Indeed, turnout rates appear to have been restored to their earlier high levels as of 2008.

Since the turn of the century, more and more people are voting. These means more and more people are interested in the voting process, which is important, especially to the context of this book (as we will see later).

## Death of a Democracy?

Reporter Brett Arends recently presented an article *Death of a Democracy* which is quite interesting. It raises some poignant questions: "Will anyone even bother voting in future elections? Will they get involved in political causes? Will they spend one dime of their savings supporting a political candidate or a campaign? When you look at what is happening with money and politics in 2010, these are not idle questions." He's referring to a Jan. 2010 Supreme Court ruling made in a 5-4 decision in the case of *Citizens United v. Federal Election Commission*, which permitted unlimited campaign contributions by corporations and unions. That decision overturned a 20-year-old ruling that forbade corporations from funding campaigns out of their general funds and also opened the door for labor unions and other groups to pump more money into campaign ads. This is good news for corporations and unions, but bad news for voters.

This ruling means that corporations and unions can now effectively spend freely on political campaigns, including during elections. Loopholes in the tax code, particularly pertaining to 501(c)4 nonprofits, mean they can do so secretly through nonprofits. Arends goes on to state "It doesn't matter whether you are a Republican or a Democrat, whether you hate the president or like him. Under this system, the game is over. Our democracy is dead. We just don't know it yet." The Supreme Court has finally let the proverbial "genie out of the bottle" and there is no going back. If elections can be bought and sold, then they can actually can be bought or sold by corporations and unions— the people with the most money. CEOs can cut checks for millions, even tens of millions, without blinking.

According to data from FactSet, there are around 350 companies on the U.S. stock market that have more than $750 million on hand just in cash and equivalents, such as short-term Treasury bills. Exxon Mobil Corp. has $13.3 billion in ready money. That's 18 times as much as Obama raised in all of 2007-08. Johnson & Johnson has $12.7 billion. UnitedHealth Group Inc. has about $10 billion. So, under the new law, the chief executive of any of these companies could spend hundreds of millions of dollars on a campaign in a matter of minutes.

No one company will have to pay the full tab to buy each election for corporate America anyway: The bill will be shared. How many companies could chip in $20 million or $50 million without even noticing? You think Goldman Sachs Group Inc. or Citigroup Inc. or Bank of America Corp. can't find that cash around to buy off reform? So, in addition to lobbying, corporations will now be able to have some measure of control over who gets elected. Corporations are only just waking up to the good news. In the last few months, money has started pouring into outside groups. According to *The Center for Responsive Politics*, a remarkable $180 million has gone into independent political organizations. Most of that, about three-quarters, has gone into organizations on the right.

What sort of clout does this money buy? According to data tracked by *Media Matters for America*, the 10 biggest independent right-wing groups aired 60,052 political ads nationwide between Aug. 1 and Oct. 11 2010. At 30 seconds a commercial, that's about 500 hours of commercials. The Chamber of Commerce spent $10 million running 4,700 adverts during a single week.

Here's yet another way your tax dollars are showing up in all sorts of unexpected ways. In one of the biggest outrages of all, your taxpayer dollars are going to fund campaign commercials for Democrats. While this is great if you're a Democrat, taxpayer money isn't supposed to be used for partisan politics. The *American Federation of State, County and Municipal Employees (AFSCME)* is a labor union representing government employees. Since government employees are paid with tax dollars, this union is directly funded by taxpayers. Your tax dollars go to government employees, who then use some of the money to pay union dues. These union dues then go to pay for political advertisements for Democrats (the only candidates most unions support). As if by magic, your tax dollars paid for some of the vilest campaign commercials of the 2010 election.

And the 2010 election is just the beginning. Expect the amounts spent in the future to be vastly greater. Political ads are merely the tip of the iceberg. The real action will come from hundreds of millions spent in areas of propaganda that you'll never see. Various experts will try to tell you the new system of unlimited secret corporate donations can't survive. "I don't believe secretly funding our elections can be sustained," Fred Wertheimer, head of reform group *Democracy 21*, told the New York Times. "It won't hold up. The public won't stand for it. This is guaranteed corruption."

As Arends writes at the end of his piece "I'm glad he's so optimistic. But who is going to stop it? There are no gatekeepers left with any power. How can someone in manacles strike off his own chains? How can you fix a broken political system with a broken political system?" That statement rings true for much more than elections.

(Source: Death of a Democracy, by Brett Arends, MarketWatch, October 19, 2010. Used with permission)

## *Politicians argue over who will be worse, not better*

An article by Lynda Gorov *Political ads mean and getting meaner before Nov. 2ⁿᵈ* chronicles some of what has been going on over the air-waves. The mud-slinging was worse than ever in the 2010 election. And it went very personal, with filth aimed at the private lives and even the religious beliefs of opponents. There was, for instance, Kentucky Democrat Jack Conway's ad suggesting that not having Christian beliefs disqualifies Republican Rand Paul for a U.S. Senate seat or public office at all. For his part, Rep. Alan Grayson played ugly with an ad equating his GOP opponent in Florida's Eighth Congressional District with the Taliban for his opinions on women. The tagline: "Taliban Dan Webster: Hands off our body — and our laws."

"Candidates have told me that every dollar spent on a positive ad is a wasted dollar in 2010," Larry Sabato, director of the *Center for Politics* at the University of Virginia told Yahoo! News. "In other years voters might have been interested in seeing the candidate's spouse, kids, and pets, or hearing about all the great things the member of Congress has done for the district, but not this year." In other words, all but gone are the biographical spots of the past, with a candidate walking in a field or through a factory. Forget voter-in-the-street testimonials. What's coming through the TV screen these days is mostly mud.

"In addition to the personal attacks, Democrats are blasting Republicans by accusing them of wanting to privatize Social Security and Republicans are blasting back with claims that healthcare reform has reformed the United States into a socialist state. Sex, religion – even federal funding for research on ants – have popped up in campaign ads aimed at fueling the electorate's already considerable anger. Illegal aliens and terrorists are other hot button topics."

While attack ads have always existed, politifact.com. editor Bill Adair says they are amplified this year by the ease of distributing them to millions of voters via the Internet rather than to thousands through mass mailings. And anonymity in advertising is now both legal and prevalent, which only emboldens people to put out negative ads. "There is a bigger megaphone now thanks to technology and interpretations of the law that allow these negative ads to be spread far and wide without allowing us to know who's behind them," Adair says.

Despite the usual headshaking, analysts say candidates engage in this ugliness because it works, especially on undecided voters. "There's no gentleman's decorum anymore," says Dave Levinthal, spokesman for the Washington,

D.C., -based *Center for Responsive Politics*. "Voters remember the ads that are scary or hilarious or beating someone up. That's why groups use this technique to bash the other guy."

Among the ads that have made Democratic political consultant Karen Finney flinch this year was one in which Democratic Congressman Bruce Braley of Iowa's Republican challenger implied that Braley supports a mosque near Ground Zero — when the issue had never before been raised in the campaign. "There's more of a market for it than there used to be. . .," Finney says. "If it gets where it's too ugly, I hope it will correct itself. I hope we'll know it when we see it and pull it back ourselves." That's not likely to happen, however. Politicians get more mileage out of spewing filth than they do from discussing the issues or being positive.

"It shows how competitive the races are, because if all the races were foregone conclusions, there wouldn't be all this outsider spending," Levinthal says. "The amount is a constant moving target. Millions upon millions literally every day are coming in" for campaign advertising.

"It also may be that the electorate is in the mood for more ugliness than usual. Concerns over the economy, employment and healthcare, among other issues, have added to voters' anger, and analysts say that few care to hear touchy feely ads that pitch positives not present in their own lives." CBS News political consultant Dotty Lynch, a communications professor at American University, says she's heard of one campaign advisor telling candidates they would do more good giving money to charity than running positive ads. She says another campaign consultant tells candidates they can run a single positive ad in their own cable TV market to feel good about themselves — and then go negative.

This is what passes for campaigning in this century. Politicians are finally showing their true colors. There is more and more money being spent, throwing mud and accusations at their opponents, and a viciousness not seen before. And corporations and unions can spend unlimited amounts of money on this garbage, all in an effort to elect someone who will be their conduit to untold billions or hundreds of billions of government spending directed their way once they get elected. The whole thing is an absolutely corrupt system, and is only becoming more corrupt as the years pass. This is what passes for democracy and elections these days? What's a voter to do?

(Source: *Political ads: mean, and getting meaner, before Nov. 2*, By Lynda Gorov, Yahoo News; Sun Oct 24, 2010, Yahoo.com. © 2010 Reprinted with permission from Yahoo! Inc. YAHOO! and the YAHOO! logo are trademarks of Yahoo! Inc.)

## *The Election Won't Bring Any Changes...*

It's the same old story. Angry at the way the country is going, the public votes for the party that promises change. And then, once the election is over, not much changes. The success the Republicans had this year in tapping into the public's anger is the mirror image of the success the Democrats had in 2006 and 2008. Back then, a majority of people were fed up with the way the Republicans had mismanaged the country. Katrina, Iraq and the recession were all you needed to know to predict the outcome. And remember when the last Republican landslide happened? It was after Hillary Clinton tried to reform healthcare (and failed). The next congressional election saw angry voters put more Republicans into office. It's the same thing over and over, with the voting populace expecting different results. Remember also the definition of insanity: Doing the same thing over and over and expecting different results.

It's pretty much the same plot line this year (2010), with a new villain. Now, a majority of people are fed up with the way the Democrats are mismanaging things. Stimulus, ObamaCare and recession are all you need to know. The politicians and the media like to pretend that these elections are a referendum between contrasting political ideologies. That America turned sharply to the left in 2008, and reversed field to the right in 2010. It makes a good story, and it motivates the voters.

Neither party challenges the status quo in any serious way. Once the new guys get in, they move the government's center of gravity an inch to the left or an inch to the right. An inch can make a big difference, but, no matter which party is in power the government spends more money than it takes in, is influenced by and funnels money to special interests and lobbyists, and continues to subsidize millions of people not to work.

Most Americans don't think in terms of political philosophies. We want results. We like our government to be big enough to keep our food safe (they haven't) and our cities protected (they aren't) from floods and terrorists. But we also like it small enough that we can do whatever we want, whenever we want. If politicians can keep us safe and not screw up the economy, we're fine (apathetic) with whichever party is in power. But if the government doesn't do those minimal things, we're ready to throw the bums out.

Lately, we've been more inclined to throw the current bums out and take a chance with the other guys (the new bums). This will be the third throw-the-bums-out election in a row. Does this suggest that politicians are bums or are we fools to expect them to change? Could it be time for a transformational election? A nice idea, but transform into what? Elections have become like changing seats on the Titanic.

## *Americans Are Angry, But who's Listening?*

Washington was transformed by the 2010 vote, but America wasn't. The America that voted for Republicans in 2010 isn't so different from the America that voted for Democrats in 2008. The politicians that were elected may not be that much different than those they replaced either. The voting was more like a reluctant, lesser-of-two-evils pick. We just want a government that's competent, but is that what we're going to get?

The politicians and the talking heads don't get it. They tell us the election was about big changes, a new direction, a return to our core conservative values, a repudiation of the Democrats and a coronation of the Tea Party. But most people haven't changed their minds in the past two years; most voted the same way they had two years ago.

Nobody wants to pay more taxes; those that are being supported and getting money from the government don't want to give up the services, benefits and free money that the government provides. We want to eat, drink, sleep, work, travel and enjoy the benefits of liberty. Can the government provide this anymore? The Great Recession has revealed cracks in our economic system, and our national and personal debt and continued deficit spending in the trillions make our problems today unlike anything the U.S has ever faced. Instead of cutting spending, reducing deficits, and repairing our economy, politicians are doing the exact opposite.

Polls show that voters don't trust or like either political party; that's why Americans have voted against the party in power for three straight elections. Come 2012, it could very well be four elections in a row. It was the poor economy — not the wisdom of the Republicans' ideas or the brilliance of their tactics — that assured they would retake control of the House.

Politicians are listening to the Tea Party. The Tea Party's actual electoral victories in 2010 were few, but the Tea Party has captured the Republican Party's attention nonetheless. Every Republican incumbent will remember what happened to Mike Castle, Robert Bennett and Lisa Murkowski: No matter how conservative you are, or how much you've done for your state or your party, crossing the Tea Partiers is political suicide. Even Republican leaders John Boehner and Mitch McConnell understand that.

The Tea Party insists on ideological purity. Republicans who even think about compromising with Democrats will be punished with primary challenges from the Tea Party next election. So the Republican leadership is promising never to compromise. Not that the Republicans are inclined to compromise anyway. The history of the past two years proves the political genius of having said no to everything the Democrats proposed. The Republicans knew they would gain politically if Obama failed, and they've done all they could to make that happen.

If there was one thing American voters made abundantly clear on Nov. 2, 2010, it's how unhappy they are with politicians and the way things work — or more often don't work — in Washington. Survey after survey has shown that the majority of voters want their elected representatives to do a much better job of coming together to solve the country's problems.

So will things improve after the "shellacking" that voters gave to Democrats in handing control of the House over to the Republicans?

Few Americans appear to be counting on it. In a November 2010 ABC News/Yahoo! News poll after the election, most say they have little expectation that things will get better as a result of the recent midterms. Respondents were asked if they thought the election was more likely to move the country in the right direction or the wrong direction. The largest number of respondents, some 40 percent, said *they didn't expect the election to make a difference at all*. Only one-third of those polled, 34 percent, thought the results would move the country in the right direction, while another 21 percent said they thought things were headed the wrong way.

An even more telling sign: a whopping 81 percent thought that gridlock — in which the two political parties cannot agree and thus don't pass any meaningful legislation — is likely to occur in the two years leading up to the next presidential election. If the three weeks since the election are any guide, they look to be dead right. "The idea that there will be any kind of bipartisan cooperation is naïve," says Greg Valliere, chief political strategist for *Potomac Research Group*. "Both parties are purging moderates who have had the temerity to compromise; we've never seen such a vacuum in the center."

We can expect more of the same in the next two years. The prospect of total gridlock is an appealing one for many cynical people, but it would be a disaster for the country and for the economy. With the economy so weak, we can't afford to squander two years playing political games. The same problems remain after the election as before—government spending, poor economic growth, joblessness, foreclosures, and anger among the voting public. The lobbyists are still in Washington, just waiting to bend the ears of the newly elected officials. Let's see if they've learned what the past three elections should have taught them. Voters still show up at the polls, and even with political party-change and new politicians, most voters polled (61%) didn't think the election made any difference at all or that it made things worse; and they're right. Voters are finally realizing just changing politicians isn't going to solve anything.

## Public Optimism Hits a 36-year Low in Views of the 'System of Government'

Optimism in the country's system of government has dropped to a new low in polling going back 36 years, and the public's sense that America is the greatest nation on Earth, while still high, has fallen significantly from its level a generation ago. Both results in the October 2010 ABC News/Yahoo! News poll suggest that public disenchantment extends beyond its economic and political roots to encompass broader views of the country's governance.

The bottom hasn't fallen out of national pride: Seventy-five percent call the United States "the greatest country in the world." But that's down from 88 percent when the same question was asked in 1984. And nearly a quarter, 23 percent, now take the alternative, saying America used to be the greatest country, "but isn't any more." That's up from 9 percent.

Optimism about the system has taken an even bigger hit in this poll, produced for ABC and Yahoo! News by *Langer Research Associates*. Back in 1974 – shortly after Richard Nixon's resignation in the Watergate scandal – 55 percent of Americans were optimistic about "our system of government and how well it works." Today just 33 percent say so, the fewest in nearly a dozen measurements across the decades. (None, though, was done in the early '90s, the last time economic disgruntlement was as high as it is now.)

There's better news on two fronts. First, while optimism is down, pessimism about the workings of government hasn't risen; 20 percent are pessimistic, about the average in those 36 years of polls – and it peaked much higher, at 28 percent, in 1996. Instead more now are "uncertain" about the system and how it's working, a new high, 46 percent.

In a new follow-up, this poll asked pessimistic or uncertain Americans what the problem is – the system itself, or the people in government who are running it. Answer: The people running the government, not the system itself, by a 3-1 margin, 74 percent to 24 percent. This means that just under half of Americans, 49 percent, are pessimistic or uncertain about the system and how it's working, and mainly blame the people running it. Sixteen percent are pessimistic or uncertain and blame the system itself. And nearly all of the rest, 33 percent, are optimistic about the system.

(Source: *ABC NEWS/YAHOO! NEWS POLL: ASK AMERICA #4 and #5,* ABC News/Yahoo News: poll #4 was conducted Oct. 2010. Poll #5 was conducted Nov. 2010. Langer Research Assoc., Langerresearch.com)

## Who Will Work for the disappearing Middle Class?

Is there really the possibility of a transformational election? Every few generations has an election that moves the country in a different direction. Jackson's election shifted political power toward the West and toward the common man, Lincoln's election put an end to the barbarity of slavery, the election of FDR established Washington as a counterweight to big business, and the elections of JFK and LBJ completed Lincoln's task (for women's and civil rights).

What's at stake now? The disappearance of the middle class. The problem isn't just the recession — as bad as it's been. This has been a long time coming. Our economy isn't producing enough good jobs to sustain a middle class. We're working as hard as ever (those that do work), but more and more of our national income and wealth is flowing offshore or to the few ultrarich. The largest holder's of our $13.8 trillion debt are Middle-Easterners and China, who got most of the money they loaned back to us *from us*. Decades of massive trade deficits put trillions into their pockets, which we had to borrow back from them to support government spending.

The right says that big government is squeezing the life out of us. The left says it's the global corporations that are to blame. Perhaps both have a point. Together, the corporations and the government have distracted us with bread and circuses while the fruits of the labors of the many go into the pockets of the idle few, oil nations or to corporations in Japan, Korea, and China. Few politicians or Wall Street mavens feel sorry for an out-of-work person driving a gas-guzzling Toyota truck (from Japan), watching a Samsung big screen T.V. and washing clothes in an LG washer and dryer (from Korea), with a house full of products made in China. The loss of middle class jobs has happened over decades, and most of those jobs aren't coming back, no matter what politicians say or do.

Will the election of 2010 change that? Not likely. Voters can't vote on the next big thing that will create millions of good jobs in this country. All big things in this country started as small things. Bill Gates and Microsoft started with two guys. HP started with two guys in a garage. Google was started by two guys—Sergey Brin and Larry Page. Sam Walton started Walmart with one store in Arkansas. Ray Kroc started McDonald's with only a handful of restaurants in Southern California. It is the entrepreneurs that will generate the next big thing that will propel America forward, not the government, and certainly not politicians. Our only hope is to vote for anyone who will support small business. It's only from small business that big businesses come from.

**In conclusion**, we have not only the right but the duty to vote. It's the only thing we have left. The thing that needs to happen is the *separation of voting from the election process.* While this sounds counterintuitive, it is the only thing that will work. We must be able to vote in real time for things that effect us like taxes, entitlement spending, healthcare, laws and regulations, government subsidizes and all the other things that are destroying our country. All we can vote for is *politicians* in elections every two years—all we can vote for is the problem, not the solution, so the problem continues to grow. The faith, trust and patience of the American people are still a marvel despite what politicians do when they get elected. The faith and patience of the voters is running out, however—there is only so much they can take. We need another option.

Elections, like politics in general, have become corrupt. There is more money than ever in elections, and the politicians aren't shy about taking as much money as they can get. As with getting money from anyone, there are always strings attached. Many politicians have become like puppets on the ends of strings of money. The politicians are more beholden than ever to the corporations, unions, lobbyists and special interests that give them money. How do they show their gratitude? Once they get to Washington, they vote however their money-men want them to vote. They give our tax dollars to whoever they owe, or whoever is going to give them more money. And what do voters get? We get a huge tax bill every year, huge deficits, federal programs and laws that don't work, less income, fewer jobs, less security. Somebody is making out well. One can only imagine how many of that "top 1%" of income earners have their hands in the government's pocket (thus our pocket). We know the bankers and Wall Street got their share of $3.3 trillion, and someone got $870 billion in stimulus spending. Again, the 1,997 lobbyists who registered to lobby on this $870 billion bill know where the money went—into the pockets of the people that paid them to lobby.

Polls continue to show that people are angry, and some even think the U.S. is no longer the greatest country, although it used to be. It's not surprising. We have many catastrophic problems facing us, and a voter's only option is to put more or different politicians into office. As the poll showed, voters believe the politicians *are* the problem. How is *a problem* going to solve *the problem*? Except for voting, what other options do we have?

We have to find a better, less corrupt way to run things. What we have now in anything from a plutocracy (def: *government by the wealthy: a controlling class of the wealthy*) to an oligarchy (def: *government by the few: a government in which a small group exercises control especially for corrupt and selfish purposes*), you can decide for yourself which one is correct (or both). What we need is a real democracy. What we have is the power to vote, and despite what has been presented, that means everything. We haven't exercised that power very well in the last three decades. The political process, elections, and politicians have overwhelmed the voters. There is a better way than simply throwing out the current bunch of politicians. A broken political system isn't going to be fixed by a broken political system. It's not broken if you're one of the entitlement recipients or government employees or corporations or unions or lobbyists or special interests reaping hundreds of billions of dollars from this system. But the average voter, the average American, who this country was established for, has to do something and must have a better option. We don't have many options now—left or right, in or out of office, it doesn't make much difference. Most voters already know this, but it doesn't stop them from being angry and looking for something better. We can't just give up and let our greatness slip away, we have to take back the rights that our great forefathers gave us. There is a better way.

# CHAPTER 8

# *The Romans and the U.S.*

**If there is one principle more deeply rooted in the mind of every American, it is that we should have nothing to do with conquest.**

*Thomas Jefferson*

## *The United States and the Roman Empire*

Everyone from historians to junior high school teachers like to compare the U.S. to the Romans. Although it is an interesting academic exercise, it also angers many people—because Rome fell. Back in the day, Rome was the greatest power the world had known. Although the U.S. hasn't been around as long as Rome, are we making some of the same mistakes that lead to their demise? Nearly four decades before the birth of Christ, the Roman orator Cicero offered this sound advice: "The budget should be balanced, public debt should be reduced, the treasury should be rebuilt, the arrogance of officialdom should be tempered and controlled, and assistance to foreign lands should be curtailed, lest Rome fall." The Romans didn't take his advice and Rome fell. That advice, more than 2000 years ago, is certainly applicable today.

At more than $13.8 trillion, our government's national debt represents an ominous recurrence of just what Cicero warned against twenty centuries ago. Our politicians are equally arrogant and regard voters as bigots and idiots. Government in ancient Rome grew to mammoth size for some of the same reasons ours has. The philosopher George Santayana once said, "Those who ignore history are condemned to repeat it." Many people wonder if we're just repeating history. Long before Christ, a Roman politician named Clodius was elected to public office on a platform of "free wheat for the masses." When Julius Caesar came to power, he found 320,000 persons in Rome — a city of 1 million — on government grain relief (food stamps?).

Emperor Nero once declared, "Let us tax and tax again. Let us see to it that no one owns anything!" He may also have been the architect of the first urban-renewal program. He burnt a large portion of Rome to make way for a number of construction projects. A few years later, another emperor dabbled in farm policy. To reduce production and raise the price of wine, he ordered the destruction of half of the vineyards in Rome's provinces. The ancient government assumed the responsibility of providing the people with publicly funded entertainment and arts programs. One historian estimates the modem equivalent of $100 million a year was poured out in circuses and gladiator duels alone.

Welfare was as loved then as it is by politicians today. In A.D. 274, Emperor Aurelian made the right to relief hereditary and boosted welfare benefits considerably. Businesses were pulverized under a burden of public hostility and excessive taxation and regulation. The masses demanded their handouts, and the most productive in Roman society were made to pay up. Some of them, thinking they were buying time, actually supported those politicians and funded those institutions which were dedicated to their very destruction. What was left of their businesses was eventually confiscated and nationalized (they must not have been able to offshore their businesses for protection).

City administrations within the empire spent themselves silly and, beginning with the emperor Hadrian, were bailed out through a kind of "federal revenue sharing," To satisfy special interests (lobbyists?) and a soaring debt prompted the government to debauch the national currency. It imposed wage and price controls, seized the people's gold holdings, took the silver out of the coinage and manufactured junk money like there was no tomorrow (Federal Reserve printing money?).

The great empire expired in A.D. 476. It fell like a lead balloon to foreign enemies. When the barbarians walked into the city, many Romans actually welcomed them in the belief that anything was better than the tyranny of their own tax collectors and regulators. It has been said that many civilizations have run their course by this pattern: <u>From bondage to individualism to great courage to liberty to abundance, then from abundance to complacency to apathy to dependency and finally back to bondage again.</u> It would seem that, given Welfare, Disability, and other entitlement programs, we are in the dependency stage now—with everyone looking to the government for a hand out, when the government is the cause of many of the problems that we find ourselves in.

More to the point, what is called *Kershner's First Law* sums up what happened to Rome pretty well: "When a self-governing people confer upon their government the power to take from some and give to others, the process will not stop until the last bone of the last taxpayer is picked bare." Today, we have most certainly conferred upon the government the power to take from some and give to others, via subsidizes, ear marks, pork spending, tax and regulation breaks, entitlement programs and all the other government hand-outs. People today are starting to realize it isn't going to end until the bones of the last taxpayer are "picked clean."

---

## Trends in U.S. Policies Parallel Those of Later Rome

---

The most remarkable civilization to date is still the Roman Empire. It began around 500BC as the Roman Republic and would survive for almost 1,000 years. The Empire went through various phases and peaked during the second century. It controlled over 2.5 million square miles of land and about 100 million people (half of the world's population). Rome ceased to be an Empire in 476 when the Western Roman Empire fell to Germanic invaders. But much of the influence of Roman culture would remain for another 1,000 years in the form of the Byzantine Empire. Many historians have undertaken to discover what caused the demise of this once great Empire. The most noted historical reference is the book by Edward Gibbon: The *Decline and Fall of the Roman Empire.* This was a mammoth six-volume series, the first volume published in 1776. Gibbon's main theme was that Rome's decline was the result of a weakened military that had spread its resources too thin.

Despite this mammoth work, historians and sociologists have come to some different conclusions surrounding the mysteries of the dissolution of the Roman Empire. One historian, Peter Heather, recently published a book called *The Fall of the Roman Empire*. He suggests that one of the main reasons for the Empire's decline was the continuing entanglements with Persian Gulf and Mideast Empires. Others now believe that Roman economics also played a much greater role in the demise of the Empire than was originally believed.

The greatest nation on earth today is the United States. The two main factors supporting this are that, at the moment, the U.S. is the economic leader of the world. Also, at this point in time, the U.S. has the strongest military of any nation. Is there any relevance with what is happening in the United States today and what occurred during the fall of the Roman Empire?

One common and provable fact is that history does have a tendency to repeat itself. After all, governments and their entities are made up of people. And as part of human nature, people are prone to make the same mistakes again and again. There are four main areas of similarity when contrasting the United States with the Roman Empire. These are: government spending, military, taxes and inflation. The following is a comparison of what happened in the later stages of the Roman Empire and the related trends occurring in the U.S. today.

## Government Spending

The most significant structures in the Roman Empire were built between 100BC and 200AD. Some were made of solid marble and many still stand today. The famous network of roads, aqueducts, and public baths were also constructed during this time and at great expense. Then in the third century, Rome was forced to spend more on military operations to protect its foreign interests and expanding Empire. Greater amounts of money were spent on social services to keep a restless public happy. Less was spent on civic building projects. The infrastructure became neglected. Supporting an army of over 500,000 was a continuing drain on resources. And with promises of pension payments to retired bureaucrats and soldiers, Rome soon dug itself an immense financial hole.

Many of the cities in the U.S. are experiencing a crumbling infrastructure (despite stimulus spending). Every year, despite what the figures may say, the government spends more than it takes in and continuously promises to make payments in the future to millions of its citizens in the form of pensions and Social Security benefits. Never mind that these obligations are currently non-funded and will require future taxation to meet. What about the other government colossus, Medicare and Medicaid? Every day the population of this country ages as millions of baby boomers are retiring. An ever increasing cost of healthcare combined with an aging population that will require more of it, will create a tremendous burden on government resources. The recent healthcare bill (ObamaCare) will only add to Medicaid and grow the government. Paying for this social health and welfare entitlement-promise will, by itself, have the power to break the government. Throw in Medicare healthcare spending and the costs associated with military operations and upkeep.....who is going to pay for all these promises?

## Military Obligations

Many historians believed that it was the constant fighting with the northern Germanic tribes and the Huns from Eurasia that helped to weaken Rome's military. But newer studies have concluded that more pressure came from the east. Rome battled the Parthian and Persian Empires for over 600 years. This is now modern day Iraq and Iran. Eventually Rome would end up fighting with most of the Middle Eastern countries as we know them today. These wars lasted until about 650 and became a huge drain on financial resources.

Flash forward to today and we find this same region is the cause of much of the world's turmoil. The U.S. now has a direct presence in the Middle East which is draining hundreds of billions of dollars from taxpayers. Further involvement might be required to protect American oil interests in the region. In his book *World War IV, the Long Struggle Against Islamofascism*, author Norman Podhoretz says we are actually fighting WWIV now, against Islamic fascists, radicals and terrorists. He further states "we won WWIII, the Cold War", but we are already fighting our next world war. Fighting terrorism is indeed a world-wide affair, and we are spending hundreds of billions a year. The Romans fought in the Middle East for 600 years, how long and how much is it going to cost us?

Several additional military encounters might be forced upon the U.S. such as protecting Israel or invading Iran. Then there is North Korea to consider, as more than 28,000 U.S. military personnel are now permanently stationed in South Korea, with many more in bases in Japan. The U.S. military machine is stretched across the globe. And with no foreseeable end to the threat of terrorism and Middle East conflicts, Americans will forced to pay up in the form of higher taxes.

## Escalating Taxes

In early Roman times, taxes were minimal and often inconsequential. The Roman Empire was able to create economic prosperity for its citizens. The economy continued to grow until the burden of maintaining the military forced Rome to raise taxes. Land and inheritance taxes were substantially increased forcing many of Rome's middle class into bankruptcy. Middle-class bankruptcies were then followed by upper classes bankruptcies as overall tax burdens became too great. Soon, government revenues began to decrease because fewer citizens could afford to pay taxes. This led to Rome's ultimate demise since it could no longer pay its military or the hired mercenaries protecting the northern borders.

Despite what the politicians say about taxes, most Americans are still burdened by over-taxation. The average worker spends the first four months of the year working for Uncle Sam (tax freedom day, remember?). After that, he gets to keep his hard earned wages to some extent, right? Until he has to pay state taxes, local taxes, property taxes, sales tax, and consumption taxes. To support such a massive federal deficit, along with military and social entitlement programs, somewhere down the line, taxes will have to be significantly raised. Or, benefits will have to be drastically reduced. When was the last time the politicians had the nerve to do either?

Their main goal is to maintain popularity, not by making the difficult choices. There is a way out though......
inflation!

## Over-inflating the Economy

The Roman government was no different than any other in the history of the world. To attempt to pay for its obligations, it simply created more money. This debasing of the currency was seen in Rome's most common coin. The *denarius* had 90% silver content during the age of Nero in about 60AD. Two centuries later, its silver content was only 0.2%. The value of silver exploded and so did commodity prices. The Romans tried to inflate their way out of their financial problems, and the results were disastrous. This type of irresponsible government policy has occurred throughout history. The results are always the same.

The politicians and many economists would have us think the real rate if inflation is this country is only about 3%. Energy, housing, schooling, medical, and insurance costs, to name a few, are rising much faster than 3%. Yet, our government says inflation is under control. In the year 2000, a dollar could buy 1.21 Euros. Today, it only buys .70 cents. The U.S. dollar is becoming one of the weaker currencies in the world. The currency only matters when you travel abroad, right? If the government starts printing money (it already is with "quantitative easing"), it will further devalue the dollar, and the holders of our national debt (treasury bills) may be diluted. So will the millionaires and billionaires, as inflation and hyperinflation may dilute their holdings. The government knows it is backing itself into a corner that will leave no way out. To pay for its towering debt, obligations and future promises it can only raise taxes or inflate the economy. There is always hope that the economy can continue to grow and produce enough tax revenue to out-pace the financial burdens. But this will not occur when tax dollars are spent on military and social entitlements. And the government insists on spending more than it takes in thus creating a negative cash flow. Somewhere down the line someone will have to pay off these crushing debts, or go bankrupt.

These trends have been continuing for many decades. It does not matter which party is running the show. We are still very much in a tax-and-spend-then-inflate situation. This same scenario has been played out in one form or another throughout history. Just because we are the greatest nation on earth today doesn't mean we will escape economic catastrophe. Irresponsible governments and their policies cannot survive indefinitely. It might have taken 1,000 years for Rome to eventually suffer the consequences. However, today's world moves much faster than in Roman times.

## Just like the Roman Empire?

So you say "Are we just like the Roman Empire, headed for the same kind of fall?" We hear this question sometimes when someone wants to make the point that the United States is doing something that will lead to its ultimate decline. The comparison between Rome and America is an intriguing one. Here are some more similarities between Rome and America:

1. Both began as small republics without much influence. Then they expanded "to the sea," by conquering or coercing the peoples who occupied the heartlands. Both continued that expansion beyond the seas. The Romans spread throughout the Mediterranean and beyond. The U.S. expanded from only a handful of states to conquer our country as we now know it, Alaska, Hawaii, the Philippines and parts of the Caribbean.

2. Both claimed important political traditions such as the rule of law and fair government. Both believe that they were providing a much better government to those they conquered.

3. Both established transnational trading systems. In the areas of the Roman imposed peace, they established road networks, a postal system, and commercial stability. Similarly, the U.S. has led the way in bringing about a global system of commerce and trade.

4. Both had long conflicts with major rivals, ending in triumph and unrivaled power. Rome won its long war with Carthage; the U.S. over Nazi Germany and the U.S.S.R..

5. Both borrowed their basic culture from predecessors. Rome from Greece. The U.S. from Britain and Rome.

6. Both dominated the rest of the world with military superiority.

7. Both took advantage of advanced technology to improve the lives of their peoples.

8. Both attracted substantial numbers of immigrants from other parts of the world.

9. Rome often used local leaders to manage the local populations. The U.S. does the same.

10. Both are responsible for a "transnational language." Latin in the case of Rome. English in the case of the U.S.

11. Both experienced a movement to centralize political power. This centralization has been accompanied by a decline in the politics of participation and an increase in the politics of the spectacle. Games and pleasure took the place of a civic life. A few elite families tended to dominate the national political life.

12. Both developed an increased reliance on a professional military, depending less and less upon the citizen soldier.

13. Finally, both experienced growing opposition at the boundaries. The resulting conflicts increased dependence on the military. The costs of military preparedness and defense strained the basic economic systems.

There are, of course, some important differences between Rome and America, including:

1. The U.S. has relatively few colonies compared to Rome.

2. The U.S. has an expanding human rights agenda.

3. The U.S. has maintained a "Democratic" form of government, unlike the Romans whose republic was transformed into rule by an emperor.

4. While Romans took pride in their empire, Americans generally reject the term "empire" as it applies to them.

The question that really matters is do the American people still have control over how our country is evolving? Or, are we like Romans at the time of the end of their republic when events were out of control of the people? Looking to Washington, and their frequent disregard for the will of the people, one can only wonder.

## *A Dominant Economy?*

How can the West possibly be regarded as being in decline when it is so economically dominant in the world? Today the combined output of the six biggest Western economies—Canada, France, Germany, Italy, the United Kingdom, and the United States—exceeds half of total global output. Gross domestic product (G.D.P.) per capita in the United States is more than 30 times higher than it is in the economies of East Asia and the Pacific.

Yet the difference between the West and the Rest is much narrower than it once was. As recently as 1968, American G.D.P. per capita was 127 times higher than that of East Asia. By this measure alone, the gap between West and East has narrowed dramatically in our time. And it will continue to narrow. The International Monetary Fund estimates that the Chinese economy is growing at a rate roughly three times that of the United States. According to Goldman Sachs, China's G.D.P. will overtake Britain's soon. By 2040 it is likely to be the biggest economy in the world.

At the same time, the Western economies have vulnerabilities that have been largely obscured by the debt-financed boom of the past nine years. America's gross federal debt now exceeds $14 trillion. Moreover, the officially stated borrowings of the federal government are only a small part of the U.S. debt problem. Ordinary American households, too, have gone on a borrowing spree of unprecedented magnitude. U.S. household credit-market debt has risen from just above 45 percent of G.D.P. in the early 1980s to more than 70 percent in recent years, although it has declined a small amount since the Great Recession. . The remarkable resilience of American consumer spending in the past 15 years has been based partly on a collapse in the personal savings rate. No longer able to use their house as an ATM, consumer spending has collapsed, as has the economy.

The Federal Government has much larger unfunded liabilities than official data imply. If you compare the current value of all projected future government expenditures—including debt-service payments—with the current value of all projected future government receipts, the gap is about $66 trillion, according to calculations by economists Jagadeesh Gokhale, of the CATO Institute, and Kent Smetters, professor at the Wharton School and data already presented.

Perhaps our most perplexing vulnerability, however, is cultural. In *Decline and Fall of the Roman Empire* Gibbon wrote that while "the corrupt and opulent nobles of Rome gratified every vice that could be collected from the mighty conflux of nations and manners, the most lively and splendid amusement of the idle multitude depended on the frequent exhibition of public games and spectacles." Orgies and circuses are not precisely the favorite pastimes of Western society today. But if you substitute pornography and NASCAR, the parallel is not so far-fetched.

Outwardly, it is true the institutions that exist to preserve and propagate our culture are in good shape. Never has the percentage of young people attending college been higher. Never have American universities dominated higher education and academic research as they do today. Our museums and concert halls offer more exhibitions and recitals than the enthusiast can possibly hope to attend. And to enter any branch of Barnes & Noble is to be overwhelmed by the sheer number of books being published.

Yet beneath this upper crust of high culture there simmers a less appetizing stew. Few children read for pleasure. Teens and tweens can barely communicate except by text messaging. Most boys would rather fritter away their time on video games. Girls no longer play with dolls; they are themselves the dolls, dressed according to the dictates of the fashion industry. Endlessly gaming, chatting, and chilling with their iPods, the next generation already has a more tenuous connection to "Western civilization" than most parents appreciate.

For our culture's sedentary character—our strong preference for watching over doing, for virtual over real action—seems closely correlated to our changing physical shape. When we think of Romans we mainly think of gladiators. We, by contrast, are being transformed into actual giants. We are certainly taller on average than past generations, a consequence of improvements in nutrition. But we are also fatter, since we now consume significantly more fat and calories than we actually need. The percentage of Americans classified as obese is 30%. Another 30% are officially considered overweight. Obesity adds hundreds of billions of dollars to healthcare spending, and results in massive increases in morbidity and mortality in our population. Obesity is a health epidemic the likes of which the Romans never had to face.

# WHAT ABOUT THE AMERICAN EMPIRE?

*"The decline of Rome was the natural and inevitable effect of immoderate greatness.*
*Prosperity ripened the principle of decay; the causes of destruction multiplied*
*with the extent of conquest; and as soon as time or accident had removed*
*the artificial supports, the stupendous fabric yielded to*
*the pressure of its own weight."*
**Edward Gibbon** – *Decline and Fall of the Roman Empire*

In his editorial about *Decline and Fall of the Roman Empire*, James Quinn presents some compelling arguments. "After ruling much of the known world for centuries, Rome fell due to a number of factors that proved terminal. Military overspending and overreach, an untenable economic system, and currency debasement all played a role. As has been well documented, the Roman emperors attempted to distract the populace from the increasingly dire reality of their situation by providing bread and circuses. But entertainment could not stop the nation-state from yielding to the pressure of its own weight."

There are numerous parallels between the end of the Roman Empire and the path the 226-year-old American republic is on now. The Roman Empire took a long time to collapse. Since the dawn of industrialization followed by the rise of digital technology, empires can now rise more rapidly, but are also likely to decline more rapidly.

## Conquest & Overreach

"The decay of trade and industry was not a cause of Rome's fall. There was a decline in agriculture and land was withdrawn from cultivation, in some cases on a very large scale, sometimes as a direct result of barbarian invasions. However, the chief cause of the agricultural decline was high taxation on the marginal land, driving it out of cultivation. Taxation was spurred by the huge military budget. The Roman Empire's economy was based on the plunder of conquered territories. As the empire expanded, it installed remote military garrisons to maintain control and increasingly relied on Germanic mercenaries to man those garrisons."

Ultimately, as its territorial expansion waned and began to contract, less and less booty became available to support the empire's widespread ambitions and domestic economy. The outsourcing of the military and the cultural dilution from the bloated empire led to lethargy, complacency, and decadence amongst the formerly self-reliant and hard-working Roman citizenry. Sound familiar?

In the modern context, as the only major power whose productive capacity was not destroyed during World War II, the American Empire emerged as victorious, as did The Soviet Union. Rather than plunder, the U.S. used its unique status to dictate terms that made the U.S. dollar the world's *de facto* reserve currency and positioned its robust new manufacturing sector to supply the world with the cars, machinery, appliances, and electronics it so desperately needed.

The U.S. trade surplus with the nations of the world led to escalating U.S. wealth and prosperity. Lately, nobody can even remember the last time we had a trade surplus. "*Prosperity ripened the principle of decay.*" Prosperity did indeed become ripe. In the 50's, everyone had a job as we manufactured things, even electronics. We became victims of our own prosperity. So at some point, under pressure from unions, labor became too expensive here, or companies simply wanted to make more profits, and started exporting jobs and whole industries. First was electronics, we sent those jobs and technology to Japan. The Japanese simply copied our electronics then overtook our entire electronics industry. The same happened to much of our auto, machinery, and appliance industries. Our industrial centers began to decay and manufacturing waned and many, many jobs are gone now, and probably won't be coming back.

Meanwhile, the U.S. military was increasingly asked by the nation's politicians to take on the role of the world's policeman, leading to action in dozens of conflicts. And even where no direct military role was taken, the U.S. has shown a keen willingness to exert coercive power – including threats, sanctions, and even invasions of other nations. We haven't had to rely on "mercenaries" yet (although we pay millions to "military contractors"), as the Romans did, but we are finding it increasingly difficult to pay for our massive military.

## Bread and Circuses

"Already long ago, from when we sold our vote to no man, the People have abdicated our duties; for the People who once upon a time handed out military command, high civil office, legions — everything, now restrains itself and anxiously hopes for just two things: bread and circuses." Roman Poet Juvenal – 77 AD

The Roman government didn't have proper budgetary systems, and so it squandered resources maintaining the empire while producing little value. When the spoils from conquered territories were no longer sufficient to cover its many expenses, it turned to higher taxes, in effect shifting the burden of the immense military structure onto the back of the citizenry. The higher taxes forced many small farmers to let their land go barren. To distract its citizens from the worsening conditions, Roman politicians played the populist card by providing free wheat to the poor and entertaining them with circuses, chariot races, and other entertainment.

The American Empire has reached the point where it now faces similar structural imbalances, but to pay its bills, it has largely chosen to borrow from foreign countries in recent years. And the bills are large. The $700-plus billion of annual military expenditures by the United States almost equals the military expenditures of the rest of the world combined.

The social safety net put in place over the decades by politicians attempting to get reelected has resulted in a massive number of Americans now totally dependent upon the almighty state for their well-being. Once a country that used to value hard work and thrift, many now wait for their government hand-outs every month. Threatening to rip apart the country's social fabric, the "new American" will vote for anyone who promises to sustain his dependency even as the nation increasingly struggles under the weight of $66 trillion of unfunded liabilities.

The non-farm workforce in the United States totals something like 226 million people. Of that number, the government directly employs 18.5 million. Millions more are employed by industries heavily dependent on government spending, such as defense, construction, and healthcare. The annual maintenance cost of the country's safety net now costs American taxpayers more than a trillion dollars. People on Welfare, Social Security, Disability, food stamps, and those that lost their job (unemployment) get hundreds of billions of dollars not to work, and hundreds of billions are spent on health benefits for people who don't work (while many who do work can't get health benefits). Americans have evolved away from being rewarded for hard work into becoming increasingly dependent on government hand-outs.

America has evolved from a nation of savers to a nation of consumers with a throw-away mentality and driven by little more than the desire for instant gratification. Worse, large segments of our society are convinced that they are owed something. To most, civic duty has become a quaint, outmoded concept. Happy to accommodate – in exchange for a reliable vote come election time – the government keeps the public satiated and sedated by providing them with an ever-increasing list of "public services."

Roman poet Juvenal described how the Roman citizens abdicated their duties to the state and turned to bread and circuses. Many huge entitlement programs represent just some of the bread that American citizens now feel entitled to. Here in America, we know how to provide circuses on a grand scale. Roman citizens were satisfied with a good chariot race. In these modern times, Americans can find entertainment and distraction with 24-hour-a-day TV, the Internet, iPhones, iPods, Blackberries, Facebook, YouTube, 1.1 million retail stores, 1,100 malls, 17,000 golf courses, E! TV, Food TV, Sports TV, Housewives of Orange County, New York, Atlanta, and New Jersey, American Idol, 660 stations with nothing on, Las Vegas, Disney World, MLB, NFL, NBA, NHL, WWF, WEC, porn, and mega-churches all competing to fill the void in people's lives.

There isn't enough time in the day to take in all of the circuses, but with what little spare time we have available, we are now able to check our email anywhere on Earth and stay in constant contact with the office even in the middle of the night. And we can text and twitter our every thought to our circle of friends and followers, providing next to no lasting purpose or benefit to anyone.

Approximately 16% of the U.S. population (36 million people) is considered poor, and many of them are totally dependent upon the state. Yet that term seems out of sync with the fact that many of those individuals have cell phones ($500/yr.), cable TV ($900/yr.), Internet access ($500/yr.), cars ($5,000/yr. lease), houses ($6,000/yr.), eat fast food ($1,000/yr.), and can smoke a pack a day ($1,500/yr.).

## Debasement

"In Rome, the supply of foodstuffs in the cities declined. The people in the cities were forced to go back to the country and to return to agricultural life. Consequently, the emperors made laws against this movement. There were laws preventing the city dweller from moving to the country, but such laws were ineffective. As the people did not have anything to eat in the city, as they were starving, no law could keep them from leaving the city and going back into agriculture. The city dweller could no longer work in the processing industries of the cities as an artisan. And, with the loss of the markets in the cities, no one could buy anything there anymore." From Ludwig von Mises – *Human Action*. Economist Ludwig von Mises argued that flawed economic policies played a key role in the impoverishment and decay of the Roman Empire. He contended that interventionist economic policies, including price controls that resulted in prices substantially below their free-market equilibrium levels, ultimately led to inflation.

Further, Rome was spending more than it could afford. The free food rations/welfare for the poor of Rome and Constantinople – as well as the many entertainments – were costing a fortune. The purchasing of exotic spices, silks, and other luxuries from the Orient bled Rome of its gold... gold that didn't return. Soon Rome didn't have enough gold to produce coins. And so it debased its coins with lesser metals until there was no gold left.

To cover the trillions it is spending each year propping up its empire, the U.S. government is now increasingly forced to rely on printing and borrowing the funds, steadily debasing the currency in the process. But the nation's currency debasement is nothing new. Rather, it began in 1913 with the creation of the Federal Reserve. It accelerated when FDR confiscated all the gold in the country in the 1930s. When Richard Nixon took the U.S. off the gold standard in 1971, the show really got on the road, as that freed the Federal Reserve to print unlimited amounts of dollars. As a result, the dollar has lost 93% of its value versus gold since 1970. And the process has already started again – The Federal Reserve has started "printing money," and continues to do so with its quantitative easing (QE) policy.

## The Military-again

Lessons from ancient Rome regarding the cost of maintaining a far-flung empire have been ignored. Today, U.S. soldiers are on the ground in at least 117 countries, with permanent bases in more than 40 countries. Even the use of mercenaries, in the form of thousands of Blackwater guards and other private contractors filling roles formerly left to the military, has become commonplace.

Using military assets to pursue political goals, as is the norm in empire building, has led to unintended consequences and wasted opportunities. One of the most egregious of those lost opportunities came following the bankruptcy and collapse of the Soviet Union. The United States had won the Cold War, but failed to recognize the cautionary signs on the path ahead. As the only remaining superpower on earth, America fell into the same trap that has befallen previous empires. Instead of concentrating on proactively confronting domestic challenges, such as unfunded Social Security, Welfare and Medicare liabilities, and developing a comprehensive energy plan to wean ourselves off Middle East oil, we continued to intervene in costly foreign adventures.

Seeking to maintain its widespread interests and to defend itself from the many enemies created by building and protecting those interests, the American military complex has grown to the point where it now spends an amount equal to at least 40% of all taxes collected from its citizens. Since 1991 alone, the U.S. has interceded in Kuwait, Somalia, Bosnia, Sudan, Afghanistan, and Iraq, among others. Over that period of time, the U.S. has spent $7 trillion on defense. The National Debt in 1991 was $3.2 trillion. Today, it is $14 trillion. In 2001, spending on defense was 17% of the government budget. In 2008, defense, Homeland Security, and war spending accounted for 26% of government spending.

## *The Collapse*

History books will likely mark 1980 as the year that the rapid phase of the decline of the American Empire began. That's when the first wave of the Baby Boomers reached the age of 35 and turned its attention to living the American dream – on borrowed money. Since that year, household debt has surged from $1 trillion to $14 trillion, while the savings rate has plunged from 12% to 0%.

There are many ways to use credit, some quite intelligent and practical, but using credit card debt to buy the latest stuff is not included. Today in America, there is at least $950 billion in credit card debt outstanding, or $9,000 per household. The average American has nine credit cards. A credit card allows every person to live above their means for awhile.....just as did the home equity loans taken against elevated house prices on mortgages people couldn't afford. The cost of higher education has resulted in student loan debt now almost equaling credit-card debt – $833 billion.

This is where reality and fantasy meet. People can only borrow and spend if the Federal Reserve and bankers provide the funds to do so. By creating money out of thin air and handing it out to people with no means of repaying it, the financial elite and politicians in Washington played a key role in bringing the U.S. economy to its knees via the sub-prime debacle. Unable to borrow anymore, consumers have cut spending and the economy has yet to recover.

Yet, for all the evidence, a large swath of Americans still believes the nation hasn't gone off course. They expect the government to save them when they get into trouble and think that taxing the rich to pay for a bigger and bigger safety net is a reasonable idea – Income redistribution for a progressively remade society. Those that get paid by the government for not working expect the gravy-train to continue forever (via taxes). The crushing levels of debt resulting from decades of excess; the far-reaching military presence; the politically motivated social safety net and other popular but unaffordable programs have now reached the point that the economic decline of the American Empire is almost a foregone conclusion.

The current downturn is not like previous recessions that lasted on average 16 months. Even as the government responds by trying to borrow and spend the country back to prosperity (via stimulus spending), there is no ignoring that much of the economic base has been gutted and future social program and entitlement liabilities could essentially bankrupt the country. As was the case in the final stages of the Roman Empire, the unsustainable military, social, and political excesses have reached the point that, in combination, they are now likely to prove catastrophic.

(Source: DECLINE AND FALL OF THE AMERICAN EMPIRE, by James Quinn, Financial Sense Editorials, August 2, 2009. Financialsense.com/editorials. Used with permission)

---

## *Technology*

---

The US has learned a second lesson from Rome, realizing the centrality of technology. For the Romans, it was those famously straight roads, enabling the empire to move troops or supplies at high speeds – many of these roads have lasted a thousand years. It was a perfect example of how one imperial strength tends to feed another: an innovation in engineering, originally designed for military use, went on to boost Rome commercially. Today those highways find their counterpart in the American interstate system and in the information superhighway: the Internet also began as a military tool, devised by the US Defense Department, and now stands at the heart of American commerce. In the process, it is making English-the Latin of its day - a language spoken across the globe. The US is proving what the Romans already knew: that once an empire is a world leader in one sphere, it soon dominates in every other.

But it is not just specific tips that the US seems to have picked up from the ancient Romans. Rome understood that, if it was to last, a world power needed to practice both hard imperialism, the business of winning wars and invading lands, and soft imperialism, the cultural and political tricks that worked not to win power but to keep it. So Rome's greatest conquests came not only at the edge of a blade, but through its power to seduce conquered peoples. The conquered natives seemed to like togas, baths and central heating - never realizing that these were the symbols of their "enslavement."

Today the US offers the people of the world a similar cultural package. It's not togas or gladiatorial games today, but Starbucks, Coca-Cola, McDonald's and Disney, all paid for in the contemporary equivalent of Roman coinage, the global hard currency of the 21st century: the dollar. People visit the U.S. to see the Mecca's of Disney World and Las Vegas. When the process works, you don't even have to resort to direct force; it is possible to rule by remote control: satellite T.V. Not that it always worked. Rebellions against the empire were a permanent fixture, with barbarians constantly pressing at the borders. Some accounts suggest that the rebels were not always fundamentally anti-Roman; they merely wanted to share in the privileges and affluence of Roman life. Our southern borders are similarly pressed with those seeking a better way of life.

There are some large differences between the two empires, of course - starting with self-image. Romans reveled in their status as masters of the known world, but few Americans would be as ready to brag of our own imperialism. Most would deny it. But that may come down to the US's founding ideals. For America was established as a rebellion against empire, in the name of freedom and self-government. Raised to see themselves as a rebel nation and plucky underdog, we cannot quite accept our current role as master. One last factor scares Americans from making a parallel between themselves and Rome: that empire declined and fell. The historians say this happens to all empires; they are dynamic entities that follow a common path, from beginning to middle to end.

We can learn from the past, or we can repeat it. We have clear indications of what lead to the collapse and fall of the Roman Empire. Yet, we are in many ways following down the same paths that caused collapse. The influence we have over the world will remain—some people like our culture and our way of life—many try to get here every day. We have the best higher education system in the world, and often train many foreigners who return to their own countries. We have to avoid the mistakes of the past, while keeping all that is great about our country. We, as a nation, have to focus on our economy and our political system. We are going to have to work our way out of our problems, not delegate power to our politicians who got us into this mess in the first place. Can the U.S. last another 750 years? That will be about amount of time needed to equal the Roman Empire.

## 10 Signs The U.S. Is Losing Its Influence

Sadly, we won't be the greatest economy in the western hemisphere forever. Even if the U.S. hadn't crashed into a financial crisis, there are demographic, material, and political forces that have been spreading power around the Americas for decades. Brazil is first among the BRICs (Brazil, Russia, India, and China) – four economies that are supposed to overtake the six largest Western economies by 2032.

Mexico is first among the MAVINS (Mexico, Australia, Vietnam, Indonesia, Nigeria, and South Africa) – six economies we expect to blow away expectations and become leading powers in their regions relatively soon. Canada and Venezuela are oil powers of the not so distant future. Peru and Chile are sitting on a fortune of metals and minerals. All these countries are cranking up, while America faces plenty of fiscal and demographic problems at home. So what is happening? Take a look:

### Our most powerful regional ally – Brazil – refuses to follow our orders on Iran

Hillary Clinton went to Brazil to beg support for sanctions against Iran and came away empty handed. Now the UN is counting on Brazil, which is friendly with America and Iran, to lead nuclear diplomacy.

### The World's Richest Man is now a Mexican, not an American.

For the first time in 16 years, the World's Richest Man is not an American. Carlos Slim, worth $54 billion, is the first Latin American to hold that title and one of many emerging market billionaires to eclipse the U.S.

*Three years after a US financial crisis, Latin America is again growing rapidly. The U.S.? Not so much.....*

Compare this to what happened during the Great Depression. Latin America was devastated when U.S. investment dried up and the export market soured in the 30's. A League of Nations report said Chile, Peru, and Bolivia suffered the world's worst depression. Today is quite different. Brazil, Argentina, and Mexico have led a buoyant recovery from the global recession, according to Reuters. The regional economy is expected by the UN to grow 4.3 percent in 2010. If the American consumer remains weak, Latin American exports will move elsewhere.

*Chile produces 300% more copper than America — the former world leader in copper production*

America used to lead the world in copper production. We produced 49% of the world's copper in 1929. Today we produced 1.2 million tons yearly, compared to 5.4 million tons in Chile.

*Brazil now produces over four times as much iron ore as the U.S.. We used to lead that industry, too.*

America once led the world in iron mining. In 1892 we discovered the world's largest mine at the Great Lakes Mesabi Range. It was a wellspring for America's industrial might and the foundation of the rust belt. Now we claim reserves at 2,100 metric tons. Seven countries claim higher reserves, including Brazil at 8,900 metric tons. We produce only 54 metric tons yearly, while Brazil produces 250 metric tons.

*Canada and Venezuela will pass the U.S. in oil production in the next decade*

America produces around 9 million billion barrels of oil a day. Venezuela and Canada each produce around 3 million. But America's reserves are 21 billion barrels and may last less than a decade. Our oil-rich neighbors claim 99 billion barrels and 178 billion barrels, respectively, and will keep producing oil into the distant future.

### *Now Brazil exports over twice as much beef as we do*

America used to lead the world in beef production. Although we still do, America exports only 800,000 metric tons of beef per year. Brazil exports 2,200,000 metric tons. Here's some ironic excerpts from a 1911 NYT article: "American-Canadian syndicate to have world's largest beef plant in Brazil..... The chilled beef industry had never been tried before in Brazil and has only recently gotten under way in Argentina."

### *Brazil is now a critical partner for Russia, India, and China*

The acronym coined by Goldman Sachs to describe the four key emerging powers has taken on a life of its own. Brazil, Russia, India, and China have held several summits and even discussed making a supranational currency — that would pull the rug out from the U.S. dollar. What's important here is that global emerging powers have good relations and are inclined to work together. For instance, China just signed major contracts to build factories and high-speed rail in Brazil.

### *Brazil, Canada, and Mexico all invest a greater share of GDP in clean energy*

A Pew survey found that Brazil invests 0.37% of its economy in clean energy. Canada invests 0.25% and Mexico invests 0.14%. America is eleventh in the world at 0.13%.

(Source: *10 Signs The U.S. Is Losing Its Influence In The Western Hemisphere*, by Gus Lubin in Recession, Emerging Markets, Sep 27, 2010, Yahoo Finance, courtesy of Market Insider, Market Insider .com, used with permission)

### *Some of the things we invented, know and love, that America doesn't make anymore*

Not to put too fine a point on it, but the U.S. has lost production of many of the things we either invented or we consider unique to our culture. We can still continue to buy most of these items, but their production is gone.

## Here are 19 Iconic Products That America Doesn't Make Anymore:

**Rawlings baseballs**            Last production date: 1969

Rawlings is the official supplier of baseballs to Major League Baseball. The St. Louis shop was founded in 1887 by George and Alfred Rawlings. In 1969 the brothers moved the baseball-manufacturing plant from Puerto Rico to Haiti and then later to Costa Rica.

**Gerber baby food**            Last production date: 1994

Gerber was founded in Michigan in 1927 by the owner of the Fremont Canning Company. The brand grew in popularity and in 1994 merged with Novartis, a Swiss pharmaceutical company. Then in 2007, Gerber was bought by Switzerland's Nestle, the world's largest food company. Today the brand has more than 80% of the American baby food market and the largest supplier of baby products in the world. Ever since the merger with Novartis, all Gerber products have been manufactured overseas. Even Anheuser Busch, maker of America's beer—Budweiser, is now owned by a Belgian drink consortium (Bud is still made in the U.S. though).

**Etch a Sketch**            Last production date: 2000

Etch A Sketch, an iconic American toy since the 1960s, used to be produced in Bryan, Ohio, a small town of 8,000. Then in Dec. 2000, toymaker Ohio Art decided to move production to Shenzhen, China.

**Converse shoes**            Last production date: 2001

Marquis M. Converse opened Converse Rubber Shoe Company in Massachusetts in 1908. Chuck Taylors—named after All American high school basketball player Chuck Taylor— began selling in 1918 as the show eventually produced an industry record of over 550 million pairs by 1997. But in 2001 sales were on the decline and the U.S. factory closed. Now Chuck Taylors are made in Indonesia.

**Stainless steel rebar**            Last production date: circa 2001

Many forms of this basic steel product are not available domestically. Multiple waivers to the Buy America Act have allowed purchase of rebar internationally.

**Mattel toys**            Last production date: 2002

The largest toy company in the world closed their last American factory in 2002. Mattel, headquartered in California, produces 65 percent of their products in China as of August 2007.

**Minivans**                    Last production date: circa 2003

A waiver to the Buy America Act permitted an American producer of wheel-chair accessible minivans to purchase Canadian chassis for use in government contracts, because no chassis were available from the United States. The waiver specified: "General Motors and Chrysler minivan chassis, including those used on the Chevrolet Uplander, Pontiac Montana, Buick Terraza, Saturn Relay, Chrysler Town & Country, and Dodge Grand Caravan, are no longer manufactured in the United States."

**Vending machines**           Last production date: circa 2003

You know that thing you put bills into on a vending machine? It isn't made in America, according to a waiver to the Buy America Act. Neither is the coin dispenser, according to this federal waiver.

**Levi jeans**                 Last production date: Dec. 2003

Levi Strauss & Co. shut down all its American operations and outsourced production to Latin America and Asia in Dec. 2003. The company's denim products have been an iconic American product for 150 years.

**Radio Flyer's Red Wagon**    Last production date: March 2004

The little red wagon has been an iconic image of America for years. But once Radio Flyer decided its Chicago plant was too expensive, it began producing most products, including the red wagon, in China.

**Televisions**                Last production date: Oct. 2004

Five Rivers Electronic Innovations was the last American owned color TV maker in the US. The Tennessee company used LCoS (liquid crystal on silicon) technology to produce televisions for Philips Electronics. But after Philips decided to stop selling TVs with LCoS, Five Rivers eventually filed for Chapter 11 bankruptcy protection in Oct. 2004. As part of its reorganization plan, the company stopped manufacturing TVs. Now there are ZERO televisions made in America, according to Business Week.

**Cell phones**                Last production date: circa 2007

Of the 1.2 billion cell phones sold worldwide in 2008, NOT ONE was made in America, according to Manufacturing & Technology publisher Richard McCormick.

**Railroads (parts including manganese turnout castings, U69 guard bars, LV braces and weld kits)**

Last production date: circa 2008. Here's another standout from dozens of waivers to the Buy America Act: railroad turnouts and weld kits. Manganese turnout castings are used to widen railroad tracks, and they were used to build our once-great railroad system. U69 guard bars, LV braces and Weld Kits, along with 22 mm Industrial steel chain are basic items that were certifiably not available in the US. *Note: The Buy America Act requires government mass transportation spending to use American products.*

**Dell computers**                    Last production date: Jan. 2010

In January 2010, Dell closed its North Carolina PC factory, its last large U.S. plant. Dell has outsourced work to Asian manufacturers in an attempt to catch up with the rest of the industry.

**Canned sardines**                    Last production date: April 2010

Stinson Seafood plant, the last sardine cannery in Maine and the U.S., shut down in April. The first U.S. sardine cannery opened in Maine in 1875, but since the demand for the small, oily fish declined, more canneries closed shop.

**Pontiac cars**                    Last production date: May 2010

The last Pontiac was produced last May. The brand was formally killed on Halloween, as GM contracts with Pontiac dealerships expired. The 84-year-old GM brand was famous for muscle cars.

**Forks, spoons, and knives**                    Last production date: June 2010

The last flatware factory in the US closed last summer. Sherrill Manufacturing bought Oneida Ltd. in 2005, but shut down its fork & knife operations due to the tough economy. CEO Greg Owens says his company may resume production "when the general economic climate improves and as Sherrill Manufacturing is able to put itself back on its feet and recapitalize and regroup."

**Incandescent light bulb**                    Last production date: Sept. 2010

The incandescent light bulb (invented by Thomas Edison) has been phased out. Our last major factory that made incandescent light bulbs closed in September 2010. In 2007, Congress passed a measure that will ban incandescents by 2014, prompting GE to close its domestic factory.

(Source: *19 Iconic Products That America Doesn't Make Anymore,* by Anika Anand and Gus Lubin in *Investing*, *Products and Trends*, *Recession*, Yahoo! Finance, posted Nov 04, 2010, courtesy of Market Insider, Market Insider .com, used with permission)

**In conclusion**, is the U.S. heading the same way as the Roman Empire? Only time will tell. We went from being a victorious country that had a trade surplus, to a debtor nation with huge trade deficits. We used to have a vibrant middle-class and many manufacturing jobs to a nation with a disappearing middle-class and many more low-paying service jobs. Like Rome, we have many more people on Welfare and social programs now than we used to, and taxes are hanging over everyone for the foreseeable future. We are even losing our influence economically as other nations step up to the plate. Taxing their population nearly to death may have been the ultimate reason Rome fell combined with runaway inflation. On the other hand, we might be more like other maturing capitalistic economies, like England, France, Spain, Italy, and Japan. While all were leaders for a time, they all slowly fell into demise. Their economies are stable, but they aren't powerhouses anymore.

Unless the U.S. addresses some of its problems, it probably won't go into slow demise, it might be more like a flame-out. Some economists in the U.S. think we are in more debt, both private and governmental, than we will ever be able to repay. We might therefore be bankrupt, as a nation, and don't even realize it. Politicians continue to pass more spending bills, increase spending on entitlement programs and subsidies, increase governmental employee pay and benefits, and push funding these programs into the future when they probably won't be in office to suffer the repercussions. It is thought by economists that many state and local governments are already bankrupt, and even now some city and local governments are hiring bankruptcy attorneys for advice. Bankruptcy will allow them to default on their municipal bond-debt and free themselves from unions and huge employee pension and healthcare expenses. Although the state and local government bankruptcy ball hasn't started rolling yet, if it does, everyone better look out.

All one has to do is look at recent collapses of entire countries, like Ireland or Greece, to see what might happen to us. Ireland had a similar housing bubble as the U.S.; their government gave out too much in Welfare and pensions and had massive numbers of government employees like the U.S. Now, the entire country is bankrupt and about to default on its debt. Associated Press sources in Nov. 2010 reported in order to get loans from the EU/IMF, of which it is a member, Ireland was forced to come up with an austerity plan. It axed tens of thousands of state jobs, trimmed welfare benefits and pensions, and imposed new taxes. The 140-page National Recovery Plan proposes to introduce property and water taxes, raise the sales tax from 21 percent now to 23 percent in 2014, and cut the minimum wage to $10.20. Ireland's bloated civil service will be particularly hard hit – seeing cuts of about 24,750 state jobs. Income tax bands will be widened so more lower-paid workers pay taxes, and higher-waged workers will see annual taxes rise more than $4,000. A raft of welfare payments will be gradually reduced and monthly pensions will fall up to 12 percent. Ireland's problems pale in comparison to what we face in the U.S. Faced with bankruptcy, Ireland's government finally started cutting Welfare, government employees, and pensions—far too late. Ireland was "rescued" with a $115 billion loan. In the meantime, in the U.S. politicians spend $150 billion *per month* that they don't have. Politicians are massively *increasing* spending for Welfare, government employees and pensions. Instead of learning from the collapse of other countries, we are doing the exact opposite. Who is going to bail out the U.S.?

Americans get very uncomfortable and angry when the U.S. is compared to Rome (or Ireland), because Rome fell. There are some similarities, however, that cannot be overlooked. By learning from the past, we might be able to avoid the same outcome. We also can't compare our dire financial situation to the Romans, because they couldn't borrow money to fund government spending the way we do. There's no telling what is going to happen to the U.S. if changes aren't made. Even with a complete overhaul, a spending freeze, and a balanced budget amendment, who's going to pay back our $13.8 trillion debt? Who is going to come up with $70 trillion that the government has promised in payments in the coming decades?

Here's something else to think about. Allan Sloan and Tory Newmyer of *Fortune Magazine* reported in Nov. 2010 that since 1995, homeowner equity has been cut in half (from about $12 trillion in 1995 to $6 trillion now).

Homeowners have less equity in their homes and less ability to borrow money, not to mention a loss of wealth of $6 trillion dollars. The total market value of U.S. stocks—the amount of money gained if *all* U.S. stocks were sold today—is about $14 trillion dollars. In addition, U.S. corporations are currently sitting on a massive amount of cash—close to $900 billion. Adding the two together equals about $15 trillion dollars—the total liquidity of U.S. corporations (stock value and cash-on-hand, not including property and equipment) is about $15 trillion. Compared to our current federal debt of $13.8 trillion, and the fact that we're adding more than a trillion to it each year (at $150 billion a month) it's not hard to see that the entire liquid value of U.S. corporations—all of them—will equal our debt in about one year. In four or five years, our debt will be equal to the *value of all U.S. corporations and ALL home equity in the U.S.* (based on current values and current spending levels).

This puts the deficit into some kind of perspective. If spending continues as it has for the last decade, we are indeed headed off a cliff. As the referenced article in *Fortune* tries to portray, our problems are not "alarmist" or "fear mongering," they are real. Politicians don't have any "magic bullets" that will cure our economy, and the government is making it infinitely worse with its fiscal policies and spending—threatening our national security and sovereignty. The truth is, somebody is going to have to pay back that deficit someday. We may be faced with taxes not seen since the days of the late Roman Empire, with debt service and taxes eating away everything we work for, and government satisfied "Not until the taxpayers bones are picked clean." There is a better way, if we will only take it.

# CHAPTER 9

# *Thomas Jefferson, George Washington, and Abraham Lincoln*

The great men that started our country as no longer with us, but their words and ideas are. They fought the revolutionary war to free us from the rule of England. Many patriots died so we could have a free and Democratic country. The form of government they created, and the ideas behind that government, along with the industrial revolution, resulted in a super-power, and has given us a standard of living second to none. Yet, all is not well in our country. Our country is in a fiscal crisis, and politicians are making it worse at every turn. We need to look back and listen to the men that started our country, the men we have to thank for our freedom and our prosperity, and who can still lead us with their ideas—we have no better teachers.

**A wise and frugal government, which shall leave men free to regulate their own pursuits of industry and improvement, and shall not take from the mouth of labor the bread it has earned - this is the sum of good government.**

*Thomas Jefferson*

A wise and frugal government? Who today could conceive of such a thing? What other entity is able to spend $1 trillion dollars in a heartbeat? Today, taxes and government regulation are choking the life out of business. People spend 1/3 or more of "the bread of their labor" for taxes to feed our government. We have one of the highest business tax rates in the world, and U.S. businesses have fled the U.S. to countries where regulations, litigation, and taxes are much lower. Of course, they have taken millions of jobs with them, jobs that foreign workers now have. Our government responds to every crisis with more regulation and more spending. The federal government has grown exponentially, not just in spending (up from approximately $20,000 per household in 2000 to $31,000 today), but in its reach. Government now intrudes into virtually every aspect of our daily lives, from the type of toilet we can purchase, to the mix of fuel we can put in our cars, to the kind of light bulb we can use. We no longer have a wise and frugal government, on the contrary.

**All tyranny needs to gain a foothold is for people of good conscience to remain silent.**

*Thomas Jefferson*

The people of this country, the ones of good conscience, have remained silent for too long. People bicker and complain about politics in this country, but have done nothing substantive about it. At least the Tea Party (whether you agree with them or not) has spoken up about the government and politicians. Without the people speaking up, the tyranny of a government of the few, benefitting the few, at the cost of the many, has taken hold in Washington and will continue to do so.

**All, too, will bear in mind this sacred principle, that though the will of the majority is in all cases to prevail, that will to be rightful must be reasonable; that the minority possess their equal rights, which equal law must protect, and to violate would be oppression.**

*Thomas Jefferson*

The majority has spoken, in opposition to government bailouts, and Washington passed the bailout anyway. The stimulus and healthcare bills—passed regardless of their popularity. The will of the majority does not prevail any longer, only the will of the few; the politicians, lobbyists, special interests, big money and political action committees. The minority has pressed their rights to an extreme, and the majority sits back and lets Washington conduct business as usual, benefiting the few with influence, money and power.

**Conquest is not in our principles. It is inconsistent with our government.**

*Thomas Jefferson*

The U.S. is certainly not an imperialistic nation. We do not colonize, but we do have a military presence in 40 countries all over the world. The politicians have made conquests all over the world, as the world's policemen, and to protect our friends and interests abroad. If we are in conquest, it is against our principals, and inconsistent with our government. It leads only to more hostility and resentment by people all over the world and huge military spending. We need to bring our service men and women home.

**Experience hath shown, that even under the best forms of government those entrusted with power have, in time, and by slow operations, perverted it into tyranny.**

*Thomas Jefferson*

This warning from Thomas Jefferson is certainly applicable today.  Over the last twenty or thirty years, and mostly in the last ten, those entrusted with power have perverted our government into tyranny by serving the lobbyists, the special interests, unions, corporations, and big money. It has happened slowly, but one look at the data from the last ten years shows how billions are spent to influence law and legislation by powerful lobbyists—that gets rewarded with hundreds of billions of our tax dollars. Our government was the "best form" for many decades, but it isn't any longer. Everyone is trying to get their hands on the federal dole, and are willing to spend millions to reap billions, and further spend billions to reap hundreds of billions. The interests of the many are no longer important to government, and the majority does not rule any longer (except when we're allowed to vote every two years).

**I have no fear that the result of our experiment will be that men may be trusted to govern themselves without a master.**

*Thomas Jefferson*

The experiment Thomas Jefferson is referring to is the new democracy he and the other founding fathers of our country started. He is not afraid that we may govern ourselves without a master, yet this has not happened. On the contrary, the federal and state governments have become our master. We are servants, supplying 1/3 of our income or more to the government, afraid of the IRS, afraid of violating regulations which have grown exponentially, afraid of losing our homes and jobs, afraid when disaster strikes that our government will not be there for us. Men can be trusted to govern themselves, when they are given the right and power. We, the people can now only vote, our majority can only elect politicians and enact ballot issues. Our government in Washington no longer listens or cares what the majority thinks; it has become our master, not our servant.

**I hope we shall crush in its birth the aristocracy of our monied corporations which dare already to challenge our government to a trial by strength, and bid defiance to the laws of our country.**

*Thomas Jefferson*

Again, Thomas Jefferson was a seer of the future. His hope was that we shall crush in its birth the aristocracy of monied corporations which dare to challenge our government. We need businesses and corporations to provide for our standard of living and jobs, but some try to challenge our government and what is right. The Democratic process, such as it is in this country, has utterly failed to combat against aristocratic corporations and their influence, their challenge by strength, and defiance to the laws of our country. If corporations don't like the current laws, they lobby politicians and get them changed. You need look no further than health insurance companies as a prime example. The strength of the corporations lies in their wealth, which has already won the battle for our government. They defy law, and when caught, use wealth to settle allegations and charges against them without admitting guilt. The monied corporations on Wall Street are always one step ahead of the law, and influence politicians in Washington at every turn. Wall Street and big banks got $3.3 trillion from the Fed, yet dumped wreckage and toxic debt on taxpayers, and are again making record bonuses of $140 billion. Corporations use their wealth to buy influence in Washington and gain massive tax breaks and subsidies from the government. And, thanks to the recent ruling by the Supreme Court, corporations and unions are free to spend and influence elections as much as they want and further influence our political processes. Anyone can tell you that the people of this country and our government have lost this battle already. Lobbyists and special interests call the tune in Washington, not the people. Thomas Jefferson would not be happy.

**I know of no safe depository of the ultimate powers of the society but the people themselves; and if we think them not enlightened enough to exercise their control with a wholesome discretion, the remedy is not to take it from them but to inform their discretion.**

*Thomas Jefferson*

Again, Thomas Jefferson foresaw were the ultimate powers of our society should lie—with the people themselves. There is an illusion, since we are still able to vote, that we still have power. Yes, we have the right to vote, but there is little or no power associated with voting anymore. The result is one elected official or another, but the system we send them to is not governed by the people, but by these politicians, whose concern is not the people they represent, but special interests and PACs—the people who give them money. Politicians and our President don't think the people are smart or wise enough to exercise "control with wholesome discretion," that power is reserved for politicians and the government, and they are trying to remake our society. Our founding fathers and Thomas Jefferson in particular, said that the people were the only *safe* depository for this power, and we can see what has happened when this power is in the *unsafe* hands of politicians and the government.

**I predict future happiness for Americans if they can prevent the government from wasting the labors of the people under the pretense of taking care of them.**

*Thomas Jefferson*

Spoken more than 224 years ago, but is applicable most assuredly today. The present unhappiness of Americans has resulted precisely from the government wasting the labors of the people under the pretense of taking care of them. Many people believe the money they pay in taxes every year is wasted. The government wastes hundreds of billions of dollars on things the people don't approve of or are not even aware of. Washington has become a black hole of spending, and not even our taxes are enough, they have to spend more than a trillion dollars they don't have each year. The government gives us the pretense that they are taking care of us, but are they? They hand out tens of billions of dollars for subsidies to businesses and people that don't need them. It provides healthcare and income to people that don't work, and penalizes those that are productive with ever increasing taxes. The government itself has grown to gargantuan proportions, all under the pretense of taking care of us. The government spending and wasting of our labor is clearly unsustainable and deleterious to an extreme. Let's rephrase this quote: *I predict future unhappiness for Americans since they let the government waste the labors of the people under the pretense of taking care of them.* It sounds a little more accurate this way.

**To compel a man to furnish funds for the propagation of ideas he disbelieves and abhors is sinful and tyrannical.**

*Thomas Jefferson*

Americans spend almost the first four months of every year working for the government. As "tax freedom" day approaches, they finally get to keep the money they worked hard for. We, as Americans, are compelled to pay taxes or go to jail. Yet polls time and again show the people of the U.S. don't support what is going on in Washington, don't approve of what the President, the House and Senate are doing. Americans don't approve of many government subsidies, the salaries, benefits, and pensions of government employees. Americans don't think government employees should be able to retire at 50 when they might never be able to retire. Most Americans didn't approve of Wall Street and Bank bailouts, stimulus spending, ObamaCare, or the massive $13.8 trillion dollar federal debt we now have. Many Americans don't approve of the massive increases in entitlement spending in the last several years. To all these things and more are Americans compelled to furnish funds—the propagation of these ideas and actions for which they disbelieve and abhor. It is utterly sinful and tyrannical, and not surprisingly, people are starting to abhor (to regard with extreme repugnance: loathe) the government.

### Leave no authority existing not responsible to the people.

*Thomas Jefferson*

A warning to the people: authority is responsible to the people. Do we have any authority that is responsible to the people anymore? Banks, Wall Street, corporations, unions, politicians, and the government itself are not responsible to the people. People have little or no say on what goes on in Washington or at state capitals, no say in legislation or the laws being passed, no say in regulations and rules that they will have to follow, no say in the tax code that will take a large share of their income. Every authority in the land is not responsible to the people, but only to the politicians and government and the laws they enact. Do we once again have government and taxation without representation? For the government to be responsible to the people, they must listen to the people. The only time government listens to the people is when the politicians might lose their jobs by getting voted out of office.

### My reading of history convinces me that most bad government results from too much government.

*Thomas Jefferson*

Our government obviously hasn't read much history and not read much by Thomas Jefferson. Our government has gotten bigger and bigger despite a century of data showing smaller government leads to increased prosperity. Government employees are living the American dream with yearly pay increases and increases in benefits and pensions while the middle class is being wiped out. Democrats have a fundamental belief that the purpose of government is cure the problems of our country, to remake our country. Reality has shown that the government can't really solve any of the problems of our country, and is only making them worse. In the meantime, the government has added trillions of dollars to entitlements, stimulus, bail outs, and subsidies to try to fix our problems—and have only succeeded in creating a massive $13.8 trillion dollar debt. The government produces nothing and creates nothing except more rules, laws, and regulations that must be followed, and creates more people in government to make new rules, laws, and regulations. We also must read history to be convinced our government has become the problem, not the solution. We have far too much government.

## George Washington

**George Washington's** *First Inaugural Address*
March 4, 1801

**But every difference of opinion is not a difference of principle. We have called by different names brethren of the same principle. We are all Republicans, we are all Federalists. If there be any among us who would wish to dissolve this Union or to change its Republican form, let them stand undisturbed as monuments of the safety with which error of opinion may be tolerated where reason is left free to combat it. I know, indeed, that some honest men fear that a Republican government cannot be strong, that this Government is not strong enough; but would the honest patriot, in the full tide of successful experiment, abandon a government which has so far kept us free and firm on the theoretic and visionary fear that this Government, the world's best hope, may by possibility want energy to preserve itself? I trust not. I believe this, on the contrary, the strongest Government on earth. I believe it the only one where every man, at the call of the law, would fly to the standard of the law, and would meet invasions of the public order as his own personal concern. Sometimes it is said that man cannot be trusted with the government of himself. Can he, then, be trusted with the government of others? Or have we found angels in the forms of kings to govern him? Let history answer this question.**

This is an excerpt from the elegant speech George Washington gave at his first inaugural address. It was when our country was still in its infancy, when people were concerned by the strength of our democracy. George Washington also uses the word experiment for our new government. He gives the people a challenge: "at the call of the law, would fly to the standard of the law, and would meet invasions of the public order as his own personal concern." The people of this country were to meet and deal with invasions of the public order, in essence to be responsible to uphold our government from the invasions of people that would try to take or pervert it. He also challenges us to be able to govern ourselves, or else angels or kings will have to do so. The experiment of Thomas Jefferson and George Washington obviously succeeded. Men did fly to the standard of the law and what was right when we fought to abolish slavery, to fight wars; and throughout history men came to the aid of the government when needed. Yet, in the last few decades, we have not been able to govern ourselves. We have been governed by the government and politicians, not by the will of the people. Polls are done all the time, the will of the people is apparent, but Washington fails to carry out the will of the people. Out of fear, the people have no choice but to accept the rule of the government, and, except for voting in or out various politicians, we are unable to even express our will to the government. We *are* ruled by angels and kings: the wealthy and the monied in positions of power and influence.

**Government is not reason; it is not eloquent; it is force. Like fire, it is a dangerous servant and a fearful master.**

*George Washington*

Our government does seem like a benign entity sometimes. People have granted the government huge latitude to conduct its affairs, partly out of fear, and partly out of resignation for not being able to do anything about it. Government has become a fearful master to most of its citizens. It has become dangerous because of its fiscal policies and deficit spending. It is an ever growing force, one that is going to become more and more desperate as there is less money to be spent or borrowed. Look at the current state governments. They can't borrow from the U.S. Treasury and can't print more money. They continue to spend, however, and now have multi-billion dollar deficits which threaten the people of the state. States have become more and more desperate, is it going to be long before the federal government becomes equally as desperate?

**The basis of our political system is the right of the people to make and to alter their constitutions of government.**

*George Washington*

Herein lies our hope. According to George Washington, *our political system is the right of the people.* It doesn't say it is the right of the politicians, the right of the President, or the right of the special interests—it is the right of the people—to make and alter their constitutions of government. Politicians spend trillions of dollars and give out entitlements and subsidizes without any mandate from the constitution as they try to progressively reshape our country. We are not powerless, although it often seems that way. Again, the people as well as the politicians have the right to alter their constitutions of government. We have to do it, as the people. Politicians are never going to alter the constitution to better serve the people. That would be self defeating for politicians. We, the people, therefore must find a way make and/or alter our constitution, if that is what is necessary, to take back our government from those that have taken it away from the people.

**The marvel of all history is the patience with which men and women submit to burdens unnecessarily laid upon them by their governments.**

*George Washington*

At one point in our history, Americans didn't even have to pay income tax. Since then, the tax burden has grown and grown until the American people and businesses are spending a third or more of the money they earn on taxes. And that's not enough for politicians, clearly, as our deficits continue to rise dramatically. The people patiently watch as politicians spend $150 billion per month more than they have. It *is* a marvel that people are submitting to the amount of spending by government, and the burden this carries. Clearly, we need a smaller government, one that will empower people, not one that further burdens people and business. Think of what we and our children and their children are going to have to pay someday. It's not a pleasant thought.

**George Washington to Bushrod Washington, 9 November 1787 : "The warmest friends to and the best supporters of the Constitution, do not contend that it is free from imperfections; but these were not to be avoided, and they are convinced if evils are likely to flow from them, that the remedy must come thereafter; because, in the present moment it is not to be obtained. And as there is a Constitutional door open for it, I think the people (for it is with them to judge) can, as they will have the aid of experience on their side, decide with as much propriety on the alterations and amendments which shall be found necessary, as ourselves; for I do not conceive that we are more inspired—have more wisdom—or possess more virtue than those who will come after us."**

A prophetic letter from George Washington. Our constitution and government is not perfect, but the imperfections can be remedied. He further states that the people, who are responsible for change as much as the founding fathers, have an "open door" to make changes. The people are as much responsible for governing as the politicians—*it is for us to judge*. That was 224 years ago, but he put faith in those that will come after him. The people, therefore, have the responsibility and the duty to make alterations and amendments, to correct imperfections in our governing system. We are supposed to have this right and responsibility, and in fact we do. But, the people have been taken out of the equation to such an extent that they feel they have lost this ability. For all practical purposes, the people have lost this ability, instead delegating it to politicians. In the horrible partisan mess that is Washington politics, no substantive changes are ever made except more spending. Or, if they are, the changes are worse than the problems they are trying to solve. Decades come and go, and business as usual is the norm, and problems never get addressed or fixed by those responsible to do so. The people, therefore, don't feel responsible and take little or no action to rectify problems and imperfections in government. The people are once again placed in a position of powerlessness, which is not what our founding fathers wanted under any circumstances.

**Democracy..... while it lasts is more bloody than either aristocracy or monarchy. Remember, democracy never lasts long. It soon wastes, exhausts, and murders itself. There is never a democracy that did not commit suicide.**

*John Adams*

Fateful words by John Adams, another of our founding fathers. Democracy, while it lasts. We are to remember that it never lasts long. It soon wastes, exhausts, and murders itself. Are there any more appropriate or meaningful words to describe our government today? The waste, fraud, special interests, and government for the few are exhausting, and greed has almost ruined our country. "There is never a democracy that did not commit suicide" Is our democracy committing suicide? Most suicides are quick and deadly, but ours has been going on for decades.

**It's not tyranny we desire; it's a just, limited, federal government.**

*Alexander Hamilton*

What Alexander Hamilton wanted has not come to pass. We have a federal government that is just for the few, and has continued to pass all limits of spending and waste. If the opposite of a just, limited federal government is tyranny, than tyranny is what we have. We have the chance to reform the government into something that is just and limited, but we must *take* that chance.

**America will never be destroyed from the outside. If we falter and lose our freedoms, it will be because we destroyed ourselves.**

*Abraham Lincoln*

It's hard to believe that anybody could destroy the U.S., but we seem to be doing a good job of destroying ourselves. Instead of creating jobs and making things easier for businesses, so they don't go offshore and to other countries, government regulates and taxes our businesses heavily, so we are bound to falter. When our government rewards people for not working, and taxes and penalizes people that do work, we are bound to falter. When our government spends a trillion dollars more than it has every year, we are bound to falter. When our government tries to solve all the problems in our country, a job it is not qualified to do, huge waste and fraud result, and we are bound to falter. When we turn our government over to lawyers, special interests, corporations, and political action committees, we are bound to falter. When the goal of our educational and healthcare system is profit, we are bound to falter. We *are* being destroyed from the inside. The clock hasn't struck midnight yet, there is still time for a rescue (not a bailout) if only we can rise from our lethargy and do it.

**Any people anywhere, being inclined and having the power, have the right to rise up, and shake off the existing government, and form a new one that suits them better. This is a most valuable - a most sacred right - a right, which we hope and believe, is to liberate the world.**

*Abraham Lincoln*

The people of the United States of America have great power—it was given to us by our forefathers, the ones that started our country. We have the right to rise up and shake off the existing government, and form a new one that suits us better. That is the whole point of this book. We have the power and ability to evolve our government into something that actually works. Abraham Lincoln hoped and believed our form of government would liberate the world. We have fought wars in Europe, Japan, Korea, Vietnam, and the Middle East to forward the cause of democracy, yet do we have democracy in the U.S. anymore? We possess the ability to have democracy; we have the right and power to change things, when necessary. Or, we can continue in the direction we've been going at our own peril. Those in power now, the politicians, don't want things to change. They are making a fortune from this system, but we can do much better, and we owe it to all those who fought and died defending democracy. We owe it to those that will come after us. We, the people, must restore what our forefathers gave us – democracy.

**I am a firm believer in the people. If given the truth, they can be depended upon to meet any national crisis. The great point is to bring them the real facts.**

*Abraham Lincoln*

Abraham Lincoln believed in the people, if they are given the facts. Are we given the real facts nowadays? Or do the media give us half-truths and slanted perspectives on things based on their liberal or conservative views? Are we ever given the truth, or just "story lines" to distract us from what is really going on? Do we get factual information over the internet? The answer is yes, if you know where to look. If the people are given the facts, Lincoln believed we could be depended on to meet any national crisis. The people responded to the financial crisis, in a huge way, and politicians over-ruled the people. They passed the financial bailout anyway, and the stimulus spending, and ObamaCare, regardless of what the people wanted. "The great point is to bring them the real facts." We must have media that is unbiased and apolitical. We have to get information that can be trusted, and if we do, we can begin to meet the national crisis we find ourselves in.

**My dream is of a place and a time where America will once again be seen as the last best hope of earth.**

*Abraham Lincoln*

What a lovely dream—"The last best hope of earth." People are doing whatever they can to get into our country and live the American dream. But for many Americans themselves (those that don't work for the government), the American dream is disappearing—they are losing their property, their jobs, their money, and their self-respect and many are descending into poverty and food stamps. Is this what has become of our country? Has it gotten so bad that people are going to start looking elsewhere for the last best hope on earth? We have the greatest country on earth, and we need to make it greater—we need to save it from those pushing us into despair. We have some big problems to solve, but so did Abraham Lincoln during his time. We have to take action and restore our American dream, not just for the elite few, but for everyone, before it's gone forever.

**Republicans are for both the man and the dollar, but in case of conflict the man before the dollar.**

*Abraham Lincoln*

He's not referring to the Republican Party here, but politicians. We lost this battle some time ago. Politicians have placed the dollar before the man. Money, power, and elections have resulted in politicians working for the interests of the few with money, while forgetting about the common man. Government has to once again serve the people it is supposed to be representing, not just the people giving them money.

**The shepherd drives the wolf from the sheep's for which the sheep thanks the shepherd as his liberator, while the wolf denounces him for the same act as the destroyer of liberty. Plainly, the sheep and the wolf are not agreed upon a definition of liberty.**

*Abraham Lincoln*

This is a very interesting parable by Mr. Lincoln. Politicians would have us believe they are our shepherds, our liberators, they will solve our problems and transform our society, they can be entrusted to borrow and spend trillions of our dollars, provide healthcare, a social safety net, stimulate the economy and keep us safe. The wolves, the lawyers, lobbyists and special interests—the thousands and thousands that circulate through the House and Senate every day, paying for influence and votes, would have us believe they know better. They believe they are using liberty to get what they want. The people think their needs are being served, but they aren't. Have those we entrusted to be our political shepherds let the wolves run our government? Obviously, since it depends on whose interests are being served.

**We the people are the rightful masters of both Congress and the courts, not to overthrow the Constitution but to overthrow the men who pervert the Constitution.**

*Abraham Lincoln*

Another vote for the people! Do "the people" today see themselves as the rightful masters of both Congress and the courts? Not on a good day, never this century. Only on Election Day, and even then, what difference is it going to make? The voters overthrow one political party and replace them with another, then do the same thing again in the next election. The voters keep trying to overthrow the politicians who pervert the Constitution, but it's not working. The problem is the voters can't overthrow the PAC's, the unions, the special interests and the lobbyists. They have become a permanent fixture, a shadow government in Washington, and everywhere else politics is involved. They are waiting to pervert the people we elect to represent us. We have to find a better way.

**Rhetoric is a poor substitute for action, and we have trusted only to rhetoric. If we are really to be a great nation, we must not merely talk; we must act big.**

*Theodore Roosevelt*

The 2010 election was an extreme example of rhetoric over action. It was probably the most negative, disgusting campaign we have ever witnessed. We are supposed to trust those people in the ads to run our country?

Would you trust them to watch your children? Are we to trust in their rhetoric and all the rest of the rhetoric in the media? Do they think we are fools? Yes, they do. If we are going to once again become what we could be—the greatest nation and democracy, "we must not merely talk; we must act big." We have to act, the people of this great nation have to act and act big, the time has come. We have an alternative, a better way is available.

**The pacifist is as surely a traitor to his country and to humanity as is the most brutal wrongdoer.**

*Theodore Roosevelt*

This quote should be taken to heart by all those people in America that can see we have a big problem but do nothing about it. As always, Theodore Roosevelt didn't mince words, *the pacifist is a traitor to his country and to humanity*, and as bad as the most brutal wrongdoer. Our democracy originated from men that took action and got the job done. We cannot sit back and hope things are going to right themselves. There is much work to be done and we have to start somewhere and we have to start *now*. Wait around for the next election? Has that worked? We have only ourselves to blame unless we stand up and move this country in the right direction. The angry pacifist, sitting at home complaining and doing nothing is "surely a traitor to his country and to humanity". People must stand up and take action, to do what is right, to restore democracy to our great country. There is a better way forward, if we will only take it.

**I do not look upon these United States as a finished product. We are still in the making.**

*Franklin D. Roosevelt*

FDR was an eternal optimist. His words offer hope, even to us in the new millennium. Maybe the U.S. is not a finished product. Maybe we haven't seen our best days already. Maybe we aren't on the steady slide into obscurity and calamity. Maybe we can save our government before it destroys itself and us. We are the people that the government is supposed to be serving, right? We have to restore our country to democracy.

**In our personal ambitions we are individualists. But in our seeking for economic and political progress as a nation, we all go up or else all go down as one people.**

*Franklin D. Roosevelt*

No truer words were spoken. We have let special interests, banks, Wall Street, predatory lending, government regulation, debt and taxes destroy our economy. There has been little political progress, as a nation. Except for governmental bailouts and takeovers, including the attempted takeover of the healthcare system, what has our government done (and except spending a trillion dollars more than it has) to progress? It is evident and true that we all are going down, as one people, in spite of or because of what our government and economy does.

**Let us never forget that government is ourselves and not an alien power over us. The ultimate rulers of our democracy are not a President and senators and congressmen and government officials, but the voters of this country.**

*Franklin D. Roosevelt*

Again, no truer words have been spoken. Many people in this country don't feel the government is *ourselves* anymore, but an onerous behemoth that is consuming everything in its path. Our government and laws have resulted in us having the largest imprisoned population in the entire world. We are taxed by the federal government, the state government, the local government, and our property and everything we buy. The ultimate rulers of our country *are* the President, the senators and congressmen. The people can throw them out, but the problem is we still have to replace them. Everyone already knows what politicians are going to do before they do it. Massive spending by the government benefits itself, the people that depend on entitlements, and the lobbyists who get money set aside for their causes. The voters of this country have been stripped of everything except the right to vote, the right to send another politician off to Washington, where they are going to do the same thing they've been doing to decades. The people, the "ultimate rulers" have become powerless pawns being pushed around the board by the kings and angels of this country, and don't see their rights and power any longer.

**The only sure bulwark of continuing liberty is a government strong enough to protect the interests of the people, and a people strong enough and well enough informed to maintain its sovereign control over the government.**

*Franklin D. Roosevelt*

"A government strong enough to protect the interests of the people." When was the last time the government was interested in the interests of the people? When was the last time the people were strong enough to exert sovereign control over the government? Nowadays, when the people speak, call, email, or fax their congress people or representatives, it doesn't matter. The people have no control over the government and what it does. It's in the hands of politicians who do what's best for them and the people paying them. We therefore are at risk of losing our continued liberty as our only sure bulwark is non-functional.

**We are not afraid to entrust the American people with unpleasant facts, foreign ideas, alien philosophies, and competitive values. For a nation that is afraid to let its people judge the truth and falsehood in an open market is a nation that is afraid of its people.**

*John F. Kennedy*

Most of what happens in Washington happens behind closed doors, in back rooms, in committees, out of the view of the public. Most or all of the legislation in Washington is not open to public debate or discussion. Washington and the politicians have become insular entities, opening their offices and influence only to lobbyists and special interests, or anyone with enough money to contribute. Washington has become a closed system of government, not an "open market." It's impossible to determine if Washington and the politicians are afraid of the people, there is no way to tell. They are only afraid of losing an election, and need more and more money to run more and more commercials, and therefore more and more willing to sell their influence and vote to the highest bidder.

**And so, my fellow Americans, ask not what your country can do for you; ask what you can do for your country.**

*John F. Kennedy*

The tens of millions of people on Welfare, food stamps, Medicaid and Medicare, on Social Security and Disability keep getting what their country can do for them. The farmers, oil companies, defense contractors, grocery stores, foreign countries, and everyone else receiving government hand-outs, tax breaks and subsidies keep getting what their country can do for them. We really do need to ask what we can do for our country, to save it from itself and our politicians. Our country was founded based on the principal of independence, hence "The Declaration of Independence." Independent people have driven the success of our country since the beginning. Now we are more *dependent* on government than ever before—we are at the mercy of our government and politicians. At the present time, we can only vote every couple of years and hope and pray things are going to change. We, the people, need to do so much more.

**Let every nation know, whether it wishes us well or ill, that we shall pay any price, bear any burden, meet any hardship, support any friend, oppose any foe to assure the survival and the success of liberty.**

*John F. Kennedy*

Liberty (def: *1. Freedom from arbitrary or despotic government or control, 2. freedom from external or foreign rule; independence. freedom from control, interference, obligation, restriction, hampering conditions, etc.; power or right of doing, thinking, speaking, etc., according to choice. 3. freedom from captivity, confinement, or physical restraint).* Liberty is freedom from arbitrary or despotic (*autocratic; tyrannical*) government. There's that word again, tyranny. Our forefathers tried to warn us about tyranny – freedom from control, interference, obligation, or restriction, hampering conditions. The very institution that is supposed to be providing us liberty, that we will protect, is taking away our liberties. The special interests that our government serves are trying to take away our liberty. As a nation, in the past, we have enjoyed the successes of liberty. In JFK's time, it seems we enjoyed liberty much more than we do now.

**The government is us; we are the government, you and I.**

*Theodore Roosevelt*

This may have been true when Theodore Roosevelt said it, but who would say that it is accurate today? The government is supposed to serve the people, do what is in the best interests of the people, to be by and for the people. The government is *not* us, it is some giant in Washington and our state's capitals, eating all that we give it and always wanting more. What Roosevelt said is an ideal, of course, not an actuality. We have long lost our connection with the government, unless they are sending us a check every month, or we are sending them money out of our paycheck every month. If we are the government, we have stood by and watched as bankers and financiers have wiped out our retirement plans, foreclosed on our houses, directed billions to people that already have billions, watched jobs go away, watched our primary educational system became weak and expensive, watched as our government handed out hundreds of billions of dollars to the perpetrators of our economic demise, watched as our government has slowly been taken over by lobbyists and special interests, watched as our government has borrowed trillions of dollars that we may never be able to repay, and watched as we have jailed more of our countrymen than any other nation on the planet. We have stood by and watched it all happen, and now the people are upset. If the people wait around for everything to fix itself, it's never going to happen. The people have to take back the government from the small minority that is reaping huge sums from the government. The people, in the end, are the only hope of our nation. Just as it was in 1776, it is now. The people have to rise up and take their power back and become the government again. Our forefathers are watching. Are we going to continue into the abyss, or are we going to evolve? The truth is the government is you and I. How you ask? As with everything that has driven the power and prosperity of our country since the dawn of the industrial revolution, the answer to our problems lies in our technology, as you will soon see.

# CHAPTER 10

# *Imagine....*

## U.S. Government to Save Billions by Cutting Wasteful Senator Program

Nearly all of the U.S. senatorial positions were categorized as inefficient redundancies.

WASHINGTON—In an effort to reduce wasteful spending and eliminate non-vital federal services, the U.S. government announced plans this week to cut its long-standing senator program, a move it says will help save more than $300 billion each year.

According to officials, the decision to cut the national legislative body was reached during a budget review meeting on Tuesday. After hours of deliberation, it was agreed that the cost of financing U.S. senators far outweighed the benefits they provided.

"Now more than ever, we must eliminate needless spending wherever possible," President Obama said at a press conference Wednesday. "When we sat down to go over our annual budget, we asked ourselves, where can we safely trim back? What programs can we do away with without negatively impacting the American people? Which bloated and ineffective institutions can we no longer justify having around?"

"The answer was obvious," Obama added. "The U.S. Senate just needed to go."

Established in 1789 as a means of overseeing the passage of bills into law, the once-promising senator program has reportedly failed to contribute to the governing of the nation in any significant way since 1964. Last year alone, approximately $450 billion was funneled into the legislative chamber, an amount deemed fiscally unsound considering how few citizens actually benefit in any way from its existence.

In fact, the program has gone unchecked for so long that many in Washington are now unable to recall what purpose U.S. senators were originally meant to serve.

"I'm sure when it was first introduced the U.S. Senate seemed like a worthwhile public service that would aid vast segments of the population and play an important role in the years to come," said Sheila McKenzie, president of the watchdog group the American Center for Responsible Government. "But in reality, this program has been a complete and utter failure."

"It simply doesn't work," she added. "We've been pouring taxpayer dollars into this outdated relic for far too long."

An analysis conducted last week revealed a number of troubling flaws within the long-running, heavily subsidized program, including a lack of consistent oversight, no clear objectives or goals, the persistent hiring of unqualified and selfishly motivated individuals, and a 100 percent redundancy rate among its employees.

Moreover, the study found that the U.S. government already funds a fully operational legislative body that appears to do the exact same job as the Senate, but which also provides a fair and proportional representation of the nation's citizens and has rules in place to prevent one individual from holding the operations of the entire chamber hostage until he is guaranteed massive federal spending projects for his home state of Alabama.

Not only have U.S. Senators cost the country trillions of dollars in misspent funds over the years, but Washington insiders claim they have also derailed a wide range of other government programs, from social welfare to job creation to environmental protection.

"Even just the space the Senate currently occupies could be put to better use," consumer advocate Michael Dodgerson said. "Were the government to open a day-care center, a homeless shelter, or even an affordable restaurant in that building, it would make more of a difference in the lives of everyday Americans than what's there now."

So far, reaction to the cutback has been overwhelming positive, with many across the country calling it a long-awaited step toward progress.

Still, a small pocket of the nation's populace vehemently disagreed with Tuesday's decision.

"This is outrageous," said Joe Lieberman, a Connecticut-area resident and concerned citizen who makes more than $150,000 a year, enjoys full healthcare benefits, and lives comfortably in a large, non-foreclosed home. "The U.S. Senate has always looked out for my best interests. It's always done right by me."

Added Lieberman, "Without it, I'll have no choice but to exploit my extensive connections in the real estate, legal, insurance, and pharmaceutical industries to obtain strictly honorary positions at large companies that, in exchange for my subservience over the years and the prestige of my name, will compensate me generously and allow me to continue living a privileged life without contributing even a moment of my time to the society that has made it all possible." A prelude of things to come? Let's hope so.

(Source: *U.S. Government To Save Billions By Cutting Wasteful Senator Program*, uncredited, originally published in The Onion, March 30, 2010, ISSUE 46•13, Reprinted with permission of THE ONION. Copyright © 2010, by ONION, INC. www.theonion.com)

**We the people are the rightful masters of both Congress and the courts, not to overthrow the Constitution but to overthrow the men who pervert the Constitution.**

*Abraham Lincoln*

## *What's wrong with Washington?*

What is wrong with Washington? This was answered by Jane Sasseen in an article that appeared on Yahoo news entitled "*poll—what wrong with Washington: It's the people in charge not the system.* "Optimism about the American system of government is at a 36-year low, yet most Americans blame the people in office — not the system itself — for all that's going wrong, according to a ABC News/Yahoo! News poll."

She goes on to write "The underlying message of the new poll seems to be that new blood on Capitol Hill is the first step in getting back on track." "In bad times, people blame those in power: It's got to be your fault — you're in charge," says Larry Sabato, head of the *Center for Politics* at the University of Virginia. There's little doubt that Americans, frustrated by the economy's woes, are plenty worried about Washington's seeming inability to successfully tackle that or many of the nation's other problems."

Only 33 percent of Americans today say they are optimistic about "our system of government and how well it works," according to the new poll, produced for ABC and Yahoo! News by *Langer Research Associates*. That's the smallest number in the nearly dozen times the question has been asked over several decades. Back in the summer of 1974 — not long after President Richard Nixon resigned in the wake of Watergate — 55 percent of Americans were optimistic that the system was working.

The numbers today suggest levels of unhappiness not seen since the worst of the Watergate crisis, and "a sense that the political system is broken," says Daniel Clifton, head of policy research for *Strategas Research Partners*. "Independants in particular think the economy is not working and the system is not working, and that has created a very anti-incumbent environment. When economic or international conditions are unfavorable, Americans naturally reflect that in their view of the system and the future," he adds. "But [those views] will inevitably change once the economy gets better, we get hold of the national debt, and we show we can accomplish some important things."

But the numbers also appear to reflect deeper levels of worry about the position of the country and how well the political system is equipped to handle the challenges America now faces. According to the poll, it's not just that optimism is declining. A far greater sense of doubt about the system also pervades much of the country. Some 46 percent of Americans say they are uncertain about how well the system is working today, well above the roughly 27 percent who reported feeling uncertain in 1974 and many other years in between.

"We live in an uncertain time, and people are responding to that," says Hank Sheinkopf, a Democratic political consultant. "As the glory of the World War II era fades, we are becoming a very different country. The economic base is entirely different; we are no longer the food basket or the industrial motor for the world. Instead, we're an overextended debtor nation, and people know that."

Regardless of what has happened in the world, people are still more upset than they have been for several decades. And Americans are clear on where fault lies: with the political class in Washington. When those who are pessimistic or uncertain were asked whether they believe the problem is the system itself or the people who are running it, a 3-to-1 majority said the people in charge. Some 74 percent said the people running the government are at fault, versus just 24 percent who placed blame on the system itself.

One commonly cited reason: *Professional politicians spend too much time looking out for their own interests*; they no longer work for the interests of those who sent them to Washington. "The underlying system is OK; [the problem] is the people who represent us. They forgot they represent us," says Dale Goodno, a 67-year-old semi-retired truck driver from Beaverton, Oregon, who voted for John McCain in 2008. "I think that if you took maybe 10 people from each state who are not professional politicians and if they ran their government like they run their own business or family budget, then the country might make a comeback and might be the great nation it used to be." Imagine that, run the government like a business. Businesses can't borrow $14 trillion, and neither should the government.

It's also the case that, even when the country's problems are at their worst, many Americans remain idealistic and believe in the efficacy of the system; to question it, argues Sheinkopf, feels almost unpatriotic. So when problems arise, "There needs to be a culpable party ..... to find a scapegoat," he says. "That means the politicians." Most voters also recognize that there's little that can be done short-term to change the system. Moreover, points out Frank Donatelli, who was the deputy chairman of the Republican National Committee during the 2008 presidential campaign, the country has rebounded energetically from previous periods, like the early 1980s, when deep economic problems also led to widespread doubts about whether the political system still worked. "In this election, voters can't do anything about the system. But they can do something about the people," Donatelli says. "It's a logical response for the public to say, 'Let's change what we can change.' "

If you've heard this before, it's because you have. A similar political climate existed in 1994 and 2006. Clifton argues that the anti-incumbent mood is even stronger in 2010 than it was in 2006 and 1994, the last two times that waves of voter anger swept Congressional majorities out of control. In a recent Gallup poll, 56 percent of respondents said that congressional representatives did not deserve reelection — higher than the 50 percent and 45 percent recorded in those prior years.

"We'll see a tremendous vote, but it's not necessarily a vote for the Republican Party; it's a vote against the status quo," says the GOP's Donatelli. "It's not that they are in love with the Republican Party; it's that we are the way they can express that unhappiness." This is, in fact, what came to pass in 2010. It's another vote against the status quo. It's sad that people still believe (3 to 1) that it's just the politicians involved. The same thing keeps happening year after year, decade after decade, and we simply change politicians. Nothing really changes in Washington, elected officials get sent off to work and are met by the lobbyist and special interests as soon as they get there. The poll showed almost half of the people were uncertain how well the system worked anymore.

It's easy to be lulled to sleep for two years, until another election presents itself. During that two years, however, it's politics as usual in Washington. Politicians continue to spend $100 billion every month they don't have. Our deficit continues to grow beyond belief. All the while, politicians support those who supported them—the people that gave them money to get elected, or those that will give them money in the future to get re-elected, or even those who will give them a job (as a lobbyist) if they don't get re-elected. Most people who follow politics think once the economy gets better, and the government gets the national debt under control, everybody will be happy again. Sadly, that day may not come.

(Source: *What's wrong with Washington? poll—what's wrong with Washington: It's the people in charge not the system*," by Jane Sasseen, Yahoo! News, Oct 25, 2010. Yahoo.com. © 2010 Reprinted with permission from Yahoo! Inc. YAHOO! and the YAHOO! logo are trademarks of Yahoo! Inc.)

## *The Democrats / Republicans are driving the nation toward insolvency.*

Are the politicians themselves to blame for how unhappy everyone is about the government? Is it the Republican's fault, or is it the Democrats? They both are, and in more or less equal measure. In 2001, when George W. Bush took office and Republicans controlled Congress, the budget was essentially balanced and the total national debt was about $5.8 trillion. Washington has run an annual deficit every year since. Over Bush's first six years, when Republicans controlled the White House and Congress, the debt rose by about $3.2 trillion. Over the last two years of the Bush administration, when Democrats controlled Congress, the debt rose by another $2.9 trillion. So over the eight-year Bush administration, the debt more than doubled, rising by a total of $6.1 trillion.

Obama, in his first two years, has added about $3.2 trillion more to the national debt. The pace of debt expansion under Obama is obviously faster, but that's due to the stimulus and to a shrinking economy that still hasn't regained all the ground lost since the recession began in late 2007. And both presidents passed programs with costs still to be tallied in the future. Still, any politician charging the other party with excessive spending could – and should – level the same accusation at his own party. Republicans and Democrats alike are addicted to spending money they don't have.

Maybe people believe it's the politicians (and not the system) that doesn't work because it's the politicians that are spending all the money. But both political parties are spending trillions of dollars they don't have. Neither party ever makes any mention of how the national debt is to be repaid, how we are going to fund Social Security, Medicaid, and Medicare, Disability, Welfare and the rest of the entitlements into the future. Politicians from both parties have just added more entitlements to these programs, which means more deficit spending and more debt. There doesn't seem to be any end in sight.

Politicians generally tend to be more popular if they hand out more money to people, but those days may be drawing to a close. The government has run out of money, and there doesn't seem to be much of an appetite for more deficit spending and more pork hand-outs. Sorry, no more "cash-for-clunkers." The Federal Reserve is currently pursuing a path that will lead our country further and further into trouble. With interest rates at zero, the Fed is buying bonds in an effort to further lower interest rates (quantitative easing). The Chinese, who hold a large percentage of our national debt, have accused the U.S. of "printing money," which seems to be what's happening. This process has the potential to cause massive increases in inflation. Inflation will further increase the cost of debt service on our national debt thus increasing government spending. This doesn't even take into consideration our unfunded liabilities for Social Security, federal, state and local pensions, Welfare and all the other financial promises the government has made.

As the poll mentioned, some people still believe in the efficacy of the system. This may have been true twenty years ago, but deficit spending and the great recession have made the situation different and untenable. It's not the same as voters remember. Instead of stimulating business and hiring, nearly a trillion dollars of stimulus spending (added to our debt) has had almost no effect. Things have changed, and voters sense this. Yet, they still look to the politicians to make things right. Why is this the case? America is obsessed with the short-term.....and the next election.

As a result of the two-year political cycle, we've become way too shortsighted in our policymaking, or lack thereof. Elections and politicians have reformed our thinking into terms of every two years. While they are in office, politicians grease as many palms as they can so they can get elected again, and that usually means special interests and political contributors. What's missing are government programs and plans set before the American people. What we have now is relentless backroom negotiations with interest groups and lobbyists.

The American people have essentially been forgotten as politicians continuously vie for the support of special interest groups. It is staggering – the special interests and their large money pouring into the campaign. The two-year campaign cycle breeds corruption in the form of politicians working for special interests and lobbyists instead of the people of the U.S. What's amazing is the gullibility of the voting public. They feel empowered every two years at election-time, but then the politicians they elect go to Washington where they are greeted by the awaiting lobbyists and special interests, and the big money.

## "If only we had the right politicians"

People may think and believe that "if only we had the right politicians" everything would be okay. Yet, more and more people think things are getting worse, not better, even after two recent elections. A majority of Americans feel that America is "on the wrong track," and that they are worse off than they were in 2008. In another sweeping poll released by *Bloomberg News* on Dec. 14th, 2010, 66 percent of respondents said that they felt that "things in the nation...have... gotten off on the wrong track," compared to just 27 percent who felt the country was heading in the right direction. 51 percent of respondents said they were worse off now than they were two years ago. A majority of voters think we are on the wrong track, and things are worse than two years ago. How much longer are we going to wait around in desperation while our politicians make things worse? When are people going to realize the *politicians are the problem*?

One year, experience counts in the election, the next election people don't want "career politicians." Politicians will continue to do what they always do: pass more legislation, laws and rules, tax and spend more money than we possibly repay, and serve the needs of their master's—not the American people, but the lobbyists and special interests. The preceding chapters have shown over and over how much politicians are insulated from the voting public, and how people are angry and disenchanted. There is abundant real and clear data that politicians caused most of our problems; that further spending is not going to solve our problems, and that *we can't rely on the politicians to get us out of the mess they created.* It's never going to end, and it's clear, at least to some people, that it's not going to work either way, or any way, or whatever way. Once the Titanic hit the iceberg, it was doomed. It's hard to say when we hit the iceberg, but it's happened. Now, politically speaking, we are just changing seats on the Titanic.

## *Even some politicians don't think our government works anymore....*

Evan Bayh, the Governor of Indiana from 1989 to 1996 and a Senator since 1999 wrote an op-ed piece for the *New York Times* "Why I'm Leaving the Senate" after he announced his retirement from the Senate. He writes "Challenges of historic import threaten America's future. Action on the deficit, economy, energy, health care and much more is imperative, yet our legislative institutions fail to act. Congress must be reformed....There are many causes for the dysfunction: strident partisanship, unyielding ideology, a corrosive system of campaign financing, gerrymandering of House districts, endless filibusters, holds on executive appointees in the Senate, dwindling social interaction between senators of opposing parties and a caucus system that promotes party unity at the expense of bipartisan consensus. Today, members routinely campaign against each other, raise donations against each other and force votes on trivial amendments written solely to provide fodder for the next negative attack ad. It's difficult to work with members actively plotting your demise. In the Senate, raising in small increments the $10 million to $20 million a competitive race requires takes huge amounts of time that could otherwise be spent talking with constituents, legislating or becoming well-versed on public policy....Because of the incessant need to raise campaign cash, we now have perpetual campaigns. If fund-raising is constantly on members' minds, it's difficult for policy compromise to trump political calculation."

Bayh further writes "The recent Supreme Court ruling in *Citizens United v. Federal Election Commission*, allowing corporations and unions to spend freely on ads explicitly supporting or opposing political candidates, will worsen matters. The threat of unlimited amounts of negative advertising from special interest groups will only make members more beholden to their natural constituencies and more afraid of violating party orthodoxies. I can easily imagine vulnerable members approaching a corporation or union for support and being told: 'We'd love to support you, but we have a rule. We only support candidates who are with us at least 90 percent of the time. Here is our questionnaire with our top 10 concerns. Fill it out.' Millions of campaign dollars now ride on the member's response. The cause of good government is not served. Our most strident partisans must learn to occasionally sacrifice short-term tactical political advantage for the sake of the nation. Otherwise, Congress will remain stuck in an endless cycle of recrimination and revenge. The minority seeks to frustrate the majority, and when the majority is displaced it returns the favor. Power is constantly sought through the use of means which render its effective use, once acquired, impossible." It's profound that a politician would go on record saying our government is "dysfunctional" and open to corruption because of campaign contributions. It's what the people are already aware of—it doesn't work anymore. Even some politicians are throwing in the towel as "challenges of historic import threaten America's future;" as with Nero, our politicians fiddle, while we all burn.

## *Online Voting Is Becoming More Common*

As a prelude to the main premise of this book – some recent information about online voting: Alex Altman of *Time Magazine* wrote an article about online voting "During the 2010 midterm elections, 33 states allowed a few million military and overseas voters to return their ballots online. Overseas voters have a tendency to be disenfranchised by distance: a 2009 analysis by the Pew Center on the States determined 16 states did not provide members of the military, their spouses and citizens living abroad enough time to vote. To remedy the problem, last year Congress passed the Military and Overseas Voter Empowerment Act, which requires states to distribute ballots at least 45 days before an election. Still, it's not hard to see why online ballot returns would seem appealing. 'The challenge has been explaining the security risk to people who desperately want to improve the plight of overseas voters,' says Pamela Smith, president of the Verified Voting Foundation."

"Yet, Washington is canceling plans to let voters return ballots digitally. But some states are undeterred. 'The system we have is totally different. You can't compare apples and oranges,' says West Virginia Secretary of State Natalie Tennant. Mountain State voters in eight counties will be able to cast ballots online next month, using a complex, privately designed system that includes a secure website, passwords and encryption codes. The process varies from state to state. In Arizona, authorized voters will be e-mailed a ballot, which they will be able to print, fill out and then upload and return. County officials will verify each voter's name, address and signature, just as they will do for mail-in ballots. 'I guess an e-mail could theoretically be intercepted, but generally speaking, we're confident,' says Matthew Benson, a spokesman for Arizona's secretary of state. Massachusetts voters will have the luxury of returning ballots over e-mail."

Online voting has become popular and will continue to be into the future. There is a tremendous need for increased security, and possibly an entirely new network or intranet system to handle online voting. The point is, the possibility to vote online exists, as it should. It's not surprising Washington is canceling plans for digital ballots. They don't want the "genie" let out of the bottle. Since everything from phones to tablets to laptops can now access the internet, anyone anywhere can vote online at anytime. This may open up a completely new chapter in the history of the U.S., if we are willing to take it.

## *Our only hope is in the clouds....*

Throughout this book, mention has been made about *a better way of doing things*. That, in fact, is the whole point of this book, and the premise is very simple: <u>Try to imagine our country without politicians</u>. Are you able to? There would be a void if they just went away, or maybe nobody would notice as they only work 80 days a year. How many people talk with their friends and workers every day with this hope? How long are people going to stand around, feeling helpless, as one party or the other fights for control of a governmental system that doesn't work anymore. The "proof is in the pudding"; the fact that people are polling to find out if people believe our system works or not is proof itself that it doesn't work.

The previous chapters have shown what our government has become—a national-security endangering catastrophic mess. It's worse than a mess, it's malignant, and malignancy usually kills the host; it's taking away all we hold dear, our way of life is slipping away, and there doesn't seem to be any treatment for the problem. Our only chance of doing anything is voting. So, we wait two years for the next election, and shuffle some politicians in and push some out. Things quiet down for awhile, but after the election is over, does anything really change? Nothing much has changed in twenty years, except its gotten worse and worse. Our government has grown into something our forefathers, Thomas Jefferson and George Washington wouldn't even recognize today, nor does anyone think they would want anything to do with it, but Theodore Roosevelt must have seen what was coming in the U.S.:

**The death-knell of the republic had rung as soon as the active power became lodged in the hands of those who sought, not to do justice to all citizens, rich and poor alike, but to stand for one special class and for its interests as opposed to the interests of others.**

*Theodore Roosevelt, Labor Day speech at Syracuse, NY, Sept 7, 1903*

It seems the death-knell rang some time ago, and people are finally beginning to hear it. What we have in our current republic is an oligarchy (*government by the few, a government in which a small group exercises control especially for corrupt and selfish purposes*). A close look at the way laws are passed, regulations are made, tax dollars are spent, and influenced is peddled in Washington, lobbyists and lawyers have almost completely taken the power in this country for their own benefit or for the benefit of whomever is paying them. The "one special class" is listed in the chapter on lawyers: the list of companies and law firms spending billions of dollars via lobbyists to control what happens in Washington. What justice have all citizens gotten in the last ten years? What benefit have they gotten for all the money they paid the government in taxes? The government has grown and grown, but at least they give us food stamps. Our politicians' addiction to spending and giving away money is threatening our national security.

Government employees make more money than the people they serve, have better health insurance than the people they serve, get to retire earlier and have better retirement plans than the people they serve. Government doctors can't be sued and some government employees apparently don't have to pay their taxes. The politicians certainly have it better than the people they serve as most are millionaires. And to make sure it stays that way, they sell their influence and power to lobbyists, many of whom were in government office or government jobs before they joined the lobbying law firms. When they get out of office, the revolving door swings and then they make the real money by becoming lobbyists themselves. Who lobbies for the average person in the U.S.? Does anybody believe that the people they elect to represent them in Washington are actually thinking of what is best for them?

Of the two parties, each has their own agenda, which corresponds to a group of people that they represent who feel entitled to whatever their party can get for them (from the government). If you want to know who it is that each party represents, look at who makes their campaign contributions. For the Democrats, it's the American Association for Justice (the American Trial Lawyers Association), for Republicans, The American Chamber of Commerce. At least The American Chamber of Commerce represents businesses, which creates jobs, products, and contributes to the economy. The American Association for Justice is lawyers trying to protect their rights to sue anyone and everyone, which wipes out jobs, GDP, products, businesses, and certainly doesn't contribute anything to our economy. On the contrary, the cost of lawsuits in the U.S. has outstripped growth in GDP for the last 50 years. In fact, lawyers and lawsuits are one of the primary reasons cited (including taxes and regulations, also created by politicians) why so many companies have moved jobs offshore. Regardless of who is paying for political influence and control of our government, the point is, the government is not working in the interests of the American people.

Elections have been seriously ugly mud-slinging filth-fests, broadcast on T.V. every other minute. Some people still care about the issues in elections, but the politicians can only seem to attack each other and make vague claims about whatever seems to be popular at the moment. People who vote know it doesn't make any difference anyway, because it's going to be business as usual once they get to Washington. Politicians spend half their time raising money for the next election to make more defamatory commercials, and the other half of their time spending hundreds of billions of our tax dollars and getting pressured by more than 13,000 lobbyists, who throw many more billions of dollars at them. It's the definition of corruption, not democracy.

Our country was started by people who thought they could make and run a better government than Great Britain. They had to fight a war to get that right, and we have just let politicians and lobbyists take it away from us. From the data presented, it's accelerating, not slowing down. The amount of money the government is consuming and spending is also accelerating, not surprisingly, as lobbying has accelerated—*they do it to get our money*. Companies that are doing the lobbying, like health insurance and oil companies, are growing at an accelerated pace. It's not going to end until the entire country is bankrupt, as their greed seems to have no limit.

**Any people anywhere, being inclined and having the power, have the right to rise up, and shake off the existing government, and form a new one that suits them better. This is a most valuable - a most sacred right - a right, which we hope and believe, is to liberate the world.**

*Abraham Lincoln*

Government has taken over the U.S. auto industry, controlled Wall Street for a brief time, controls banks (through TARP and the trillions the government gave them during the bailout), controls our largest mortgage lenders—Fannie Mae and Freddie Mac, and now the government is trying to control healthcare. The government has proven again and again, throughout history, that it can't manage anything. It can't even manage itself. Any business that took in as much money as the government and mismanaged it so badly would be out of business. More people are in poverty than in recent memory, more people are losing their houses, more people are on food stamps, and less people have jobs than has been seen for a long time. *The road to economic ruin runs right through Washington*. It doesn't work, and we can't turn back the clock three or four decades when government was less corrupt.

The people of America have given the politicians and their supporters enough rope over the last several decades, and instead of hanging themselves, they have hung us. Some people remember the talk of "campaign finance reform" and "term limits" for politicians. Neither of those programs came to pass. Did anybody think politicians were going to enact laws limiting their power, the money they get, and how long they could stay in office? In fact, with the Jan. 2010 ruling by the Supreme Court, it's worse than ever. More money is spent on lobbying and elections than ever, and it's a bigger mess than ever. Given the chance to limit lobbying and special interest influence available to politicians every session, and their utter lack of effort fighting the corruption of these influences, the politicians have only collected more money and spent more tax money. Politicians are spending $150 billion dollars a month more than they are taking in, all added to the massive $14 trillion dollar debt.

There is an old joke, maybe you've heard it—if you can't succeed in business or acting, at least you can go into politics. Some politicians may be good for the people of America; they're not all bad by any means. There are probably some politicians that don't take money from lobbyists, aren't pushed into spending on causes and companies by lobbyists, don't subsidize and hand out money to people that give them money, don't spend hundreds of billions on earmarks and pork, but they are the in the minority. Never in the history of mankind has there been an institution where people with *so few qualifications* can spend so much money. Politicians are not the best and brightest people in this country. The best and brightest want nothing to do with politics, and usually fear the government and politicians. We hear from these people on a daily basis as they offer their comments and ideas to the press. They write books and publish on websites and magazines. They teach and do research at some of our most prestigious universities. There are people that know how we can solve the problems in this country, but they aren't politicians. We can do better.

**Every government degenerates when trusted to the rulers of the people alone. The people themselves are its only safe depositories.**

*Thomas Jefferson*

An excellent quote by Thomas Jefferson: the people themselves are the only safe depository of the government. Currently, the exact *opposite* is true: our country is trusted to the rulers of the people alone, *and it has degenerated*. Washington has become an entity unto itself alone, being fed by our tax dollars, and being controlled by lobbyists and special interests. This book has shown over and over how our government has become mismanaged and corrupt, how the people of this country, for whom this country was set up, have become marginalized and removed from the political process over and over again. The will of the people doesn't matter in Washington, only the will of whoever is paying for play with our politicians.

The amazing thing is that, over time, we can get rid of the politicians. We don't need politicians. It would be so easy. Our forefathers created this country for the people, not the politicians, and the people can take control and fix everything in this country. We have the strength and the tenacity—if we are given the chance, and more importantly, if we *take* the chance. How you ask? Like everything else that has caused growth and prosperity is this country, the answer lies in technology. We have the power and right to vote, remember? We can vote anytime, 24/7 from anywhere in the country about anything. We have cell phones, laptops, tablets, home computers, work computers and a variety of other web-enabled devices. It's safe to say that everyone who wants a cell phone can have a cell phone. They actually give them away when you sign up for a plan. The technology for phones has grown incredibly in the last ten years. What phones can do, and what you can do with cell phones is amazing. We don't have to wait for the election cycle every two years!

The most important thing, for this discussion, is that they connect to the internet. You can therefore vote with a cell phone. You can also use any web-enabled device, the number of which seems to grow every month. Any web-enabled device can become your own personal voting device. If you told someone they could vote with their web device, they wouldn't be surprised. The potential to vote over the internet has existed since the mid-nineties, for at least the past 15 years, really. Back then, not everyone used the internet, not everyone had internet service or even a computer.

But, today penetration is almost complete. Wireless internet or web-enabled device-coverage is almost ubiquitous across the U.S. It would have to be, for everyone to be able to vote with their favorite device. It's obvious this would not be a hard thing to implement. We would need a completely different level of authentication, security, and applications to implement voting on devices. It would open up jobs and a new technological direction to pursue. Voting would take much less technological advance than we already have. We would have to provide devices to those that can't afford them, but it wouldn't cost very much. Imagine the technology we have today, then imagine those ridiculous voting machines we have (the ultimate analog devices). What happened? We have the technology, and technology is not going to be the problem.

The problem is going to be making people responsible enough to take their right to vote and take it to the next level. Most people spend at least an hour on the internet or cell phones every day; texting, surfing, social network sites, YouTube. If people would spend 10 or 20 percent of this time involved in the political process—in running our country—we could literally solve all our problems. Our original leaders and the brave people that fought and died so we could have independence from England wanted everyone's voice to be heard. But people couldn't leave their farms, crops and shops and go to the state capital or Washington to have their voice heard. So, they elected people to represent them in Washington. Congressmen and Senators were Representatives. They represented their constituents (the fancy name for the people that elected them).

My, how things have changed. They now represent the people that give them money. Their constituents may give them money, a few hundred dollars, or a few thousand, here and there. But big lobbying groups, political actions committees, unions and corporations give *billions* of dollars, the prospect of jobs after their political career, and the promise of riches in the private sector as lobbyists and board members. All for selling out their political capital, selling out their influence and their vote on bills and the formulation of laws and regulations in committees they oversee in Washington—for selling out our country. With the technology we have today, _we don't need anyone to represent us_, we don't need any middle men who are beholden to someone else than the people who elected them. We don't need politicians to run for re-election, <u>because we don't need politicians in the first place</u>.

Thomas Jefferson and George Washington and the rest of our founding fathers gave birth to a beautiful baby democracy. It grew, went through adolescence, and is now middle aged. Instead of maintaining its health, it has allowed a systemic cancer to take over, like brain cancer, since it's in the centralized part of the body (Washington). The rest of the body (the people) keep feeding the cancer, which has grown and grown and is threatening to wipe out everything. The people, using technology, need to surgically remove the cancer before it kills the organism. We have the technology, but do we have the will to go through with the surgery that will save us? Or will we let the cancer consume everything. We still have time, but as with cancer, the sooner it's taken out, the better.

**This country, with its institutions, belongs to the people who inhabit it. Whenever they shall grow weary of the existing government, they can exercise their constitutional right of amending it, or exercise their revolutionary right to overthrow it.**

*Abraham Lincoln*

Except for getting elected, politicians have become obsolete on many levels, for many reasons. First, they are responsible for raising and spending tax dollars (and trillions they don't have). They have proven that they are unable to be either responsible about spending, or to provide anything good or reasonable with the spending (except the growth and security of the government itself and those dependant on the government, it's pay increases, health benefits, and increased regulation and increasing taxes to finance everything). In 2010 alone the government spent $1.25 trillion dollars more than it raised in taxes, it's called the deficit. These add up year after year, and the amount of money paid just to finance this debt drains more and more money that could be spent on other things. To pay this debt, we and our children, and our children's children will be enslaved by taxes for decades, if we are *ever* able to pay it off. And politicians are unwilling and unable to stop spending money and bankrupting our country.

We need to use to technology to free ourselves from our oligarchy, our plutocracy, from the politicians, from the special interests, the lobbyists, the political action committees, the unions, and mess that is our current political system. *We need to once again become a democracy*, where each voice is heard, not just every two years, but at anytime and anyplace.

## *"The Cloud"*

**Information is the oxygen of the modern age. It seeps through the walls topped by barbed wire it wafts across the electrified borders.**

*Ronald Reagan*

A big catch-word in technology, "the cloud" represents tens of thousands of servers all over the country. These servers, along with switches, represent where we go when we are on the internet. Web sites are programs that are loaded on servers that we access with our browsers. It's called "the cloud" because it's up there somewhere, in the clouds. It's real though, more access and storage than anyone could have imagined ten years ago. It also represents freedom from software. We don't need to buy expensive software to load onto our computers or tablets, we simply need to use software that is in the cloud (loaded on a server somewhere via our browser).

The people that developed cloud computing imagined a place where you didn't need an expensive computer and expensive software, all you needed was a way to get on the internet, and they would take care of the rest. It's not free, of course, but it may allow many more people to do many more creative things without spending so much money on hardware and software. The cloud also represents freedom, because it's available to anyone who has a web-enabled device. It was the development of the cloud computing that allowed YouTube, the site where everyone downloads their videos. It was the cloud that allowed for social networking sites like Facebook. And it is the cloud that will allow for government to be free from all the corruption, filth, and greed which is not-so-slowly destroying our country.

<u>We need to return to a democracy</u> (def: *government by the people; especially: rule of the majority : a government in which the supreme power is vested in the people and exercised by them directly or indirectly through a system of representation*

*usually involving periodically held free elections, From Webster Dictionary)* <u>and we can</u>, because everyone's voice can be heard again. Does anyone even remember what democracy is? We haven't had it for so long, and people have become so disillusioned, that they have just accepted things the way they are.

But we can do so much better. Our technology has led us to this place in time, where we can have democracy again. We can all vote for what we think is important, we can make real decisions and affect real change. Or we can continue to send politicians to Washington, were they forget who and what sent them there. A democracy needs to make laws, change laws, eliminate laws, draft legislation, allocate our tax dollars, decide what our country should be doing in the world, protect and insure that the average American is being served. That's what a democracy should be, and what it should be doing.

## *Our greatest asset is our people...*

It's always been the people of America that have driven our success. The people that have had new ideas, invented things like the PC and the web. The smartest people in this country *are not politicians.* Our smartest and best people don't make laws; they don't draft legislation nor decide how to allocate our collective capital. At best, the Nobel winning economists, legal scholars, leaders in the fields of business and finance are appointed to government positions or secretary-ships, they advise but don't make things happen, the politicians do that. The smartest people in this country know what to do to solve our problems, they write books about it, they talk about it on T.V. programs, they publish research and they write articles and books. But it doesn't translate into action in Washington. Washington is an insular, self-contained place of bad decisions and more bad policy. How might this be changed?

How can we best use our human capital? We have the technology to vote, anytime and anyplace. We need a model of how a new government might look. Let's look at something in Washington that actually does work fairly well sometimes: The U.S. Supreme Court. It works well because usually the best and the brightest people are nominated to become justices. The politicians, however, always make it into a conservative vs. liberal battle, but, for the most part, the best and smartest are appointed to the Supreme Court. Once appointed, they are not influenced by lobbyists, political action committees, unions or people with money, because they don't need to run for office. They are above the cesspool of politics as usual. They hear cases and render decisions. Not everyone agrees with their decisions, but they are, for the most part, above reproach. They aren't perfect, but the Supreme Court is something everyone in this country can be proud of because it works.

Now, imagine that the people appoint the best and brightest, the smartest people in our country, to commissions or agencies, like the Supreme Court. There can be the commission for taxation, a commission for foreign affairs, a commission for banking and finance, a commission for public works, transportation, and national security, a commission for energy and conservation, a commission for everything our people need. These commissions can be nominated by their peers or the people, by the entire academic and public system that knows who the best and brightest are, who they would trust to run a commission for the good of the whole country, not because of their political affiliation or if they can be bought off and do what they're told, but because they are the best, the smartest, and will do the best job. These people will be nominated, and they will be appointed by the people, and like the Supreme Court, they will do what is right and what is best, and if they don't, they will be replaced. People not are perfect, and they will make mistakes, but they can and will make the best decisions for our country.

We cannot say that the best and brightest are running our country now, not anywhere close. The best minds in our country can finally be unleashed, not for the benefit of corporations, lawyers or special interests, but for the benefit of everyone, rich or poor. They will produce legislation that we need, that will actually solve problems—but won't have control of its passage – the people will decide if it is good or not, by voting. The smartest people in this country will produce legislation, it will first be distributed on T.V., webinars, on websites, on video, explained to the media, so the people can see, read, and understand it. Discussion forums will analyze and reform the legislation so that the greatest number may benefit, and then when all the discussion is over, the people of America will vote on it. We won't have to wait for every two years to make changes, we won't have to wait and hope and pray that somebody does the right thing. The people will vote and decide, the majority will rule, <u>we will have a real democracy</u>.

## The Best and Brightest Are Our Greatest Capital...

The best, smartest people of our great country are our greatest capital of all; our Nobel Laureates, our brightest people from the best universities, our best financial and economic minds, working to solve our problems, offering solutions, and the people voting on these issues. Our government has been built on 224 years of tradition. Many of the problems were in today are the result of rules and legislation passed 50 years ago. Federal rules and regulations never go away, they just pile up. Federal entitlements and money hand-outs never go away either (lobbyists make sure of that), they just grow and grow (like our debt), like the government itself. The greed of the few is wiping out the resources of the many. The government is squeezing the life out of our businesses and our people.

We desperately need revision, reform and change, and you can be sure it will never happen with our current model of government. It's doomed to failure, and we're all going down with it. We don't have to end up like every other great civilization in history, but we will unless we evolve. Our political system has not kept up with technology, nor does it ever want to. It wants power in the hands of the few, benefitting the few and whoever else can figure out a way to rip off the government. What we have now is corruption: politicians (who we elected) even let lobbyists (who we didn't elect) write legislation. We are going to have to take our power back and use it in a way that will benefit everyone—via a real democracy. The point is, we have the technology to do just that.

Imagine our best and brightest, the smartest people in their field, offering to the people solutions and changes that will really help everyone. Instead of lobbying, they make webinars to educate people about the problems we face and what they can do to fix them. We can have videos and T.V. stations, not spectator stations like C-span, but channels that run programs of legislation, foreign affairs, tax changes, why they need to be changed, how they can be changed, and what our options are. Present all the figures, details, and options for everyone to see so they can decide for themselves what they think is best, and on the third Thursday of the month, or every Thursday, or Wednesday mornings, everyone in the country will have open voting for the day. They can vote to see if a topic needs revision and further legislation, or if everyone is already happy with the way things are. If legislation is needed, then in a month they make the best legislation possible, and we vote again. If it's something of critical importance, maybe have a best two out of three vote. With this option, our choices are almost unlimited. Imagine being able to vote once a month, twelve times a year. We can shape public policy in real-time, and solve problems quickly and effectively.

One of the greatest things about the internet (and also one of the most annoying) is everyone can participate if they want to. Everyone can and does participate on the internet. Anyone and everyone can have their voice heard. Witness the seemingly insignificant videos that ten million people choose to view. People want to participate on the internet, but now it's not for anything that really matters. We can have websites devoted to participation and discussion on the wide range of political matters facing our country. We already have websites like this, but it's all for entertainment, nobody in Washington is listening, and they certainly aren't following the will of the people.

We can debate, educate, and move politically on the internet and T.V., and then vote and make a decision. And if what we decided doesn't work or isn't right, we can improve and then vote again next month, and *we can fix problems in real-time*, before they become huge debacles. Imagine college kids making and showing political videos competing with corporations trying to push their agenda. Another great thing about the internet: people value what's real, and most people aren't interested in corporate and big money agendas. Lobbyists, special interests, unions, and politicos will have to compete with every other person in the U.S. to shape public opinion. The most popular websites and browsers actually try to keep advertising and corporate influence to a minimum. Every person could voice their opinion on an issue, and millions of people could see their video if it's good and real. Imagine, nobody would control what we see, and more importantly, what we think.

**Vox Populi**: The Latin words for "the voice of the people." Never before in history have we had the ability to voice our opinion, share our opinion, and then decide by voting in such a robust and easy manner. Imagine the voice of the people making decisions for our country, in the clouds. We would have to insure the integrity of the system. People have tried throughout history to manipulate elections, stuff voting boxes, forge votes, rig voting-systems; the list goes on and on. We would need to monitor the authenticity of each vote from device to server. We would need to monitor voting in real time. The technology would have to be bullet-proof. This could be accomplished, however, with a little effort.

We would have to have a new branch of government in charge of our new voting system and its integrity. It would be responsible to the people they serve, the people of the United States of America. Every current branch of the government would be made into a commission or agency, which would be nominated by their peers, and voted by the people. We could wring out the ridiculous waste, fraud and redundancy in government now. Needed reforms could be made, based on the will of the people. The commission itself would have no power to make law, legislation, or spending, but would make law, legislation, and recommendations on spending, and the people would vote.

The people would have the power—what our forefathers and our greatest leaders hoped and dreamed we would have. There would be a standard period of a month, or two months, or two weeks, or whatever we decide, for debate and discussion on the laws, legislation, and recommendations of the commissions or agencies, and then everyone would vote. Majority would rule. Again, Democracy: *government by the people; especially: rule of the majority : a government in which the supreme power is vested in the people and exercised by them directly or indirectly through a system of representation usually involving periodically held free elections, (From Webster Dictionary)*. This is the definition of Democracy, and this is what we must have—Democracy. The people could reign in spending; make laws that are fair to everyone. Using our brightest minds, our most knowledgeable people, our most experienced and successful people, guiding us, followed by the rule of the majority. It could be democracy in action in real time. Can you imagine?

## *American Evolution not Revolution...*

We have to do this. We have to evolve. We can look back through the whole of history, and countries that have refused or been unable to evolve have diminished, died, or been wiped out. It's not a big change, it's a huge change. The Tea Party's favorite phrase is "take our _____ (insert word: money, government) back." Many people want to take back what is rightfully ours, *our birthright*—democracy. Many people that are running things now want us to believe we are living in a democracy, because they allow us to go to the polls once every two years, but are we really? This book has shown, in a variety of ways and circumstances that we are *not* in control of our country. People know this, maybe not always consciously, but they know this already. Nobody has offered another choice. The choice is obvious and the *choice must be democracy.*

We can use our technology to allow the free flow of ideas, the free flow of structure from our best minds, the free flow of solutions to problems that have become overwhelming. We have to use our human capital to reclaim our birthright of democracy from those who have taken it. We have to start now. Believe it or not, it can get worse, much worse.

If you can't imagine a world without politicians, then imagine this: Politicians keep racking up trillion dollar deficits every year. The Treasury starts buying our treasury bills (how we finance our debt), which they are already doing now. This is equivalent to the government printing money. For awhile, interest rates remain at zero, but inflation takes off, commodity prices soar (as they are now), our currency is worth less and less, and the Federal Reserve has to start raising interest rates. Interest rates on treasury bills then start rising, which is great for bond holders, many of which are foreigners, but costs the government more and more money to service its debt. The debt continues to grow, as does debt service—it triples in a year. Politicians keep approving higher and higher debt ceilings then vote for an unlimited debt ceiling. Afraid of an impending collapse, nobody wants to buy our treasury bills, so the government is broke in a matter of weeks. The government freezes spending on everything. The government has to raise taxes dramatically to service the increases on debt service and continued increases in entitlement spending, squeezing out jobs as millions are laid off so businesses can pay their taxes. Politicians actually double taxes immediately to get some cash flow. Businesses can't grow, can't afford to borrow money to expand, and go on slash and burn policies to preserve capital and meet tax obligations. Not wanting to pay higher taxes, most businesses announce off-shoring of the remainder of their operations and lay off millions more employees. As profits are decimated, the stock market crashes and many investors are wiped out. Individuals see their tax burden double. As the economy tanks, millions more lose their jobs and quit spending, and businesses continue to contract. They can't spend anyway, because inflation has doubled the prices of everything. People from all social classes start to declare bankruptcy at an unprecedented rate. Buried under a $20 trillion dollar national debt, and debt service more than a trillion a year, the government slashes Social Security and other entitlements as they run out of cash, and tax receipts continue to drop as more and more people and businesses declare bankruptcy, lowering revenue even further. As the economy continues to spiral downward, foreigners decide it's time to get their money out of treasury bills, as the rating on U.S. treasuries is downgraded. The U.S. can barely afford interests payments on its debt, but now bondholders are pulling out en masse, and are demanding their principal back. Bond prices sink into nothingness. This causes U.S. treasuries to go into default as the government can't afford principal payments. The Middle Easterners and Chinese, our largest bond holders, seek collateral for what they are owed, to which the U.S. refuses  The stock market crashes even further, the U.S. is unable to raise any more cash because nobody is buying our Treasury Bonds. Grocery stores refuse food stamps believing the government will be unable to pay. The healthcare system refuses Medicare and Medicaid patients, believing the government unable to pay. Banks start to refuse Social Security, Disability and Welfare checks, believing the government unable to pay. Unemployment benefits are stopped. All subsidies are stopped. Foreign governments and the International Monetary Fund (IMF) refuse to loan or guarantee loans to the U.S. The government essentially seizes, credit markets seize, U.S. banks and corporations seize, and even the ones that were bailed out by the government some years earlier refuse to loan what little money they have to the government. Pundits say the government is bankrupt, and, for all practical purposes, it is. Banks even stop taking pay checks from government employees believing the government unable to pay. The military grinds to a halt as oil companies and other suppliers stop getting paid, and so stop providing supplies to the military. What little tax income the government is getting goes to the military for national security reasons. People reluctantly leave their military service as they are no longer getting paid, and nobody will accept their credit. As the U.S. continues to print more money to try to get out of this situation, the U.S. goes into hyper inflation, which dilutes the wealth of the wealthy into nothingness. The money you have this month is worth ½ as much in two months. Unable to get food with food stamps, people riot and loot stores, emptying warehouses and delivery trucks. The National Guard is called up, but can't possibly cover all the insurrection as many have left guard service because they aren't getting paid. Police, firemen, prison guards and government employees walk off the job because they aren't getting paid. The government has no choice but to authorize local militias for protection. As people and businesses become diluted, they flee the country with whatever they have left, and try to convert what's left of their dollars to whoever will take them, for whatever they can get for them. The government tries to nationalize U.S. corporations and personal assets. Will the people and the countries that hold our debt/treasury bills just let us float away, or will they try to take some collateral from us?  Do we give them California and call it even?

If our government can't borrow any more money via treasury bills, are we going to let China, a Middle Eastern government like Saudia Arabia, or the IMF bail us out? Are we going to let one of these entities tell us how we are going to run our government and economy as they surely would if they had to bail us out?  Is this really what we want? We would have to get bailed out or the government would shut down. This scenario and hundreds of others like it are a very real possibility on the road we continue to travel down as a country. Politicians haven't taken any real action to reverse course because it takes leadership and pain, both of which aren't popular with politicians. If you think these examples are ridiculous, look at what happened to the former Soviet Union and bail-outs in Europe.

Fear does nothing productive, however. We need to change how things are done, we don't need another American "naught decade" (2000-2010) or a "lost decade" like the Japanese. We don't need to drive more and more people into poverty, or get more people on food stamps. We need to get people working. We don't seem to have a political system that has the ability to do anything to help us, but only make things worse. We face the real possibility that we, as a country and as a people, are going to have more debt than we will *ever* be able to repay. The people are going to have to look after their own interests. The politicians aren't going to look after our interests. They had their chance. The young people of this country showed great faith in the government and elected President Obama in 2008. Young people showed up to vote in higher numbers than ever, and with great hope sent him to Washington. Then politics took over, and we continue in this accelerated death spiral. We have to summon that energy and the energy of all Americans. Are we just supposed to keep summoning faith and hope every two years? Only to be rewarded with the continued debacle in Washington? And it can get much worse, because our national security is at risk. Just because it hasn't happened yet doesn't mean it can't happen. Young people have no faith that they are ever going to see a dollar from Medicare or Social Security, and for good reason, yet they are forced to keep paying into the program (those that have jobs). We must channel our energy, our hope, and our faith. We are going to have to take back our right and our democracy, and we can.

People need healthcare, but who among the politicians are going to have the guts to stand up to the health insurance companies that extract hundreds of billions in profits from healthcare every year? Who is going to make changes to our medical lawsuit/tort system? Who is going to make changes to our entitlement programs that need to be made? Do the politicians have a plan for any of this, or are they just going to continue to spend and increase programs that already don't work? There are no shortages of plans that can fix things, but the people who have developed and analyzed these plans never get heard.

Take for example the book *Seeds of Destruction* by Glenn Hubbard and Peter Navarro. Mr. Hubburd is the Dean of the Columbia School of Business, and Mr. Navarro is a business professor at UC Irvine. Their book details the disastrous real consequences of our government policy in many areas, and they offer their own plan on how to get out of the economic situation we find ourselves in. Their main thesis is illustrated on the cover of their book "*Why the path to economic ruin runs through Washington, and how to reclaim American prosperity.*" It is an easy-to-read intelligent work, and their ideas on how to solve the myriad of economic problems in the U.S. are straight forward and would undoubtedly work, if they were put into action. They show how our tax system doesn't work, our healthcare system doesn't work, our entitlement programs don't work, and why these and many other programs in Washington have lead to the U.S. being uncompetitive, and how things are unlikely to change if we continue to pursue our "business as usual" path. This and many other books have been written about the economy, our energy policy, immigration policy, defense policy, foreign policy, and many other components of our government. Yet, none of these plans are ever implemented, plans that might save this country from utter collapse and ruin. We can do better.

So, with the responsible voter on the one hand, and the best and brightest Americans on the other, this combination can't lose. Are we past the point of needing politicians and just don't know it? Our economy, tax system, business, defenses, environmental and safety problems, foreign policy, and domestic rights have become so complex that we need experts to help us deal with problems we now have. Politicians aren't experts on all of these problems, nobody is. Politicians are mostly lawyers, who may or may not be good at practicing law. Some politicians are doctors, who are probably good at practicing medicine. Others are business owners, trying their hand at power after having gotten rich. The fact is politicians *are not fit* to solve the problems facing our country, even if they had the desire to do so. We need experts, the top people in the field, to be offering solutions to problems and directing the electorate in the right direction. The commissions and agencies would be free of lobbyists and special interest pressure. They would be paid, but not receive graft, political contributions, or other "incentives" from lobbyists and special interests, and would take oaths to serve the people of the United States as their sole purpose. They would not have to run for re-election every few years, and could resign anytime they pleased. They could also be replaced at any time the electorate decides. We could easily attract the best and brightest people into these positions, because any hint of politics would be removed. They could propose solutions to our problems, and the people could make the hard decisions that must be made in order to survive and prosper as a country.

This system would work so much better than what we have now. Often times the solutions to problems are not that complicated. For example, many economists believe what lead to the sub-prime disaster and the Great Recession is the same thing that led to the Asian currency crisis, the South American debt crisis, the European debt crises, and many other financial meltdowns—*uncontrolled leverage*. By simply controlling leverage, we can avert many future "bubbles" to come, and avert another massive recession, which will come again if something isn't done about controlling leverage. Leverage is also what's wiping out our government—deficits and debts. Many people don't know how to control leverage, but I'm sure there are many economists that do.

Our healthcare system and our education system for that matter have to be made "not for profit." The current systems for both don't work. People can't get or can't afford healthcare, because hundreds of billions of dollars are being extracted by health insurance companies and many others. Kids have a tough time going to college because it has become so expensive. Kids that want to get a decent education and get ahead in life are saddled with massive debts before they even start working. People in the U.S. used to think healthcare and education were a right in the U.S., but they aren't anymore. We can return both to some form of sanity by making the entire system "not for profit" and remove the profit motive that has ruined both of these needed services.

*The changes we need in this country aren't going to be made by politicians.* They are going to fight to hang onto the current system as long as it provides huge financial incentives and jobs. Politicians don't want things to change. They don't want for the voters to have power to make decisions and change policy. Yet, <u>we don't need politicians for anything</u>, really. How many people have been sitting on the sidelines for decades, watching as our country has gotten less and less competitive, been subject to more and more litigation, watched as federal, state, and local politicians and employees have run our country into the ground? Why has nobody stood up and demanded something different? I again use the words of Abraham Lincoln *"This country, with its institutions, belongs to the people who inhabit it. Whenever they shall grow weary of the existing government, they can exercise their constitutional right of amending it, or exercise their revolutionary right to overthrow it."* This country does indeed belong to the people who inhabit it, the people of United States of America. We have grown very wary of the existing government—it has become corrupt and beholden to the few; the lobbyists and the special interests. We can exercise our constitutional rights and try to amend our government, which is what this book proposes. We also have the revolutionary right to overthrow our government, which would result in chaos and probably civil war, neither of which anybody can afford. We can evolve into a real democracy, or devolve into pitchforks, anarchy and a modern dark age. An armed populous, however, doesn't need pitchforks. We must evolve to a working democracy before time runs out.

## *Our Constitution gives us the right...*

Our government has mechanisms already in place to amend our constitution to make the changes presented here. We are no longer living in a time where we need politicians to represent us—<u>we don't need politicians</u>

anymore. The people can represent themselves. Every person of voting age has access to more information at their fingertips than any person in the history of mankind. We have to use this information to evolve our government back to a democracy of the people, by the people, and for the people. Of course we still need a president (and vice president), who would oversee our commissions and agencies, the military, and be the front man for the people. And that's about it. The president could actually do his/her job, without all the political nightmares and conflicts that they face on a daily basis. The president and vice president could only present options to the voters, not have the power to act independently. _We don't need any more politicians_. Our government has to come to the reality that it doesn't work anymore, that it can't get away with what it's gotten away with for decades, and that the people are in fact the depository for the government, in fact and in reality.

Our birthright, as Americans, is a Democracy. We fought to get it, and we've had to fight to keep it, but somewhere it has gone missing—it's been stolen from us. Prosperity has resulted in the fall of our democracy, not its rise, because we have allowed those that have prospered and those that make our laws—the rich and the lawyers to corrupt our government for their own purposes. We are at the crossroads. If we stay with the same election-driven political lottery system we have now, we are headed for a fall, the likes of which hasn't been seen in this country before. If we can slowly remake our government with the smartest and most successful people in our country, we can claw our way back to Democracy and prosperity again. No one person, group of people or party will win, but _we the people will all win_. If we do nothing to change our system, we _all_ will surely lose and time is running out. The people that win with our current system will continue to take until all the money is gone, until "our bones are picked clean."

We have the technology, first and foremost, to effect a great change in how things are done. The only limiting factor is the question of whether the voters, the people, will rise from their lethargy and take our government back from the lobbyists, politicians, unions and special interests. We have a responsibility for the handling of our country, our Democracy, and the legacy we leave our children. We have to stand up and vote and vote again until we have a real Democracy. We have to evolve and use the technology that we ourselves have developed, by adapting it for use in governing ourselves. If we fail, we will be using our technology to watch ourselves fall off a cliff into the abyss. Our forefathers were willing to fight and die for their ideals and what they believed in. This book has tried to bring them back to life, at least by their words, so they can give us direction for now and our future. We don't have to fight and die to restore Democracy to our country; we only have to exercise our right to vote. We have to take back control of what we are voting for, instead of being force-fed what we are _able_ to vote for. As a grass-roots movement, we can, by voting, effect any change in our system that would be good and beneficial for all Americans, not just the rich and those in power.

We have the ability to use a model in Washington that still works and is uncorrupted, The Supreme Court, and evolve this model to the rest of our government in the same manner. Ironically, a group of lawyers and liberals and conservatives, but a group that is, for the most-part, uncorrupted. The people, and the people alone, should have the right to decide how our tax dollars are going to be spent, and how the private sector is going to behave. We have to take our rights; nobody is going to hand them to us. Our forefathers gave us these rights, but we have to take and use them. They gave us the right and responsibility to change our government when it doesn't work anymore or is corrupted—we are clearly living with such a government now. There is such a better future available to us. It's out there, buts it's also right in the palm of our hands. We need to use the information the _age of information_ has provided us—in a governmental framework. It has not yet been done, but it's a very real possibility. It's simple and it makes sense, and it will work better than we can imagine. It's painfully obvious to everyone that it's time to move on, but we haven't had another option, no plan. Now we do, and it will work. The voters and people of this country are not the great unwashed fools that politicians make us out to be. We can process and decide great things if we are given all the facts and realities of a situation, and are then allowed to vote. It's our greatest gift, our greatest legacy, given to us by the great patriots and leaders of our nation more than 224 years ago. We once again have to follow their lead. We have to take what they gave us and evolve into something that works. Let's hope we are able to do so, while we are still able to do so.

# Post Script

I hope you enjoyed the book, and I hope that it made you angry. Anger is energy you can work with, something that can get you involved, motivated and active; in this respect, it may be useful. If you are angry and do nothing, then it is just as destructive as those you are angry at, and you are helpless. I implore you to use your anger in a positive way, channel it into something good, by taking action. This book provides options that you may pour your anger into for positive results. We, the people of America, have everything we need to evolve and solve our problems; we have the tools, they were given to us by great men. We *must* use them now to save ourselves.

I am not some academic or elitist sitting in an ivory tower lamenting the decline of our country. I am not some pundit on T.V. or radio, removed and insulated from the people of this great country. I have worked directly with the people; helping the poor for more than 15 years. First in medical training—most medical training is done with the poor; two years as a medical student and three years as an intern and resident. Then, I've worked in a primary-care rural-health clinic in Southern Illinois for the past ten years. I've also worked in an area with the highest per-capita number of Welfare recipients in Illinois. What I've written has been from experience, of seeing the problems we face, and how our government has created many more problems than it has solved, especially with the poor. I've worked in the Medicaid, Medicare, Social Security and Disability systems for 15 years, and understand their many limitations very well. I've also had to work with health insurance companies for 15 years, and, as a doctor, it's been a very unpleasant experience. I have also been involved in the medical tort system, and although I've never been sued, it remains one of my and many doctor's greatest fears. I've seen doctors quit medicine altogether after having been sued only once for malpractice—it's a devastating blow from which some cannot recover. I have certainly made mistakes in my life, but I've often learned more from my mistakes than my successes. Maybe we can learn, as a country, from our mistakes and evolve into something better. Or, we can keep repeating our mistakes and collapse.

As far as I'm concerned, hope rings eternal. I hope this book gave you hope that things can be better. It is obvious to me that we can't just wait around and hope things will get better, we must get active. Imagine back to 1776, what those men were facing. They wanted to govern themselves, and had the nerve to think they could actually do it. Whatever the cost, they were determined to rule themselves, and tell England "no more". It's hard to imagine the fear they must have faced, and the courage they needed to overcome this fear. They knew what they were doing was right and just, but were facing one of the "superpowers" of the day. Yet, they summoned the courage to fight for what they believed in, and some sacrificed their lives. Their courage in the face of fear should inspire us today, to do what we have to do to restore our country to Democracy. We have to tell the politicians "no more" and be determined to rule ourselves. We must join together, rich and poor, left and right, whatever race or color, and stand up, call ourselves Americans and take our rights back. We have to work together, to evolve our government into something that works for us again. We cannot let fear defeat us, because it surely will. Fear didn't defeat Thomas Jefferson and George Washington. "We have nothing to fear but fear itself" FDR's encouraging words in the face of the Great Depression inspired millions. We, the people of the United States of America have a choice and we have the ability. Our course is set before us: one road leads to tyranny, ruin and darkness, the other to prosperity, health, and liberty. Which path will you choose?

# REFERENCES

## *Chapter 1: 1776*

Constitutioncenter.org."THE CONSTITUTION of the United States," National Constitution Center.

Merriam-Webster.com/dictionary, Merriam-Webster, an Encyclopedia Britannica company, © 2010 Merriam-Webster, Incorporated.

Famousquotesandauthors.com, Copyright © 2010 Famous Quotes and Authors.com. All Rights Reserved.

En.wikipedia.org "List of countries by GDP {nominal}," From Wikipedia, the free encyclopedia.

John J. Gibbons and Nicholas de B. Katzenbach "Confronting Confinement: A Report of The Commission on Safety and Abuse in America's Prisons," June 2006, pgs. 6-18. Copyright © 2006, Vera Institute of Justice.

Michael Snyder "The Middle Class in America Is Radically Shrinking. Here Are the Stats to Prove it," by Yahoo! Business, Jul. 15, 2010, courtesy of Business Insider. Businessinsider.com.

Strategyone.net "StrategyOne Public Opinion Survey: The 'American Dream' in today's economy," contact: Bradley Honan Senior Vice President, StrategyOne , October 19, 2010.

Scott W. Allard and Benjamin Roth "Strained Suburbs: The Social Service Challenges of Rising Suburban Poverty," Metropolitan Policy Program at Brookings, October 2010, pgs. 1-33. The Brookings Institution, Brookings. edu.

Bruce Katz and Robert Puentes "Affluent, but Needy (First Suburbs)" Brookings, October 30, 2010. The Brookings Institute, Brookings.edu.

Robert Rector, Katherine Bradley, and Rachel Sheffield. "Obama to spend $10.3 Trillion on Welfare: Uncovering the Full Cost of Means-Tested Welfare or Aid to the Poor," SR-67, Sept. 16, 2009, pgs. 1-53. Heritage Special Report, Published by The Heritage Foundation, Hertitage.org.

Glenn Hubbard and Peter Navarro "Seeds of Destruction." First printing: August 2010. Copyright 2011 by Pearson Education Inc. publishing as FT Press/Financial Times, FTpress.com.

Gus Lubin "10 State Pension Funds that May Run Out of Money," The Business Insider, October, 18, 2010. businessinsider.com.

Kurt Erickson "Police, fire pension revamp headed to Quinn's desk" The Southern Illinoisan, The Southern Springfield Bureau, December 2, 2010. Thesouthern.com.

Nina Easton "Prosperous Pensioners, the start of the next populist storm?" Fortune-Opinion, Fortune Magazine, Oct. 18, 2010.

Cato.org "State and Local Government Debt Is Soaring," Tax Policy Studies, No. 37 • July 2006, The CATO Institute , copyright The CATO Institute.

Laurence J. Kotlikoff "Is the United States Bankrupt?" Federal Reserve Bank of St. Louis Review, July/August 2006, 88(4), pp. 235-49. © 2006, The Federal Reserve Bank of St. Louis.

## *Chapter 2: The Federal Behemoth*

THE FACT BOOK: FEDERAL CIVILIAN WORKFORCE STATISTICS 2007 Edition, U.S. Office of Personnel Management (OPM), pgs. 1-109. OPM.gov.

Michael Snyder "12 Facts That Will Blow Your Mind – Federal Employees And Members Of Congress Are Getting Rich While Those Of Us Who Pay Their Salaries Suffer," The Economic Collapse, posted 11-22-10. Theeconomiccollapseblog.com.

Chris Edwards "Overpaid Federal Workers," The CATO Institute, Downsizing the Government, copyright The CATO Institute. downsizinggovernment.org.

Dennis Cauchon, "Federal Pay Ahead of Private Industry," USA Today, March 8, 2010.

David Cay Johnston "Free Lunch; how the wealthiest Americans enrich themselves at government expense (and stick you with the bill)", The Penguin Group 2007, Pgs. 20-25. Copyright David Cay Johnston, 2007.

James Gattuso , Diane Katz and Stephen Keen "Red Tape Rising: Obama's Torrent of New Regulation," The Heritage Foundation, October 26, 2010, Backgrounder #2482. Heritage.org.

Molly Dahl and Noah Meyerson "Social Security Disability Insurance: Participation Trends and Their Fiscal Implications," Economic and budget issue brief, a series of issue summaries from the Congressional Budget Office, July 22, 2010. CBO.gov.

David H. Autor and Mark G. Duggan "The Growth in the Social Security Disability Rolls: A Fiscal Crisis Unfolding," Journal of Economic Perspectives, Volume 20, Number 3, Summer 2006; Pages 71–96.

## *Chapter 3: Government Subsidies*

Ken Cook "Government's Continued Bailout of Corporate Agriculture," farm subsidy database, The Environmental Working Group, Dec. 10, 2010. Farm.ewg.org.

Chris Edwards "Agricultural Subsidies," Downsizing the Federal Government, June 2009, The CATO Institute, copyright The CATO Institute, Cato.org.

Dan Morgan, Gilbert M. Gaul and Sarah Cohen "Harvesting Cash: A year-long investigation" The Washington Post, July-December 2006. Washingtonpost.com.

Tad DeHaven and Chris Edwards "Business Subsidies," Downsizing the Federal Government, The CATO Institute, February 2009, copyright The Cato Institute. downsizinggovernment.org.

ELI.org. "Estimating U.S. Government Subsidies to Energy Sources: 2002-2008," Environmental Law Institute, September 2009, pgs. 3-29.

David Kocieniewski "As Oil Industry Fights a Tax, It Reaps Subsidies," New York Times—Business Section online, July 3, 2010. NYtimes.com.

Adam Isacson , Abigail Poe, Lisa Haugaard, and Joy Olson "U.S. Aid from Foreign Military Financing, Entire Region, 2006-2011," Just the Facts, Dec. 3, 2010. justf.org.

State.gov "Foreign Military Financing Account Summary," U.S. Department of State, June 23, 2010.

Laura Rowley "Is the College Debt Bubble Ready to Explode?"Yahoo! Finance, Friday, December 3, 2010. Finance. yahoo.com.

Reid Wilson "Anti-earmark Tea Party Caucus takes $1 billion in earmarks," National Journal, Dec 2, 2010. Nationaljournal.com.

## Chapter 4: Our Litigious Society

Legalreform-now.org "Lawyer Reform: Reduce the Number of Lawyers," December 2, 2010.

John Gaylord Wells "Every Man His Own Lawyer: And Business Form Book," Nabu Press, February 16, 2010. Original publication date: 1879, original Publisher: J.G. Wells, 618 pages.

Stephen R. Elias and Ralph Warner "Lawyers Try to Reestablish Their Monopoly" Legal Reform Now! Dec. 2, 2010. Legalreform-now.org.

TowersPerrin.com "2008 Update on U.S. Tort Cost Trends," 2008, copyright Towers Perrin.

Jan Hatzius "Employment and Real GDP ," Calculated Risk: Finance and Economics, Sunday December 06, 2009. Calculatedriskblog.com.

Vern Wuensche "Respect the Constitution, restore checks and balances to our three branches of government," © Copyright 2010 Voter Reports, Inc. Voteoutlawyers.com.

Craig Holman "Origins, Evolution and Structure of the Lobbying Disclosure Act," May 11, 2006. Published by Public Citizen, citizen.org.

Larry Makinson and Sheila Krumholz et al. "Lobbying: Influence Inc 2000," Influence and Lobbying, 2000, The Center for Responsive Politics. Copyright The Center for Responsive Politics. opensecrets.org.

David Cay Johnston "Perfectly Legal; the covert campaign to rig our tax system to benefit the super rich—and cheat everybody else,"The Penguin Group 2003. Copyright David Cay Johnston, 2003.

Dave Levinthal "Congressional Members' Personal Wealth Expands Despite Sour National Economy," opensecretsblog: Investigating money in politics. Contact: Dave Levinthal. By communications on November 17, 2010. Opensecrets.org.

David Weidner "Banks to Taxpayers: Get Over It: Commentary: Moral hazard is the payoff of Fed's emergency lending,"Yahoo! Finance courtesy of MarketWatch, December 7, 2010. Finance.yahoo.com.

## Chapter 5: Healthcare

David U. Himmelstein, Elizabeth Warren, Deborah Thorne, and Steffie Woodhandler

"Illness and Injury As Contributors To Bankruptcy," Market Watch—Health Affairs, 2005 Project HOPE-The People-to-People Health Foundation Inc. Bdp.law.harvard.edu.

Melissa B. Jacoby & Elizabeth Warren "Beyond hospital misbehavior: An alternative account of medical related financial distress," Northwestern University Law Review, Vol. 100, No. 2, pgs. 536-580. Copyright 2006 by Northwestern University School of Law.

Arlengroup.com "Usual, Customary and Reasonable," Benefits Factsheet, 3/28/08. Arlen Group Employee Benefits, arlengroup.com/facts/fact_ucr.pdf.

Kathleen Sebelius "Health Insurers Finally Get Some Oversight," The Wall Street Journal, Opinion Journal, Sept. 28, 2010. Online.wsj.com.

Fred Charatan "US doctors' incomes are falling, new survey finds," BMJ. 2006 July 1; 333(7557): 11, Pubmed Central. ncbi.nlm.nih.gov/pmc/articles/PMC1488748/.

Ricardo Alonso-Zaldiva "Employers looking at health insurance options," Associated Press, Sun Oct 24. Ap.org.

Medicaid Enrollment: December 2009 Data Snapshot, Kaiser Commission on Medicaid Facts; Medicaid and the Uninsured. Publication #8050-02, The Kaiser Family Foundation. kff.org.

Brian Blase "Obamacare's Medicaid Policy: Putting the Doctors in Another 'Fix;'" October 4, 2010, WebMemo #3031, The Heritage Foundation. Copyright The Heritage Foundation. Heritage.org.

WSJ-Online "Big Insurance, Big Medicine," Opinion Journal, review and outlook: October 26, 2010. WSJ.com.

UNITEDHEALTH GROUP INCORPORATED, Commission file number: 1-10864, UNITED STATES SECURITIES AND EXCHANGE COMMISSION, Washington, D.C. 20549. FORM 10-K, ANNUAL REPORT PURSUANT TO SECTION 13 OR 15(d) OF THE SECURITIES EXCHANGE ACT OF 1934 FOR THE FISCAL YEAR ENDED DECEMBER 31, 2009.

Wendell Potter "Deadly Spin: An insurance company insider speaks out on how corporate PR is killing health care and deceiving Americans," Bloomsbury Press, New York, pgs. 121-123 and cover. Copyright 2010 by Wendell Potter Consulting, LLC.

Noam N. Levey "Health insurers pour money into GOP campaigns, hoping to limit new regulations," Chicago Tribune – Washington Bureau, October 05, 2010. Articles.chicagotribune.com.

## Chapter 6: The Natives are Restless

Brian Montopoli "Tea Party Supporters: Who They Are and What They Believe," CBS News-Politics, April 14, 2010. CBSNews.com.

Becky Quick "As America's deficit crisis looms, fiscal hawks and doves need to make peace," Fortune Magazine-Opinion, Sept. 27, 2010, pg. 55.

David Weidner "Banks to Taxpayers: Get Over It: Commentary: Moral hazard is the payoff of Fed's emergency lending," Yahoo! Finance courtesy of MarketWatch, December 7, 2010. Finance.yahoo.com.

Aaron Task and John Cassidy "Bailout Nation: Banks Got the Goldmine, Consumers Got the Shaft," Yahoo! Finance Tech Ticker, Dec. 3, 2010. Finance.yahoo.com/tech-ticker.

Todd J. Gillman "Debt limit will be test of resolve for GOP freshmen from tea party," The Dallas Morning News, November 21, 2010. Dallasnews.com.

Martin Crutsinger, "November federal budget deficit highest on record," Associate Press/Yahoo! Finance, December 10, 2010. Finance.yahoo.com.

News.yahoo.com "Earmarkers feast on pork one last time before diet,"courtesy of Associate Press, Dec. 14, 2010.

Elizabeth MacDonald "US Debt a National Security Issue," Fox Business, October 11, 2010. Foxbusiness.com.

Tom Coburn "100 Stimulus Projects: A Second Opinion," Senator Tom Coburn, 111th Congress, June 2009. Coburn.senate.gov.

Tom Coburn "Dr. Coburn Introduces Bills to Prevent Lawmakers, Staff and Federal Employees from Cheating on their Taxes," press release, Senator Tom Coburn, 111th Congress, Sep 16 2010. Coburn.senate.gov.

Brian Riedl "10 More Examples of Government Waste," The Heritage Foundation, April 4, 2005, Backgrounder #1840. Copyright The Heritage Foundation. Heritage.org.

Dana Priest and William Arkin "A hidden world, growing beyond control," The Washington Post, July 19, 2010. Projects.washingtonpost.com/top-secret-America.

Air.org "Finishing the First Lap: The Cost of First-Year Student Attrition in America's Four-Year Colleges and Universities," American Institutes for Research, October 11, 2010. Media Contact Larry McQuillan.

Finance.yahoo.com "Survey: Investors Fear Government Far More than Inflation, Terrorism," Monday October 11, 2010. Finance.yahoo.com/news.

Nicole V. Crain and W. Mark Crain "The Regulation Tax Keeps Growing," Wall Street Journal Online-Opinion, Sept. 27, 2010. WSJ.com.

Brian Riedl "Why Government Spending Does Not Stimulate Economic Growth," The Heritage Foundation, November 12, 2008, Backgrounder #2208. Copyright The Heritage Foundation. Heritage.org.

Daniel Mitchell "The Impact of Government Spending on Economic Growth," The Heritage Foundation, March 15, 2005, Backgrounder #1831. Copyright The Heritage Foundation. Heritage.org.

Zhou Xin, Simon Rabinovitch and Kevin Yao "U.S. fiscal health worse than Europe's: China adviser," Yahoo! Finance, courtesy of Reuters, December 8, 2010. Finance.yahoo.com.

## Chapter 7:Voting

WSJ.com "Blaming the Voters," Wall Street Journal Online-Opinions, Sept. 30, 2010.

Jann S. Wenner "Obama in Command: The Rolling Stone Interview," Rolling Stone, Sep 28, 2010; pgs. 1-7. Rollingstone.com/politics.

Thom File and Sarah Crissey "Voting and Registration in the Election of November 2008," Current Population Reports, U.S. Department of Commerce Economics and Statistics Administration, U.S. CENSUS BUREAU, May 2010; pgs. 1-20. Census.gov.

Brett Arends "Death of a Democracy," MarketWatch, October 19, 2010. MarketWatch.com.

Lynda Gorov "Political ads: mean, and getting meaner, before Nov. 2," Yahoo! News, Sun Oct 24, 2010. Yahoo.com.

Langerresearch.com "Public Optimism Hits a 36-year Low In Views of the 'System of Government,'" ABC NEWS/YAHOO! NEWS POLL: ASK AMERICA #4, produced for ABC and Yahoo! News by Langer Research Associates. Tuesday, Oct. 26, 2010.

Langerresearch.com "Fans of Congressional Gridlock Cheer the Election's Outcome,"

ABC NEWS/YAHOO! NEWS POLL: ASK AMERICA #5, produced for ABC and Yahoo! News by Langer Research Associates. Tuesday, Nov. 23, 2010.

## Chapter 8: The Romans and the U.S.

Edward Gibbon and David P. Womersley (editor) "The History of the Decline and Fall of the Roman Empire," Penguin Classics; abridged edition, January 2, 2001, 848 pages. Originally published in six volumes between 1776 and 1788 by Edward Gibbon.

Peter Heather "The Fall of the Roman Empire: A New History of Rome and the Barbarians," Oxford University Press, December 1, 2005; 608 pages.

Norman Podhoretz "World War IV," First Vintage Books Edition, 2008. Copyright 2007, 2008 by Norman Podhoretz. Published by Vintage Books, a division of Random House.

James Quinn "DECLINE AND FALL OF THE AMERICAN EMPIRE," Financial Sense Editorials, August 2, 2009. Financialsense.com/editorials.

Gus Lubin "10 Signs The U.S. Is Losing Its Influence In The Western Hemisphere," Yahoo! Finance Courtesy of Business Insider, Sep 27, 2010. Yahoo.com.

Anika Anand and Gus Lubin "19 Iconic Products That America Doesn't Make Anymore," Yahoo! Finance, courtesy of Business Insider, Nov 04, 2010. Yahoo.com.

Allan Sloan and Tory Newmyer "Why can't Washington magically fix the economy? Let us tell you an ugly truth about the economy," Fortune Magazine, Economy section, Nov. 1st. 2010; pgs. 96-110.

## Chapter 10: Imagine

TheOnion.com "U.S. Government To Save Billions By Cutting Wasteful Senator Program," The Onion, March 30, 2010, ISSUE 46•13. Copyright by The Onion. Theonion.com/articles.

Media.bloomberg.com "Bloomberg News National Poll," Selzer & Company, study #2004, Dec. 13th, 2010; pages 1-8.

Evan Bayh "Why I'm Leaving the Senate," New York Times-Opinion, February 20, 2010. NYTimes.com.

Jane Sasseen "What's wrong with Washington? poll—what's wrong with Washington: It's the people in charge not the system," Yahoo! News, Oct 25, 2010. Yahoo.com.

Alex Altman "Will Online Voting Turn Into an Election Day Debacle?" Time Magazine Online, Oct. 15, 2010. Time.com/time/politics.

# ACKNOWLEDGMENTS

I would first like to thank Brian Riedl, the Grover Hermann Fellow in Federal Budgetary Affairs, Robert Rector, Katherine Bradley, Brian Blase, Rachel Sheffield, Daniel Mitchell and everyone at the Heritage Foundation for the excellent work they do and everything they provided for this book.

Extra special thanks to The Center for Responsive Politics and Dave Levinthal, Larry Makinson and Sheila Krumholz. Without opensecrets.org, this book would not have been possible. Keep up the good work.

Very special thanks to Robert Garber, Chris Edwards, Tad DeHaven and everyone at The CATO Institute, also without whose help and information this book would not have been possible.

Thanks to Leeann Brown and the Environmental Working Group, your data and assistance are greatly appreciated.

Thanks to Brett Kitchen and the Environmental Law Institute for their dedicated work.

Please provide whatever support you can to the above organizations. They help us all.

Thanks to Kanani Kauka and the Kaiser Family Foundation.

Thanks to authors Wendell Potter, David Cay Johnston, and Norman Podhoretz.

Thanks to Scott W. Allard, Benjamin Roth and The Brookings Institute, Towers Perrin, Langer Research, John J. Gibbons and Nicholas de B. Katzenbach of the Commission on Safety and Abuse in America's Prisons.

Thanks to Craig Holman of Public Citizen, StrategyOne, Glenn Hubbard and Peter Navarro, Senator Tom Coburn (R-Okla.), Peter Heather, James Quinn of financialSense.com, Arlengroup.com, TheOnion.com, and Laurence J. Kotlikoff.

Many thanks to Lynda Gorov, Brett Arends, Anika Anand, Jane Sasseen and especially Gus Lubin of Yahoo! News and Business, and the other organizations they work for.

Very special thanks to Elizabeth Warren, Co-Director, Bankruptcy Database Project at Harvard. Ms. Warren is a tireless advocate for the rights of the middle class, and is an inspiration to all Americans. I have enjoyed and been inspired by several of her lecturers I had the pleasure of attending.

Thanks also to Ariel Turner for the original cover design and her excellent work. arielturnerdesign.com.